D1072811

Reindustrializing New York State

Strategies, Implications, Challenges

HC
107
N7 R45
1986

Reindustrializing New York State

Strategies, Implications, Challenges

Edited by

Morton Schoolman

STATE UNIVERSITY OF NEW YORK AT ALBANY

and

Alvin Magid

STATE UNIVERSITY OF NEW YORK AT ALBANY

State University of New York Press

Published by
State University of New York Press, Albany
© 1986 State University of New York
All rights reserved
Printed in the United States of America
No part of this book may be used or reproduced in any manner whatsoever
without written permission except in the case of brief quotations embodied in
critical articles and reviews.
For information, address State University of New York Press, State University
Plaza, Albany, N.Y., 12246

Library of Congress Cataloging in Publication Data
Main entry under title:

Reindustrializing New York State.

Includes index.
1. New York (State)—Economic policy—Addresses,
essays, lectures. 2. Industry and state—New York
(State)—Addresses, essays, lectures. 3. New York
(State)—Industries—Addresses, essays, lectures.
I. Schoolman, Morton. II. Magid, Alvin, 1937—
HC107.N7R45   1986   338.9747   85-14771
ISBN 0-88706-177-X
ISBN 0-88706-178-8 (pbk.)

10   19   8   7   6   5   4   3   2   1

Contents

For Our Parents

Preface

To an unusual extent there is agreement as well as grave concern among social scientists that deindustrialization is a fact of American life and that cities and communities in the Northeastern, Midwestern, and Sunbelt regions of the United States are undergoing economic decline. In response, a variety of economic redevelopment strategies have been forthcoming from researchers in both the public and private sectors. Proposals have been crafted which range from industrial policies seeking to assign government a permanent and comprehensive planning function to supply-side formulas aiming to greatly diminish government's role. Incorporating elements of both are proposed collaborative or partnership relationships among government, business, labor, the academic community, and representatives from interest groups within the community at large.

Further research as well as policy making is complicated increasingly by the basic issues of industrial restructuring. Rapid technological and organizational changes in international markets require dramatic new departures in our industrial structure so that the United States can compete successfully. Restructuring is dependent upon the development of new techniques and technologies and their adaptation to mature as well as fledgling industries, upon the reorganization of education to allow for the education and retraining of a highly flexible labor force, and upon greater public awareness of new economic imperatives and their social and political exigencies.

Higher education has begun to contribute to the research effort. Since traditional relationships within well-defined disciplines have permitted educational institutions to evolve only gradually, however, changes in research agendas and curricula are slower than events external to the academic community warrant. At the same time, there is no topic of greater fundamental importance to our domestic policy than the reindustrialization of the United States. As the significance of this issue will not diminish over the next decade, reindustrialization requires a sustained response from major U.S. institutions. Our educational agenda cannot afford to incorporate slowly the academic contribution to this challenge. Nor can it ignore the problems left unsolved by a conventionally organized research and curriculum that can neither integrate reindustrialization's many dimensions nor master the sweep of its detail. The academic response must be at least as creative and as decisive as that of the public sphere. If it is not, the university cannot contribute to the task of economic revitalization the indispensable qualities which it alone possesses.

Reindustrializing New York State: Strategies, Implications, Challenges is the first volume in a series on Reindustrialization to issue from the Multicampus Consortium for the Study of New York's Economic Revitalization. The Consortium is a cooperative effort among several campuses within the State University of New York, organized to reconstitute disciplinary relationships among social scientists on each campus and among the campuses belonging to the Consortium. It is designed to promote the systematic research in political economy that is mandated by the present stage of economic development. The Consortium encourages a comprehensive, interdisciplinary study of the essential characteristics of rapidly changing state, national, and international economies and of their structural interdependencies. And while this volume is largely the product of social science research within the State University system, the Consortium integrates its research program with an equally serious commitment to curriculum. At each of the Consortium's campuses, participating faculty cooperatively teach courses devoted to a study of contemporary political economy as it is conceived and examined in their research. The Consortium was developed in the belief that only a multicampus-multidisciplinary approach to the problems of political economy could meet the intellectual challenges to research and education posed by the phenomenon of deindustrialization and by the necessity for a reindustrialized economy.

Reindustrializing New York State attempts to examine systematically the broad spectrum of problems brought by the deindustrialization of New York's economy, the State's policy response to these problems, the impact and consequences of its economic policy, and possible new directions for its improvement. This anthology will be followed by specialized studies which focus upon issues central to the reindustrialization debate, especially as it pertains to New York. Foremost among these are the restructuring of the State's industry, human resource policy, the evolution of new institutional forms accompanying the revitalization of the economy, capital planning policy, the impact of national economic policy on the State's strategic economic goals, and others. The overall objective of these studies is to monitor the State as it meets the challenges to its social progress and economic prosperity.

The State University of New York Multicampus Consortium was founded in the belief that this period of reindustrialization will neither be shortlived nor will socioeconomic and political changes be at the margin. Moreover, the technological reorganization of the U.S. economy makes knowledge and its distribution within society a most significant factor for economic growth. Accordingly, the university is in a unique position to encompass new approaches to education and research that will augment its intellectual resources in the social sciences and permit the social sciences to contribute uniquely to facilitating the difficult process of social and economic transition.

M.S., Albany, N.Y.
January, 1985

Acknowledgements

The editors would like to gratefully acknowledge the generous support of several organizations and individuals who have made this study of New York's economic revitalization possible. The Research Foundation of the State University of New York, the State University of New York Nelson A. Rockefeller Institute of Government, and the State University of New York at Albany Institute for Government and Policy Studies provided indispensable financial support at all stages of production and composition. Special appreciation is extended to Warren F. Ilchman, Director of the Rockefeller Institute and Provost of Rockefeller College at the State University at Albany; John W. Kalas, Assistant Vice President for Planning, and Herbert McArthur, Assistant Vice President for Research Development, the Research Foundation; and Robert Quinn, Director of the State University at Albany Institute for Government and Policy Studies, for their enthusiastic intellectual as well as professional interest in our efforts. For the past three years, there have been many more members of the academic community and of the public and private sectors of New York who have enriched our study of New York's political economy than we possibly can identify. As the project unfolds in the future, our good friends and colleagues from New York University, Columbia, Cornell, several State University of New York campuses, from the New York State Government and Legislature, private sector and general public will be thanked appropriately. We also are grateful to Marilyn McCabe, Cheryl Wainwright, and Suzanne Hagen for their careful preparation of the final draft of this manuscript.

I

Introduction:
New Directions

ONE

Solving the Dilemma of Statesmanship:

Reindustrialization Through an Evolving Democratic Plan

Morton Schoolman

> And if judgments are to have value, policy
> decisions have to be made early, when the
> magnitude of the problem is only dimly
> perceived, but when there is still latitude
> for action; when the crisis is clear, it is
> often too late to act. That is the dilemma
> of statesmanship and the possibly fatal
> flaw in the political process that can act
> only when it is too late.
>
> Felix G. Rohatyn
> *The Twenty-Year Century*

"Comprehensive," "strategic," "coherent," "long-term," "cohesive," "consistent," and "integrative." These terms, and others of similar cast, have become increasingly prominent since economic "decision making" has been transformed gradually into a process of economic "policy making" and the design of "programs." Certainly, the precise history of this incomplete transformation of relatively independent and discrete economic decisions into more or less coherent policy positions and programmatic areas is one that only the most persistent scholar could reconstruct. Nevertheless, even a casual study of the decision-making process at any level of government since the New Deal would disclose that a definite vocabulary has emerged steadily, a "framework of political discourse" within which the character of economic decisions is at least partially shaped. To put it quite simply, these are terms which connote economic planning. To claim that decisions are presently taken within a framework of discourse that connotes planning is not to argue that government now *plans*. Rather, it is to point to a development that suggests a tendency toward organized, rational planning, though not necessarily economic planning of the sort so often objected to in libertarian and republican ideologies. Although this claim, controversial as it may be, cannot be defended adequately within the confines of an introductory essay, it is at least possible to establish its credibility by means of a serious effort to examine the manner in which a complex and exceedingly worrisome area of public policy is being managed collaboratively by the public and private sectors of New York State.

Planning discourse is especially rife at the level of state government, and increasingly so in many states—particularly in the Northeast and Midwest—during the past two decades. Moreover, there is no indication that it will abate, or that it is being used rhetorically or incorrectly or without some awareness that economic decisions procedurally and substantively are much different than economic policies and programs in the past. In fact, the terms that introduced this discussion are taken from public statements on the economy and on the state of New York State made between 1981 and 1984 by the present governor of New York, Mario Cuomo, and his predecessor, Hugh Carey.[1] An identification of the planning tendencies in the evolution of New York's economic policy and an appraisal of the significance of economic planning cannot be based, however, upon a vocabulary adopted by political leaders and public managers to describe the State's proposals for economic development. Rather, the tests for economic planning eventually must focus on the implementation of these proposals and the institutional arrangements and practical consequences to which they give birth. In the course of this analysis it will become evident that the economic policies of New York during the past ten years are coming to share many of the characteristics usually associated with planning. Most important among these characteristics are the strategic, long-term intentions of economic policy, the new and, perhaps, permanent institutional forms which have emerged to formulate and implement economic policy, the gradually more explicit recognition of the structurally interdependent nature of the economic problems with which economic policy is contending, and the development of policies in light of the structurally interdependent nature of economic problems and institutions (that is, economic policy in one area should not be developed in such a way as to frustrate the objectives or offset the gains in another area).

The examination of economic policy in New York must be preceded by a concise account of the gravity of the economic conditions which provoked the response that has become ever more comprehensive, strategic, coherent. . . .

THE DECLINE AND RISE OF THE EMPIRE STATE

The practice commonly observed among economists and most other technical analysts who are called upon to evaluate the health of a state's economy is to weigh its growth rates against those of the nation as a whole. By this general measure, and by nearly all of the economic criteria which it entails, since the beginning of the last decade New York's economy only can be judged to have been chronically ailing.[2]

Several telling examples of the disabling performance of New York's economy between the years 1970 and 1982 are readily available. New York's 1.5 percent nonfarm employment increase compared very poorly with the 26.4 percent advance for the nation. Likewise, nationally the labor force grew by a third while the State's workforce increased by less than a tenth. Employment in the retail industry, one of New York's largest employers, increased by 3 percent, though nationally growth approached 40 percent. In transportation, communications, and utilities 15 percent of the industries' jobs were eliminated—nationwide a gain of 12 percent was posted. Employment in the finance, insurance, and real estate (FIRE) sector increased by 13 percent, but was outdistanced considerably by the nation's 46.8 percent increase. Its manufacturing sector, which until 1973 had held the State securely in the first position in manufacturing among all states in the nation, lost a total of 386,500 jobs between the years 1970 and 1982. From the midpoint of 1970 until the close of 1981 New York's unemployment rate exceeded that of the nation by a rate in excess of two percent halfway through the decade. Hourly earnings for New York's manufacturing workers in 1982 were $8.35, compared to $8.50 for the United States. In 1970 more than 25 percent of the country's leading industrial companies were based in New York State; by 1981 less than 18 percent remained. Per capita income increased by two-thirds of the national growth rate from 1970 to 1981. Finally, as the population increased in the United States by more than 17 percent during the past decade, New York State's fell by nearly 4 percent. Population decline in New York's major cities appears to verge on the catastrophic—New York City declined by 10.4 percent, Buffalo by 22.7, Rochester by 18.1, Syracuse by 13.8, and Albany by 12.1

percent. Additional criteria relating state to national trends would offer a more complete economic portrait, though hardly one measurably less dismal. Taking all of New York's economic sectors together, for instance, would not produce a match, much less an improvement over, a single national counterpart.[3]

Undoubtedly, if New York continued to move along the trajectory outlined by these figures, or even if the trajectory turned upward though growth consistently remained beneath national rates, the entire State progressively would become a depressed area. Yet, straightforwardly comparing New York's growth rates with the nation's over the twelve-year span, 1970–1982, is an injustice to the State. The greatest part of the decline actually occurred during the first half of the last decade and it bottomed out at the conclusion of the 1974–1975 recession. Beginning in 1975 New York State clearly reversed its economic direction and in several important economic dimensions narrowed the gap between national and State growth patterns. To fully appreciate New York's new departures, though, requires that we compare New York's post-1975 growth rates with the record already described. Focusing on periodic growth rate patterns within the State, rather than confining our attention to growth in the State relative to that of the nation, provides a much different outlook for New York's future than the forecast implied earlier.

New York's unemployment problem has receded since 1975 when it had surpassed 10 percent. By 1979 the State's unemployment figures had dropped to nearly 7 percent. Although the nation's unemployment began to recede earlier than New York's and continued to recede during the same period, the State's rate declined more precipitously. Furthermore, when joblessness once again climbed in New York and the nation through the 1980–1981 recession, New York's increase was considerably less steep than the country's as a whole. In 1982 it registered 8.2 percent, continuing the trend initiated two years earlier of remaining below the national unemployment rate, a trend that has been sustained to the present. These developments are indicative of the formation of a sturdier economic base, specifically a transition from manufacturing to services.[4]

Upstate areas of New York, notably Poughkeepsie, Albany-Schenectady-Troy, and Binghamton maintained significantly low rates of unemployment while downstate recorded marked improvement, particularly in New York City where 40,000 fewer than in 1975 were listed as jobless in 1982. A few urban areas historically dependent upon older industries continued to suffer from severe unemployment. To its distress, the steady nationwide decline in the metals and automobile industries continued to plague Buffalo, whereas the growth of high-technology industry (and the stability of IBM) contributed decisively to its 17.2 percent employment gain.[5]

As intimated, much of New York's progress since 1975 is due to the especially sound performance of the service sector, which has replaced manufacturing as the State's employment base. Finance, insurance, and real estate posted an increase in employment of nearly 17 percent between 1975 and 1982, a substantial improvement over its 25 percent employment decline for the decade's first five years. Education, business, and legal services experienced employment growth rates in excess of 20 percent between 1975 and 1981, and for the same period social services and computer-related services recorded growth figures of 52.7 and 108 percent, respectively. Though still declining, manufacturing did so more slowly, and construction, an especially weak sector of New York's economy, also moderated its employment decline when compared to its steep 22 percent fall in employment from 1970 to 1975.[6]

In other economic sectors, the reports were relatively favorable as well. Wholesale and retail, for instance, improved its performance somewhat over 1975. More general economic indicators also proved agreeable. By the close of 1982 personal income growth in the State had exceeded national growth. Total nonfarm employment at 6.3 percent between 1975 and 1982, though continuing to remain behind the national growth rate, nevertheless had made strides toward closing the deficit. Overall, New York State's economic turnaround after that fearful midpoint of the 1970s enabled it to make "slow progress", according to several appraisals, toward recovering its reputation as a growth state.[7] (Figures 1 through 7 may be consulted for growth trends extending from 1970 to 1982, 1970 to 1975, and 1975 to 1982.)

It is not possible to distinguish with much confidence the factors which accounted for New York's post-1975 economic recovery from those which contributed to the nation's. Since it is not within the power of a state to isolate itself entirely from national economic policies or trends, at the same time that its economic fate was being decided by state public and private sector policies New York both fell victim to and subsequently benefited from the national business cycle. But while factors contributing to the State and the nation's recession and recovery cannot be differentiated with precision, there is sufficient evidence to indicate that there clearly were factors present in New York which were unique to the state level. This claim appears warranted for at least two reasons. Although New York's rate of recovery from the mid-1970s recession initially lagged behind the nation's along several lines, such as unemployment and personal income growth, New

Figure 1.

Annual Average Unemployment Rates For United States and New York State
1970 - 1983

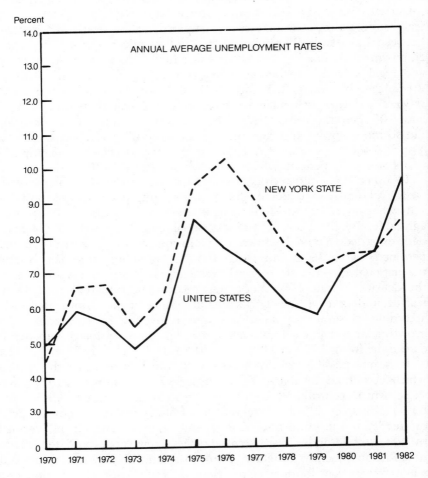

Source: New York State Department of Commerce

York's rate of improvement eventually surpassed the nation's. New York also weathered the recession of 1980–1981, the severest decline since the Great Depression, better than the nation as a whole.[8]

Figure 2.

Employment Trends-Manufacturing & Services
New York State (1970 - 1981)

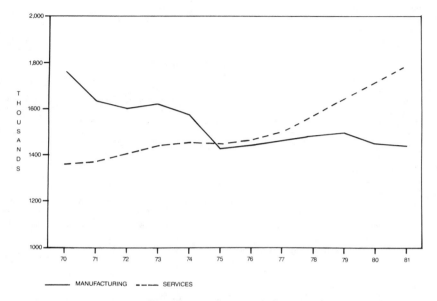

MANUFACTURING ---- SERVICES

Source: New York State Department of Commerce

According to this argument, an effort to sort out factors at the state level which may have played some special part in New York's recovery from one—and greater resistance to a second—recession requires that attention be directed to factors which appeared half-way through the State's recovery and thereafter. For it was at those times that New York and the nation's economy behaved differently; as suggested by certain common measurements New York's economy appeared stronger. Among the factors affected by State policies during this period, perhaps the one subjected most extensively to public management and reform was New York's "business climate." The business climate had been a perennial topic in the discussion about New York's economy.[9] Beginning in 1975, however, when the complete spectrum of the damage inflicted by the recession and longer term decline had become fully visible, it appears to have moved to the forefront in the debate over the cause of the State's economic problems.

Figure 3. Rate of Unemployment by Place of Residence, New York State and Major Labor Areas, Selected Years

	1975	1980	1981	1982
New York State	9.5	7.5	7.6	8.6
Downstate	9.8	7.4	7.7	8.1
New York City Area	10.1	8.0	8.3	8.8
New York City	10.6	8.6	9.0	9.6
Westchester County	6.9	4.2	4.5	5.0
Rockland County	6.8	5.8	6.0	6.1
Putnam County	8.2	5.9	5.9	6.6
Nassau-Suffolk Area	8.8	6.0	5.9	6.2
Albany-Schenectady-Troy Area	7.4	5.8	6.1	7.0
Binghamton Area	7.5	6.5	6.6	7.8
Buffalo Area	10.8	9.7	9.6	12.8
Elmira Area	9.4	7.7	7.8	11.7
Glens Falls Area	11.3	8.8	8.7	9.8
Newburgh-Middletown Area	9.3	7.7	8.0	8.4
Poughkeepsie Area	5.7	5.3	5.7	6.0
Rochester Area	7.5	6.0	6.0	7.5
Syracuse Area	9.2	7.3	7.0	8.2
Utica-Rome Area	9.4	7.4	7.6	9.0

NOTE: The rate of unemployment is the total number of unemployed residents as a percent of the combined total of unemployed and employed residents.
SOURCE: New York State Department of Labor.

Figure 4. Rate of Unemployment, United States, New York and Selected States, 1975 and 1982

	1975	1982
United States	8.5	9.7
New York State	9.5	8.6
California	9.9	9.9
Florida	10.7	8.2
Massachusetts	11.2	7.9
New Jersey	10.2	9.0
North Carolina	8.6	9.0
Pennsylvania	8.3	10.9
Texas	5.6	6.9

NOTE: Total unemployment as a percent of the combined total of unemployment and employment.
SOURCE: U.S. Bureau of Labor Statistics and North Carolina Employment Security Commission.

The blame for the condition of New York's economy was laid squarely on the business climate. In retrospect, this seems clear given the economic policies enacted by the State through the remainder of the decade. Not all components of the business climate were the targets of remedial action. The labor environment—meaning wages, the avail-

Figure 5. Changes in Nonagricultural Employment by Sector, United States and New York State, 1970, 1975 and 1982

Sector	Percent Change 1970–1975 U.S.	N.Y.S.	Percent Change 1975–1982 U.S.	N.Y.S.	Percent Change 1970–1982 U.S.	N.Y.S.
Total	8.6	−4.6	16.5	6.3	26.4	1.5
Services	20.3	6.3	36.8	25.8	64.5	33.7
Manufacturing	−5.4	−19.2	2.9	−3.4	−2.7	−22.0
Government	17.0	9.1	7.5	−2.3	25.7	6.6
Retail trade	14.5	−0.9	20.6	4.0	38.1	3.0
Finance, insurance, real estate	14.3	−2.5	28.5	15.9	46.8	13.0
Wholesale trade	10.6	−7.4	19.9	5.3	32.6	−2.5
Trans., comm., pub. utilities	0.6	−13.3	11.3	−2.3	12.0	−15.3
Construction	−1.8	−21.7	11.0	−1.8	9.0	−23.1
Mining	20.7	−6.3	49.2	−17.6	80.1	−22.8

SOURCE: U.S. Department of Labor and New York State Department of Labor.

ability of a skilled workforce to meet the needs of industry, unionization, labor unrest and work stoppage rates—was either at or below the average for leading industrial states and the nation generally.[10] One study, in fact, pointed out that in the 1970s work stoppage rates had reached their lowest point in thirty years, while another simply called into question the presumed relationship between these factor costs (labor and wages) and economic growth and decline. The business climate factors held primarily responsible for the erosion of New York's economy were taxes and public spending, in short, fiscal policy.[11]

Surveys of New York's business climate strongly and invariably correlate two factors: one of the nation's least desirable business climates and one of its highest expenditure and tax rates.[12] According to labor and management officials, taxes proved to have a negative impact on business are the State's individual income tax, the corporate franchise tax, sales taxes (state, county, and local), and local property taxes.[13] "Negative impact" is not a term that lends itself to strict definition. Studies for the past twenty years have demonstrated consistently that the absolute level of taxes is important as a factor affecting business costs, though negligibly so in the case of certain taxes. Yet, its real significance is as an indicator of the general receptivity of an environment to the task of meeting a wide range of business interests and needs. A tax cut, paired with restraint on spending, is the approach most often adopted by states to radically improve their business climates. New York pursued tax cuts while giving merely rhetorical weight to

11

Figure 6.

Personal Income Growth-New York State vs. United States
(Percent Change from Previous Year)
(1973 - 1982)

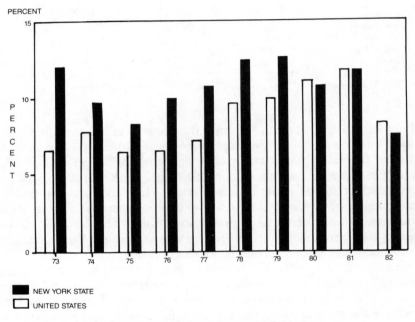

Source: New York State Department of Commerce

the necessity for reduced spending and better balanced budgets. The
outcome was a far more favorable, albeit unstable, business climate.
In the view of the business community, the instability of the business

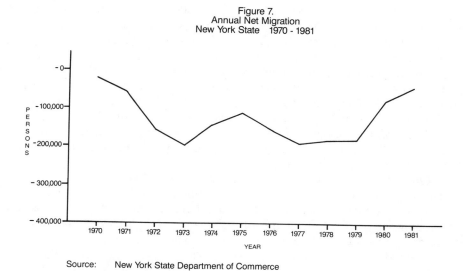

Figure 7.
Annual Net Migration
New York State   1970 - 1981

Source: New York State Department of Commerce

climate derived from the unpredictability of a tax structure which was poorly coordinated with spending policy.[14]

Between 1977 and 1979 New York State legislated two billion dollars in tax reductions, with more than 75 percent of the reductions in effect by 1980, and introduced an important complement of business tax incentive programs.[15] By the end of the decade, tax policies and promotional schemes to attract, retain, and subsidize new industry and the growing service sector had collaborated to recover—with some degree of success—New York's reputation as a growth-oriented state. But a dramatically altered business climate, substantial tax reductions, promotional campaigns, and the growing service sector could not contend with problems which, it was discovered at the turn of the decade, had resulted from the deindustrialization of the national, as well as State, economy. Profound economic difficulties were dimly perceived beneath the brighter signs of recovery. Real growth no longer could be stimulated incrementally but required policies which would restructure the economy.

REBUILDING THE EMPIRE STATE

At the close of the 1970s there was serious recognition among State policy makers that the customary policy levers were no longer sufficient

13

to revitalize an ailing economy. Fiscal policy, or for all intents and purposes tax policy, had become the virtually exclusive vehicle used to spur economic growth. State tax policy, however, was neither consistent with other areas of fiscal policy (and could not be so long as social and economic policy remained uncoordinated), nor was it more than a useful short-term, supply-side aid to selective industrial sectors. It certainly was a poor antidote for problems whose causes lay elsewhere than in high taxes and business climates of ill-repute, such as the chronic decline of manufacturing, structural unemployment, economically distressed areas, a decaying physical infrastructure, and other forms of deindustrialization.

One of the several unmistakable signs that there was a new understanding that current and unconventional economic problems extended beyond the reach of conventional macroeconomic policy was a bill sponsored in 1980 by the New York State Senate and Assembly. According to the legislation, the governor would be required to present an annual economic report to the legislature evaluating the state of the economy and mapping proposals to strengthen it. The legislature, in turn, would respond to the governor's message with public hearings on the document, the results of which could serve as the basis for legislative debates on the economy and cross-fertilization between the legislature and the executive branch. Its intent was to initiate a continuous dialogue on economic policy in order to enlarge its analytical focus and to devise substantive programs with sophistication equal to the complexities of an economy in transformation to a new level of organization and development.[16] For a variety of reasons which have no bearing on this inquiry, the bill was not enacted into law, even though it appeared on several legislators' agendas each year after it was first proposed.

In good faith with the intent of the bill, and for other reasons to be described shortly, Hugh Carey chose to present an economic report to the legislature for the last two years of his second term as governor. Each of these reports, *The New York State Economy in the 1980's: A Program for Economic Growth* (1981) and *Building From Strength: A Program for Economic Growth and Opportunity* (1982), was followed by public hearings conducted by the New York State Joint Senate-Assembly Commerce Committee.[17] The governor's messages constituted a qualitatively different approach to economic policy than any taken before in New York. Economic policy ceased to be one area among many others in the public agenda. In a very theoretical as well as practical way it became the nucleus of policy discourse, the vital center to which all other policy areas—the budget, energy, infrastructure, intergovernmental relations, the environment and other central regulatory fields, education and crime—had to be related. Perhaps most important, economic and social policy were integrated as a unified set of concerns. No longer would the objectives of either one be defined independently and at the possible expense of the other.

Carey's messages asserted unequivocally that New York's economy was in the throes of being restructured and that the structural transition was rooted in the very base of society. The production of goods had given way to the management of information. Manufacturing, in other words, had been replaced by services. Compared to manufacturing, however, service industries comprised a far more fragile economic base. The technological revolution that had been partially responsible for weakening the competitiveness of manufacturing contributed to the geographical flexibility of services. Service businesses, or the service component of businesses, such as the so-called "back-office operation," were highly vulnerable to relocation to other states offering economic incentives. The tactical approach mandated for a state already rich in service industries was to adopt a policy aimed at retention. A policy orientation toward the service sector meant a shift away from manufacturing support to the support of service development programs.

The programmatic shift from manufacturing to service support could be misread easily as the launching of a "sunrise and sunset" policy. In fact, as Carey's messages were presented in the context of a national debate about economic winners and losers in a society taking its first awkward steps toward reindustrialization, the 1982 report stated explicitly that the "strategic emphasis on services should not be interpreted to mean neglect of manufacturing."[18] Manufacturing was declining, but the decline and its costs were inevitable unless policies were conceived which accelerated the decline in a manner which was favorable to the growth of the State's economy and to *each* of its principle actors, present *and* past. By devising policy tactics which both conform to a negative tendency and which anticipate and mediate its consequences, a negative tendency such as a decline in manufacturing can paradoxically be turned into an advantage. Rather than design policy for manufacturing in general, an approach that would be discarded, manufacturing was divided into specific sectors—urban center manufacturing, technological manufacturing, and traditional ("smokestack") manufacturing—each with its own special problems and needs, each with its own policies. Macroeconomic policy would be replaced by microeconomic policy, by industrial targeting that did not, however, rely upon a zero-sum calculus.

15

Only a full-length study of strategic planning in New York could do justice to the extent to which the State has developed microeconomic policies for each targeted industrial sector. Nevertheless, what can be underscored here is that quite productive strides have been made in designing policy "clusters" intended to fit the idiosyncrasies of discrete economic sectors and subsectors. Clusters have emerged not only for services and the manufacturing sectors, but for agriculture, wholesale and retail trade, fire, insurance, and real estate, construction, and others. And following the example of manufacturing, sectors were divided further with policies devised accordingly. Without attempting an exhaustive analysis of microeconomic policy as it developed during the Carey administration, two modest undertakings can help to define the contours of the State's strategic economic planning. By selecting one strategic economic category, small business development, which includes businesses from several of the economy's many sectors, such as manufacturing, retail, and agriculture, the proliferation of policy clusters which respond to the particular problems and needs of small business, and the breadth of the policy areas represented by the policy clusters, can be seen clearly. Next, by singling out one type of small business, high-technology manufacturing, it is possible to see how microeconomic policy becomes further specialized, though as it does so it remains well coordinated with other sectors of the economy. This second example will also bring to light a negative economic tendency as well as the strategic approach through which it is developed in a way advantageous to the State.

Although it is evident that its economic strategy implicitly committed New York to a competition with other states for migrating business firms, a working premise of the strategy is that resources are much better utilized if invested in the birth of new firms and the expansion of firms already in existence. Underlying this premise is the understanding that competition among states is intense, that it leads frequently to abatement policies which injure the fiscal stability of communities attempting to lure business facilities, that the number of firms involved at any one time in interregional migration is small, and that jobs created through new locational decisions based upon the most lucrative offers are not "real" jobs because they may well be enticed elsewhere.[19] New business development is therefore a crucial and fertile area for microeconomic policy. In 1981 alone new and small businesses benefitted handsomely from State tax reduction policies especially targeted for this category. Extensive reductions included refundable investment tax credits and employee incentive tax credits for new firms in need of a greater cash flow before their earnings make them eligible for other tax credits, reduction of the State's capital gains tax for designated investments, and a substantial increase in the amount of income allowed for officers' salaries exclusion under the corporate franchise tax.[20]

The capital needs of business development are greater, however, than those provided for by tax credits and incentives. Development finance emerges as a second area of small business microeconomic policy because business start-ups, due to the high financial risk involved, cannot be adequately supported by private capital markets. The State's role in development finance is not to supplant private capital but to supplement private sources and to aid business in obtaining loans and technical assistance. During the past several years the State has explored many avenues for development finance. One of the most promising is the reform of public employee pension funds to broaden investment portfolios to include small business, venture capital projects, and ailing but sound businesses in need of new infusions of capital. In other areas, development finance policy focuses on the special needs of small business in rural and distressed areas, on the provision of export financing for small and medium businesses, and on permitting industrial and commercial lenders to insure loans against the higher costs and risks associated with small business lending. While each of the policy clusters contends with important needs and problems of small business, the development finance area is particularly significant, as we shall appreciate more clearly further on.[21]

Small businesses will also benefit from reforms in both the statutory bases and the administrative apparatus of regulatory policies. In New York, as in most other states, state as well as national regulatory constraints protect the competitive advantages of big business in many sectors of the economy. New York's efforts to tailor procedural regulations to enhance the efficiency and predictability of regulatory administration, and its elimination of the duplication of regulatory mechanisms among national, state, and local systems, will help restore the ability of many sectors' small businesses to compete effectively with larger concerns, particularly with respect to product innovation and development. Microeconomic policies have been particularly successful in the transportation, telecommunications, and other information intensive sectors, where policy reform has removed regulatory impediments to the growth of new technologies, abolished statutory constraints on investments, and deregulated prices.[22]

Taken together, tax programs, development finance proposals, and regulatory reforms constitute three distinct clusters of microeconomic policies which are directed specifically to the needs of small businesses. Although it could be argued quite correctly that policies have always been formulated in relation to the particular needs and particular sectors of the State's economy, the argument would seriously overlook the great extent to which economic policy has become rationalized. If space permitted, continuing to confine our attention to small business, it would be a simple matter to aggregate policy clusters by examining how State policies are formed cumulatively to meet the special energy needs of small businesses, their needs for special types of technical assistance to develop and expand export markets, and their requirements for a specially educated and trained workforce. The examination would demonstrate that there are increasingly few private dimensions of this small business economy which are not socialized, that is, underwritten by microeconomic policy. Moreover, as rationalized as small business policy may appear to be from just this cursory review of microeconomic policies targeted to its economy, the true extent of policy rationalization is appreciated only when the actual concentration of policy clusters directed to a single sector of the small business economy is considered. Studying the formation of policies designed to nurture the growth of high technology and to coordinate its growth with other manufacturing sectors in New York State reveals very quickly how economic planning is evolving steadily through the proliferation and rationalization of microeconomic policy.

High-Technology Policy in New York State

New York State always has possessed great strength in the area of high technology, as the presence of industries such as IBM, General Electric, Eastman Kodak, Grumman, Xerox, Corning, and Bausch and Lomb will attest. Without question, it was the comparative advantages which New York enjoyed, particularly in the first two decades following the Second World War, that allowed it to become established as one of the leading high-technology states. A collection of now priceless economic resources, the seeds for which had been sown at different times since the turn of the century and for much different purposes and which had matured at various rates of development, eventually provided a fertile groundwork for high-technology firms to flourish. Once a state can lay claim, as New York could, to one of the most advanced university and research networks in the country, a well educated and trained labor force, an elaborately designed infrastructure, especially its system of transportation, and a functionally diverse set of financial institutions, there are few preconditions which remain to be met for a free market to prosper. Perhaps the most important remaining factor, and one originating beyond the boundaries of New York State, was not the absence of competition from other states but rather of *organized* competition for high-technology industry. Certainly, several other states also could boast of a very sound high-technology sector. And their success, too, was largely the consequence of the same accidental collection of factors which ultimately served as an excellent foundation for the growth of high technology. If New York occupied a national leadership position in high technology, it did so for reasons similar to the nation's international leadership in this sector. Both were as much due to the *comparative underdevelopment* of other states and nation-states, such as Japan and Germany, as to the development of New York and the United States.

During the second half of the 1960s, however, several state governments targeted the high-technology sector in order to accelerate its growth. New York took scant notice of these efforts until the mid 1970s when it began to search about for ways to initiate a recovery from the recession and to develop sturdier economic defenses against future downturns. New York was impressed particularly with the number of research parks which had been created across the country, with public sector support, to foster the development of high-technology firms.[23] New York's northeastern neighbor, Massachusetts, was one of the primary examples looked to for economic development guidance.[24] Other states, though, notably North Carolina and California, drove home the same strategic lessons. The evidence of their success was most dramatic for new high-technology firms. Both sales and employment growth for this sector of manufacturing so far exceeded that of traditional manufacturing that the long-range tendencies indicated a comprehensive restructuring of state economies. Regardless of the reasons for the decline of traditional manufacturing, the long established base of New York's economy, within the context of national and international economic restructuring the State was compelled to accomplish considerably more than the revitalization of traditional industry. Even restored traditional manufacturing would not restore the competitiveness of the State's economy. Only rebuilding the economy along restructured lines could accomplish that task.

To the extent to which public sector efforts were largely responsible for other states' high-technology growth records, as was the case in Massachusetts, California, and North Carolina, New York was unprepared to compete effectively. The shallowness of New York's investment in new high-technology enterprise is as well illustrated by what it did, as by what it did not do. In the early years of the 1960s, the State created an Advisory Council for the Advancement of Industrial Research and Development that in turn sponsored the legislative enactment of

19

tax deductions to spur investments in research and development and the establishment of the New York State Science and Technology Foundation. For the first ten years of its existence the Foundation's work was confined to subsidizing science and engineering programs in the State. While this was an important contribution to the development of high technology, alone its contribution was tenuous because complementary programs in addition to tax credits, such as those which would help finance the new firms, were necessary if its impact was to be measurable and sustained.

This apparently disinterested and let-the-market-work-its-will attitude toward high technology ended abruptly in the bright light of the combined achievements of the high-technology growth states and the equally impressive combination of recession and long-term economic decline. Within a few years following the end of the 1974–1976 recession, New York completely reversed its minimalist position and adopted the standpoint that the future of new high technology will depend greatly on the role assumed by State government. As is clear from State policy maker's evaluations of New York's high-technology situation relative to that of other states, the State realized that it now would have to act much more aggressively than had other state governments, for at least the following two reasons.[25]

In the fast growing high-technology states, standard macroeconomic policy notwithstanding, state government had been drawn into high-technology economic development to catalyze new growth that already had made extensive progress through strategies initiated by the private sector. In Massachusetts, North Carolina, and California, for instance, new high-technology firms were enterprises which originally had splintered off major universities and maintained a symbiotic research and development tie. New York, despite its unquestionable wealth of high-technology resources, did not possess institutional arrangements equivalent to the MIT-Harvard, Stanford-Berkeley, or Duke-Chapel Hill-North Carolina State complexes. As those in the governor's office—who were moving swiftly to evaluate New York's opportunities for the growth of high-technology industry—knew, the

closest New York can come may be the Stony Brook-Brookhaven area and the technologically intensive industries on Long Island. Of course, New York City with Columbia University, the CUNY Graduate Center, NYU and many existing technologically oriented businesses cannot be considered weak in this regard. . . . Commerce has had discussions with parties at SUNY at Binghamton about a possible SUNY-Commerce linkage to provide high technology/small business services at that campus. Whether or not any other areas of the State have such resources is unknown, although the Capital area does have General Electric and Rensselaer Polytechnic Institute and the University Center at Albany.[26]

And in addition to the absence of specific entrepreneurial private sector-university networks, New York also received substantially less research and development funds from the federal government. While there is some debate over the extent to which federal support contributes to the cumulative success records of high-technology firms, there can be little doubt that federal R & D money was an indispensible subsidy in high-technology growth states during the embryonic stages of new high-technology companies and their cooperative relations with educational institutions.[27] Because of the conditions distinguishing New York from the paradigmatic high-technology states, the State resolved to *reorganize* its high-technology assets in order to establish market relations comparable to those at work in Massachusetts, North Carolina, and California. Creating these market conditions necessarily involved the State in complex microeconomic strategy, the first major step on the road to economic planning.

Comparative state high-technology evaluations, upon which New York's new high-technology initiative was based, formally originated in the executive chamber with the Economic Affairs Cabinet (EAC) in June, 1978. EAC, basically a predecessor of and counterpart to Mario Cuomo's Council on Fiscal and Economic Priorities, was created by Governor Carey in late 1977.[28] Its mission was to define and implement economic development strategies and projects. In this regard its membership is particularly important. It was comprised of the highest officials in each of the agencies directly involved in economic development. Not only were all economic development policy areas to be incorporated into redevelopment strategies, but EAC was charged as well with their coordination. Structural interdependency, comprehensiveness, and consistency, essential characteristics of strategic economic planning, were present from the first stages of the State's high-technology initiative.

These characteristics were carried over into the planning apparatus that was designed by EAC to formulate a growth strategy for young high-technology firms. EAC's consideration of high-technology growth in other states produced, in August 1978, the High Technology Opportunities Task Force and the Advisory Council on High Technology. State government agencies represented in Task Force membership were the Department of Commerce, the Department of Environmental Conservation, the Department of Taxation and Finance, the Job Development Authority, the Urban Development Corporation, and the State University of New York. Cooperatively, these agencies and organizations would shape high-technology strategy through the Carey and into the Cuomo administrations, which will become evident as their economic development proposals over the next half-dozen years are examined. The Advisory Council was composed of representatives from business, labor, and the academic communities throughout the State. The Council's function was to aid in the formulation of high-technology development by contributing ideas informed by a statewide perspective and by appraising those of the Task Force. Together, the Task Force and the Advisory Council laid the groundwork for high-technology development policy through public-private sector cooperation.

Several economic development proposals were promptly forthcoming from the Task Force and Advisory Council partnership. One of the first and most important was the revitalization of the New York State Science and Technology Foundation. With great dispatch, in January, 1979, the governor announced the revitalization program and, after extensive legislative-executive discussions, a newly endowed Science and Technology Foundation was enacted into law in 1981. In the ensuing years, the Foundation became the umbrella organization under which many long-range economic development projects could be conceived and initiated.

As outlined by the Task Force and Advisory Council, the powers of the Foundation enabled it to assume a central role in stimulating the growth of new high-technology firms. Among others, it was given the authority to identify new or emerging products and industries requiring and warranting support; to partially subsidize and provide technical assistance to private research organizations, small high-technology businesses, entrepreneurs, educational institutions, and inventors whose R & D projects held promise for further industrial and commercial development; to provide financial or technical assistance in obtaining funds for the demonstration and subsequent commercialization of new and innovative technologies; to maintain a register of scientific and technical personnel and facilities in New York to regularly update the State's strengths and weaknesses in this area; and to serve as a liaison to promote cooperation among the private sector, the university community, and government.[29]

The Science and Technology Foundation also was authorized to organize efforts to secure R & D funding from the federal government, which was the object of the second high-technology development proposal made by the Task Force and Advisory Council. At the time when New York's Science and Technology Foundation was proposed for revitalization, the State ranked fourth behind California, Maryland, and Massachusetts for total R & D expenditures (defense, space, health, energy, agriculture, natural resources, science, transportation and commerce, and the environment). At least part of the reason for New York's poor standing relative to the abundance of its resources in high-technology research and development, the Advisory Council argued, was its success in the areas of *commercial* high-technology industry. High-technology corporations on the order of IBM, General Electric, and Xerox, whose projects flourished with commercial R & D funds, had no need for federal R & D expenditures comparable to that of young, high-technology firms. New York's new emphasis on young high-technology development mandated new and ambitious efforts in the direction of attracting federal expenditures.[30]

To that end, the Science and Technology Foundation was doubly urged to forge the closest possible coordination among government, industry, and the university community. Such a tightly coordinated cooperative relationship could integrate a unified front of research and development resources with the technical and political leverage to obtain funds. Beyond the responsibilities assigned to the Science and Technology Foundation, State agencies involved in economic development were encouraged by the Advisory Council to supplement the State's lobbying efforts in Washington to seek funds for high-technology industries not vying for R & D monies in other states, thus providing New York with a competitive advantage for federal subsidies in certain high-technology areas, and in a variety of ways to act as a conduit to the federal government for New York's high-technology businesses, presenting these projects and proposals collectively to pair a cost-effective approach with a concentration of political pressure.

The High Technology Task Force and Advisory Council also generated proposals for the development of high-technology and research parks after the examples of California and North Carolina, for state and federal venture capital assistance and state tax incentives for high-technology firms, and for a host of additional aids to inventors and entrepreneurs. The intense energies expended by the public-private sector partnership in a short period of time produced results which can only be described as prolific. Yet, the most far-reaching proposals for targeting new high-technology growth industries evolved from the legislation establishing the Science and Technology Foundation.

Shortly after the revitalization of New York's Science and Technology Foundation, legislation was passed enabling the Foundation to designate Centers for Advanced Technology in technical fields which have significant potential for productivity improvement and economic growth in New York State. The Foundation targeted seven areas of technology as having development potential for the State's economy and designated a different university center as the development site for each field. Cornell University was identified as the center for the advancement of agricultural biotechnology, Columbia University for the development of computers and information systems, the State University of New York Centers at Stony Brook and at Buffalo for medical biotechnology and medical instruments and devices respectively, Syracuse University for computer applications and software engineering, the University of Rochester for advanced optical technology, and the Polytechnic Institute of New York for telecommunications technology.[31] The Centers for Advanced Technology provide the basic framework for the State's attempts to foster university-private sector cooperation. Within this framework New York's academic institutions and industry can enhance their combined research and development potential in high technology as well as their potential for technology transfer. The linkages formed through the Centers for Advanced Technology have strengthened graduate programs, created faculty positions, and contributed scientific equipment to the universities. In return, small high-technology firms have access to university research, scientific and technical resources, and personnel beyond the capacity of business R & D facilities. The linkages thus allow for academic research to be procured in areas of high priority for New York's industry and for modern technologies to be diffused rapidly throughout the State. From the standpoint of New York's economic redevelopment, the result, quite simply, is increased productivity and competitiveness.

New York's complex network of microeconomic policies facilitating the development of high-technology industry, of which CATs are the most visible institutional expression, is potentially damaging to traditional manufacturing if State support for the two industrial sectors becomes asymmetrical. Indeed, regardless of the intellectual and financial resources invested in planning the growth of new high-technology firms, it would be a sign of very poor planning and coordination if the consequences for another sector were not anticipated and mediated. High-technology policy, however, integrated the dual objectives of small high-technology firm growth with increasing the productivity of traditional manufacturing. As part of the legislative package that created the Centers for Advanced Technology, New York's Urban Development Corporation was authorized to support the development and construction of a Center for Industrial Innovation at Rensselaer Polytechnic Institute, located in Troy.[32] With UDC's financial contribution of 30 million dollars, to be secured through the issuance of bonds, and with the additional support of private sector financing, the Center for Industrial Innovation would be charged essentially with the task of developing technologies which would be adopted by industries to increase their productivity. The development and application of "productivity-enhancing technologies" offered traditional manufacturing, among others of the many industrial sectors to be served by CII, the opportunity to reverse its steady decline. Designed specifically for the purpose of enhancing the productive capacity and efficiency of established industries, CII already possessed strong foundations in RPI's Center for Interactive Computer Graphics, Center for Manufacturing Productivity and Technology Transfer, and Center for Integrated Electronics. As with the Centers for Advanced Technology, CII would institutionalize further cooperative or partnership relationships among business, government, and the academic community, while contributing significantly to educational purposes.

Just as the already precarious situation of traditional manufacturing could have been endangered further by an asymmetrical promotion of the new high-technology growth sector, the problem of structural dislocation could be exacerbated through the adaptation of productivity-enhancing technologies to traditional manufacturing. Productivity-enhancing technologies serve manufacturing by increasing productivity and competitiveness, but in many, particularly labor intensive, cases, firms would be saved at the expense of jobs. Structural dislocation is the inevitable byproduct of technology transfer, and the more so on the scale envisioned by the Center for Industrial Innovation and similar projects that will certainly issue from technology policy in New York.

Consequently, at this point the question is whether State economic development policy continues to recognize the degree to which microeconomic supports for new high-technology and traditional manufacturing are structurally related to the displacement of the labor force. Once again, the singular mark of strategic economic planning is the care with which policy makers map out the structurally interdependent links. Blindness to the consequences caused by newly designed policies will generate political opposition to economic policy as such, i.e., to "industrial policy," as it unwittingly favors groups who benefit from one-sided policies. Policy that narrowly focuses on a particular problem, such as developing new high-technology firms or enhancing the productivity of a declining manufacturing sector, without concern for the problems that such an exclusive focus creates, constitutes an incremental approach that works successfully only when the problem is not structurally related to other problem areas. As is apparent, though, structural interdependency in the high-technology area requires a comprehensive, well-integrated, and coordinated planning approach and rejects incremental solutions. This argument can be substantiated further by the way in which the State attempts to manage the problem of labor force dislocation.

Beginning in 1981, New York passed legislation and implemented programs based on federal legislation which would provide a wide range of training opportunities generally related to changing labor market conditions. Included among these opportunities are programs designed to meet the vocational needs of the structurally unemployed and of employers requiring technically trained labor. Two programs specifically designated for the structurally unemployed exemplify State policy efforts in this area.

New York's community colleges have been authorized to enter into contracts with business and labor organizations to develop curricula that would meet their specific occupational needs, particularly for retraining in technical areas. In addition to these "contract courses," where occupational training and retraining is the responsibility of the educational institution, the federal Job Training Partnership Act, which replaces the Comprehensive Employment and Training Act (CETA), sponsors retraining programs for dislocated workers which are conducted jointly by employers, educational institutions, and community organizations.[33] The JTPA invests responsibility for program development and administration in "Private Industry Councils" (PICs) which are located within "Service Delivery Areas" (SDAs), the local governmental unit intended to promote effective delivery of training services.[34] (New York State has 34 SDAs.) Business, labor, academic institutions, and related service organizations hold membership in the Private Industry Councils. Local vocational retraining programs are developed cooperatively by the PICs and local officials representing the SDAs. The contract courses and JTPA partnership initiatives are decisive steps toward a comprehensive employment and training strategy. The dimension that must be stressed, however, is that while both initiatives equally distribute authority for program development among the public and private sector organizations, the private sector has the determinative influence over programmatic definition. Consequently, structural dislocation policy could remain in step with tendencies of the economy as it passes through successive stages of industrial restructuring, a natural outcome of a policy process that, like its technology-based economy, is becoming decentralized.

ADMINISTRATIVE CONTINUITY
AND POLITICAL CHANGE

Without exception, each of the programs and policies examined thus far, as well as the discernibly steady movement toward comprehensive economic planning, was the result of the combined efforts of the governor's office and the State Legislature during the Carey administration. It must not go without saying, however, that there could be no claim about the *State*—as an administrative entity—being engaged in economic planning unless there were a political commitment made by Carey's successor to continue to pursue strategic planning as the vehicle for economic revitalization. To a considerable extent, of course, this argument holds true only as long as the programmatic initiatives of the administrative units involved in economic development do not develop the deep bureaucratic roots that cannot easily be torn up by new political leadership. In such cases, economic planning could, for a time, prevail even against hostile political forces. While having passed successfully through the embryonic stages of legislative and bureaucratic development to become fully institutionalized and operational, Carey's economic planning efforts nevertheless were quite new and untested when he passed the governorship to Mario Cuomo. Because the previous administration's economic strategies were neither complete nor mature, it would have been a relatively simple matter for the new governor to ignore politely the accomplishments of the Carey administration and to begin afresh. To do so would not necessarily have earned him political or bureaucratic opposition if his own economic policy initiatives were to have more or less addressed the same problems, albeit in different ways, such as the substitution of tactical objectives and immediate political gains for strategic initiatives and long-term, but deferred, economic gains. Potentially and, at least, in the short run, there was more political capital to be won by the new governor by introducing his own economic program than by perpetuating one that he inherited from his predecessor.

To his great credit, and as a decisive indication that the State continues to be immersed in economic planning, Cuomo retained Carey's economic strategies intact. Furthermore, as we shall discover, it would not be an exaggeration to say that Cuomo's economic strategies were authored, *for the most part,* by the Carey Administration.[35] Since it may appear as if Cuomo has neglected economic policy simply because very few *new* strategies have been forthcoming, there can be no doubt that the new governor's acceptance of Carey's economic plan could draw criticism. Unfortunately, this has been the case. In his 1983 and 1984 ("State of the State") *Message to the Legislature,* Cuomo presented a collection of economic policies which completely reproduce the Carey programs and, subsequently, the governor has been taken to task for being insufficiently aggressive in State economic policy.[36] What must be stressed to the contrary, though, is that from a strategic planning perspective—which is the only viable perspective in the context of an economy contending with deindustrialization—Cuomo's replication of Carey's plan is a policy strength, not a weakness stemming from a lack of imagination and determination, in short, from a lack of political leadership. What requires some consideration, therefore, is the extent to which the new governor's economic strategies preserve the former governor's economic plan.

Among the many characteristics common to the approach to economic policy making taken by Governors Cuomo and Carey is an avoidance of ideology and a depoliticization of the policy process. In the first instance, the issue of whether or not to develop an industrial policy is no longer contestable. As Cuomo categorically stated, "we have gone ahead with an economic development strategy that has nothing to do with ideologies and everything to do with common sense."[37] Put differently, government intervention versus the free market and the many variations on this ideological theme are anachronistic. They belong to an earlier stage of economic evolution when the "pace of technological innovation" was not "unforgiving."[38] Technology presents circumstances which annihilate conventional ideological choices and which impose a pragmatic inertia on economic policy. Ideals and interests, no matter how precious or powerful, cannot prevail over the constraints of the new technologically ordered economy. Technology requires "common" sense reasoning that cuts across divisions and overrides differences. For Cuomo, as for Carey, this subordination of ideology means agreement not through the *quid pro quo,* through the politics of interest group negotiations, but through a cooperative relationship among interests which defer to a good greater than the sum of its parts.

"Partnership," therefore, would continue to serve as the framework for all economic policy and economic policy also would remain comprehensive and strategic.[39] As evidence for the continued significance of this framework and of its breadth of responsibility, the partnership concept was speedily embodied in what was intended by the new governor as the single most influential policy apparatus, the Council on Fiscal and Economic Priorities. The Council's role, of course, is advisory. It is the counterpart to, and replacement for, Hugh Carey's Economic Affairs Cabinet discussed earlier. Following the example of EAC and its High-Technology Opportunities Task Force and Advisory Council on High Technology, it is comprised of representatives from the business, labor, government, and academic communities and includes representatives from community organizations and minority groups as well. The Council distributed its responsibilities among a collection of task forces and working groups which formed a highly rationalized division of labor. An overview of the core policy areas which they covered—industrial redevelopment, human resource development, and the rebuilding of public capital facilities—will illustrate the extent to which the previous administration's approach to economic development policy has been reproduced, with changes occurring only at the margin.

Industrial redevelopment includes both the support of new high-technology growth industries and the development of productivity-enhancing technologies and their application to conventional manufacturing. Although essentially the industrial redevelopment focus of the Carey administration, Cuomo's policy apparatus has realized a few changes. The background for one particularly noteworthy difference had been prepared by the Carey administration. Within the context of the national debate over sunrise and sunset industries, Carey had moved policy discourse forward in New York from a discussion of "declining" industries to "mature" and "older" industries, and from "high-technology" to "technology-based" industries.[40] Industries which had ceased to be competitive had reached a threshold stage of product cycle development—they had matured, not declined. Adopting new technologies would turn older or mature industries into technologically-based industries, thereby permitting them to regain the competitiveness of *other* high-technology industries. Carey had been so successful in shifting the terms of economic policy discourse that there are the barest traces of concern with "declining" industries in the Cuomo administration. Cuomo's policy apparatus formalized this advance in economic policy discourse. As a result, in principle there is no sector of the State's economy as it is now approached by policy makers that cannot be modernized.

Cuomo's formalization of economic policy discourse is indicative of the substantive redevelopment programs supported by the new administration. Most important among them, the Science and Technology Foundation, Centers for Advanced Technology, Center for Industrial Innovation, incubator and technology parks are pivotal, and familiar, components of the technology-based industry growth policy. Each of these initiatives has been extended through several apparently new programs. To a great extent, the programs, such as the Innovation Finance Corporation, are additional supports for the development of productivity-enhancing technologies.[41] Other programs focus on the economic redevelopment of distressed areas, regional high-technology development, and—again following the example set by Massachusetts—the formation of an Industrial Cooperation Council, which will be discussed shortly. The Council will explore and facilitate alternatives to plant closings, such as employee ownership, local management buyout, and other forms of industrial refinancing and reorganization that would preserve potentially viable businesses and the economic stability of local communities.

Human resource policy remains as closely coordinated with industrial redevelopment as it was under the previous administration. As Governor Cuomo has stressed, the Job Training Partnership Act provides an opportunity to assure that the education and retraining programs it allows the State to support are consistent with its overall economic strategy. And Cuomo's human resource policy, like Carey's, is attuned to the shifting needs of industry as it undergoes restructuring.[42] Perhaps as a result of his New Deal leanings, though, Cuomo has permitted the economic redevelopment human resource policy to be supplemented by a welfare-state employment policy. While the coexistence of Neoliberal and New Deal programs is a necessary short-run, stop-gap measure until education and retraining programs are developed statewide, a coherent human resource policy will require that the majority of income support mechanisms are replaced by programs synchronized with reindustrialization. Anything less would condemn certain social groups to marginal status in a transformed economy. With the exception of the present governor's somewhat more generous employment policy, Cuomo and Carey share virtually identical human resource policies, at least through 1984, which rely primarily upon the JTPA. Cuomo's policy apparatus, however, has refined the microeconomic features of the retraining programs for the structurally displaced.[43]

Finally, the economic development policy area that has been improved upon considerably since the Carey administration is capital planning policy, more commonly known as "infrastructure." Cuomo has called upon his Council on Fiscal and Economic Priorities to prepare a five-year capital plan which will determine the State's infrastructure needs in view of its economic strategy and balanced against its fiscal constraints. Infrastructure has become and will continue to be, at least for the next two decades, New York's fiscal albatross. Projected capital planning costs are staggering.[44] Perhaps because there are, as yet, no definitive studies on the relationship between declining infrastructure and economic decline, it will be difficult for the State to settle confidently on capital plant priorities which are known to respond directly to the evolving demands of an economy in the process of being restructured. Despite the empirical uncertainties in this area, what is nevertheless very significant is the determination on the part of the new administration to strategically integrate capital planning and economic planning. Given the planning practices in other policy areas, infrastructure planning should become increasingly targeted to economic sectors. And what then will prove to be most interesting is the degree to which fiscal restraints on infrastructure development will compel the State to choose between meeting the infrastructure needs of the community at large and supporting those of the economy. Policy choices here will have a determinate impact on the success of New York's long-term economic strategy.

From this brief overview of New York's strategic economic development policy under the present governor, two tendencies are indicated. First, in central areas of economic policy there is strategic continuity from the Carey to the Cuomo administration. The essential elements of New York's economic plan as it was conceived between 1978 and 1982 are being retained intact. Second, recent changes in the strategic plan, such as those introduced into industrial redevelopment or human resource policy, are marginal, though Cuomo's capital planning strategy is a more aggressive approach to rebuilding the State's infrastructure than that of his predecessor. It would be a simple matter to provide additional evidence for the continuity of economic strategy. Cuomo's economic policy reincorporates Carey's support of small business, export and development finance and assistance, the service sector, tax and regulatory reform, and so forth. At the same time, Cuomo's approach is not only as comprehensive, but as structurally coordinated as Carey's. The one remaining dimension of Cuomo's strategic economic approach requiring consideration is the extent to which it maintains the practice of industrial targeting characteristic of Carey's plan. Since high-technology policy already has provided a basis for an analysis of targeting, it offers an excellent comparative perspective for gauging the degree to which this planning method continues.

New York's Urban Development Corporation has designed several projects which will make a very important contribution to the long term growth of high-technology industry and enhance the capacity of the State to promote high-technology development. A project that furthers both of these ends is UDC's proposed Governor's Association of High-Technology Executives (GATE). GATE's purpose is threefold. An essential function will be to identify both existing and emerging high-technology businesses in New York in need of some form of assistance that could be provided by state agencies. At the same time, the Association will develop a statewide network of permanent communication channels between high-technology firms and State agencies from the highest levels of policy making down through the agency hierarchy. Lastly, GATE will serve as a liaison between new high-technology firms and all other organizations which assume some leadership role in economic development.[45] The logic underlying UDC's

GATE project is sound. States which have achieved prominence in high-technology have, without exception, also had State policies which supported high-technology development over the long term and which were formulated through interaction with high-technology firms. State high-technology firm interaction also enriched and expanded the capacity of state agencies to shape effective high-technology programs. Public-private sector partnerships, especially communication networks, create an information flow whereby the intelligence quotient of the policy process increases through interaction that indirectly promotes economic development by contributing to an improved business climate, directly as a consequence of substantive policies collaboratively designed, and that enhances the capacity of policy-making institutions to initiate subsequent, and more sophisticated, interactive formative processes.

Just as the Urban Development Corporation targets high-technology industry, among the many sectors of the economy for which it develops policy, by establishing communications networks which provide a foundation for a wide range of high-technology policy initiatives, it targets specific high-technology sectors as well. Information technology is perhaps the fastest growing, most highly developed, and largest of New York's high-technology industries. There are, of course, many agencies in New York charged with promoting economic development which also target this sector. The rationalization of their combined efforts is illustrated accurately by UDC's microeconomic focus on information technology.[46]

UDC's overall policy objective is to promote economic diversification as well as growth in the information processing industry. A particularly ambitious proposal is the construction of a high-technology research institute that will carefully target research and development investments exclusively in information technology. UDC's rationale for this proposal is that the history of the State's economic development policy for information technology has consisted in the distribution of limited resources to a variety of institutions. Consequently, quite promising technological discoveries are under-funded at all stages of research and development. The institute would pool the existing research expertise of many State institutions in the information and decision sciences. UDC also proposes a statewide videotex service, the purpose of which would be to more fully utilize information technology in delivering services to, and involving citizens in, government. The idea here is that the use of information technology will improve the efficiency of State service delivery, much as it has in the private sector. Finally, UDC intends to develop an information technology mart to help market New York's information technology products. Market supports are perhaps the single most important contribution to the information technology economy that can be made by the State. Without market supports, New York will neither compete with states and nations which do underwrite their information technology markets nor will it enable this sector to continue to expand.

The Urban Development Corporation's GATE project, high-technology research institute, statewide videotex service, and information technology mart coordinate high-technology development policy inputs, assist information technology research, development, production and application, and the marketing of information processing technology. Yet, these are only a few of the microeconomic policy initiatives that originate with UDC. And as impressive as such an intensive concentration of resources from a single state agency is, other recent targeting efforts are equally so.

Although as of 1973 New York was forced to relinquish the nation's highest ranking in manufacturing to California, and the State's manufacturing sector subsequently conceded to services as its new economic base, New York's economic stability remains dependent upon reversing the plight of traditional manufacturing, of so-called older, mature, or, figuratively, smokestack industry. Earlier noted, it will be recalled, was Carey's commitment to the revitalization of conventional manufacturing so long as programmatic initiatives did not proceed at the expense of promising new trends (services) and developments (new high-technology firms).[47] In this area, as in others considered, the new governor has kept faith with his predecessor's decision not to abandon the traditional sector. Cuomo, however, has begun to investigate the dilemma of older industries more systematically. Evidence for this inquiry is found in the *Report on Adaptation of Older Industries,* a policy study completed by the governor's Economic Development Subcabinet working group on older industry.[48]

Submitted to the governor in late 1984, the *Report* explores possible answers to three very difficult questions:

How can New York encourage the adaptation of new technologies to its traditional industries to raise productivity and increase competitiveness?

What can the State do to eliminate competitive disadvantages to older industries?

What can New York do to avert or minimize the loss of jobs when plant closings are threatened?[49]

Because the working group's policy recommendations are extensive, only a few will be mentioned specifically to highlight the industrial targeting approach to the conventional sector.

Despite the significant progress Carey's approach to older industries had made with its substitition of "technology-based" industry for the distinction between high-technology and declining industries and with the creation of the Center for Industrial Innovation, New York had failed to devise a strategy to implement Carey's proposed comprehensive program for assisting in the transfer of technology to traditional industry. In particular, there was not even an effective institutional framework for providing technical assistance to increase productivity. The *Report* proposed a program whereby selected industries are to be used to demonstrate how new technologies can be adapted. The demonstration projects will be organized on a regional basis encompassing all industry categories and also on an industry-specific basis. The logic here, clearly, is that the regions which are suffering economic distress do not overlap, in all cases, with industries hardest hit by competition. The institutional framework for the demonstration projects consists of a partnership or collaborative relationship among specialists from the academic community and the public and private sectors. Among other forms of collaboration, they will sponsor industry seminars and conferences, provide assistance to industries on such matters as patent litigation, technical standards, and regulatory matters, and develop an industry library and computerized technical base of industry pertinent data. Both the industry (printing, New York City) and the region (Buffalo) selected for the pilot demonstration projects are excellent test cases. Despite the new images created by recent changes in policy discourse, both have been steadily declining.[50]

A second set of policy recommendations contained in the *Report* is concerned with avoiding plant closings. An important and explicit intention of these proposals is to coordinate targeting initiatives with other economic objectives. Specifically, the working group sought to prevent plant closings while not undermining other State policies designed to improve the business climate and stimulate investment. Consequently, the legislative path requiring firms to provide workers and communities with advance notification of the intention to close or relocate and with compensation once such decisions are implemented— a path endorsed by several political economists and considered seriously by many states—is not a policy alternative open to New York State. Rather, the study argued for an expanded definition of the responsibilities to be assumed by the governor's Industrial Cooperation Council.

According to the *Report,* the ICC should have at its disposal a Plant Closing Adjustment Fund that would be used to subsidize feasibility studies of the potential for the continued operation of a manufacturing facility scheduled to close and of the possibility for new management by its employees, or to conduct nationwide marketing campaigns to locate buyers or operators for such facilities. In the event of employee-management takeovers, the Adjustment Fund would provide legal, financial, and management assistance. The Fund would be made up of contributions from the State, manufacturing firms, and perhaps from employees. In addition to the Plant Closing Adjustment Fund, the working group proposed the establishment of funds to partially finance employee ownership and, in certain instances, to enable the State to make equity investments.[51]

Finally, the Economic Development Subcabinet working group laid stress on the need to "coordinate employment and training activity with the overall attempt to assist business adapt its equipment, management, products, and work force." Moreover, coordination between the adoption of productivity-enhancing technologies and consequent structural dislocation retraining programs is extended to complement other State and private sector worker occupational education initiatives, such as the JTPA Private Industry Councils, and those of the Departments of Labor and Education, unions and employer associations. For the first time, in fact, in this all important area of technology adaptation the Council has made coordination the substantive focus, and not simply the form, of structural unemployment policy. The working group proposes that the State identify geographical, industrial, and product areas which will be affected by "a specific plan for adaptation."[52] In other words, the practice of forecasting introduced here transforms economic strategies for increasing competitiveness and labor force flexibility into a strategic economic plan. The approach will obviate the danger that locational decisions, industrial and product investments, and training programs will be based on forms of production and production techniques which are rapidly being replaced by more advanced technologies.

The policy initiatives proposed by the Urban Development Corporation and the working group of the governor's Economic Development Subcabinet hardly exhaust the extent to which the Cuomo administration has continued the industrial targeting begun by the previous governor's policy apparatus. Further examination would show, for example, that high-technology policy and the adaptation of the older industries project also include an energy initiative, tax and regulatory policy, an infrastructure program, and development finance proposals, as well as the strategies in the UDC and older industry categories which already have been discussed.

REINDUSTRIALIZING NEW YORK:
STRATEGIES AND IMPLICATIONS

Since the latter part of the last decade New York State has been in the process of acquiring a history, theory, and vocabulary of strategic economic planning. New York did not begin its economic recovery in 1977–78 with an elaborately conceived plan complete to the last detail. Rather, planning terms of the sort noted at the very outset of this essay at first appeared gradually and, as the State's economy increasingly began to take on the shape of relations coordinated through administrative fiat, the administrative reorganization of the economy has been molded steadily to the structure of these relations as the structure evolved. Accordingly, this "dialectic" between the State's economy and its government, which originated with actions taken by the State, has shaped the State government into an agency that plans. It is no surprise, then, that the governor's 1985 *Message to the Legislature* proposes "long-range planning"—not only in the area of economic development but in a "variety of fields."[53] Whether or not it was the governor's intention, an economic policy process that has evolved into a strategic planning process now has been recognized and acknowledged formally as planning. From this point on, it is very likely that an accumulated experience and discourse will be regularly embodied in a systematic statement of principles and practices relating to the planned revitalization of New York's economy.

"Dialectic" is the most appropriate concept for the dynamics of this evolutionary process. Unfortunately, like "planning" and "industrial policy" it is encrusted with ideological meanings which have no place in a discussion that wants to point to new and quite positive developments which certainly will crystallize as the planning process matures. In the course of discussion it will be useful to clarify what is meant and what is gained by referring to the process as dialectical.

In the late 1970s, the State was faced with an economic predicament offering three choices. New York could maintain its conventional relationship to the market and define policy in broad macroeconomic terms. That approach, in essence, would defer to the forces and tendencies of the market. The result: rapid deterioration in all sectors and most regions of the economy, bankruptcies, accelerated plant closings in manufacturing, unemployment, population migration, and the abandonment of communities. Or, in order to insulate some industries from the pressures of competition, the State could seize upon the protectionist precautions available to it and design *ad hoc* policies to retard or alleviate the immediate symptoms of long-range decline. Here the results would be an uncoordinated set of policy efforts which would discourage the necessary industrial restructuring and introduce economic distortions and social inequities into the market. As a final choice, New York could enable established businesses to recapture their competitiveness, subsidize the development and growth of new businesses, and retrain and, if necessary, relocate workers who are unemployed or structurally displaced. New York has followed the path of the third alternative. By assisting businesses in financing research, risks, and investments, by sharing the costs of developing export markets, and by funding job training and education, the State has reduced considerably the short-term costs of capital and labor. Unlike what has occurred in other states which have relied heavily on their own or federal macroeconomic policies, powerful businesses, urban areas, or regions have not been permitted to dominate economic policy in New York. Rather than succumb to the pressures and temptations to form politically expedient policies, New York's strategies have been devoted to the long-term restructuring of its economy.

There should be no mistaking the significance of New York's approach. In restructuring its economy, the State government has become one of the institutional structures upon which its economy centrally depends. While the objection could be raised that there is nothing new or special about a dependency arrangement that in the past has characterized all economic policy to an extent, it is a unique dependency at this stage of the State's economic development. As has been clear in the preceding analysis, New York's economy is being restructured throughout *technologically*. Whether industry manufactures high-technology products or manufactures products through high-technology processes, the decisive factor in both cases is continual technological advance. Once this process of technological restructuring is set into motion, as it was by New York in the second half of the 1970s, the State, as policy making apparatus, becomes integrated into the economy as an organic part of its overall structure. Integration of this structurally interdependent type does not result because the State has socialized capital costs by means of microeconomic policy and industrial targeting. If capitalization were the issue, the dependency relationship between the public and private sectors would remain as contingent as it has been in the past when it was defined by *ad hoc* initiatives. To the contrary, the State has become integrated structurally into the economy because of the very institutional formations which it has newly designed to meet the needs of technologically restructured economic processes. These new institutional forms—the public-private sector partnerships—and all that they provide in the way of information, legal, technical, and financial assistance, and most importantly, the part they play in facilitating the organizational adaptation of participating institutions (government, business, labor, education, community associations, and so on), constitute the *indispensable* organizational framework without which a technologically based industry could not compete nor a technologically restructured economy evolve.[54]

By creating and nurturing the "partnership," New York State has contributed to the restructuring of a technologically based economy that which only the state can contribute—the reorganization of the framework in which competitive production and its technological evolution is made possible. As the reorganization unfolds, through—and as—the development and elaboration of the public-private sector partnership, the State is drawn into a dialectic. The policy process, which in response to economic crisis formally initiated the reorganization of the framework of production through the formation of Carey's Economic Affairs Cabinet, the High Technology Opportunities Task Force and High-Technology Advisory Council, and through related proposals, has itself now become a division of the production process. Within the partnership framework, there can be no policy that contributes to the evolution of production that does not, at the same time, contribute to the rationalization of economic policy. A technologically restructured economy requires this partnership framework, and as the framework develops the economy it is likewise developed by the economy. Put differently, a high-technology based economy gives birth to state planning.

Neither political economy nor democratic theory yet possess concepts or categories which unambiguously grasp the political form that this partnership or framework of production to some extent already has become and into which it fully will evolve. "Partnership," or public-private sector cooperation, denotes only the formal status of the participants before the policy process within the framework is launched. Once the partnership begins to formulate and implement policy and economic development is underway, an analytical distinction between the public and private sectors or among government, business, education, labor, and community organizations can be insinuated, perhaps, though certainly not an equally precise *empirical* distinction. In practice, the boundaries between the participant's formal identities become blurred; their roles, far more than interchangeable, are doubled. As part of a framework where production and policy are two facets of a single process, each participant is both policy maker and a party affected by policy decisions. Yet, while laying bare its internal dynamics, this analysis largely describes, rather than evaluates, the new institutional formations. For an evaluation to take place, it must begin with an acute awareness that traditional theoretical discourse is inadequate to capture the essential nature of this partnership framework. Concepts and categories of political economy and democratic theory can be used, though cautiously, with the understanding that the political relations entailed by the partnership framework are not exactly what conventional discourse leads us to believe. Rather, the terms of traditional discourse offer us perspectives of the sort which follow.

When Mario Cuomo spoke of "creating new partnerships for economic growth," like Hugh Carey before him who was the author of New York's new policy discourse on partnerships and the architect of this new institutional form in New York State, the governor intended for economic planning to proceed democratically.[55] And the partnership framework does incorporate democratic values and practices. New York's industrial targeting and microeconomic policy functions quite differently from macroeconomic formulas and *ad hoc* political remedies for ailing economies and industrial sectors. New York's economic strategy eliminates, while macroeconomic and *ad hoc* policies promote, the inequities, distortions, and disincentives in the market which result from an absence of coordination and cooperation. Equity and equal opportunity, therefore, are two values imbedded in the restructuring of the market. For an illustration, we have only to recall the State's symmetrical targeting of growth industries and mature industries or its general hostility to a zero-sum calculus for economic growth.

Equity and equal opportunity considerations are extended, not only to industrial sectors, but to the employees of these sectors in the form of job training. With the State's attempt to pair job training with skills specifically required by industries, labor ceases to possess that abstract quality assumed in macroeconomic policy. The consequences of this shift in the meaning of labor are quite significant. Retraining structurally dislocated workers raises the right to work issue to the level of the public agenda in a way radically different from the treatment of employment by the welfare state. When the State targets human resource policy to industrial sectors, it actually redefines its obligations to the unemployed. As human resource policy, employment is not simply a matter of the individual's social security. It is no longer a personal welfare or distributive issue, but one directly pertaining to "investment" in human productive capital. As such, employment is tied now to the country's economic prosperity. Responding to the technological imperative for flexible system production the State will not long be able to resist the transformation of human resource policy into a full employment policy—indeed, into *skilled* full employment policy. Now that economic policy is embodied in the partnership framework of production and has become part of the economic division of labor, many other welfare policies will follow the example of human resource (or human capital) policy, which may thus put an end to welfare state policy, as such. This development is inevitable within the new framework, for as human development and economic development become integrated, the former will be viewed as a necessary condition for the latter, just as a flexible labor force is a necessary condition for value-added production and competitiveness. The "next American frontier," as Robert Reich calls it, will end the welfare state by ending the cultural and economic conditions which sustain it.

This last point requires elaboration. As Reich argues, correctly, social welfare issues have had a precarious existence in virtue of their identification with a "civic culture" that has been viewed consistently as being opposed to the basic values of a "business culture."[56] The two cultures articulate different norms, though not merely in a theoretical or philosophical sense. The normative division between social justice and prosperity, government or the free market, community or freedom, also has been expressed pragmatically in the state and national policy process since the birth of New Deal democracy. Public welfare, community, and social justice necessarily were subordinated to what appeared, according to this dualistic cultural matrix, as an unavoidable choice between the rational and the practical side of liberalism, or, as some may contend, between liberalism and capitalism. In either case, in the history of welfare state policy social welfare never finished better than an often impoverished second on a list of priorities led by economic security and prosperity. By integrating human development, social welfare and social justice, and community with economic development, economic security and prosperity, and the market, the new partnership framework offers to merge the traditionally opposed cultures into a new cultural form.[57] This is the real meaning and deeper historical significance of such neo-liberal propositions as that stated by Mario Cuomo—"Economic Development: The Priority That Supports All Other Priorities."[58]

There is one other democratic perspective on the partnership that deserves attention, not only for its own merits but because it also may well be the organizational foundation for all other democratic qualities that are to be associated with the new framework of production. Until recently it was the prevailing view among social theorists that technological evolution, particularly as it unfolds through economic growth, gives birth to highly centralized forms of economic and political decision making.[59] Briefly, the argument is that technological units of production can be exploited most effectively by being bound progressively together into an organic whole. All parts contributing to the technological process of production—individuals, groups, classes, machines, corporations, and so on—constitute its division of labor. The logic of technological development is a logic of unification and concentration, with ever larger but more rationalized subsystems of production obedient to fewer centers of control. Government follows this pattern laid down by the technological organization of production as it expands, centralizes, bureaucratizes, and rationalizes at a pace set by the exigencies of technologically determined productivity. The state-capital collaboration that, until recently, has been indicative of modern capitalism, emerged to insure economic growth originally made possible through technological achievements.

With the development of new high-technology growth industry, technology continues to exert the same organizational pressures on economic and political decision making, albeit in a substantially altered form. Functionally independent and, most importantly, specialized high value-added advanced technologies, which are proving to be the preferred—and economically necessary—alternative to the high volume standardized method of producing wealth, *decenter* economic production and decision making and *decentralize* political decision making. And once again, the collaboration of business and government follows the new organization of production. Although economic development and redevelopment initiatives may originate in New York State's capitol, in the final analysis all important economic decisions regarding the process of production, and their implementation, will be made by "partnerships" located statewide. The new downscaled organization of technology requires such downscaled government planning and downscaled corporate planning. It would not be an exaggeration, but only in keeping with the structural dynamics of technology, then, to say that downscaled government—local democratic decision making—can be established statewide because of the new downscaled technological mode of production. Consequently, to encourage the development of decentered technology is, at the same time, to promote the development of local democracy.[60]

Within a decade New York could become the paradigmatic example of this radically new political form, and for good reason. New York's potential leadership position in the new, democratic political economy is rooted, paradoxically, in its initial backwardness in the development of new high-technology industry. Because New York could not boast, as of 1978, of collaborative public-private sector and university-industry complexes through which high-technology industries and markets could evolve rapidly, the State had to design and develop these complexes in order to prepare a fertile soil for growth industry. To accomplish this, as we already have seen, economic, educational, and political resources and institutions widely scattered throughout the State were called upon to serve as the multicentered bases for New York's public-private sector partnerships. The seven Centers for Advanced Technology and the Private Industry Councils distributed among the thirty-four service delivery areas designated by the Governor are but two of the many examples of the new institutional arrangements which emerged from the State's initiatives. Herein, then, lies the crucial difference between New York and many other high-technology growth states. In states other than New York, high-technology complexes were, and continue to be, concentrated in a very few geographical areas within state boundaries (Massachusetts' "Route 128," North Carolina's "Golden Triangle," California's "Silicon Valley"). In New York, the opposite has occurred. High-technology partnerships are distributed throughout the State and this distribution contains the potential for New York's leadership in decentralized and local democratic forms of decision making.

Democratic perspectives on the partnership framework explicated here certainly are not exclusive of other significant democratic qualities which could be developed in a much more elaborate analysis. But neither are they exclusive of several undemocratic features, only two (and the most important of which) will be noted at this time. The greatest danger arising from the partnership relation is that the democratic potential of the new framework simply will be overwhelmed by economic interests. Coinciding with this corporatist spectre is the possibility that the substantive and procedural integrity internal to the partnerships' participating institutions—local government, universities and colleges, community organizations, and others—to some extent will be compromised as they address, in good faith, the needs of the other participants and the collective needs of the partnership as a whole.

At this early stage of economic redevelopment, it is impossible to predict whether the democratic or the undemocratic tendencies of New York's partnership will prevail. Yet, there are judgments that can be made without being premature.

First, unless New York State and its industry is prepared to withdraw from competing in the national and international economy, the partnership framework is an unavoidable necessity. Without the collaboration entailed by the partnership, there can be no development of technology-based industry, and without the development of technology-based industry the economy of New York will decline irreversibly.

Second, the partnership will not automatically become either democratic or undemocratic only by virtue of its structural dynamics. Whether or not it evolves democratically and into a democratic form ultimately will depend upon the willingness of the individual members of each of the framework's institutions—elected officials and public managers, faculty and administrators, industry, labor, and community leaders—to participate in shaping the substantive and procedural outcomes of the partnerships. If particular philosophical viewpoints from within the participating institutions are not articulated, at least to that degree the partnership framework will be less representative and less responsible to its publics' interests. Blame for this outcome will lie partially, therefore, with those parties who absent themselves from participating in a development that is ineluctable so long as a growth economy is the imperative.

Finally, terms such as democratic, undemocratic, or corporatist may well offer perspectives which can alert us to possible evolutionary outcomes of the new economic development partnerships, but these perspectives are hardly adequate to comprehend the theoretical or practical implications of this development. As yet, there are no concepts or categories which can bridge the gap between the present, new form of economic redevelopment and its future. To be sure, a new political vocabulary will emerge in time. Until that time, the familiar terms of political discourse will enable us to remain attentive to the possible consequences of policy decisions and to the political forms which make and implement them. But these terms should neither pose obstacles to our commitment to new and promising institutional forms nor make us sanguine about their success and their respect for what should be preserved.

If it seems peculiar that the state, rather than the Union, may have become the cradle of democratic as well as economic renewal, then New York's present initiatives must be appreciated within the broader political context. It is easy to point to complex political, bureaucratic, and ideological obstacles to national initiatives in strategic economic planning. No matter how sympathetically we study the embattled terrain of national economic policy, however, several basic facts remain. What has passed for national industrial policy—slaughtered programs, emasculated agencies, tax cuts favoring social rather than economic "sectors," fiscal and monetary policy generally—has introduced distortions, inequities, and disincentives into the national market place. For instance, economic growth has resulted from the artificial creation of a domestic market that prospers by managing foreign competition while crushing American export industries. And, to pursue the logic of this example, when monetary policy harms American export industries, it harms New York's exporting industries. New York State, in other words, can labor overtime to aid its business in the development of export markets, but national macroeconomic policy can pose an insurmountable hurdle to its success. In most other areas of the State's strategic planning, national macroeconomic policy could be equally as detrimental. All things considered, then, national economic policy has two opposite effects on New York, one actual and one potential. On the one hand, it has forced the State to design its own comprehensive economic policy, in essence, to plan. Planning, in turn, has laid the groundwork for the evolution of new economic and perhaps democratic institutions. On the other hand, if the difficulties faced by the State's export initiatives offer any lesson, it is that national economic policy may possibly lay this evolution to waste. To return to the sentiment expressed by Felix Rohatyn, New York State has made strides toward solving the dilemma of statesmanship through an evolving democratic plan.[61] Yet, there can be no enduring solution at the State level until another dilemma is faced.

CHALLENGES TO THE PARTNERSHIP

No actions undertaken by states, however, can constrain the national government to address, much less publicly acknowledge, its own dilemma of statesmanship. It is true as well, though, that if the national government were to attempt to bring economic policy into line even with the broad objectives of states' initiatives, there would remain crucial areas in which state and national aims and strategies are necessarily incongruent. Nevertheless, regardless of the obstacles posed by the federal government, New York State clearly has made impressive strides toward economic planning.

At the same time, it is far too early, certainly, to determine the extent to which New York's initiatives will succeed or fail. Economic impact studies as yet are either too few in number or too narrow in scope to yield corrective evaluations. On the other hand, it seems that the State already has anticipated—and responded to—particular criticisms of its strategic approach. For example, the explicit coordination of policies, programs, and agencies, for which critics have pressed ever more aggressively as coordination actually has increased, and which has been evolving steadily as a deeply rooted structural force within the economic policy process, soon will be institutionalized as a result of the governor's decision to appoint a Director of Economic Development.[62] And if there could be any further doubt that the State is engaged in strategic economic planning, it should be erased by the governor's request that the new super-commissioner "describe [New York's] overall economic strategy."[63]

While it is too early to subject the State's strategic economic policy to a systematic critical study and evaluation, the time is highly appropriate to identify, as precisely as possible, the challenges it must meet. Many of these challenges, perhaps the most difficult, are those produced by long-term economic decline, in effect, by deindustrialization. Others have surfaced more recently in the wake of the State's economic reversal and have resulted from State policies, past and present, where the strategic cures it has provided have proved worse than its economic afflictions. Still others are challenges to be additionally creative where State policies have either achieved or promised some new measure of economic success.

Our first three essays identify bench marks which may offer reference points for State policies focusing upon declining industries and distressed communities or, in the other direction, affecting broad Statewide trends. Unfortunately, these essays may also implicitly outline the limits to State economic policy, that is, indicate the types of problematic areas upon which the State can have little or no impact. This last point is particularly true of Barry Gewen's "Imports and Apparel: From Riches to Rags," where the State may be powerless to reverse the decline in the apparel industry—once the State's largest manufacturing employer. In the near future, the State's task will be to prevent other industries from suffering the same fate, or at least to spare their workers the same pains. For the State to finally confront the necessity for a declining industry policy obviously will be a tragic way to repay its indebtedness to one of its oldest basic industries. "Industrial Devolution in New York State," by Glenn Yago and other members of his Industrial Research Project at the State University of New York's Stony Brook campus, distinguishes categories of industry most likely to abandon the State's communities and to impose the economic hardships of rapid disinvestment. Again, perhaps the only course of action here open to the State is to encourage its communities to avoid a hostage relation to certain industry types or to equip them to withstand the shocks delivered by industrial outmigration. Ed Renshaw's "Trends in Manufacturing Employment and Reflections on Infrastructure Investment, Tax and Expenditure Policy in New York State" concludes this section on an upbeat note by underscoring definite steps that the State can take to capitalize on efforts to reindustrialize its economy. The argument proceeds from an analysis of policies which are not yet, but could be, designed within a framework of strategic economic development.

Renshaw's essay also provides an appropriate transition to the following section on local and regional economic problems, trends, and policies. Whereas he leads us to a consideration of general economic policy areas where reforms in the policy process are necessary preconditions for state and local reindustrialization efforts, in "Strategic Planning in a White Collar City: The Case of Albany," Todd Swanstrom refines that argument by endorsing the selective adoption of strategic planning techniques as an approach to enhancing particular dimensions of growth trends within local economies. Swanstrom's argument points up the fallacy of interfering in the market where negative market forces are powerful and policy resources are modest. It implicitly offers a stern measure of the enormous resources which must be at the State's disposal if its attempts at strategic planning are to reverse the tendencies toward economic decline as well as nurture growth trends. Like Swanstrom's, the contributions by Mark Kasoff and Mark Soskin, "Economic Development Prospects for New York's St. Lawrence River Basin," and by Lawrence Southwick, "Local Economic Development and the State," carve out special areas of economic development where regional communities can prosper. Prosperity will occur, though, only if the State is judicious when forming policies that will have an impact on local development initiatives. Both articles evaluate the effect of a range of State programs and institutions on local development priorities. They also recommend State reforms that would improve the efficacy of statewide revitalization strategies as well as the capacity of local units to achieve their own *and* State objectives. The issues examined in these pieces closely resemble those which arise in discussions about the relationship between state and national economic policies. As is evident from the two studies, however, the State is far more reflective about its relation to local and regional areas than the national government is about its policy impact on the State. As a consequence, New York State stands a better chance than the nation as a whole for the eventual creation of a sturdy economic foundation anchored among its many local and regional centers. Such a foundation cannot but strengthen the long-term prospects for the State's strategic economic goals.

Yet, if New York had no other incentives to rebuild its economic foundations through state and local initiatives, the intense pressures of international trade would provide more than sufficient motivation. This is true not merely in the obvious sense that stresses the importance of sectoral restructuring to enhance the competitiveness of the State's industry. It also is true from the standpoint of New York's ability to exploit the far greater potential of its already highly favorable international economic position. This is the decisive lesson contained in Walter Goldstein's "The Changing Impact of International Trade on the Economy of New York State" and in Prem Gandhi's "Foreign Direct Investment and Regional Development: The Case of Canadian Investment in New York State." Goldstein's comprehensive analysis of New York's trade relations establishes a new strategic imperative—a renewed effort on the part of New York to integrate the revitalization of its economy with its international trade policy initiatives. The deeper implication of his argument is that international trade is not just one dimension among others of the State's economy, but a sector whose development defines the limits and possibilities for the development of the State's entire economy. New York cannot hope to restructure industry to make it more competitive unless it first develops international trade policy as an incentive to restructure industry. Consequently, New York can no longer afford an economic policy that does not place international trade at the forefront of strategic concerns. Likewise, Gandhi causes us to raise similar questions about the potential benefits to the State provided by foreign direct investment. Neglecting policy initiatives which would attract foreign direct investment may undermine economic revitalization efforts generally. For Gandhi, however, there is not the same degree of structural interdependency between economic revitalization and foreign direct investment as there is for Goldstein between strategic economic development and international trade.

With "Building the Twentieth Century Public Works Machine: Robert Moses and the Public Authority," Jon Lines, Ellen Parker, and David Perry pose a more fundamental challenge to the partnership policy framework. Reconstructing the obstacles that must be overcome by policy makers to rebuild another pillar of the State's economy, the infrastructure, the authors demonstrate how the powers aggregated by the public authority together with the pragmatic leadership exercised by Robert Moses are prerequisites for designing and implementing infrastructure policy. If they are correct, then one major implication of the essay may be that only policy institutions and forms of leadership which many social scientists would consider to be substantially less democratic than the partnership framework can revitalize the State's economy. Such an implication, however, would be greeted with irony by Michael Black and Richard Worthington. In "The Center for Industrial Innovation at RPI: Critical Reflections on New York's Economic Recovery," they argue that basic principles for democratic representation were violated when the decision was made by the New York partnership under Hugh Carey to commit the State to a high-technology economic redevelopment strategy and to develop the Center for Industrial Innovation. In light of the last two essays, therefore, the partnership policy framework is either too democratic or too undemocratic to be a procedurally or substantively effective policy-making apparatus. While John Kalas' "Reindustrialization in New York: The Role of the State University" is not intended to resolve this dispute about the democratic qualities of the partnership, it does lay to rest many of the corporatist fears raised by Black and Worthington about the influence of business on State economic policy. Kalas not only brings into view the entire range of contributions made by the State University to New York's revitalization efforts, but reveals as well the extent to which the University has been developed in the process of making its contributions. And perhaps most important within the context of the normative debate provoked by the previous two essays, Kalas' work enhances our confidence in the University's ability to preserve the integrity of its values and institutions while not insulating itself from the State and relinquishing its public responsibilities.

The analyses of defense spending, of the so-called "New Federalism," and of acid rain focus attention on serious problem areas for which solutions ordinarily would not be forthcoming at the state level. They are included in this volume for two reasons. First, despite the fact that viable state solutions are rare wherever problems originate largely beyond its geographical and political boundaries, in a few cases there are important exceptions to the rule. Second, each of these three problem areas is a central concern for New York's economy, although in virtue of their geographical and political points of origin they cannot be easily incorporated into the State's strategic economic policy. In fact, it appears unlikely that federal procurement policy could become a cornerstone of New York's economic development, as it has in other states. The failure of the State to improve its federal procurement standing is to be regretted, for according to James Ryan's "Defense Procurement and the Reindustrialization of New York State" even a modest redistribution of federal funding toward New York would make a significant difference to the health of its economy. Ryan's argument not only helps us to understand the economic impact of federal procurement policy, but proves that Department of Defense procurement is an industrial policy rather than simply procurement policy. Richard Silkman's "Old Federalism and New Federalism in New York State" identifies an area of federal intervention where New York may be only somewhat more successful in deriving new advantages. New Federalism has created a highly ambiguous predicament for New York's revitalization and, while offering certain bright prospects, on the downside may force the State to make costly economic trade-offs. In the final analysis, New York's capacity for seizing the economic redevelopment opportunities provided by the New Federalism will depend upon the speed with which a revitalized economy will either remove fiscal burdens from the State or enable the State to bear up under them. To conclude this special issues section, "Acid Rain: Public Policy in the Face of Uncertainty," by Roman Hedges and Donald Reeb, takes up the most controversial of the three areas. In addition to evaluating the impact of acid deposition on New York's economy, Hedges and Reeb explain why the State has been able to initiate important steps toward managing a problem that, in a practical sense, lies outside of its domain. Each successive essay shows State policy to be increasingly capable of corrective policy measures in relation to the absence of necessary, or the presence of obtrusive, federal initiatives.

Alvin Magid brings our study of New York's reindustrialization to a close with a reconsideration of industrial democracy. Drawing upon comparative evidence, Magid's analysis is especially important at a time when the State is considering industrial cooperation as an organizational strategy for retaining industries in communities where deindustrialization introduces its familiar decay. Magid offers a balanced perspective on the appropriateness of industrial cooperatives for New York's industrial structure.

There can be no doubt that these are formidable challenges to strategic economic policy in New York State. Each is a priority; each must be managed in due course. Moreover, these are challenges which can be managed only by an economic plan, because as Hugh O'Neill, New York State's Deputy Secretary for Economic Development, has argued, "the pressures for economic revitalization are enormous; consequently, the temptation to do anything is enormous."[64] To resist the temptation to do anything in the short-run is as important as long-term economic strategies. New York already has displayed resistance to expediency, but its future good judgment may well depend upon the progress of New York State's partnership and upon all those who contribute to it.

II

Bench Marks:
A Declining Industry,
Industries Contributing to Decline,
State Policies and State Decline

TWO

Imports and Apparel:

From Riches to Rags

Barry Gewen

The apparel/textile industry never has had a particularly good public image. To many people it is still the "rag trade." In the past, apparel manufacture conjured up images of slumbs, poverty, and men, women and children toiling endless hours over sewing machines for pennies a day. The word "sweatshop" was coined to describe conditions in the industry.

Unions arose to combat the sweatshop and, in combination with a government that was willing to harness the power of law against industrial evils, they largely succeeded in cleaning up the worst conditions. Most recently, sweatshops have reappeared to plague both workers and law-abiding employers. Yet, the negative image one hears at present is not of a "sweatshop industry" but of a "sunset industry." The apparel/textile industry, as well as other smokestack industrial sectors of America, we are told, is fated to decline, to sink into the sea like the setting sun. Foreign competition will determine its fate. What is more, in its efforts to preserve itself and the jobs of millions of Americans from a deadly flood of imports, the industry merely is retarding economic growth and weakening the U.S. vis-à-vis its international competitors. Apparel is not only in miserable shape, it is making everyone else miserable, too.

Two of the most prominent advocates of this view are the influential economists Lester Thurow and Robert B. Reich. Writing in the *New York Review of Books,* Thurow declared that "with the loans to Chrysler and Lockheed, Congress decided upon a strategy of keeping declining and ultimately doomed 'sunset' industries open—while real industrial policies would speed up the closure of the sunset firms." Thurow went on to present a stark choice for America's future.

> There are only two possible responses. A country can have an industrial policy of protecting its sunset industries and watch its national economic sun set as it prolongs the agony of decline. Or a country can have a policy of promoting sunrise industries so that there are new and better job opportunities for the workers of sunset industries.[1]

And writing in the same periodical a few months later, Reich expressed similar ideas.

> The United States has consistently used its tariffs, quotas, "orderly marketing agreements," tax breaks, and bailouts of various kinds to protect older industries that have long since become uncompetitive in world markets. These policies have retarded change in the structure of the American economy.[2]

To those who work in the apparel/textile industry these views are not only misconceived, they are factually incorrect. For while the concept of "sunset industry" is relatively new—having entered public discourse only in the last three years or so, along with such related terms as "Atari Democrat" and "Reindustrialization"—the sunrise/sunset policy is not. America has been pursuing such a policy for years. The apparel/textile industry is being allowed to disappear. If trade agreements reached under the internationally recognized Multifiber Arrangement and sanctioned by GATT have slowed the decline, they have neither halted it nor are they designed to do so. The trend has been in a single, inexorable, and downward direction. The sunrise/sunset opponents could wish for little more than a speedier demise.

THE DECLINE OF AN INDUSTRY

Twenty-five years ago imports accounted for one out of every 20 garments purchased by American consumers—4.9 percent of the domestic market. Ten years ago imports constituted one out of five apparel purchases—20.6 percent of the American market. In 1982, imports accounted for two out of every five garments bought in American stores—41 percent of the domestic apparel market. Today almost 50 percent of all apparel worn in the U.S. is made overseas. In women's apparel the figure is already over 50 percent.[3]

The seriousness of the situation is highlighted further when these numbers are translated directly into unemployment statistics. In 1958 the number of U.S. jobs needed to produce the imported apparel was 51,700. By 1983, the number of job opportunities lost to imports reached approximately three-quarters of a million. For the past 25 years the unemployment rate in apparel never fell below the national average. In 1958, a recession year, overall unemployment was 6.8 percent; in all manufacturing it was 9.2 percent. In apparel, the unemployment rate was 12 percent. Ten years ago total unemployment was 4.9 percent. The average for manufacturing was below that figure at 4.3 percent. In apparel, however, unemployment was 7 percent. And that was the lowest percentage it reached during the decade of the 1970s. The recession year of 1982 was particularly grim. Overall unemployment was 9.7 percent, not quite double digits. Manufacturing did reach double digits—12.3 percent. But in the garment industry, unemployment reached an appalling 15.4 percent. When the rest of the country is in recession, the apparel industry suffers depression.

Nowhere have the industry's problems been more apparent or more severe than in New York State.[4] In 1948 the industry was the State's largest manufacturing employer, providing jobs for 424,000 workers, more than the second and third largest industries combined. One out of every five New Yorkers in manufacturing was an apparel worker. About one out of every 12 nonagricultural employees was an apparel worker and, conversely, more than one out of every three apparel workers in the country was a New Yorker. The industry was thriving. New York City's apparel center, the Mecca of fashion, was a source of pride for the City and the State.

By 1980 this prosperous and vital sector of the State's economy was in serious trouble. The workforce had shrunk to 170,000, a loss of a quarter million jobs. The industry, though still a major employer of New Yorkers and providing jobs for 12 percent of manufacturing workers in the State, was no longer number one. Among manufacturing industries it had been beaten out narrowly by the machinery sector. Similarly, New York's nationwide share of apparel workers had dropped from 36 to 13 percent. In 22 years the number of apparel shops in the State had been cut in half, from 14,806 in 1958 to 7,302 in 1980. The New York State Department of Labor concluded that the movement of employers to other states and other countries in search of cheap labor and the rising flood of imports "has had a disastrous effect on the industry in New York."[5]

One might imagine that after so much damage has been done there could be little more left to do. In fact, the sunset is still very much in progress. Though the apparel/textile industry lost over 700,000 jobs in the latest decade alone, the reduction came from a total of almost 2.5 million positions. There remain 1.8 million American workers employed in apparel/textiles.

Very few people realize the size of the "rag trade." Because it is spread out through so many locales and made up of thousands of small shops averaging 50 workers each, the industry does not command the same attention as more visible giants like steel and autos. Yet apparel/textiles remain the nation's largest industrial employer. The industry provides work to one out of every eight American production workers, more than the total number of production workers in basic steel, auto assembly and chemical refining combined.[6]

In thousands of small towns across the country, the loss of a garment shop can devastate an entire community. Last year the people of Highland County, Virginia—population 2,600—saw their unemployment rate jump from 12 percent to 23 percent when a women's apparel plant, the only industrial employer in the entire county, shut down. The reason for the closing was competition from imports.[7]

The human face behind the statistics is recorded in the files of the International Ladies' Garment Workers' Union. In 1982, ILGWU shops in the New York towns of Homer and Oswego closed their doors because of imports. Officers of the union described what happened to some of the workers affected.

Deborah K. had to go on welfare because of losing her job. Debbie has four children and an unemployed husband.

Claudia M. had to go on welfare after she lost her job. Claudia speaks very little English. She is 60 years old and very bitter because all she knows how to do is sew garments.

Carolee W. has had to move into cheaper housing and go on welfare since the factory closed. Carolee has five children and is pregnant again. Her husband is unemployed.

Rita B. had to go on partial welfare. She lives with no electricity and no central heating. She is sickly and cannot get better housing because she is all alone. She cuts her own wood, carries her water from a well.[8]

It is necessary to be clear about the precise nature of the threat to these workers and their industry. Imports are a problem for a number of American industries, but the problem is not the same everywhere. Labels like "free trade" or "protectionism" obscure more than they describe. What is happening in steel is not the same as what is happening in autos. And what is happening in apparel/textiles is different from what is happening in steel and autos. The sunrise/sunset proponents argue that the older industries have become uncompetitive on the world market and obsolete. How does this apply to the import-devastated apparel/textile industry?

Often the trade question is posed in terms of quality. Americans are said to buy imports because they believe they are getting better value for their dollar. Yet quality is not an issue in the apparel/textile industry. There are no country-by-country, garment-by-garment consumer reports on apparel, nor could there be. The enormous diversity of the industry, its hundreds of thousands of small shops worldwide and the rapid turnover of styles and products preclude such comparisons. Consequently, we can measure quality best by looking at declared consumer preferences. And what the preference polls report is that American consumers believe American-made clothing to be superior to imports. In a University of Missouri telephone survey of areas in the eastern United States, 64 percent of those polled preferred American apparel to imports. Only 10 percent said imported clothing was superior and 26 percent felt there was no difference.[9] Other polls show similar findings. Put simply, no one enters a store deliberately intending to buy a shirt made in South Korea or a sweater made in Thailand. If importers are taking an ever larger share of the American market, it is not because consumers are specifically asking for them, but because that is what they are being offered.

Productivity has been a source of considerable discussion over the past several years, with the argument that American industry must improve its productivity in order to compete in the world market. Productivity, however, is not an issue in apparel/textiles. American technology is "state of the art" and productivity has been increasing steadily. The U.S. International Trade Commission estimates that the same quantity of men's shirts requiring 3.5 direct labor hours to produce in the United States requires 5 direct labor hours in Hong Kong, and 6 in both Singapore and Thailand.[10] Indeed, most plants overseas are using American methods of production, encouraged to do so by American companies that have their work done overseas. Because of the nature of the industry—labor-intensive with relatively low capital investment—any innovation in production travels quickly around the world.

Related to the productivity issue is the claim that imports force flabby, oligopolistic American firms to rejuvenate by bringing needed competition. But there is no flabbiness in an industry where 20,000 domestic shops vie for a share of the domestic market. Apparel/textiles

57

is one of the nation's most competitive sectors. Its fluidity and ease of entry assure a steady stream of new entrants aspiring to turn their rags into riches. "Monopoly" and "oligopoly" are words that are foreign to this industry.

Finally, it is said that American workers have priced themselves out of the world market with their incessant demands for higher wages. This argument approaches the real heart of the import problem. Apparel production in particular is a labor-intensive industry, with wages accounting for 30–40 percent of total costs. Any wage difference, therefore, is an important, indeed crucial, competitive advantage. Third World countries have been able to undercut American firms because of the lower wages paid in those lands. This does not mean that American wages are too high. On the contrary, the problem is that Third World wages are too low.

In 1981, when the average U.S. manufacturing wage was over $8.00 an hour, the average for an apparel worker was $4.94. That amounts to $172.90 for a 35-hour week. Is there anyone in the United States who would consider such earnings excessive? Yet, in Hong Kong, which supplies about one-fifth of all apparel imports, the 1981 hourly wage for garment workers was $1.18. In South Korea, the third largest supplier, the wage was 63 cents an hour. In the People's Republic of China, with the potential to become the top supplier by far, the average wage paid to garment workers is 16 cents an hour. Other examples are equally striking—84 cents an hour in the Dominican Republic; 38 cents an hour in India; 32 cents an hour in Thailand; and in the Philippines, 25 cents an hour.[11] It is impossible for American workers to compete with these wages. Once all of the rhetoric of the trade debate is eliminated, a single fact stands out. The only reason imports are devastating the American apparel/textile industry and turning it into a sunset industry is the incredibly low wage paid to workers in the Third World countries.

Although that is the most essential fact about the plight of the apparel/textile industry, there is another fact to bear in mind. We are in the midst of a dynamic situation. If we choose to do nothing about low-wage imports the problem will only get worse. Further job destruction is certain. Indeed, one can fairly predict that every job which *can be* exported *will be* exported.

The reason for this is that manufacturers and retailers have learned to shop around for the cheapest labor they can find anywhere in the world. If the environment is right, deals are made, plants are constructed, and production begins. Some American workers are losing their jobs to 16-cents-an-hour labor. More manufacturers then follow, forced to close their U.S. facilities because of this competition, and more Americans are sent to the unemployment lines.

It is well to remember that such international "shopping around" is far removed from the traditional free trade arguments of the classical economists. When they spoke of "comparative advantage," the basic point the Smiths and Ricardos were trying to drive home was that nations should not ignore other nations' natural advantages. It was folly for England to try to grow grapes rather than buy wine from Portugal. These writers never foresaw a world in which workers in Birmingham were pitted directly against workers in Seoul or Manila. Certainly, they never imagined a situation where capital moved as freely as it does today. David Ricardo wrote:

Experience, however, shows that the fancied or real insecurity of capital, when not under the immediate control of its owner, together with the natural disinclination which every man has to quit the country of his birth and connections, and intrust himself, with all his habits fixed, to a strange government and new laws, check the emigration of capital. These feelings, *which I should be sorry to see weakened,* induce most men of property to be satisfied with a low rate of profits in their own country, rather than seek a more advantageous employment of their wealth in foreign nations.[12]

Our world has changed considerably since Ricardo's time, and it is safe to assume that if he were alive today, any theories associated with his name would look very different from those that have made him famous.

THE CHANGING THIRD WORLD

There is a second side to the modern movement of capital that makes the process even more devastating. If manufacturers are eager to move their production facilities abroad to take advantage of low-wage labor, Third World nations are as eager to have them. A profound shift has occurred in the growth policies of Third World countries, a shift that began in the 1960s and that has been accelerating ever since. As a result, policy decisions made in Taipei, Peking, and Colombo are having seriously detrimental effects on our domestic economy.

Until the 1960s manufactured exports played only a small role in the economies of Third World nations. Governments for the most part concentrated on building up their home industries. But after the hoped-for development frequently failed to take place, new policies were set in motion. As a study for the World Bank reports, "there has been a widespread shift in less-developed countries' policies away from inward-looking industrialization around the home market, toward a systematic effort to export industrial products."[13] Outside investment became an avidly sought prize. Foreign manufacturers were assiduously courted.

The countries that pioneered the change included those on industrial Europe's rim—Spain, Portugal, Greece, Yugoslavia, and Israel—as well as the Asian nations of South Korea and Taiwan. (Hong Kong, though not a nation, also should be mentioned here.) They, in turn, were imitated by Brazil, Mexico, and Singapore. These nations, especially the ones outside of the European orbit, are today considered the success stories of the Third World, and a new category, newly industrializing countries or NICs, has been created to distinguish them from the rest of the emerging world. Now others are looking to export-oriented growth policies to pull themselves out of poverty. Among the nations currently initiating export-promotion measures to attract foreign business the World Bank includes Colombia, Argentina, Uruguay, Chile, Sri Lanka, Tunisia, Morocco, Haiti, Dominican Republic, Cyprus, Malta, Mauritius, and some Central American republics.[14] This list is not exhaustive.

In the cases of some of the larger of these countries, such as Brazil and Spain, economies of scale together with other factors have enabled them to export machinery and transportation equipment. But generally, the path of success in exports has been through the labor-intensive industries where a poor nation's abundant labor supply provides a comparative advantage against the developed countries. The prime example of such an industry is apparel manufacture, which has been called a locomotive for growth. The prime examples of nations or states that have climbed aboard this locomotive are Taiwan, South Korea, and Hong Kong. Together, the Big Three account for approximately 60 percent of all apparel imports into the United States.

The successes of the Big Three are well known around the world. Consequently, others are rushing in to build their own export-oriented apparel industries. In reporting on the growth of the apparel/textile industry in Indonesia, Thailand, and the Philippines, the *Far Eastern Economic Review* explains the thinking behind this push.

The textile industry allows relatively easy entry to the newcomer, both technologically and financially, particularly at the downstream end of production. It has thus provided a textbook illustration of how an underdeveloped country can catch up with and sometimes overtake an advanced country, starting with labor-intensive processes such as knitting and simple garment making and gradually moving upstream into more designer-conscious garment production.[15]

Seth M. Bodner, Executive Director of the National Knitwear and Sportswear Association, is already anticipating problems with the new suppliers only now coming on line, "like Sri Lanka or some place like the Maldive Islands. . . . This is where the future conflicts are going to be joined, and admittedly it's a hard perception to get across."[16]

Sri Lanka provides a good example of the policy changes now taking place in the Third World in imitation of the NICs. "The whole thrust of our development strategy is to become like Singapore," a government official told the *New York Times*.[17] The policy began in 1977. Industrial zones were established where foreign investors were lured with promises of tax holidays and cheap labor. The tax breaks were for 10 years. Wages, the government proudly declared, "are even lower than in India."[18] At Katunayake Garments, an industrial zone enterprise making gloves for the American market, 290 young women work two shifts, often rising at 3 or 4 in the morning and not getting home until the middle of the night.[19] By 1982 about 25 apparel factories employing 15,000 people were located in Sri Lanka's industrial zone. Another 65 factories with 27,000 people are outside the zone.[20]

Though Sri Lanka is not one of the major shippers at the present time, its growth has been striking. In late 1978, a journalist for *Women's Wear Daily,* the newspaper of the women's apparel industry, reported:

Since Sears and Eagle Shirts broke ground here for apparel production four years ago, this small nation is now doing business with everyone, but there has been a virtual explosion of trade with the United States in the past 18 months, says D. N. Thurairajah, deputy director of the Ceylon Textile Manufacturers Association. The list includes retailers, importers and manufacturers: Sears, J. C. Penney, KW International, Oxford Industries, Phillips-Van Heusen, Triton, BVD, Campus, Englishtown and others.[21]

In 1976, before its new economic policy, Sri Lanka's cotton, wool, and man-made fiber apparel exports to the U.S. totalled 1,288,107 square yards equivalent (SYE). By 1979, its shipments amounted to 25,415,711 SYE, and by 1982, in the midst of world depression, it was exporting 58,050,525 SYE of apparel.[22] Its apparel workforce nearly trebled, expanding from 15,000 in 1974 to 42,000 in 1982, and the U.S. International Trade Commission reported that "Sri Lanka will most likely continue its efforts to expand exports of apparel during the next five years, partly because of the need to reduce its relatively high level of unemployment and partly because the success of its free trade zone largely hinges on the production of apparel for export.[23]

If Sri Lanka is a classic example of a new apparel-exporting nation, perhaps the most ominous example as far as the future of the American industry is concerned is the People's Republic of China. With one quarter of the world's population, this predominantly rural nation had an *urban* workforce of 90 million people out of a total workforce of 430 million in 1975. Between 1957 and 1975 its total labor force grew at a rate of 2.4 percent per year, faster than its overall population, and estimates are that labor force growth will be even faster throughout the 80s.[24]

To cope with these population and employment pressures, China has embarked on a massive development plan of its own and it, too, sees exports as a key source of growth. With its unmatched numbers and incredibly low wages, its potential to undercut competitors in labor-intensive industries is unparalleled. As one excited U.S. apparel manufacturer who has been doing business with Peking since the Nixon opening put it, "You've got 900 million people there and I bet there's a hundred million of them that can sew."[25] A more precise and sobering statistical estimate was provided by *Women's Wear Daily*. It reported that the "two Chinese enclaves of Hong Kong and Taiwan supply 45 percent of all U.S. apparel imports from a skimpy population base of 21 million. That is barely 2.2. percent of China's teeming masses." It also cited the President of the American Apparel Manufacturers Association as calculating, in light of these figures, that "theoretically, China can have an output 50 times larger than two of the largest suppliers combined."[26]

The Chinese government obviously is aware of the importance of its apparel/textile industry for the nation's development plans. In 1980 five million workers were employed in the industry, with three million in textiles and two million in apparel. That year, textiles and apparel together made up one-fourth of China's total exports and one-third of its exports to the United States.[27] Peking has been actively promoting export growth by seeking out foreign investors, setting up industrial zones, and pursuing joint ventures with foreign companies. Its success in attracting business—lured by one of the lowest hourly wages in the world—has been nothing less than phenomenal.

From a standing start in the mid 1970s, China's apparel trade has been growing so rapidly that the country is now the fourth largest supplier to the U.S. Expansion has been almost geometric, as these tables clearly indicate.

CHINESE APPAREL EXPORTS TO U.S. (S.Y.E.)

	1976	1977	1978	1979
Cotton	19,813,414	23,098,521	48,629,577	104,231,435
Manmade Fiber	2,614,612	5,028,016	12,686,640	37,137,377
Wool	318,783	276,172	600,301	458,668
TOTAL	22,746,809	28,402,709	61,916,518	141,827,480
	1980	1981	1982	1983
Cotton	110,283,468	140,989,343	155,827,803	204,558,733
Manmade Fiber	46,794,064	95,155,179	191,717,523	212,383,115
Wool	9,086,481	6,705,278	9,168,369	12,211,368
TOTAL	166,164,013	242,849,800	356,713,695	429,153,216

Source: U.S. Bureau of the Census; ILGWU Research Department

Over 10 percent of all U.S. apparel imports now come from mainland China. The International Trade commission points out that "the government will continue to emphasize, at least in the near term, the growth of the textile and apparel industries as an important supplier of consumer goods and foreign exchange earnings."[28] If these shipments are not controlled adequately, it will be only a few years before China becomes the number one source of apparel imports. How long the American apparel/textile industry can last beyond that is a matter for conjecture. Clearly, though, the Chinese example emphatically demonstrates the weaknesses of the free trade argument. It proves beyond a doubt that unregulated trade is a prescription for disaster.

From the standpoint of American industry free trade does constitute a serious threat. Yet it is important, as well, to understand that for the Third World free trade is at best a mixed blessing, a double-edged sword. With Taiwan, South Korea, and Hong Kong as examples, exports seem to offer a bright future of smooth development and rapid advance. But there is a dark side to this picture. Keeping uneasy company with the new skyscrapers of Seoul and Taipei are all the old evils of industrialization. The sweatshop conditions that the developed countries successfully battled during the past century have reemerged in the Third World in a more virulent form than before. According to a *Washington Post* correspondent, "While Korea has gleaming new factories and a growing middle class, it remains a land of miserable poverty and Dickensian wages and employment conditions for the working class." One Korean textile worker told the *Washington Post* she worked nine and ten hours a day, seven days a week.[29] A candy worker described 84-hour work weeks which increase during the busy seasons to 14-hour days, Mondays through Saturdays, and 18-hour days on Sundays.[30] For Hong Kong, the story is identical.

Many young workers in Hong Kong, especially those employed in the smaller factories that dominate every local industry, work in cramped, unhygienic and dangerous conditions that would not have surprised Shaftesbury or Dickens. Even those who work in larger factories often do so in conditions that would be totally unacceptable in Britain.

Child labor and homework are common.

In any Hong Kong resettlement (housing) estate, from early morning to late at night, whole families, from children of five to grandparents of 70, can be seen sewing, snipping, assembling and painting not just toys but also denims and plastic flowers.[31]

All of these products are made for export.

The newer exporting nations are reproducing these conditions. According to the *Washington Post,* Thailand has a thriving if illegal commerce in "child slaves." Children as young as 10 are sold by their parents for $50–$150 in return for one year's employment. The youngsters, under the complete control of their employers, are kept virtual prisoners. They work 12 hours a day seven days a week, and are beaten if they prove uncooperative. The *Washington Post* reports that:

Some were sick and partially crippled from long hours in poorly lit and ventilated factory halls, where their work included making batteries, wrapping candy and sewing cheap shirts. Among others, who have not been lucky enough to be rescued, there are reports of deaths.[32]

It is a mistake, however, to assume that sweatshops, child labor, inhuman conditions, and exploitation will eventually disappear from these countries, or that the evolution of these societies will necessarily follow the path of the Western democracies. For one thing, almost without exception trade unions, one of the major forces for progress in the developed nations, are strictly controlled or totally repressed in the export-oriented nations. In "socialist" Singapore, where wages are set annually by government edict, issues of promotion, hiring, firing, and assignment of tasks are by law nonnegotiable. Unions are left to organize blood drives and productivity campaigns. Days lost through strikes and other labor unrest have fallen from 411,000 in 1961 to 1,011 in 1977 to 0 in 1978.[33] Similarly, in South Korea "emergency" decrees prohibit strikes and any union activity is closely watched by the Korean Central Intelligence Agency. Church groups that try to assist workers are regularly "cautioned" by the government.

But undoubtedly the most important factor preventing social improvements is a competitive momentum that fosters the proliferation of sweatshops. In the global race to attract labor-intensive manufacture, the decisive lure is low wages. Businesses stay in a country only as long as they cannot do better elsewhere. If a nation that has become dependent on garment exports allows wages to rise, the "normal" course of development in the West, plants will simply pick up and move. To keep industry within its borders a government must hold wages down. Ultimately, the only people who benefit are the importers of the First World and the entrenched elites of the Third. Third World workers are victimized by the very economic development policies that were supposed to benefit them. As more and more countries seek to reproduce the Taiwan-Hong Kong-South Korea model, the pressure to match or outbid competing nations becomes intense.

Economists sometimes speak of situations where a few can benefit from an activity that, if followed by everyone, would make things worse than before. The example often given is of a crowd watching a parade. If a few people stand on their toes, they will see better. But they will force the people behind them to do the same until everyone is standing on his or her toes. At that point, no one can see any better than before. Likewise, if a few countries like South Korea and Taiwan employ low wages as a "comparative advantage" to attract industry, they will be better off than the rest. But as every developing nation attempts to use this "comparative advantage," sweatshops and government repression will proliferate around the world. This is the nature of the international competition now emerging, and it promises not development but prolonged misery.

Today, even the pioneers in apparel export are beginning to feel the heat. Workers earning a dollar an hour are threatened by workers whose wage is 50 cents an hour. They, in turn, are being undercut by workers making a dollar a day. Hong Kong's apparel/textile industry, says the *Far Eastern Economic Review*, "is now at a more critical stage than at any time in its 30-year history."[34] Taiwan currently is hoping to upgrade its products and diversify its markets to preserve its industry. Most telling is the action of South Korea as it responds to increased competition by tightening the screws even further on its workforce. The government has ordered banks to refuse loans to companies that raise wages above government-decreed limits, and it has issued new labor laws designed to crack down on unions. According to the *Wall Street Journal*, "government officials make no bones about their efforts to hold down wages." As one member of Korea's economic planning

65

board explained, "we've just got to have a year of restraint to regain our competitiveness."[35]

Even those Third World countries with more humane traditions have been forced to retrench in order to meet the competition of the sweatshop economies. Sri Lanka, once considered a model for Third World social justice because of its education, health, and nutrition programs, has drastically reduced social expenditures in order to attract business. An international Gresham's law is driving out the good for the sake of the bad.

What is the least common denominator? How far down can nations be dragged? There is practically no bottom. The World Bank estimates that under the most favorable conditions of economic growth, 260 million people will still be living in absolute poverty by the end of the century. A more likely prediction, the Bank claims, is 600 million. With such a pool of desperate people ready to accept any conditions offered for the sake of food in their mouths, the global competition for labor-intensive industries like apparel will remain fierce as far into the future as anyone can see.

This is a zero-sum game that shows no signs of stopping and that the United States cannot possibly win. Jobs overseas are being created at the expense of unemployment at home and almost two million American workers are threatened directly. Through no fault of its own, the apparel/textile industry is faced with a near-extinction that many sunrise/sunset theorists seem so devoutly to desire.

But the danger is not to apparel/textiles alone. The prospect for this industry is shared by other labor-intensive industries as well, because the same economic processes are at work. Where labor is a significant cost factor in production, manufacturers and merchandisers have a special incentive to seek out low-wage countries. Along with apparel/textiles, among the threatened industries are shoes, electronic assembly, furniture, paper and wood products, and toys. These sectors—all sunset industries—constitute 42 percent of America's manufacturing employment, about 8 million jobs.[36] To these must be added the jobs indirectly dependent on the sunset industries; it has been estimated that for every two jobs directly created by the apparel/textile industry one additional position is created to supply materials such as chemicals, machinery, and paper and to provide services like transportation, shipping, and maintenance.[37] There is a ripple effect extending far beyond the industries now fighting extinction.

Starkly put, the choice that confronts the American public and American policy makers is to do nothing and allow millions of jobs to disappear overseas, or to take steps to tie our trade policy to a full-employment policy. On its face, this is not a choice at all. No policy maker can allow these jobs to drain away with no alternative in sight except large-scale, permanent structural unemployment for millions. But in the current debate over industrial policy, what makes the sunrise/sunset perspective so visible and influential is that it seems to offer an alternative and therefore a way to avoid tackling this uncomfortable problem head-on. That alternative is the sunrise of high technology. Workers who lose their jobs in the dying sectors are to be retrained for slots in the emerging sectors.

THE FALSE SUNRISE

This happy vision raises many questions, though perhaps the first thing that should be said about it is the most personal. It is hard to escape the thought that one reason the apparel/textile and other labor-intensive industries are so readily dismissed as sunset is that the workers who depend on them are low-wage, often minority, often female. In women's apparel, for instance, over 80 percent of the workforce is female. Many advocates of the new technology, it must be said, display a lack of sympathy for the low-income workers whose jobs are immediately on the line. That attitude is quite simply a kind of arrogance or elitism. So entranced are they by their dreams of the future that they have no patience for the knotty realities of low-income families who may stand in the way of or slow down the march to technotopia.

This elitism is readily apparent when labor-intensive workers are described as "secondary wage earners," implying that their positions are not important, either to their families or to the country. It is also apparent when it is said that these jobs should go overseas precisely because they are low-wage positions, which presumes that Americans should not be doing this sort of work, and when Americans are called upon to make sacrifices for the poor of other lands, as if there were not poor in the United States. There may be overtones of racism and sexism here, albeit of a most genteel kind. One cannot imagine millions of white, male, middle-class jobs being regarded so cavalierly.

In speaking of the apparel/textile industry a few years ago, former Congresswoman Shirley Chisholm provided the irrefutable answer to such insensitivity.

Regrettably, there is easy talk about the need for us to give up these jobs so that workers in the poor lands of the earth shall have a chance for gainful employment. Usually this is put in terms of affluent Americans making sacrifices for the indigent

Third World. In reality, however, it is not affluent America that makes the sacrifice when a job is wiped out in a textile mill or in an apparel shop. It is the nonaffluent American who is sacrificed. We dare not induldge in an impossible policy where we pit the people of the Third World against the people in our own Third World.[38]

Yet this is precisely the policy that we are asked to pursue.

To be sure, not every spokesman for a high-technology future is insensitive to the needs of America's Third World. Robert Reich, for one, has made an exemplary statement stressing the importance of providing jobs for sunset workers that are at least as good as the jobs they are being permitted to lose.

In America the "losers" must be compensated. They must be given generous job training, help in relocating, new industries within their regions in which they easily can gain employment at wages as high as they had before. . . . The workers who are being threatened must be included in the process of industrial policy making itself. Anything less, and they will resist—and will have a right to resist.[39]

The key here is that no one in the present should be sacrificed to a mere vision of the future—and least of all the most vulnerable members of our population. Nor must labor-intensive workers be asked to bear the costs of great economic changes for the society as a whole. If there are better positions for workers in our labor-intensive industries to go to (and the necessary adjustments are carefully arranged), few would "resist." Unfortunately, what actually is happening is that the sunrise/ sunset notion has become a shibboleth in which words substitute for realities and low-income families are compelled to accept long range promises as compensation for immediate losses. In the name of fairness, this should be turned around. Benefits must be at hand before sacrifices are called for. Those who promise a new sunrise job for every sunset position destroyed should be obligated to meet their commitments.

Meeting commitments, however, will not be easy. Examined closely, the sunrise/sunset perspective quickly loses its allure, for as a policy it depends on a straightforward proposition. Jobs must be created in the new industries as rapidly as they are destroyed in the old. Yet this is extremely unlikely. Creating jobs is a slow, difficult, expensive, time-consuming, and uncertain process. Needs must be assessed, money allocated, workers retrained, families relocated. Destroying jobs through imports, on the other hand, is easy. The technology for production does not have to be developed. It is already known, and easily exportable. The skills are quickly learned, much more quickly than skills in the new high-technology industries. No new product must be tested or advertised. The market for the goods already exists.

Generally, the very real problem of job-creation in sunrise industries is simply assumed away. The positions will just automatically be there when the two million apparel/textile workers and the millions more in other sunset industries come asking. The call is for "retraining," but without much attention given to what these workers will be retrained for. Yet the questions about retraining are manifold. No one has shown that workers in sectors like apparel/textiles, who frequently have limited education and mobility, can in fact be retrained for the promised high-tech positions. No one comments on possible techno-logical displacement in the sunrise jobs. Should sunset workers be retrained to do office work at a time when predictions are being made that one-third of all office jobs may disappear in the next ten years? Put simply, when someone says "retrain," the first question must always be, "for what?"

Apparel/textile workers have a special reason to be skeptical. They have heard it all before. As far back as the late 1950s and early 1960s they were confronted with an import problem, at that time from Japan. But they were told that there was no reason for alarm because any workers who lost their apparel jobs could find positions in related industries like shoes. The transition would be painless. Then, when all of the related industries began to feel the pressure of low-wage imports, and the domestic shoe industry was practically wiped out, a new explanation was offered together with a new solution. If labor-intensive industries, because of the nature of their production processes, faced a special import problem from low-wage countries, opportunities existed in the capital-intensive sectors where capital-rich America enjoyed a "comparative advantage." The industries commonly cited as safe havens for displaced workers were steel and autos.[40]

That experience should teach a lesson. We should never sacrifice what we have for rosy though unreliable predictions about the future. If we allow imports to enter the United States unrestricted and with no concern about their relation to domestic employment, we can be certain that millions of people will be without work. Furthermore, they may well be without hope for work regardless of what the economic prognosticators promise will occur in the long run.

In any case there is no reason to be optimistic about the future. Not so long ago, microchips were said to be the very epitome of a sunrise industry as well as an American stronghold. In 1972, the Japanese did not produce a single commercial microchip. Now they dominate the world market in the most advanced chips and are expected to maintain their positions when the next generation of microchips becomes available. Meanwhile, the U.S. industry is stagnating and American producers are complaining about Japanese imports.[41]

Computer technology shows signs of going the same way. *The Economist* reports that Fujitsu, Japan's largest computer manufacturer, "is preparing for a strong push into America's computer and telecommunications markets."[42] It expects a 50 percent growth in the coming year and 100 percent in the following two. Experts argue that with the concentrated business-government effort the Japanese are making in the computer field, the current American lead in this staple of high technology, calculated at approximately three years, is being steadily eaten away. In their *Fifth Generation*, Feigenbaum and McCorduck propose that "our planning vacuum at the national level is causing us to squander our valuable lead at the rate of one day per day."[43] Gordon Bell, one of the great innovators of the U.S. computer industry, asks whether there will "even *be* an American computer industry in 10 years if we don't make the right response to Japan."[44]

A Congressional task force of U.S.-Japan trade, noting the energy with which the Japanese are moving into the sunrise industries, concludes that "the Japanese threat in these high-technology areas may soon become the most explosive economic issue between our two nations."[45] And another Congressional study emphasizes that the threat is not solely a Japanese one. "In the future," it stresses, "the United States will confront intense foreign competition across the full range of manufactured products."[46] The advanced nations such as France, Germany, and Great Britain will challenge us in the high-technology fields, the newly industrial nations in the traditional capital-intensive smoke-stack sectors like autos, steel, and chemicals, and the emerging nations in the labor-intensive areas. There is no escape from the problems of the growing global economy, certainly not in high technology, and this prognosis suggests the special danger of relying on a sunrise/sunset strategy. For if we allow our bottom to fall out by permitting our labor-intensive industries to go overseas, we simply increase the pressure on ourselves to out-compete our allies for the scarce "sunrise" jobs. What is more, if every advanced nation follows the same industrial strategy, as indeed they are being advised to do and for exactly the same reasons as the U.S., then the contest for technological superiority will almost surely degenerate into a life-and-death struggle for economic survival.

Meanwhile, as foreign competition increases erosion is occurring at home. Production jobs in high-technology fields are being exported out of the United States just as they have been in the case of the older industries. In a much publicized news story of March, 1983, headlined "High Technology Jobs Going Overseas as U.S. Costs Rise," the *New York Times* reported that Atari was shifting 1,700 of its jobs from California to Hong Kong and Taiwan, following the example of Apple Computers and Wang Laboratories. Other high-technology companies were reluctant to discuss their own plans with the *Times,* but it was known that some firms were looking at Malaysia, the Philippines, and Mexico as possible locations. As the chief economist for Chase Econometrics explained, "What people have tended to forget is that eventually high-technology industries become competitive, like any other industry. And keeping labor costs down is a crucial part of being competitive."[47] No company, no matter how advanced, is immune to the attractions of a 50-cent-an-hour wage.

Some observers who have been identified with the sunrise/sunset argument offered their own comments on Atari's move. These were particularly revealing. Former Massachusetts Senator Paul Tsongas declared that "what Atari did underscores the need to stay ahead of the wave, to develop new products continuously."[48] Such a vision of an endless and precarious technological treadmill provides small comfort to those jobless who have been assured that companies like Atari were their tickets into the future. No more helpful was Professor Reich, despite his declarations about the displaced poor. Confronted with a situation in which a sunrise became a sunset before anyone had a chance to bask in the warmth of midday, he suggested shifting "our labor force into higher skill-intensive jobs, which do not move offshore as quickly."[49] His assumption is that U.S. citizens can acquire skills which others cannot. But there is no reason to believe Americans will always win this particular race—and what should the loser do?

The point is not to deny the importance of high technology to America's future. Nor is it to suggest that international trade is somehow evil or self-defeating. Its virtues may have been overrated, but a knee-jerk protectionist response to every blip on the import charts is no less irresponsible than is a mechanical free trade answer to the vastly heterogeneous reality of modern economics. Examining the present plight of apparel/textiles is valuable because it highlights the superficiality of much current thinking. "Free trade" will do nothing except guarantee a widening pool of unemployment in this industry. "Sunrise/sunset" is an empty promise. In both instances slogans are employed in place of thinking.

THE ROAD TO SOLUTIONS

Any serious industrial policy must address the question of trade with flexibility and pragmatism. What program will assure prosperity and full employment? What is fair to all Americans? What will work? The answers will not be the same in every situation. Some industries may need temporary relief from import surges. Others can be aided by export-promotion schemes. Still others, vital to our national defense, must be preserved regardless. No modern nation, for example, can do without a steel industry.

In the case of the labor-intensive industries like apparel/textiles, the present quota system must be revised in light of current realities. Because the enormous wage differential between the industrialized and the developing countries is not going to improve markedly any time in the near future, temporary measures would not be effective—except temporarily. Similarly, tariffs are no solution. To cope with a 16 cent-an-hour wage, tariffs would have to be raised to utterly unrealistic levels. Export supports are meaningless to labor-intensive industries, which can never hope to sell in countries with massive labor pools. And assistance designed to increase capital investment and productivity is, while desirable in itself, equally irrelevant to the problem.

A quota system can be designed to preserve jobs without undermining trade. At present, a resolution is being considered in Congress to limit apparel imports to 25 percent of the American market, an enormous percentage by the standards of almost any other industry, yet a significant reduction from current levels in apparel/textiles. The advantage of such a proposal is that it safeguards jobs in the United States and at the same time allows imports to grow in line with growth in the American market. Everyone would be able to benefit from an expanding U.S. economy. The present zero-sum game would be terminated.

In addition, a quota system would encourage the development of global policy on apparel imports rather than the patchwork quilt with which we are currently burdened. Instead of responding after the fact whenever another emerging nation begins shipping to the United States, at the stage when jobs were lost and markets disrupted, we would be able to anticipate and accommodate. A Sri Lanka would be able to increase its exports to us, but only after a Taiwan or Hong Kong had decreased theirs. There is an advantage here even for the dozens of Third World countries eager to export to the U.S. but only now coming on line. A quota system brings orderliness and regularity into what is a chaotically cutthroat business. Disruptive surprises would be eliminated both for importers and exporters. Nations would be able to plan with certainty, knowing in advance what their allowances would be.

Objections will be raised to the idea of quotas as a feature of a rational trade policy by those who misapply the teachings of Adam Smith and David Ricardo. But the free traders then have the obligation of proposing genuine solutions of their own to a problem that is not about to go away. Resistance will also come from those opposed to government involvement of any kind in the operations of the "market." This broader objection raises a philosophical and ultimately an ethical question. The battles waged against nineteenth-century laissez-faire produced the accomplishments of the welfare state. Social Darwinism was replaced by the belief that it is an appropriate role of modern government to protect its citizens against poverty and economic hardship. Few would choose to return to the conditions and convictions of the nineteenth century, even if we could. Today, trade is the last bastion of the old *laissez-faire* ideal, and even those who accept the necessity of intervention in the domestic economy sometimes balk at the idea of regulating trade. But if it is right to protect citizens against the woes produced by our domestic economy, it is surely right as well to protect them against the stresses and strains of the global economy.

New York State in particular stands to gain from a rational trade policy both because of the size of its apparel industry and because of its continuing role as a port of entry for immigrants to this country. The garment industry has always contained a large immigrant population. Millions of Germans, Irish, Jews, Italians, Hispanics, Eastern Europeans, and Asians first gained a foothold in American society and the American economy through their jobs at the sewing machine and the spreading table. As millions of newcomers from Latin America and Asia now stream onto our shores in search of the same opportunities that awaited our parents and grandparents, we have an obligation to them no less binding than our obligation to native-born and naturalized Americans. If we allow the apparel/textile industry to be washed away, we will have condemned these arrivals to a desperation worse than that which awaited the newcomers at the turn of the century.

Our immigrant populations always have represented much that was brightest about America's future. Today, as in the past, their jobs in the rag trade are among the few openings available to them in their new, bewildering, often frightening environment. Far from being an anachronistic remnant of the past, the apparel/textile industry of the 80s remains a foundation stone of the future—for hundreds of thousands of Americans spread across the country, and for the countless Americans-to-be who have recently arrived or have yet to come.[50]

THREE

Industrial Devolution in New York State*

Glenn Yago, Hyman Korman, Gail Lerner,
Sen-Yuan Wu, Michael Schwartz, Charlene Seifert

> History boils over there's an economic
> freeze sociologists invent words that mean
> 'Industrial Disease.'
>
> Mark Knopfler
> *Dire Straits*

Ever since the term "reindustrialization" was coined by Columbia University sociologist Amitai Etzioni in the Carter White House, it has become the basis of competing visions of economic recovery that seek to revitalize old industries and create new ones. Government policies as diverse as those of President Reagan and Mitterrand have used the term to characterize their efforts to undergird basic industries and adjust to new structural conditions of the world economy. The term's lack of analytical precision, therefore, invites us to examine what it seeks to remedy.

It takes no analysis at all to see that closings of individual plants, decline of whole industries, and deterioration of regional economies are increasing in the State. Job loss might have been considered a transitory problem in the context of post-war economic growth. In the context of economic decline that began in 1973, however, job loss has become a fixture of the 1980s. In the abstract, plant closings and relocations are part of the ongoing process of structural change in society. This

* Research for this chapter was supported by the National Science Foundation, grant number SES8310190.

change becomes a major social problem when closings and relocations of manufacturing facilities cluster in a single community or region. Disinvestment occurs, triggering unemployment, declining incomes, and degeneration of public services.

Since 1980, researchers have spotted numerous instances of industrial and geographical reorganization of the economy, but the evidence supporting this, such as numbers of jobs lost and population redistributed, simply maps the contours of manufacturing and employment decline. Unanswered are a number of analytical questions about the current watershed of social change in industrial society. Why do plants shut down? What are the social, economic, and political causes? What are the causal relationships among plant closings, unemployment, local economic conditions, social disorganization, and local fiscal problems?

Sociological interest in plant closings began during the Depression of the 1930s, and most case studies in the subsequent two decades were accounts of individual, family, and community responses. In the late 1950s and 1960s, a second round of research saw disinvestment as an aspect of the automation and modernization of U.S. industry. These studies focused upon the specific adjustments of individuals and companies to brief and unavoidable periods of structural unemployment in the context of national economic growth. Since then, case studies sought to understand community and individual responses to permanent unemployment caused by the long-term decline of steel, automobile, and other industries. For the most part, despite the importance of industrial decline and disinvestment, the literature contains studies on the social and psychological responses of individuals facing the stress of unemployment.

Only recently have studies begun to focus on the generic historical and social processes affecting industry restructuring. In the United Kingdom, studies have examined the way that workplace reorganization, as the result of new technology, intensified labor production processes, and relocation, have affected industrial, firm, and job migration. Case studies of textile, automobile, steel, and other industries—as well as cross-sectional data based on factory inspection efforts—have yielded major insights into how these technological and organizational factors affect industrial decline and job loss.[1]

In the United States, the debate over deindustrialization has revolved around the issues of how capital mobility and disinvestment in manufacturing have affected manufacturing productivity, competitiveness, and national economic performance. Structural shifts and linkages among economic sectors are only now beginning to be explored.[2]

Current national data sources, like the U.S. Department of Commerce's *Census of Manufacturing*, are too infrequent or too highly aggregated for rigorous analysis of localized industrial decline. Employment data from the Bureau of Labor Statistics, which are based upon a rotating national sample, are statistically unreliable when applied to units smaller than states or to particular industrial sectors. Other federal data sources such as reports required by the Adjustment Assistance Act or the Equal Opportunity Employment Commission are too limited in the kinds of firms included. Dun & Bradstreet Corporation data (prohibitively expensive and incomplete) contains insurmountable coding problems. In short, data limitations at the national level make it impossible to verify the various theoretical perspectives on plant closings. Moreover, industrial and social policy decisions derived from these perspectives preclude systematic research.

Data sources for investigating plant closings and industrial migration are limited by many factors. There is neither an appropriate nor accurate measurement at state, county, and community levels. Also lacking is systematic examination of the correlations between firm characteristics and incidents of plant closings. The impacts of a plant closing upon local employment, fiscal conditions, and social costs are largely undocumented. Finally, there are no comparative perspectives on how different communities are affected by plant closings.

THE CAUSES OF DEVOLUTION

Most theories of economic and social change associated with industrial decline are based upon nationally aggregated figures that obscure social changes in specific regions. Our unique data set on New York State enables us to consider competing theories in an effort to understand the kind of social changes deindustrialization causes.

Post-Industrial Theory

A swing from manufacturing to service employment generally is seen as the benchmark of post-war economic change. The trend towards a post-industrial society characterized by dramatic growth in the tertiary and quaternary sectors of the economy became predominant when manufacturing employment began to decline. The post-industrial perspective views plant closings as necessary in the transformation from a manufacturing to a more complex service and administrative economy, so plant closings alone do not indicate economic decline. They are indicative of restructuring toward new areas of productivity and economic growth.

Traditional location theory suggests that firms are more likely to close plants in areas where either costs rise relatively quickly or market prospects deteriorate and sales revenues fall. Probably also important, though, are the spatial patterns of employment decline and the geographical distribution of industrial decline, factors that have not received much attention.

The neoclassical approach to explaining the distribution of industry is based upon observing factor cost differentials, among them labor, raw materials, and transport. The central concern of this perspective is how variations of a firm's production costs affect distribution and profits. With respect to metropolitan regions, this view maintains that technological innovation produces a spatial transfer in the location of industries. New technologies require different resources and production skills, access to newer markets, and beneficial business climates.[3]

Redistribution of industry and population among regions is the result of technological diffusion and adaptation, as well as negative costs associated with the concentration of industries in specific regions, for example, in the Northeast. Plant closings occur when failing, unprofitable firms do not adjust to major economic and technological changes. Disinvestment is, therefore, both natural and necessary—even though it can be highly disruptive.

Product Cycle Theory

The focus of post-industrial theory and the associated spatial distribution of factor costs and their impact upon industrial location has been criticized. Changing industrial structure greatly influences the demand for factor costs and production and distribution. Cost differentials of production factors vary considerably over time as a consequence of changes in the composition, concentration, and diversity of industries within the economy.[4]

Product cycle theories have addressed shifts in products, growth paths, and occupational structures over time and demonstrated how these effect changes in industry location based upon demands for land, labor, and capital costs. Regional patterns of growth and decline are linked to cycles of product mix and development just as technological changes in product development and production greatly affect the gravitation of basic industries to certain locations. Accordingly, industry itself is antecedent to and determinant of factor cost allocation and distribution spatially.

Product cycle research in economies and geography is critical to understanding how and why new products develop, influence industries, and locate in specific regions. Plant closings and openings, therefore, could be affected greatly by firms flexible enough to adapt to new product cycles, promote them, and diversify their product mix.

Capital Mobility and Industrial Organizational Theory

A final perspective sees plant closings as a consequence of increased capital mobility and economic concentration in industrial organizations. Change in business organizations, specifically in the increasing domination of multilocal and multinational corporations, is the ultimate source of disinvestment. With both resources and expertise, firms can seek out the most profitable investment opportunities regardless of location. Their large size and multilocal character makes them less accountable to any particular locale, thus freeing them from traditional constraints of local government or unions. So, this phenomenon results in the withdrawal of investment in certain regions in favor of more profitable and faster-growing sectors of the industry. In this view, the rise of multinational corporations, large conglomerates, and absentee-owned firms increases capital mobility and essentially changes the national character of industry-wide investment decisions.

Research focused upon business organization has linked together changes in capital concentration, technology, production, and location. Internal industry changes that occur through rationalization, intensification of production, or technical innovation are known to generate closings and job loss. Institutional and spatial limits also explain how older firms inhibit new industry formation.[5]

INDUSTRIAL DECLINE IN NEW YORK STATE

The New York State economy was one of the first to experience the end of post-war economic growth. Nonagricultural employment peaked in 1969, four years before the national high, and has declined ever since (see Table 1). While manufacturing employment accounted for a disproportionate share of the decline in total employment, New York's total manufacturing output has declined each year since 1970. Although earlier periods of economic growth saw declines in manufacturing offset by increases in trade and service employment, this appears not to have been the case during the 1970s in New York State. This relationship between declining manufacturing and total employment is one that requires further theoretical and empirical exploration. Unemployment rates above 5% have been consistently higher than the national average since 1971, as indicated in Graph 1. This is relevant to job decline in relation to the industrial and geographic distribution of plant closings.

The Industrial Migration File, an annual data set collected by the field offices of the New York State Department of Commerce, is one of the few organized reporting systems utilized by government to monitor economic changes. The opening, closing, expansion, and contraction of industrial facilities are recorded and classified in considerable detail. Industrial facility changes are coded by company name, parent company name, Standard Industrial Classification code, employment, investment, and other plant characteristics. While this data cannot answer all of the theoretical questions raised above, it contributes to our data base. Combining other firm and county level information with Commerce figures, we designed this data base to clarify linkages between population and industrial redistribution.

For analytical purposes, all industrial activity changes have been grouped into the following categories: closings, contractions, openings, and expansions. The timing and character of these industrial migration activities demonstrate that an overwhelming number of openings and expansions were consonant with the State's economic crisis. The past two decades reveal many changes (see Graph 2). The 1960s began with a relatively high number of closings that decreased by 1967 and were reestablished at the initial level by 1970. Until 1974 plant closings remained relatively stable (about 300 per year), but were declining by the end of the decade. While plant openings were initially lower than

Table 1. Nonagricultural Employment and Manufacturing Decline in New York State, 1969–77 (thousands)

Year	Total	Manufacturing	% Manufacturing
1969	7182.0	1970.8	27.4
1970	7154.8	1760.6	24.6
1971	7005.2	1633.4	23.3
1972	7038.5	1602.2	22.7
1973	7132.2	1619.1	22.7
1974	7076.0	1574.6	22.2
1975	6826.8	1421.0	20.8
1976	6778.8	1438.8	21.2
1977	6628.4	1413.1	21.3

SOURCE: *New York State Statistical Yearbook, 1980* (Albany: State of New York, Department of Commerce, 1980).

Graph 1.   New York and United States Unemployment Rates, 1970-1980

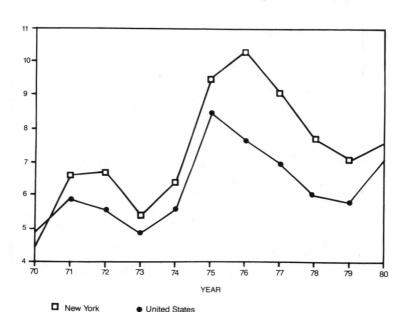

YEAR

□ New York   ● United States

Source: *Resident Employment Status Of Civilian Labor Force,* Bureau of Labor,
Market Information Report No 85 (Albany: State of New York,
Department of Commerce, 1981).

closings, they gradually rose until the 1973–74 economic crisis, then declined. Expansions in existing plants superseded plant openings for most of the 1970s. The faltering industrial position of the State has been associated largely with the decline in new openings and expansions.

By 1980, the frequency of industrial migration activities was 45 percent of their peak during the boom years of the 1960s. While expansion activities characterized industrial migration in the 1960s, the 1970s generally saw an increase in plant closings and contractions in relation to openings and expansions.

We looked at the size of reported activity using employment figures (see Table 2), then at the distribution of migration activities between openings/expansions and closings/contractions shifts (see Table 3 and Graph 3). Most of the expansions and openings, perhaps indicative of reindustrialization, represent low employment gains, while the larger number of closings represent medium and high losses.

Graph 2.   Industrial Migration Events in New York State,1961 - 1980

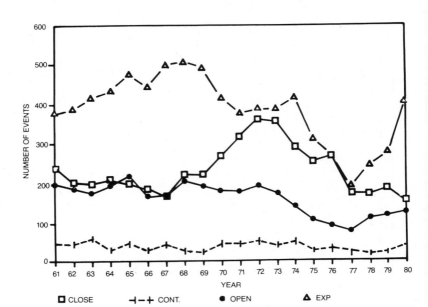

□ CLOSE   ┤─┼ CONT.   ● OPEN   ▲ EXP

Source: Compiled from the New York State Department of Commerce Industrial
           Migration File by the Industrial Research Project, SUNY-Stony Brook.

The greatest period of decline in the industrial employment base occurred in the late 1960s and early 1970s. Moreover, the high level of closings and contractions was sustained until 1977.

When we examined the regional distribution of industrial migration, other interesting patterns emerged (see Table 4). New York City represented 37.7 percent of the industrial migration activity and more than 50 percent of all plant closings (nearly double the State average). In openings and expansions, New York City fared less well than the rest of the State. The Capital District and Suffolk County performed better in openings, while Buffalo, Elmira, the Northern Region, Rochester, and Syracuse all exceeded the State average in expansions. Significantly, however, the difference between New York City and other regions decreased when project size was compared. The many openings and expansions had restricted economic impact since they were mostly of small size.

Table 2. Industrial Activity Employment Effects in New York State, 1960–1980

	All changes in physical plant		Closings		Contractions		Openings		Expansions	
Size	No.	%	No.	%	No.	%	No.	%	No.	%
Low Gain or Loss (0 to +/−30)	8237	50.7	1333	32.0	116	17.8	1818	62.3	4970	80.5
Medium Gain or Loss (+/− 31 to +/− 100)	3867	23.8	1867	44.8	248	38.0	833	28.5	919	14.9
High Gain or Loss (+/−101 and over)	1814	11.2	972	23.2	288	44.2	270	9.2	284	4.6

SOURCE: Compiled from the New York State Department of Commerce Industrial Migration File by the Industrial Research Project, SUNY-Stony Brook.

Table 3. Industrial Migration Activity in New York State, 1960–1980

Activity	Frequencies	Percent	Total No. Jobs Gained or Lost	Average No. Jobs Gained or Lost
Closings	4642	28.5%	−397,249	−95.2
Contractions	700	4.3%	−127,892	−196.1
Openings	3186	19.6%	+143,554	+49.1
Expansions	7719	47.5%	+169,474	+27.4
TOTAL	16247	100%	−212,113	−15.2

SOURCE: Compiled from the New York State Department of Commerce Industrial Migration File by the Industrial Research Project, SUNY-Stony Brook.

The State's economic deterioration is signaled by the distribution of industrial migration by industry (see Table 5). Textile, apparel, lumber, furniture, fabricated metal, paper, and leather industries all showed higher than average rates of plant closings. Openings and expansions of plants were higher than the State average in machinery and electrical machinery (17.5 percent and 15.5 percent compared to averages of 11.4 percent and 11.6 percent). The scope of closings and contractions by industry, however, clearly shows that the number of large-size closings and contractions far exceeded the number of openings and expansions. In no industrial category did small-scale openings and expansions compensate for the job loss resulting from large-scale closings

Graph 3. Industrial Migration Employment Impacts in New York State, 1961-1980

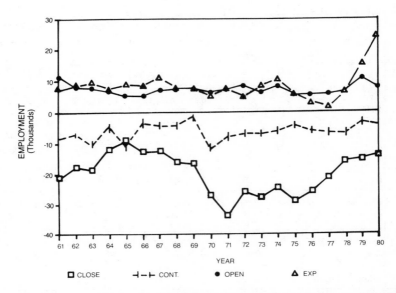

Source: Compiled from the New York State Department of Commerce Industrial
Migration File by the Industrial Research Project, SUNY-Stony Brook

and contractions. Moreover, the mix of industrial activities represented during earlier years has declined increasingly.

Our final discussion concerns the different rates of industrial migration by local and multilocal firms (see Graphs 4 and 5). The industrial migration file indicates (by the parent code) whether or not the plant is a branch, part of an out-of-state corporation, or, if local, a single branch facility. There is a higher rate of plant closings among parent-controlled plants than locally-owned plants (34.3 percent compared to 24.4 percent). Without a parent company, there are more openings and expansions. Contractions for local plants are almost half that of branch plant subsidiaries.

At this stage in our research, we can say that size was a factor for local firms performing better than multilocal ones. In the context of overall industrial decline, however, local plants also experienced difficulty during the past decade.

A great deal remains to be investigated in the State's economic and social changes. Our further research will be geared to spotting changes

Table 4. Industrial Activity Employment Effects by Region in New York State, 1960–1980

Region	Closings		Contraction		Opening		Expansion		Total	
	Employment	Mean	Employment	Mean	Employment	Mean	Employment	Mean	Employment	Mean
Binghamton	−3551	−55.5	−3791	−151.6	2843	39.5	7263	38.6	2764	7.9
Buffalo	−28143	−147.3	−12635	−203.8	7480	45.6	21433	28.5	−11865	−10.2
Capital District	−16464	−114.3	−5199	−152.9	6580	37.8	6677	20.8	−8406	−12.5
Elmira	−2837	−105	−2745	−305	2080	74.3	5923	40	2421	11.4
Mohawk Valley	−8113	−108.1	−2120	−141.3	1721	23.9	6956	35.5	−1556	−4.3
Mid Hudson	−15407	−69	−4049	−139.6	8900	35	9160	24.8	−1396	−1.6
Nassau	−29832	−83.6	−9710	−313.2	14005	38.4	12186	23.7	−13351	−10.5
Suffolk	−16625	−87.2	−4080	−291.4	30745	50.2	18167	30	28180	19.8
New York City	−227250	−92.1	−64134	−191.4	43018	59.6	36574	19.4	−211792	−39.2
Northern	−4714	−81.2	−763	−69.4	2116	23.5	5414	26.2	2053	5.6
Rochester	−19176	−136.9	−7544	−243.3	5275	41.2	15907	36	−5448	−7.3
Syracuse	−8764	−136.9	−5501	−250	5097	69.8	12192	50.1	3024	7.5
Westchester-Rockland	−16346	−95	−5621	−165.3	13694	82	11532	37.3	3259	4.8

SOURCE: Compiled from the New York State Department of Commerce Industrial Migration File by the Industrial Research Project, SUNY-Stony Brook.

Table 5. Industrial Activity Employment Effects by Industry in New York State, 1960–1980

Industry	Closings		Contractions		Opening		Expansion		Total	
	Employment	Mean	Employment	Mean	Employment	Mean	Employment	Mean	Employment	Mean
Food & Kindred	−37879	−123.8	−11430	−184.3	10960	67.6	11586	25.7	−26763	−27.3
Textile Mill Products	−21618	−92.4	−6342	−181.2	8744	44.6	4676	16.7	−14540	−19.5
Apparel	−43605	−74.5	−5562	−99.3	14860	46	9711	22.2	−24596	−17.5
Lumber and Wood	−4347	−53.6	−330	−82.5	2117	25.8	1504	13	−1056	−3.7
Furniture and Fixture	−12295	−76.4	−1864	−116.5	3477	36.2	3473	19.9	−7209	−16.1
Paper and Allied	−19317	−93.3	−4265	−118.5	7239	47.6	5442	17.3	−10901	−15.3
Printing and Publishing	−25187	−94	−9075	−137.5	8504	56.7	7883	17	−17875	−18.8
Chemical and Allied	−21043	−90.7	−11877	−182.7	6069	42.4	11131	25	−15720	−17.7
Petroleum and Coal	−645	−129	−5145	−735	1882	156.8	333	15.8	−3575	−79.4
Rubber	−14040	−94.8	−1988	−142	5233	35.1	3828	17.8	−6967	−13.3
Leather	−12675	−91.2	−2658	−139.9	3732	63.3	3280	26.5	−8321	−24.4
Stone, Clay	−7805	−92.9	−2168	−144.5	2924	37.5	2427	17.3	−4622	−14.6
Primary Metal	−13174	−121.9	−6570	−285.6	3700	38.9	6495	27.6	−9549	−20.1
Fabricated Metal	−25218	−84.6	−4661	−179.3	9399	41.4	11027	21.1	−9453	−8.8
Machinery	−28227	−93.2	−10903	−181.7	12915	46.6	20159	30.7	−6056	−4.6
Electrical Machinery	−54509	−120	−26841	−339.7	19669	55.8	32817	45.3	−28864	−17.8
Transportation Equipment	−9057	−104	−7858	−392.9	5926	82.3	10194	54.2	−795	−2.1
Instruments	−17878	−109.7	−6335	−287.9	7719	64.8	14786	44.2	−1708	−2.6
Miscellaneous	−25835	−87.6	−1731	−72.1	8353	49.1	7878	25.8	−11335	−14.2
Column Total	−397249	−95.2	−127892	−196.1	143554	49.1	169474	27.4	−212113	−15.2

SOURCE: Compiled from the New York State Department of Commerce Industrial Migration File by the Industrial Research Project, SUNY-Stony Brook.

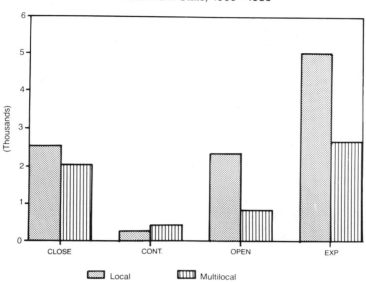

Graph 4. Employment Effects, Multilocal/Local Firms, Events in New York State, 1960 - 1980

Source: Compiled from the New York State Department of Commerce Industrial Migration File by the Industrial Research Project, SUNY-Stonybrook

in New York State's industrial infrastructure that have social impacts, specifically private and public investment patterns and unemployment. These empirical connections are expected to clarify some issues of the current industrial policy debate.

SUMMARY

Many analysts have argued that industrial decline, as indicated by plant closings, is a major cause of social, political, and economic problems throughout the Northeast. Associated with plant closings, we believe, are increasingly severe problems of regional unemployment, social welfare expense, deteriorating public services of regional economies, and local fiscal crises.

Until our work, there was no systematic study of plant closings in New York State and their social and economic effects because of the absence of relevant data. The State of New York Industrial Migration

Graph 5. Employment Effects, Multilocal/Local Firms, Jobs
in New York State, 1960 - 1980

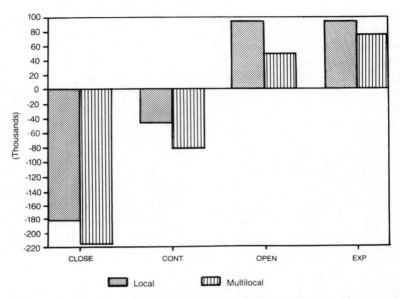

Source: Compiled from the New York State Department of Commerce Industrial
Migration File by the Industrial Research Project, SUNY Stony Brook.

File offers a unique opportunity to examine many disinvestment issues, provided it can be merged with other state and local data sources. This kind of research could well inform the debate over industrial policy in New York State, where deteriorating economic conditions require bold initiatives for economic reconstruction.

From our developing data base, preliminary analysis indicates that in 1965–75 expansionary activity decreased while closings and contractions maintained a high level. There were many more expansions and openings than closures and contractions, but the closures tended to be larger and frequently involved several hundred employees. Contractions were much smaller in scale, yet they were most dramatic in New York City. The Capital District and Suffolk County were less severely affected. Certain industries (apparel, textile, lumber, furniture, fabricated metal, paper, and leather) declined disproportionately, although machinery expanded. Finally, plants which were subsidiaries of larger, multilocal companies were more likely to contract or close. Those which were independent or locally-owned were more likely to open or expand.

Our investigations thus far indicate that policies must be crafted to answer specific questions in some problem areas. Concerning economic dislocation, for example, we need to know how the impacts of deindustrialization are distributed across the State's regions and population, who are at greatest risk, and what kind of new jobs and wages can workers find? If education and training were required, how can programs keep pace with strategies for productivity, and who will absorb the cost? How can populations and, more broadly, regions and industries be targeted for assistance?

Unarguably, fostering job and firm growth is the State's top priority, but its reindustrialization depends on new capital formation. What kind of programs will encourage this, and how can they be coordinated among local and regional businesses? With world markets as a prime goal, what impetus do State firms need, and how can public and private investment strategies be developed to leverage financing for overall economic growth?

The size and complexity of New York State mandate detailed examination, but decision makers must solve these policy questions without introducing new bureaucratic structures. Data among our early findings suggest that New York State needs integrated policies focusing on both new and mature industries. Linkages are needed among capital programs for business, job development, training, and community assistance. In the meantime, however, a rigorous research effort should be encouraged among the State's higher education and research institutions.

In fact, we believe an important parallel can be drawn. The breadth of our own unique data base, which is drawn largely, though not exclusively, from the New York State Commerce Department's Industrial Migration File, illustrates what can be learned from existing government institutions once a more comprehensive base has been developed from a wide variety of supplementary sources. At the same time, drawing on research results from the State's colleges, universities, and other institutions, policy experts and business professionals should capitalize on this knowledge base to generate realistic policy options and to address the short-term and long-term needs of the New York State economy.

FOUR

Trends in Manufacturing Employment and Reflections on Infrastructure Investment, Tax and Expenditure Policy in New York State

Edward F. Renshaw

I first want to examine trends and changes in the composition of manufacturing employment in New York State. Data for two and three-digit industries indicate a continuing erosion of New York's share of total manufacturing employment in the remainder of this decade. Loss of market share has been particularly spectacular in such touted industries as scientific instruments and office and computing equipment. If Atari, the leading producer of video games, has been forced to move its video and small computer production operations to the Orient in order to remain competitive, can Coleco be far behind?

Next, I will focus on three types of infrastructure investment—rail, water supply, and education. The problems in each of these areas are sufficiently unique to merit separate policies. It is not unreasonable to suppose, however, that the best way to promote economic development is for New York to recognize that there is a cost minimizing trade-off between repair and replacement and to try to solve its crumbling infrastructure problem in the most cost-effective manner possible.

A third part of this inquiry is concerned with tax policy. The State's tax policy is short-sighted and biased against real investment in new plant and equipment with a long life expectancy. It also is biased against income from wealth as opposed to income from labor. Firms in long-standing, capital intensive industries, such as primary metals and paper, have little incentive to modernize their facilities and can be expected to abandon their New York based plants when they deteriorate to the point of not yielding a profit.

Finally, I want to consider government employment and the future of business services in New York. The number of persons employed in New York State government almost has tripled since the great depression of the 1930s. Manufacturing employment, on the other hand, has trended downward since 1943. At the present time there are almost as many persons employed in government as in manufacturing. The upward surge in government employment has been facilitated by a progressive income tax structure and a fairly steady increase in employment in finance, insurance, and business services. Some large corporations with headquarters in New York City are now in the process of moving their back office operations from high rent districts in Manhattan to Suburbia. Long Island has turned out to be an early winner. With the revolution that is now taking place in telecommunications, however, the exodus might as easily be to California or the suburbs of Washington, D.C.

MANUFACTURING EMPLOYMENT

In 1948 almost two million people were employed in manufacturing in New York State. This figure has since decreased to less than 1.5 million in 1981. The loss of employment is even more dramatic when the New York figures are expressed as a percent of U.S. employment (refer to Table 1).

New York's share of total U.S. manufacturing employment has shrunk from 12.7 percent in 1948 to only 7.1 percent in 1981. More New Yorkers are now employed in service industries and in wholesale and retail trade than in manufacturing. Instruments and related products, apparel, printing and publishing, and leather products are now the only two-digit industries where New York State still has an above average share of U.S. manufacturing employment.

Just after World War II more than 21 percent of New York's industrial employment was concentrated in apparel and other textile products. By 1981 this percentage had been reduced to only 11.6 percent as a result of an aggregate loss of more than a quarter of a million job opportunities in the garment industry (see Table 2). Apparel is still our second largest two-digit manufacturing industry, but its relative importance could easily slip to fourth or fifth by the end of this decade if past trends continue.

Table 1. New York's Share of Manufacturing and Total Non-Agricultural Employment, in Percent by Two Digit Industries, Selected Years, 1948–1981

Industry	1948	1953	1960	1969	1973	1981
Total Non Ag Employment	12.5	11.8	11.4	10.2	9.3	8.0
Total Manufacturing Employment	12.7*	12.1*	11.2	9.3	8.0	7.1
Instruments & Related Products	31.4*	17.6*	25.2*	23.2*	22.3*	31.2*
Apparel	35.6*	31.9*	25.9*	19.4*	15.2*	13.3*
Printing & Publishing	21.5*	20.4*	19.0*	16.8*	14.5*	12.3*
Leather & Leather Products	19.3*	17.9*	16.9*	14.1*	12.6*	11.9*
Electric & Electronic Equipment			12.3*	9.9	8.2	7.7
Paper & Allied Products	13.9*	12.9*	11.5*	9.3	7.7	7.2
Machinery, Except Electrical	10.4	10.4	7.6	9.0	7.9	6.9
Chemicals & Allied Products			10.5	8.6	7.4	6.4
Stone, Clay & Glass Products	8.6	8.4	8.0	7.3	6.3	5.7
Food & Kindred Products	10.1	9.4	8.8	7.3	6.2	5.7
Fabricated Metal Products			8.1	6.0	5.5	5.0
Furniture & Fixtures					5.9	4.7
Primary Metal Industries	7.2	7.2	6.5	6.2	5.6	4.5
Rubber & Misc. Plastics Products			5.9	5.2	4.7	4.3
Textile Mill Products	7.7	7.4	6.8	5.6	5.7	4.2
Tobacco Manufactures	3.9	4.3	3.0	3.6	3.2	4.2
Transportation Equipment	6.7	6.9	5.8	4.7	4.4	3.8
Petroleum and Coal Products	6.0	6.1	6.0	5.9	4.6	3.0
Lumber & Wood Products					2.1	2.1

* New York's share of manufacturing was above New York's share of total non-agricultural employment.
SOURCE: U.S. Department of Labor, Bureau of Labor Statistics, *Employment, Hours and Earnings, States and Areas, 1939–78 and 1977–81.*

It will be noted that there are only two major industrial categories—machinery (except electrical) and the instruments and related products industry which is dominated by Eastman Kodak—where employment was at a new high in 1981 as compared with 1948, 1960, and 1973. Relatively stable employment in two other major industrial areas—electric and electronic equipment, printing and publishing—has helped to compensate for the more dramatic employment losses in the apparel industry and has left New York with a more diversified manufacturing base.

Some statistics on average hourly earnings in the various two-digit industries are presented in the first column of Table 2. Production

93

Table 2. Hourly Earnings and the Composition of Two-Digit Manufacturing Employment in New York State 1948, 1960, 1973 and 1981

Rank 1981	Industry	Hourly Earnings 1981	Thousands Employed				Percent of Total			
			1981	1973	1960	1948	1981	1973	1960	1948
1	Machinery, Except Electrical	$ 8.80	171.9	164.2	159.1	143.2	12.0	10.1	8.5	7.2
2	Apparel & Other Textile Prod.	5.62	165.7	218.6	318.9	423.9	11.6	13.5	17.0	21.4
3	Electric & Electronic Equip.	7.49	160.5	160.6	177.3	N.A.	11.2	9.9	9.4	N.A.
4	Printing and Publishing	9.76	156.1	160.9	172.9	158.7	10.9	9.9	9.2	8.0
5	Instruments & Related Prod.	9.07	133.6	124.0	105.5	93.0	9.3	7.7	5.6	4.7
6	Food and Kindred Prod.	7.64	88.9	106.6	156.7	181.6	6.2	6.6	8.3	9.2
7	Fabricated Metal Prod.	7.75	80.0	91.0	99.7	N.A.	5.6	5.6	5.3	N.A.
8	Transportation Equipment	10.93	71.7	84.0	98.6	85.0	5.0	5.2	5.2	4.3
9	Chemicals & Allied Equip.	8.46	71.4	76.8	87.1	N.A.	5.0	4.7	4.6	N.A.
10	Primary Metal Indust.	10.69	51.0	70.0	77.1	89.2	3.6	4.3	4.1	4.5
11	Paper and Allied Prod.	7.31	49.8	54.3	69.4	65.7	3.5	3.4	3.7	3.3
12	Stone, Clay and Glass	8.60	36.2	45.3	48.6	47.0	2.5	2.8	2.6	2.4
13	Textile Mill Prod.	5.52	34.9	57.7	63.3	102.5	2.4	3.6	3.4	5.2
14	Rubber & Misc. Prod.	6.47	31.8	32.7	22.3	N.A.	2.2	2.0	1.2	N.A.
15	Leather and Leather Prod.	4.96	27.7	35.9	61.4	79.6	1.9	2.2	3.3	4.0
16	Furniture and Fixtures	6.19	21.9	29.7	N.A.	N.A.	1.5	1.8	N.A.	N.A.
17	Lumber and Wood Prod.	5.91	13.9	15.9	N.A.	N.A.	1.0	1.0	N.A.	N.A.
18	Petroleum and Coal Prod.	—	6.4	8.9	12.8	13.7	.4	.5	.7	.7
19	Tobacco Manufactures	—	2.9	2.5	2.8	4.4	.2	.2	.1	.2
	Total Manufacturing Equipment	7.84	1,432.0	1,619.1	1,878.7	1,976.5	100.0	100.0	100.0	100.0

SOURCE: U.S. Department of Labor, Bureau of Labor Statistics, *Employment, Hours and Earnings, States and Areas, 1939–78 and 1977–81.*

workers in the leather and leather products industry earned less than $5 per hour in 1981 while those persons lucky enough to be employed in the transportation equipment and primary metal industries earned more than $10 per hour.

Benjamin Stevens has noted that the rubber, apparel, plastics, and instruments industries all seem to be rather sensitive to relative wage costs. He believes that a gradual convergence of wage and energy costs will tend to halt the shift of manufacturing jobs from the frost belt to the sun belt in the United States, but perhaps not to the many developing nations in the rest of the world.[1] The loss of employment opportunities has been particularly great in low-paying manufacturing industries such as apparel, textile mill and leather products.

Significant employment losses also have occurred in New York's three highest paying two-digit manufacturing industries—transportation equipment, primary metals, printing and publishing. Technological differences between the United States and the rest of the world have narrowed dramatically in these industries and in some cases the United States is no longer the technological leader. Japan and many other rapidly developing nations have ceased to target our textile and apparel industries. They now are focusing more squarely on steel, autos, and other high cost unionized industries with aging factories where workers have become accustomed to feather bedding and above average wages.

Their success at capturing a larger share of the U.S. market has led Phil Keisling, an editor of the *Washington Monthly*, to suggest that industrial America is on the verge of committing suicide. Rather than let its marginal plants drop into the abyss, he believes that the U.S. should be creating a type of "social safety net" that will allow for their orderly transfer to "the hands of those with a much greater stake in their survival: local investors and—even more so—their own workers."

Those that decry such local buyouts as "lemon socialism" are missing the point altogether: they actually represent the best aspect of entrepreneurship by letting those most affected by a business share in both the risks and the rewards of operating it.[2]

Ownership can sometimes make a noticeable difference with regard to productivity and overall profitability. A carefully controlled study of the restaurant business found that franchisee-ownership boosted profits about 15 percent compared to similar corporate owned establishments that were operated by hired managers.[3]

Many persons apparently are willing to accept less compensation if they can own their own business or are in a better position to influence decision making. If wage concessions, productivity improvements, and/ or changes in ownership are not forthcoming in some of New York's highest paying industries, job losses might very well escalate. Either outcome in conjunction with a continued rapid loss of low paying manufacturing jobs could have the effect of helping to narrow the dispersion of hourly earnings in manufacturing.

The emphasis to this point has been on two-digit manufacturing industries. The statistics on employment trends are not much brighter at the more detailed three-digit level (refer to Table 3). Published figures for 1981 show only 21 three-digit industries where New York State had 10 percent or more of U.S. manufacturing employment. In all of these premier industries New York's share was less in 1981 than in 1960. The loss of market share was stunning in the rapidly expanding office and computing equipment industry. More than a third of all the persons employed in this industry were New York residents in 1960. By 1981, however, New York's share had been reduced to 12.3 percent. The loss of market share was even more spectacular in the case of engineering and scientific instruments, where New York's share of national employment shrank from 44.5 percent in 1960 to only 14.6 percent in 1981.

The New York State Department of Commerce contends that more than one half of the State's manufacturing workforce now is employed in jobs which involve high-technology goods and services. The fierce competition in the scientific instruments, office and computing equipment industries, however, raises serious doubts as to whether new jobs in high technology reasonably can be expected to offset continued erosion of job opportunities in more prosaic industries, such as handbags and personal leather goods, women's and misses' outerwear, costume jewelry and notions, blankbooks and bookbindings, toys and sporting goods, and women's and children's undergarments.

While there is a great deal of charm associated with new technology it must be stressed that jobs in high-tech manufacturing industries are not necessarily good jobs. Massachusetts and other New England states have been quite successful at capturing a disproportionate share of the employment growth in office machines, computer manufacturing, and a number of other high-tech areas. Bennett Harrison has found, however, that the industries which are growing in New England tend to display low average earnings and low average job attachment, while those industries that are declining tend to pay higher average wages and evidence lower turnover. He noted that jobs are being redesigned to eliminate the need for semi-skilled labor. Engineers, research scientists and higher level managers clearly benefit from new technology. The

Table 3. New York State's Premier Three-Digit Manufacturing Industries, Selected Years, 1960–1981

SIC Code	Industry	New York Employment Thousands				Share of US Employment in Percent				Hourly Earnings Dollars 1981	Share Rank 1981
		1960	1969	1973	1981	1960	1969	1973	1981		
386	Photographic Equip. & Supplies	43.6	68.4	74.2	81.9	62.9	61.2	59.6	60.0	$10.50	1
317	Handbags & Personal Leather Goods	19.1	17.7	12.8	10.1	52.9	48.2	38.0	33.6	4.50	2
272	Periodicals	25.4	27.8	24.4	27.7	36.1	36.9	37.4	28.8		3
391	Jewelry, Silverware & Plateware	11.9	17.3	16.9	15.5	27.3	32.6	31.3	27.2	6.63*	4
273	Books	20.1	24.6	22.9	24.8	28.8	25.0	24.0	24.8	7.49	5
385	Ophthalmic Goods	9.5	9.2	9.4	8.5	33.5	26.8	23.3	20.9	6.33	6
233	Women's & Misses Outerwear	131.5	119.7	98.7	81.0	35.4	27.6	21.9	19.9	5.83	7
279	Printing & Trade Services			9.0	8.8			22.0	19.7	12.16	8
238	Misc. Apparel & Accessories	20.9	18.2	15.5	10.4			23.4	18.2		9
296	Costume Jewelry & Notions	21.6	19.4	14.4	7.0	36.2	31.4	23.2	15.1	5.21	10
381	Engineering & Sci Inst	25.7	15.3	11.8	11.5	44.5	19.2	18.0	14.6	9.16	11
278	Blankbooks & Bookbinding	14.6	15.2	11.5	8.9	30.9	26.3	19.4	14.1		12
239	Misc. Fab. Textile Prod.	37.8	34.0	27.6	24.8	27.0	19.5	14.6	14.1		13
284	Soaps, Cleaners & Toilet Goods	16.5	19.0	17.3	19.0	18.1	15.4	13.7	13.0	7.69	14
231	Men's & Boys Suits & Coats	31.1	28.4	21.2	9.7	26.0	21.5	18.5	12.7	6.64	15
251	Engines and Turbines	12.9	16.5	18.6	16.8	14.9	14.7	15.3	12.6	9.47	16
364	Electric Lighting & Wiring Equip.	22.5	28.3	27.3	24.9	16.4	13.8	12.3	12.3	7.21	17
357	Office & Computing Equip.	51.0	60.2	49.4	57.0	34.8	21.8	12.9	12.3	7.83	18
394	Toys & Sporting Goods	23.1	19.9	20.3	13.4	23.2	16.1	15.0	11.4	5.76	19
283	Drugs	23.3	23.9	22.0	22.0	21.4	16.7	13.6	11.0	8.29	20
234	Women's & Childrens Undergarments	31.8	22.7	16.6	9.8	27.0	18.2	14.7	10.8	5.03	21

* Earning Figure is for 1980

SOURCE: U.S. Department of Labor, Bureau of Labor Statistics, *Employment, Hours and Earnings, States and Areas, 1939–78 and 1977–81.*

gradual disappearance of middle-layer jobs makes it less clear, though, whether there are sizable social benefits to be expected at the manufacturing end of high technology industries.[4]

The average hourly earnings of production workers in electric and electronic equipment, New York's third most important two-digit manufacturing industry, was only $7.49 in 1981 or 35¢ less, on the average, than for all manufacturing employment in the State. The average earnings in non-electrical machinery, New York's most important two-digit manufacturing industry, on the other hand, was $8.80 or almost $1.00 more per hour than for all manufacturing.

Industry in New York certainly must strive to be technologically competitive. It is by no means clear, though, that public policy should be focused primarily on the promotion of "high-tech" as opposed to "low-tech" industries. Many of New York's premier industries hardly can be considered high-tech industries. In the leather goods, jewelry, and apparel industries the best hope of remaining competitive is to emphasize high fashion and merchandise that is of high quality.[5] New York is such a costly place in which to live and work and so lacking in basic energy resources that we should probably be pleased to relinquish the image of a manufacturing center that produces cheap goods for a mass market.

PUBLIC INFRASTRUCTURE AND MANUFACTURING EMPLOYMENT

New York was once a gateway to the West and the cradle of American industry. Those who profess complete faith in the power of private enterprise to initiate economic development will perhaps be startled to learn that before the Civil War about 70 percent of the capital invested in canals and probably more than 30 percent of the capital invested in railroad building was contributed by local, state, and federal governments.

The most general impressions left by the record of public promotion are, first, the strength and persistence of the desire to promote economic growth and, second, the pragmatic willingness to make use of whatever means seemed likely to be effective in the particular case. The variety of expedients was extraordinary. Public action was taken at every level of government, from the nation to the township, and sometimes by combinations of different authorities. Still more varied were the relationships between public and private participation. The improvements were constructed sometimes as purely government undertakings, but more often by combinations of public and private funds of governmetal and individual initiative. The sources varied widely; there were even cases in which a single connected line of communication was constructed partly as a public work, where the difficulty was the greatest, partly by mixed enterprise, and perhaps partly by unaided private investment. Government support might take the form of subscriptions to stock, or of loans to the companies or guarantees of their own obligations or of direct subsidy in cash or kind or credit.[6]

It is estimated that the cost of shipping a ton of wheat or flour from Buffalo to New York City fell from $100 to $10 with the construction of the Erie Canal.[7]

The old zest for promoting economic development via public infrastructure investment has waned considerably since the construction of the canal and it is only in recent years that the State legislature has begun to appreciate the need to repair and modernize some of its ports and railways. In the remainder of this section we will consider briefly the railway infrastructure problem and then go on to examine some other problem areas.

The Transition from Oil to Coal

New York is still more than fifty percent dependent upon petroleum to meet its energy needs. Electricity generation is the single largest consumer of primary energy in the State and is relatively more dependent upon oil than the electrical power companies in most other industrial states. The New York State Energy Master Plan advocates a conversion of some oil-fired generating plants to coal as a means of reducing the State's dependence on imported oil and lowering the cost of electricity to consumers and industry. Approximately 82 percent of the coal tonnage delivered to the State in 1980 was by rail.

During the planning process for the State's first energy master plan, concern was raised regarding the ability of the rail transportation system to deliver required volumes of coal to New York electric utility sites for both conversion and new plants. It now appears, though, that only minimal investments will be required to improve transportation facilities and that the tonnage requirements of coal-fired plants are generally attractive enough to stimulate the needed investment without government financing.[8]

The more significant problem with respect to rail infrastructure is what to do with low density branch lines which may be serving just a few industrial customers. The Northeast Rail Service Act of 1981, which is designed to help Conrail achieve self-sufficiency, allows it to abandon any lines with only ninety days notice. In a recent report to Congress, Conrail has identified forty branch lines totaling 394 miles which have been selected for future abandonment in New York.

Rather than have the State become involved heavily in subsidizing the uneconomical portion of Conrail and other Eastern railroads that are experiencing financial difficulty, it might be better for the State to require the major railroads to sell or lease for a very nominal sum— perhaps $1.00 per year—any abandoned branch line for which there is a consortium of local interests, such as railroad employees, local governments, banks and private enterprises, willing and able to assume the financial responsibility of operating and maintaining their own local, short-line railroad.

The average hourly earnings of non-supervisory production workers employed by class 1 railroads is almost 50 percent greater than the average earnings for all non-supervisory workers employed in non-agricultural industry in the United States. The railroad industry, moreover, is notorious for its feather bedding practices. Consequently, it could be very costly to maintain little used branch lines under existing institutional arrangements.

Short-line railroads can sometimes be operated cheaply by utilizing services of part time workers, railroad buffs, and retired engineers who are more interested in having something worthwhile to do than in the size of a monthly pay check.[9] If the employment and local property tax concessions that are likely to be associated with new institutional arrangements for hauling freight and coal on little used railroad track are not sufficient to make short lines competitive, then the independent truckers probably ought to be given a fair chance to acquire the traffic. While the taxes paid by truckers to support roadways may not cover all of the damage to our highways, they clearly go a long way toward meeting that objective.

Educational Infrastructure

U.S. automakers, homebuilders, and most good manufacturers are now in the process of substantially down-sizing their products in response to smaller families, higher energy prices, congressionally mandated improvements in energy efficiency, financial deregulation, and a fundamental change in monetary policy which is keeping long term interest rates substantially above the inflation rate. This down-sizing is being aided and abetted in many cases by a revolution in microelectronics.[10] The net result is a pressing need to reengineer almost everything and to retrain workers in shrunken material producing and handling industries, such as autos and steel, who are now unemployed and cannot reasonably expect to get their old jobs back.

Pierre du Pont, the governor of Delaware, has noted that the focal point for reacting to changes in skill needs in the workplace has been our educational system.

Each new generation was sent into the marketplace with a set of skills that would serve it usefully for a lifetime of productive employment. But the skills now required for continued employment are changing so rapidly that "one-skill-per-generation" is no longer sufficient.

Many officials have spoken of the need for improved training and retraining programs. But many seem to be referring to the jobs of 1933.

The answers of the '30s are not the answers for the '80s and '90s. The jobs of tomorrow require new skills and different education than the jobs of yesterday. Traditional depression-age employment programs will do little to impart technical skills to space-age workers.[11]

The problem of obsolete job skills is not limited to people with relatively little education. Louis Smulin, a professor of electrical engineering at M.I.T., has noted that each year some 10,000, or 5 percent, of the nation's electrical engineers transfer out of their field, many because they feel useless or technologically obsolescent. A year long study by a four-man committee at M.I.T. has concluded that the

problems we are facing cannot be solved simply by incrementally improving and expanding current educational programs. A quantum jump is needed, amounting to a revolution in engineering education.[12]

The committee proposed a new alliance between industry and the academic community under which, on company time and at company expense, engineers would continue their graduate-level education in at least one 15-week course per year. It recommended that as much as 10 percent of an engineer's working time be devoted to continuing education.

New York has made a very sizable investment in its educational infrastructure. Advanced technical education, for the most part though, has been left to the private sector. In the mid 1970s, after a very substantial expansion of the City and State Universities of New York, almost half of all the bachelor degrees in the State were being awarded by these two institutions of higher learning but less than a quarter of all the engineering degrees. It was not until 1982 that the State established a New York Center for Industrial Innovation at Rensselaer

Polytechnic Institute and passed legislation authorizing the establishment of Centers for Advanced Technology at other universities.

The reluctance of public institutions of higher learning to become involved in technical education raises an interesting question whether the more numerous private universities and technical institutes with engineering programs are adequately equipped to keep abreast of the technological changes which are occurring in their own specialties. For more than a decade the realization has been growing in the nation's universities that much of their scientific instrumentation is obsolete, has not been replaced or upgraded for years, and is frequently down for repair.[13] The cost of new instruments that might lead to important breakthroughs are so high, in some cases, as to be beyond the reach of many colleges and universities. In such cases it makes sense to encourage universities and technical institutes to collaborate with private enterprise in the establishment of joint research and equipment programs. The State of New York could facilitate such ventures by exempting jointly used equipment and associated buildings from local property taxes.

Tax relief for educational training and equipment sharing with the private sector should not be limited to colleges and universities. There is a need to extend the concept to the elementary and secondary level, where basic math and science education is rather appalling. Performance scores in these two subject areas declined during the 1970s, especially among high achieving students.[14] Margaret Farrell, who chairs the Department of Teacher Education at the State University of Albany, has noted a disappearance of qualified mathematics and science teachers all over the United States and has suggested that basic education in New York is falling short in its high-technology preparation.[15] The gap between what a person with analytical ability can earn in industry and in high-school teaching is now so great that most school districts find it increasingly difficult to hire and retain qualified persons to teach math and science. One implication is that the State Education Department and the various school districts in New York should consider seriously new and more efficient ways to instruct students in these subjects. Along these lines, however, the teaching profession has been understandably resistant to educational television, teaching machines, and other innovations which might lessen the need for qualified teachers. The dramatic reductions now occurring in the cost of personal computers, though, would suggest that much of the task of teaching basic math and science ought to be turned over to machines and perhaps livened up a bit with some computerized gaming. The role of the teacher would become similar to that of a librarian, projectionist, and expert counselor rather than a subject matter expert.

The most pressing problem is not physical infrastructure, since most schools do have computers and projection equipment, but getting some decent software to go with the hardware that industry is all too willing to provide. Software development and testing is the area where private enterprise is falling short in its effort to improve education and where incremental public dollars probably can be put to the best use.

Water Supply

New York possesses more than 70,000 miles of rivers and streams and over 3.5 million acres of lakes. Annual precipitation is substantially higher than the national average. The federal Water Resource Council has concluded that New York's available water supplies are well in excess of what will be needed through the end of this century. A survey by the U.S. Commerce Department has found, moreover, that water supply and fire protection, which often depends on an adequate supply of water, are among the critical factors taken into consideration by large corporations in locating industrial plants. In fact, a recent report to the governor of New York by the Council on State Priorities has concluded that water is perhaps the State's most important natural resource. Drought, ground water pollution, and aging delivery systems, however, have helped to make urban water supply a lively infrastructure issue in New York State.

Economic analysis suggests that water conservation is often more cost effective than investment in additional capacity when the problem is drought induced water shortages.[16] Since the oil embargo of 1973 there has been a revolution in the home plumbing industry that promises significant savings in both water and energy. One company which is headquartered in New York, the Park Electrochemical Corporation, manufactures a line of water pinchers and other low-cost plumbing devices that can reduce water consumption by as much as 50 percent without any significant alteration in life style. In the case of industry, water shortages have sometimes been a blessing in disguise. Russell's study of water conservation investments made by industrial establishments in Massachusetts during the prolonged drought of 1962–66 found that many of these investments were quite profitable and easily could be justified on their own merit.[17]

The U.S. Army Corps of Engineers has studied the urban water supply systems of Buffalo and a number of other New York cities. The City of Buffalo collects revenue for only 44 to 56 percent of the water it produces. The water not producing revenue is either lost through leaking water mains or is not accounted for by the City's metering system. Pipe line capacities, moreover, have been reduced by as much as 75 percent because of the accumulation of internal corrosion during the 80-year average life of the distribution system.

While rehabilitation is needed, it is by no means clear that the major improvements should begin on a crash basis. There is, after all, a cost minimizing trade-off between repair and replacement. When this type of analysis was applied to Buffalo's water mains it was found that only 17 miles or less than 2 percent of the distribution system "warrants replacement at the present time."[18]

The traditional method of financing improvements in local water supply systems has been to issue tax exempt bonds. Debt financing will tend to shift the cost of the additional water supply to those persons that benefit from the expansion and, if the expected growth takes place, a large part of the cost of repaying interest and principal can be funded by expanded revenues from additional water sales.

Water supply improvements in many states are financed with revenue bonds, though municipalities in New York are not authorized to do so. Article 8, Section 2, of the State Constitution provides that no indebtedness of a municipality may be contracted unless such municipality shall have pledged its faith and credit to the payment thereof. To get around this limitation it has been proposed that the State create a water Finance Authority which would be empowered to issue revenue bonds for water and sewerage facilities. The Authority would be authorized to issue up to 4 billion dollars in bonds. Participation in the program would be voluntary and operation and maintenance of the systems would remain the responsibility of the participating municipalities.

Assistance from the Authority would be conditioned upon the statutory creation of an independent local water board which would own all the revenues of these systems and would be required to set user fees and rates at a level sufficient to pay any debt service, operating costs, and other agreed-upon costs of the facilities so as to place these systems on a revenue sustaining basis. In essence, this legislation would create a revenue bond financing capacity for all municipalities throughout the State, while avoiding legal and procedural obstacles in the State Constitution.[19]

While it does make sense for the State to create a Water Finance Authority to assist localities in financing water and sewers, it is by no means clear that debt should always be used to fund the rehabilitation of aging distribution systems that can be gradually replaced in small increments in a cost minimizing fashion over long periods of time. The interest that must be paid on debt issues will about double the longer run cost of replacing the distribution system and will tend to eliminate an older city's comparative advantage in having a reasonably satisfactory water supply system that is largely paid for.

Tax exempt bond financing, moreover, is no longer as "costless" a way to finance infrastructure investment as it used to be. The yield on Moody's Baa municipal bond index was usually less or, at most, only about one percentage point more than the average annual growth rate for hourly earnings in New York manufacturing from 1948 to 1980 (see Table 4). Baa rated communities that had to borrow money to finance infrastructure investments in 1981 and 1982, on the other hand, paid interest rates that were about four percentage points above the respective growth rates for hourly earnings. The implication is that we may have entered a new era where taxpayers will be forced to incur a real financial burden that will not be offset by inflationary increases in income, if communities use new bond issues to defer the cost of infrastructure rehabilitation.

Highway improvements, for the most part, have been financed on a pay-as-you-go basis by motor vehicle and fuel taxes. This type of financing has helped to reduce traffic congestion, preserve the financial integrity of mass transit, and encourage energy conservation.[20] The financing of the rehabilitation of urban water supply distribution systems on a pay-as-you-go basis also offers social advantages since, if metering is in effect and water is priced on a usage basis, it encourages households and industrial establishments to conserve water. Water conservation will in turn save pumping and water treatment cost and also will make it possible for communities to survive recurring droughts with less strain and fewer adjustment costs. Pay-as-you-go financing would seem particularly appropriate in the case of New York City's third water tunnel. This is an investment that, like insurance, will take a long time to complete and when finished will not provide additional revenues to repay bondholders.

TAX POLICY

New York State's tax policy is short sighted. It also is biased against income from wealth as opposed to income from labor. Persons who have inherited financial assets or are good at the business of buying and selling such assets have an incentive to live in other states, even if they work in New York, to avoid a differentially high marginal tax

Table 4. The Real Burden of Municipal Debt, 1948–83

Year	Average December Yield, Moody's Baa Municipal Bond Index in Percent	Percentage Change in Average Hourly Earnings in New York Manufacturing	The Real Burden of Municipal Debt[a]
	(1)	(2)	(3)
1948	2.8	7.5	−4.7
1949	2.5	3.5	−1.0
1950	2.1	2.0	.1
1951	2.5	7.2	−4.7
1952	2.9	4.3	−1.4
1953	3.4	5.3	−1.9
1954	3.0	2.8	.2
1955	3.2	3.3	− .1
1956	4.2	4.7	− .5
1957	4.0	4.5	− .5
1958	4.1	3.8	.3
1959	4.4	3.2	1.2
1960	4.0	3.6	.4
1961	4.0	3.0	1.0
1962	3.6	2.5	1.1
1963	3.6	3.3	.3
1964	3.5	3.2	.3
1965	3.8	3.1	.7
1966	4.3	3.4	.9
1967	4.7	4.3	.4
1968	5.2	5.9	−1.7
1969	7.2	5.9	1.3
1970	5.8	6.8	−1.0
1971	5.6	7.8	−2.2
1972	5.4	6.7	−1.3
1973	5.4	5.5	− .1
1974	7.5	7.9	− .4
1975	8.0	8.4	− .4
1976	6.7	7.3	− .6
1977	6.0	7.6	−1.6
1978	6.8	7.2	− .4
1979	7.4	8.1	− .7
1980	10.6	9.3	1.3
1981	13.3	9.2	4.1
1982	10.8	6.5	4.3
1983	10.3	5.9[e]	4.4[e]

[a] Column (1) minus column (2).
[e] An estimate.
SOURCE: *Economic Report of the President, 1984* and the New York State *Employment Review.*

on "unearned income." Although the capital gains tax has been eliminated for long-term investment in new businesses, there is an important sense in which this type of highly discriminatory tax policy will simply make it easier and more advantageous for the successful entrepreneur to sell out at a profit and retire to a sunnier climate. There is also a possibility that a continuation of the recent bull market for stocks and bonds will make it more advantageous for the owners of old business not entitled to tax free capital gains to sell out and retire to other parts of the country.

Inflation is the primary determinant of interest rates and a large part of the price appreciation to be expected from owning common stock or selling an ongoing business to someone else or another corporation. If the Federal Reserve's tight monetary policy is successful at keeping the inflation rate in the 4 to 7 percent range for the next several years, one can imagine a further increase in price earnings ratios for most corporations and a climate where the temptation to sell out and retire to a better climate is irresistable. The eroding taxable wealth base will in turn make it more difficult for the State to finance the generous health benefits currently available to senior citizens in New York who were not willing or able to save or lucky enough to buy common and preferred stocks when prices were very low.

New York's tax code is not only biased against financial wealth but also is biased against real investment in new plant and equipment with long life expectancy. Leonard Sahling of the Federal Reserve Bank of New York has shown that for equipment investments with service lives of ten years or less the corporate tax burden in New York State turns out to be no heavier and is sometimes actually lighter than in most other states. For long-lived investments, though, New York's tax laws drive the after-tax rate of return on new investments far below what it is in other places.[21]

Relatively high corporate taxes in New York State have been partly offset by a 6 percent investment tax credit which has been raised to 10 percent in the case of new facilities for research and development. Investment tax credits, however, are much more advantageous to firms that invest in short-lived assets than to firms that are dependent upon long-lived assets. In the case of an asset that lasts only one year the credit in effect will be available to help reduce corporate income taxes every year, in contrast to once in a century if an asset has an expected life of 100 years. Firms in long-lived, capital intensive industries, such as primary metals and paper, thus have little incentive to modernize their facilities and often abandon their New York based plants when they deteriorate to the point of not yielding an adequate profit. Disengagement is being hastened further in some cases by relatively high local property taxes.

Since the abandonment of obsolete manufacturing facilities can impose very high social costs on local governments and persons that are forced to move elsewhere to find employment, it makes sense for the State of New York to seriously consider new types of tax abatement for long-lived assets that are more conditional upon the assets being replaced. Instead of using outright tax forgiveness to promote tax abatement, the State might require firms that benefit from property tax abatement, investment tax credits, and accelerated depreciation charges to establish special reserve accounts. These accounts would be matched by IOUs to government that only will be forgiven after the assets in question have been replaced or an equivalent investment has been made elsewhere in New York.

It should be recognized that New York is located in a rather harsh climate and is forced to import most of its mineral resources. Since imports constitute a financial leakage that can have an adverse multiplier effect on the State's economy, one can make a case for accelerated depreciation allowances and perhaps other types of special tax abatement for long-lived investments that save energy, recycle old materials, or utilize indigenous supplies or renewable energy. The State Energy Office has noted that

New York State is excessively dependent on high-cost imported energy supplies. Less than 10 percent of the total energy consumed in New York State is supplied by indigenous resources, while approximately 90 percent is imported from other domestic and foreign sources.

Net consumption of energy costs New York's economy an estimated 23.4 billion dollars in 1980, 65 percent (or 16 billion dollars) will pay for oil alone. If 1 billion dollars of this amount was spent within the State for indigenous energy resources, economic activity would increase significantly. The 1 billion dollars could create an estimated 381 million dollars of earnings and 22 thousand employee years.[22]

Energy that is saved as a result of insulation and investment in more efficient energy converters can also be expected to have a favorable multiplier effect since part of the saving in expenditure is likely to be spent on other goods and services that are produced in the State of New York.

Effective ways to save energy are cogeneration and district heating systems that are often very expensive to construct but can be expected to create savings for many decades. This is one area where public participation and tax abatement (especially property tax abatement) is needed to insure an optimal amount of private investment.[23]

While the major steel producers in the United States are in a state of retrenchment and probably will continue to abandon primary production facilities in New York, there are currently about 60 minimills, mostly in the South and West, that are able to turn out steel at costs rivaling the price of imported metal and still make a profit. These mills are essentially in the recycling business and produce specialized steel products in small plants by melting scrap metal in electric furnaces and pouring the hot metal into highly automated continuous-casting machines that crank out ready-to-use steel in a matter of minutes.[24] With most cities running out of landfill sites it makes sense for state and local government to pay special attention to new ways of economically recycling old materials. In some cases public subsidies can be justified in connection with recycling on the grounds that it would be more costly for public entities to safely bury waste material.

Now is an especially good time for public officials in the State of New York to carefully examine tax expenditures and subsidies to business to make sure that existing policy is not biased against recycling, indigenous industries, and long-lived investments. Some of the subsidies currently available to business are discriminatory. The Power Authority of the State of New York, for example, currently provides sizable subsidies to the aluminum industry in the form of very cheap power from the Niagara and St. Lawrence River projects.[25] Comparable subsidies are not available to other hard pressed industries such as steel.

GOVERNMENT EMPLOYMENT AND THE FUTURE OF BUSINESS SERVICES IN NEW YORK

Statistics on total employment in nonagricultural establishments by industry division in New York State are presented in Table 5 for selected years from 1939 to 1981. Manufacturing employment appears to have peaked out in 1943 and has been trending downward ever since. In that year there were more than three times as many persons employed in the production of goods as in government. Government employment, on the other hand, has sharply increased, especially at the state level, and at the present time there are almost as many persons employed in government in New York as in manufacturing.

In 1980 the state and local governments in New York had more full time equivalent employees per 10,000 population than any other state except Wyoming, which is able to shift a large portion of the cost of its government to persons living in other states by means of

109

Table 5. Thousands of Employees in Nonagricultural Establishments by Industry Division, New York State, Selected Years, 1939–1982

Year	Total Employment	Manufacturing	Mining	Construction	Transportation & Public Utilities	Wholesale & Retail Trade	Finance Insurance & Real Estate	Services	Government
1939	4,131	1,356	7	146	430	860	374	505	453
1943	5,226	2,189	10	125	458	851	350	572	672
1945	5,061	1,990	8	109	492	863	335	603	661
1948	5,596	1,976	10	212	544	1,139	383	709	622
1949	5,472	1,853	10	209	510	1,133	384	732	640
1953	5,936	2,119	11	223	517	1,164	413	768	721
1954	5,828	2,006	10	238	492	1,161	422	776	724
1957	6,179	2,024	10	261	516	1,239	457	881	790
1958	6,027	1,867	9	256	491	1,228	466	900	810
1960	6,182	1,879	9	266	482	1,251	480	978	838
1961	6,158	1,823	8	259	480	1,248	491	997	850
1969	7,182	1,871	8	269	497	1,442	590	1,329	1,176
1971	7,011	1,634	7	276	472	1,422	589	1,372	1,240
1973	7,132	1,619	7	283	470	1,460	586	1,438	1,269
1976	6,790	1,439	7	189	428	1,414	575	1,463	1,274
1979	7,179	1,493	6	210	434	1,477	605	1,643	1,311
1980	7,207	1,445	6	209	431	1,465	626	1,710	1,314
1981	7,287	1,433	6	213	430	1,466	655	1,784	1,300
1982	7,234	1,362	6	214	422	1,454	670	1,816	1,290

SOURCE: State of New York, *Employment Review.*

taxes on out-of-state shipments of coal and oil. The statistics on government employment understate the tax payer burden in New York since a large portion of those people who are employed in the mushrooming service industry are dependent on government contracts and payments for services rendered. Medicaid expenditures per capita in New York are more than twice the national average and most of these payments are to private physicians, non-profit institutions, and proprietary health care facilities.

New York, more than any other state, was the swiftest to embrace the ideals of the Great Society and in the process has become so burdened with all manner of taxes as to be on the verge of not only destroying its manufacturing base but its finance, insurance, and business services industries as well.

The president's efforts to build a strong national defense establishment at the expense of social welfare spending and the possibility that New York City might lose a good part of its business service industry means that public officials will have to reexamine the financing of vital services and also address the question as to whether New York can afford to remain a welfare state.

Higher education is one area where rising costs are forcing price increases for services rendered, which in turn are being partially offset by a system of family income-conditioned subsidies that are based more on financial need than academic ability. One suspects that price discrimination based on the ability to pay may soon be applied to other types of governmental services besides education and publicly subsidized housing.

Transit users, as a group, apparently possess about as much income, on the average, as non-users.[26] That being the case it would seem only fair and reasonable to raise fares to the point of covering most operating costs and mainly use public funds to provide special transportation allowances for persons on welfare and other low income groups that need the subsidies the most.

One suspects that New York's enthusiastic embrace of Medicaid and other Great Society welfare programs in the late 1960s may have had a deleterious effect upon employment growth. From 1969 to 1979 more than 19 million new non-farm employment opportunities were created in the United States. During the same period of time New York State lost about three thousand jobs in non-agricultural industries. In trying to guess what might happen in the remainder of this decade it is helpful to construct an employment multiplier model for the State's economy.[27] The model which is presented in Table 6 indicates that there has been a high correlation between average annual changes in non-agricultural employment in New York State since 1947, and corresponding changes in U.S. employment when an adjustment is made for divergent behavior in the government, construction, and durable goods manufacturing sectors of the New York economy.

The negative constant term in our employment multiplier model implies that in the absence of any change in national employment and the three explanatory variables that are specific to the State, there will be a loss of about 15 thousand jobs per year in New York. When increases in government, construction, and durable goods manufacturing employment were *just sufficient* to offset this negative constant term, New York was able to capture about 2.9 percent of any increase in national employment.

The decimal fraction .029, or 2.9 percent coefficient for the change in total U.S. employment, can probably be regarded as an upper limit to New York's likely future share of total U.S. employment growth. This is likely to be true since employment in durable goods manufacturing almost is certain to continue the downward trend that began toward the end of World War II. If the back office operations of large corporations headquartered in New York City are partially decentralized

Table 6. An Employment Multiplier Model for New York State, Where the Dependent Variable is the Average Annual Change in Total Nonagricultural Employment in Thousands of Employees from 1947–80

Independent Variable or Type of Statistic	Regression Coefficients and Related Statistics*
Constant Term	−14.68 (14.68)
Change in Total U.S. Nonagricultural Employment in Thousands	.029 (.008)
Change in Total Construction Employment in New York State in Thousands	2.37 (.57)
Change in Durable Goods Employment in New York State in Thousands	1.12 (.24)
Change in Government Employment in New York State in Thousands	1.19 (.34)
Coefficient in Determination	.885
Standard Error of the Regression	40.5
Durbin Watson Statistic	1.111

* The figures in parentheses are standard errors.
SOURCE: Basic Data are from the New York State *Employment Review*.

to other parts of the country, in much the same manner that much of the manufacturing employment that was once located in the city has been decentralized, that could reduce considerably the need for the construction of new office buildings in New York City and force public officials to reduce the number of government employees every time there is a national recession whether they want to or not.

The problem is that when total employment ceases to grow, or grows at a slow rate, many young people will leave their parents behind and move to other states to find jobs. The net result is that business establishments and the State's remaining work force must bear the burden of providing high cost health care services and nursing homes for other people's parents. When the president's offer to take over the cost of financing Medicaid is viewed from this perspective it is quite clear that every circumspect public official in the state of New York ought to hope and pray that he is successful at getting his New Federalism through Congress.

CONCLUDING REMARKS

Manufacturing employment in New York is likely to continue to move downward in the future as productivity is increased and goods production is shifted increasingly to the rapidly growing Sun Belt and countries with lower labor costs. The economic and financial health of New York also is threatened by a communications revolution which will make it more feasible for financial institutions and manufacturing corporations that are now headquartered in New York City to decentralize some of their record keeping functions. Slow employment growth in conjunction with an aging public infrastructure and an older population that requires more health care services will make it very difficult for governments in New York to provide adequate services without having an adverse feedback effect on employment opportunities and the growth of the tax bases that support government services.

There is no simple solution to this conundrum. It should be recognized, however, that tax rates are high in New York and that tax policy is biased against income from financial wealth and investment in new plant and equipment with a long life expectancy. Tax reform is needed, but if it is to be successful at helping to retard the decline in manufacturing employment in New York it must be targeted with greater care.

Given the harsh climate, a scarcity of energy resources, and the high cost of rebuilding infrastructure in such congested areas as New York

City, it is not unreasonable to conclude that the best way to further reindustrialization in New York State is for the state and local governments to put their own house in order by striving to be as cost effective as possible in maintaining infrastructure and providing public services.

III

Foundations

FIVE

Strategic Planning in a White Collar City:

The Case of Albany

Todd Swanstrom

S trategic planning originated in military thinking, which conventionally has made a distinction between strategy, the long-term plan necessary for winning the war, and tactics, the day-to-day decisions necessary for winning individual battles. While some form of long range planning has been a relatively well established part of the management of large corporations in the private sector, strategic planning only emerged as a distinct discipline in schools of business administration in the 1960s. The first major wave of adoption of strategic planning techniques by corporations occurred in the United States from 1962 to 1965. Nevertheless, for years American corporations have been criticized for taking a short-term, bottom-line approach to planning. They have been less willing than Japanese corporations, for example, to accept losses in the short run in order to gain entry into profitable markets in the long run. Partly in response to such international pressures, U.S. corporations have increased their use of strategic planning techniques since the 1960s. Today, most major U.S. corporations have a staff specifically for the purpose of strategic planning.[1]

Strategic planning did not spread to the public sector until the 1970s, when state governments began to adopt formal systems of strategic planning. It was not until the 1980s that local governments began to take up the techniques of strategic planning.[2] Perhaps the best known application of strategic planning at the local level is San Francisco's plan, completed in 1983 under the sponsorship of the San

Francisco Chamber of Commerce.³ By now, however, many cities have embarked on formal strategic planning exercises, including Philadelphia, Memphis, Fort Worth, Pasadena, Chicago, and an equally impressive collection of smaller cities.

The application of strategic planning in the public sector is part of a history of reform efforts to apply formal and often quantitative methods, usually first developed in a business environment, to problems of government. The progressive era at the turn of the century inaugurated such well-known reforms as strong mayor and city manager forms of government, the increased use of quasi-public authorities to perform productive functions for government, and the creation of independent city planning commissions—all reforms modelled to a greater or lesser extent on practices in the private sector. The goal was to remove local government decision making as much as possible from day-to-day political pressures and rationalize it in the name of economy and efficiency. More recently, efforts to rationalize the budget process have included the programming-planning budgeting system (PPBS) installed in the federal government by executive order of President Johnson in 1965, but later abandoned. This was followed by planning practices known by such familiar acronyms as MBO (Management By Objective) and ZBB (Zero-Based Budgeting).

The close relationship of strategic planning to business reforms introduced into government calls into question any claim that it is a new and distinct method. Nevertheless, strategic planning has a number of important characteristics that distinguish it from all earlier efforts. Strategic planning is extremely broad in focus. It does not confine itself to processes directly under the control of government, such as the budgetary process, nor does it focus only on physical development, as is typical of much urban planning. It could be called more accurately a form of policy planning. Even that would be too narrow, though, as strategic planning does not confine itself to public policy, but examines the practices of private actors as well—in the spirit of public-private partnership so common in cities today.

Indeed, the feature that perhaps best distinguishes strategic planning from other forms of planning is its stress on factors external to the organization. In the language of strategic planning this feature is referred to as the "environmental scan." Organizations must adapt to a changing, perhaps turbulent, environment, and strategic planning proposes to examine that environment with cold objectivity, avoiding the mistakes of planners who do not assess the compatibility of their plans with future trends. The environmental scan has increased in sophistication with advances in basic forecasting techniques, such as time series analysis, input-output models, regression analysis, and panel methods like the Delphi technique.[4]

It is precisely the claim of strategic planning that it can enable organizations to cope with a changing environment, specifically mitigating negative trends and taking advantage of positive trends, that has made it so attractive to city governments in recent years. In the past decade city governments have experienced profound environmental changes that have taxed their ability to cope. After a period of sustained economic expansion, for instance, since the mid 1970s cities have experienced much lower rates of economic growth. Many older central cities have even experienced economic contraction. Equally as important, since the halcyon days of the Great Society, federal aid to local governments has declined sharply. According to a survey of 303 cities by the Joint Economic Committee of Congress, in 1982 alone federal aid to cities for operating purposes fell 10.3 percent.[5] Finally, the economic function of central cities has been rapidly changing from a manufacturing to a service base.

The old incremental methods of decision making no longer seem adequate to the hard choices forced on cities by a changing economic environment. As cities are situated increasingly in a competitive economic environment, policy no longer can be made predominantly by responding to internal political interest groups. On the contrary, policy must respond more to the imperatives of a mobile post-industrial economy. As San Antonio's Henry G. Cisneros, one of the new breed of high-tech mayors, puts it, fundamental changes in the economy require cities to adopt "more entrepreneurial behavior" than they have been accustomed to in the past.[6] With its focus on how to take advantage of external trends, just as corporate strategic planning determines how to take advantage of market trends, strategic planning is well suited to this new sensibility of local political leadership.[7]

A great deal can be learned about the efficacy of strategic planning by applying it in a preliminary fashion, as I intend to do, to one city. In particular, such an application offers a useful approach to evaluating this newly emerging practice as a tool of local public policy. My focus will be on economic planning. Strategic planning begins by analyzing the trends which have an impact on the city. Its purpose is to separate those trends that can be influenced by policy from those that cannot. Strategic wisdom lies first in understanding the limits of what can be done. In our modern mobile economy, it is often argued, economic planning must be left to the federal government, with state or regional government playing a peripheral role. Local governments, it is believed, are too small to exercise much control over economic activity. If this is true, it makes little sense to apply sophisticated strategic planning techniques to local economic planning. The problem here, then, is to determine how much space exists for applying strategic planning to the economic dilemmas of cities, specifically central cities with a heavy reliance on service sector employment.

URBAN DECLINE IN ALBANY: CONFRONTING THE TRENDS

A quick environmental scan of Albany, New York, reveals the classic syndrome of urban decline. Population has dropped as middle-class households moved out to the suburbs, taking with them jobs and the tax base. Retailing has emigrated to the large suburban shopping centers. Wholesale operations have followed. Manufacturing employment has declined sharply. The only bright spot in Albany's economy is the growth of white-collar service employment downtown.

According to the decennial population counts by the U.S. Bureau of the Census, Albany increased in population continuously until the mid twentieth century, reaching a peak of 134,995 in 1950. Since then it has been all downhill, with population loss accelerating each decade. According to the 1980 census, Albany's population was only 101,727. Most of this population loss took place in the core city neighborhoods surrounding downtown. In the downtown area itself, for example, the population declined from 10,700 in 1950 to 1,712 in 1980.[8]

Population loss would not have been so damaging for Albany if it had affected all socioeconomic classes equally. As happened in so many other cities, though, it was the middle class that fled, leaving the poor and minorities behind. As Graph 1 shows, in 1949 Albany city median family income was approximately equal to Albany County's median family income, which includes the suburbs. By 1979 Albany's income had dropped to only 82.7 percent of the County's, reflecting the flight of the urban middle class from the city to the suburbs. In line with these trends is the changing age composition of the population. The percentage of elderly (+65) increased to 16.5 percent in 1980, compared to only 11.4 percent for the United States as a whole, while the percentage of young people to 19 years of age declined to 26.8 percent in Albany city in 1980, as compared to 32 percent for the country as a whole.[9]

Albany has suffered not only from the decentralization of population, but also from the decentralization of economic activity. Graph 2

Graph 1. Albany's Median Family Income as Percent of County's
Median Family Income

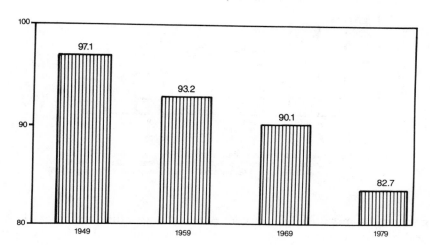

Source: United States Bureau of the Census, *1954, (1958, 1963, 1972, 1977) Census
Manufacturing, Selected Services, Retail Trade, Wholesale Trade,
State of New York,* (Washington D.C.: U.S. Government Printing Office),

summarizes the economic trends affecting the City of Albany. Between
1954 and 1977, for example, employment in the retail sector in Albany
declined 36 percent. Most of this was due to the success of suburban
shopping malls in taking business away from central city merchants.
City retail sales as a percentage of the Standard Metropolitan Statistical
Area (SMSA) retail sales declined sharply from 29.8 percent in 1958
to 14.2 percent in 1977.[10] The same can be said of wholesale
employment. The even larger drop in manufacturing employment was
due both to the migration of industrial concerns out of the city and
the relative decline in manufacturing employment generally. At the
same time that manufacturing employment dropped 47.5 percent in
the City of Albany, it fell only 14.8 percent in the SMSA.[11]

As mentioned, the only bright spot in Albany's economy has been
the expanding service sector. While Albany is typical of many older
northeastern cities in the loss of manufacturing, wholesale, and retail
employment, given that it is the capital of the second largest state
government in the country, it is not surprising that Albany has a
stronger service sector than most comparably sized cities. From 1950
to 1980, for example, the number of city residents who work in

121

Graph 2.   Employment by Sector, Jobs Located in the City of Albany, 1954-1977

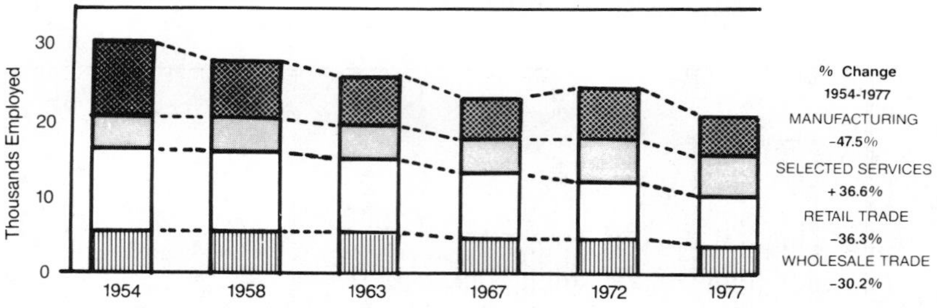

% Change
1954-1977
MANUFACTURING
−47.5%
SELECTED SERVICES
+36.6%
RETAIL TRADE
−36.3%
WHOLESALE TRADE
−30.2%

Source: United States Bureau of the Census, *1954, (1958, 1963, 1972, 1977)*
Census Manufacturing, Selected Services, Retail Trade, Wholesale Trade,
State of New York, (Washington D.C.: U.S. Government Printing Office)

government increased 56 percent. A second expanding sector has been health and hospital services, with employment of Albany residents increasing 63 percent from 1950 to 1980.[12] There is reason to believe, however, that employment in both government and health services will level off in the years ahead.

Outside of government and health, expansion of the service sector in Albany has been highly uneven. Looking at jobs located in the city of Albany in selected services, excluding government and health, employment declined in every major category except one—business services. Employment in this category increased 117 percent from 1958 to 1977.[13] Employment growth in business services was concentrated in the central business district. Between 1970 and 1980, for instance, employment in Albany's central business district increased 29 percent, while in the rest of the city employment increased only 12 percent.[14] Like many cities of the Northeast and Midwest, while suffering from a declining manufacturing base Albany is enjoying growth in the downtown service sector. Corporate headquarters, insurance, banking, and the ancillary services associated with these concerns are tending to locate in the central business district.

Notwithstanding positive trends in the service sector, the overall economic situation facing Albany has not been favorable. Specifically, there are two major problems that must be addressed by any strategic plan. (A problem is defined here as a gap between needs and resources.)

First, there is a mismatch between the job skills of inner-city residents and the types of jobs locating there. With low skills and little education, many inner-city residents qualify for jobs mainly in the manufacturing sector. But this is precisely the sector that is declining within the city and which is migrating to the suburbs and beyond. On the other hand, the kinds of service sector jobs that are locating in the city, front office jobs that are often highly skilled and professional, are beyond the reach of most inner-city residents. Routinized service sector jobs for which they would qualify are dispersing like manufacturing. Hence, residents of the inner city, who are heavily minority, have a high unemployment rate. A map of census tracts in 1982 with estimated unemployment rates above 10 percent shows inner city residents to be concentrated in the minority neighborhoods surrounding downtown.[15] Even if core city residents do have a job, however, they are often relegated to the secondary labor market where employment is insecure, low paid, and lacking in benefits.[16] Unemployment and underemployment are the fundamental causes of the litany of urban problems—housing deterioration and abandonment, crime, drug addiction, and welfare dependency.

The second major problem facing the city of Albany is the fiscal crisis of local government. The most important source of revenue for Albany city government is the property tax, accounting for 42 percent of city revenues in 1982. Yet between 1975 and 1983 the value of assessed property in the City of Albany declined 47 percent (in constant 1978 dollars).[17] Albany has a special problem in that over 71 percent of the taxable property in the city is tax exempt, primarily due to the fact that it is New York State's capital. Moreover, the decline in population has not meant a decline in demand for services. For one thing, the existing population is poorer and requires additional social services. At the same time, the city has just as many miles of streets and sewers to keep up as before. In fact, the problem of the infrastructure has worsened. The age of Albany's infrastructure mandates its replacement. Put straightforwardly, economic trends affecting Albany are placing city government, regardless of how it manages its resources, in a fiscal squeeze where expenditures tend to outpace revenues.

STRATEGIC PLANNING: THE ROAD NOT TAKEN

The solution to Albany's problems would seem to be obvious. Albany must attract investment that will provide jobs for inner city residents and boost the city's tax base so that it can provide basic services. Solutions, however are never as simple as they appear. Deep forces are shaping Albany's economy and efforts to improve the situation must work within these forces, not against them.

One approach would be to cut the cost of doing business in Albany in order to attract back the manufacturing jobs that are being lost. The primary method for doing this at the local level is to cut taxes for investors, usually through some form of property tax abatement. The problem is that local property taxes are only a minuscule portion of the costs of doing business. In Wisconsin, local property taxes were estimated at .68 percent of the value of shipments for all manufacturing industries.[18] The relative unimportance of local taxes for manufacturing location decisions is confirmed in the literature.[19] By contrast, in 1977 the U.S. Department of Labor estimated that "labor is the single most important input into the production of a firm, accounting for approximately 60 percent of all input payments on a national basis."[20] Manufacturing is dispersing to the Sunbelt and overseas primarily because of lower wage rates, not because of lower local taxes. "Smokestack chasing" is rarely successful for a city like Albany. Even if it could be made successful by adding local subsidies on top of tax breaks, in most cases the costs would exceed the benefits. It does not make sense for a city to buck a deeply rooted trend.

Perhaps, then, what cities should do is try to boost the existing trend toward the centralization of certain forms of office functions. Here, however, we run into the problem encountered earlier, that the costs imposed by local governments on business are so negligible as to make little difference in location decisions. In fact, since white-collar service functions are less capital intensive than manufacturing—labor being an even more important part of the cost of doing business—property tax incentives will exert even less leverage than in manufacturing. It is estimated, for example, that a 75 percent local tax abatement will reduce the cost of leasing space in a typical new office building by about 1 dollar per square foot per year.[21] In Albany office rents for prime space are presently in the 14–18 dollar range. This means that at best an abatement would reduce the cost of renting office space by about 7 percent. Yet office rent is only a small part of the cost of doing business.

New York City has had the largest tax abatement program in the country to boost white-collar employment. As of 1984 the city had given away more than half a billion dollars in past and future tax revenues.[22] Roughly 90 percent of the exemptions have gone to Manhattan projects, mostly white collar. There is little evidence that the subsidies had any effect on Manhattan's overheated real estate market. As Comptroller Harrison Goldin put it, "Tax incentives for this highly desirable area of the city are as necessary as additional sand for the

Sahara desert."[23] Due to such findings, the tax abatement program in New York City has been severely curtailed in certain areas.

One caveat must be added to this discussion on the futility of local incentives. While it is irrational for cities to give up their own scarce revenues to offer special incentives to investors, it may make sense for cities to utilize federal subsidies for this purpose. The Urban Development Action Grant (UDAG) program, for example, costs cities little, except administrative costs, and provides substantial subsidies to investors. It does not take sophisticated strategic planning to determine that pursuing such grants makes sense—especially when the payback on the subsidized loans usually goes to the local government sponsor, which then can spend the money as it sees fit.

In sum, efforts to attract primary economic activity through local incentives are generally ineffective. Its logic is that of the marketplace. Reduction in price, no matter how small, will attract more customers. But as David Gordon has shown, this logic is flawed. There are structural rigidities in the capital investment market which prevent it from engaging in continuous substitution at the margin, as mainstream economic analysis assumes.[24] The efforts of local government are overwhelmed by structural trends in the economy. This limited finding should not be used to conclude that local governments can raise taxes to confiscatory levels. Clearly, there is a broad range where local tax rates can vary safely.

A POSITIVE STRATEGY: CAPTURE EXTERNALITIES

Are cities powerless, then, to affect their economic future? The answer is "No." Even though cities can do little to directly influence primary economic trends, there is something they can do to attack the problems of poverty and fiscal stress. Success will come only if cities stop trying to reverse negative trends and begin riding on the advantages provided by the one positive trend.

The one positive trend that nearly all central cities are enjoying, no matter how decimated their industrial base, is the centralization of certain forms of white-collar service employment in downtown districts. It is important to understand the nature of this trend. From its founding in the 1920s until recently, urban economics has been dominated by economic base analysis.[25] The idea is that an urban economy can be divided into those industries which export and those which depend on the export sector for their income. The export sector is considered to be the basic sector and economic growth depends on its expansion.

From this point of view manufacturing concerns which export their product are the base of the local economy and the service sector, because it serves the local population, is secondary for growth. Recent work suggests that this view of the service sector as dependent on manufacturing is outmoded. Some services such as drycleaning, beauty parlors, and grocery stores do, indeed, service a local population. There is another growing class of services, however, intermediate producer services, that serve the specialized needs of business.[26] These command and control functions of corporations (and government) are the types of services that are concentrating in the central business districts of cities like Albany. The cost of these services is exported to the rest of the country and the world as a part of the final price of the product (or is paid for through state taxes).

The same advances in transportation and communication that permit the dispersion of manufacturing also enable administrative and control functions to be physically separated from the sites of production. This does not explain, however, why these functions tend to concentrate in central business districts. In truth, not all of these services centralize. Like manufacturing, back office functions tend to disperse to low wage areas. It is the highly skilled professional services concerned with planning, coordinating, and deal-making that tend to concentrate.

There still is no theoretically satisfying explanation why certain services are centralizing while most other economic activity is dispersing. Jean Gottman has offered, perhaps, the most satisfying account. Gottman argues that the old trinity of primary (processing raw materials), secondary (producing finished goods), and tertiary (services) economic activity is no longer adequate. To this he adds a fourth category, the quaternary sector, involved with abstract transactions, decision making, and information processing.[27] These highly specialized occupations apparently require concentration in one geographical location where frequent face-to-face contacts are possible. The presence of specialized business services there, such as accountants, advertising agencies, and lawyers, gives decision makers expert advice that would not be immediately available in a suburban location. The dense interweaving of quaternary activities in the cores of our central cities apparently creates a synergy that is more than the sum of its individual parts.

There is growing evidence that Albany is becoming a regional center of quaternary functions. As the state capital, it plays a crucial role in the planning and coordination function for all of New York State. Many, if not most, of the nearly 40,000 state workers in Albany fit Gottman's description of the quaternary sector as involving abstract transactions and decision making. Albany is also an educational center.

The State University of New York at Albany, the city's largest educational entity, has over 16,000 students. Finally, the city's central business district has the basis for a thriving corporate service sector, with many financial institutions, including two of the top 100 bank holding companies in the nation, headquartered there. As of December 31, 1980, eleven banks headquartered in Albany had 5.1 billion dollars in assets, much more than other cities of similar size.[28] Employment in the central business district grew a hefty 29 percent between 1970 and 1980. With a surprising 77 percent of the county's office space located in the City of Albany in 1982, it is clear that Albany still has a great attraction for office employment.[29]

The problem is that while Albany has grown robustly as a location for quaternary service activities, most of the benefits of this employment growth have leaked out of the city to the suburbs. For example, from 1960 to 1980 people who work in the city increased 30 percent while the number of people who live in the city fell 22 percent. To cite another example, while employees in the central business district increased 29 percent from 1970 to 1980, from 1967 to 1977 retail sales in the CBD declined 42 percent (not controlling for inflation). These negative trends have obvious implications for Albany's tax base. The city has been able to capture very little of its increased economic activity for the public purse because over 71 percent of the property in the city is tax exempt and because the city has no commuter income tax.

Even though the city, to date, has not been very successful in capturing the externalities and spinoffs of the growing quaternary service sector, the opportunity presents itself. Growth of service employment in the city has reached a critical mass where it has a momentum of its own. Albany has a resource which it can exploit profitably. If the city is going to offer subsidies, they should be pinpointed as spinoffs of the thriving downtown service sector where the central city has a clear relative advantage. Clearly, the existing trends for Albany to be a place of employment but not a place for other activities cannot continue indefinitely. Eventually some people are going to want to live close to where they work—regardless of the cost of gasoline. The presence of 40,000 workers downtown five days a week represents a resource of which the city can take advantage. By marketing close-in housing to these workers, the city can boost its property tax base. Moreover, if more people live in the city, retail sales, at least for convenience shopping, will revive. Cities like Baltimore and Minneapolis have shown that downtown retailing can compete with the suburbs if it projects an exciting marketplace atmosphere that is lacking in the shopping malls. Development of these spinoff opportunities is crucial to attack the inner-city employment problem. While inner-city residents often do not have the education to qualify for the professional jobs locating in downtown districts, they could find employment in a revived retail sector feeding on those white-collar jobs.

The key to urban revival in cities like Albany is the dense interweaving of different uses within a concentrated urban core. Too often in the past city planning has tended to separate uses through such devices as zoning codes. This worked for suburbs. In fact, suburbs are based on the separation of work and residence. But this principle is disastrous for cities. Cities cannot compete with suburbs on their ground. Americans only are beginning to understand the principle behind successful cities— a principle that Jane Jacobs articulated clearly twenty-three years ago.

The ubiquitous principle is the need of cities for a most intricate and close-grained diversity of uses that give each other constant mutual support, both economically and socially.[30]

Strategic planning is well suited to nurturing diversity, for diversity requires long range planning to coordinate different forms of economic activity within a limited land mass. This must be accomplished in a manner which will reinforce and not damage, each sector. The private market by itself will not bring about this result. The tendency for office functions to force out other forms of activity located on expensive downtown real estate is well established—"Manhattanization" of downtown districts. Planners are only beginning to understand how to nurture diversity. Gradually the techniques are beginning to emerge, such as the use of vertical zoning to require retail on the first floor, large mixed-use projects involving cooperation between the public and private sectors, inclusionary housing schemes requiring office developers to aid residential development, rehabilitation of historic housing stock surrounding downtown, and the revival of waterfronts to bring people back downtown. Planning for core city revitalization is a burgeoning specialization within the planning field.

It is now common to hear that cities will not prosper by cutting costs for industrial investment but need to develop the amenities that will attract skilled white-collar employment. I would argue that it is precisely the spinoffs discussed above that constitute the amenities that can aid white-collar expansion. Having close-in residential neighborhoods, recreational retailing, entertainment, and culture will make downtown all that much more attractive to the quaternary sector. While cities cannot directly influence primary economic trends, by promoting the spinoffs of white-collar employment they can, indirectly, provide effective incentives for quaternary expansion.

FINAL CAVEAT: THE PROBLEM OF DISTRIBUTION

There is an upbeat mood about cities now. James Rouse has called this "the most hopeful period in the history of the American city."[31] Private sector interest in developing central business districts as centers of quaternary service functions creates a great opportunity for formerly depressed central cities. And strategic planning can help cities to determine how best to take advantage of this opportunity. What strategic planning cannot do is solve the attendant *political* problem of urban revitalization.

Strategic planning assumes the city is a unitary actor. The question of goals is for the most part finessed. While strategic plans often have a "mission statement," it is usually exceedingly vague. Frequently it will be something like "expand economic growth and job opportunities." Economic growth is assumed to be the *sine qua non* of all other progress. In the private sector this tendency of strategic planning presents few problems because society sanctions corporations to pursue growth and profits to the exclusion of other values. In the public sector it is different. If a neighborhood is unprofitable, we cannot close it down like an unprofitable subsidiary.

Our analysis indicates that cities do have leverage to expand their economies and capture additional resources. How these additional resources should be distributed, however, has not been addressed. And strategic planning has no tools for addressing this question. Promoting residential gentrification around downtowns may be an effective overall strategy, but in most cases it will lead to the displacement of existing residents. How society should deal with this is a political question.[32] Economic analysis can show that because of the dense interweaving of quaternary functions, the downtown service sector is relatively immobile. Service employment in downtown Albany is especially immobile because state government has committed billions to fixed capital investment. A limited commuter tax, therefore, would garner badly needed revenues while causing little investment to move away; however, the State legislature will probably never vote to tax itself. Yet, the question of a commuter tax is a distributive question and no amount of strategic analysis will make it disappear.

SIX

Economic Development Prospects for New York's St. Lawrence River Basin

Mark J. Kasoff and Mark D. Soskin

W hile large in land area, two counties in the North Country of New York State, St. Lawrence and Franklin, possess small populations and for decades have been depressed economically. Spanning these two counties and reaching from Ogdensburg to Malone, New York, the St. Lawrence River Basin (SLRB) contains many small villages, such as Gouverneur in southwest St. Lawrence County and Malone in northern Franklin County. In recent years, particularly, the industrial bases of these villages have languished. On a brighter note, though, the River Basin region can boast also of the growing villages of Potsdam and Canton, as well as the Village of Massena with its strong industrial base. Ogdensburg, the only city in St. Lawrence County, should be included among these bright lights, for it now appears to have reversed its chronic economic decline as high-technology firms from Ottawa have located there.

Following a historical review of the St. Lawrence River Basin's economic development and a brief outline of its socioeconomic characteristics, we will present a detailed economic and industrial profile of the region along with a description and assessment of economic development and planning agencies. At that point, we will be in a position to consider the economic advantages and disadvantages of the region from the perspective of what the State of New York can do to improve its future prospects.

HISTORICAL OVERVIEW

The region of St. Lawrence and Franklin County is an enormous area of New York State between Canada and the Northern portions of the Adirondack Park. The two counties contain 4,370 square miles, almost 10 percent of the land area of New York State (see Table 1). Isolated from New York's commercial markets and population centers by the lack of rail and major highway arteries and by the geographic mountain barrier, the region nevertheless possesses substantial development potential owing to its proximity to the most populous areas of Canada via the two international bridge links and port facilities on the St. Lawrence Seaway.

Although the largest and fourth largest counties in New York State, St. Lawrence and Franklin represent one of the lowest population density regions in the Eastern United States. With an area of over 7,700 square miles, its population of just over 150,000 amounts to only 20 persons per square mile. The figures for New York State and the United States are 371 and 50, respectively. Of the six largest population centers, Ogdensburg, Massena, Potsdam, Canton, and Gouverneur in St. Lawrence County and Malone in Franklin County, none exceeds 14,000. The region's population total has stagnated since the turn of the century with Ogdensburg, Malone, and Gouverneur experiencing significant losses in population in the last three decades while only the college towns of Canton and Potsdam, plus a few of the smaller villages, have experienced any measurable growth in recent years. The two counties contain 0.85 percent of the State's population compared to 10 percent of New York's land area.

The region was settled in the early nineteenth century, primarily for raising livestock and field crops. Ogdensburg served as a significant regional commerce center. By the middle of the century, substantial activity flourished in the extractive industries of sandstone quarrying, copper, iron, and zinc mining, and the harvesting of the virgin stands in the northern Adirondack forest. Around these basic industries grew manufacturing complements of meat-packing plants and lumber mills, along with transport, commerce, and service area business. Rail linkages were established throughout the region and the area became an important supply source for the Northern Army effort in the Civil War. Each of the six major villages had reached sizable populations by 1870.

By that time it was already evident that economic growth for the region was coming to an end. Farmland was being abandoned for the more hospitable climate and fertile, less rocky soils of the Midwest. From a diversified agricultural base of sheep, pigs, chickens, cattle, and

Table 1. Socioeconomic Characteristics, North Country Counties

	Land Area Square Miles (1)	Population 1980 (2)	% Δ 1970 to 1980 (3)	Per Square Mile (4)	Unemployment Rate 1980 (5)	Mfg. Empl. % (6)	Per Capita Personal Income (7)	Mfg. % of Payroll (8)	Median Family Income (9)	% of Family Below Poverty Line (10)
New York State	47,377	17,558,072	-3.7	370.6	8.6	20.9	11,460	22.6	20,180	10.8
County										
Franklin	1,642	44,929	2.3	27.4	12.6	16.9	6,754	11.7	14,966	12.7
Jefferson	1,273	88,151	-0.4	69.2	11.6	22.4	8,442	24.9	16,295	10.9
Lewis	1,283	25,035	5.9	19.5	10.7	26.3	7,146	37.4	16,257	10.6
St. Lawrence	2,728	114,254	1.7	41.9	10.3	18.1	7,218	35.5	16,540	12.9

SOURCE: U.S. Bureau of the Census, *County and City Data Book, 1983* (United States Government Printing Office, 1983).

133

a variety of field crops, farming rapidly collapsed into a residual of marginal dairy enterprises dependent upon government subsidy programs.

The extractive industries fared no better. The exorbitant costs of transporting quarried stone ended the era of its use in construction in Albany and Ottawa. By 1890 half of the forests had been lumbered, leaving merely inferior secondary growth useful only for wood chips, veneers, and domestic wood stove consumption. Only a small zinc mining operation remains in the Gouverneur area, with abandoned and exhausted mines reflecting the move to abundant western and foreign sources of ore deposits. The rapid decline in these primary industries exerted harsh repercussions upon the paper mills, food processors, and the support industries in the commercial, service, and transportation trades. However, part of this decline was offset by the arrival of manufacturing to the region in the textile and metals industries.

Firms located in Massena and Malone and, to a lesser extent, in Ogdensburg and Canton, to exploit the comparative advantages of the area. Low cost power and access to rail and St. Lawrence River transport attracted ALCOA and Reynolds aluminum plants and a General Motors foundry employing several thousand employees. Prior to these developments footware and dressmaking firms located in the Malone area, employing over a thousand workers. In addition, cheese processing firms sprang up in Canton and Ogdensburg to take advantage of the ready dairy supply sources in the region. Ogdensburg retained its commercial superiority due to its locational situation at the eastern lakehead of the St. Lawrence before the completion of the Seaway in the 1950s. The extensive rail and ferry connection there also provided a suitable business environment for several small manufacturers.

The third historical period in the region's economic fortunes began immediately after World War II. The continuing decline in farming-, timber-, and extraction-related industries led to business flight, plant abandonment, and labor out-migration. This trend was exacerbated further by the opening of the St. Lawrence Seaway, construction of the interstate highways, and the shutdown of rail lines through the region. The locational isolation brought on by these events in many cases overrode the comparative advantages for business firms in the two counties. Total transportation costs, including direct expenses and other costs such as the value of time, inventory requirements, and so forth, increased the costs of doing business in the region. Finally, the aging of the physical plants for the large Massena firms together with the threats to the Malone textile industry, initially from the South and then from abroad, injected a critical element of uncertainty into the future economic prospects for the region.

During this period, the only area of growth was in the education industry. The rapid expansion of the two State University of New York colleges and two private colleges in Potsdam and Canton, especially during the 1960s and early 1970s, created an island of relative prosperity in the central part of St. Lawrence County. Thus, the Villages of Canton and Potsdam were the only ones recording population growth between 1970 and 1980 (as shown in Table 2). However, with declining birthrates and population cohorts, local colleges are planning for steady enrollments in the next five years. Overall staffing in the public colleges has been reduced over the last decade.

SOCIOECONOMIC CHARACTERISTICS

The last three censuses reveal a stable, slightly higher population for the region. St. Lawrence County rose about 2,000 between 1960 and 1980. Centers of manufacturing activity lost population while villages with strong service based employment rose. Ogdensburg's population dropped about a third to 12,375 while Massena declined by a slightly smaller proportion to 12,851. Potsdam rose rapidly in the 1960s along with increased enrollments at the campuses of the State University of New York and Clarkson College. The 1980 population was higher than 1970. The county seat, Canton, with its

Table 2. Population and Income, Principal Villages of Franklin and St. Lawrence Counties

	1980 Pop.	% 1970–1980	Median Family Income
New York State	17,558,072	−3.7	$20,180
Malone	7,668	−4.7	15,000
Saranac Lake	5,578	−8.3	16,008
Tupper Lake	4,478	−7.7	15,458
Potsdam	10,635	6.5	19,356
Massena	12,851	−8.5	20,798
Ogdensburg City	12,375	−15.0	16,117
Gouverneur	4,285	−6.3	12,959
Canton	7,055	10.3	22,909

SOURCE: U.S. Department of Commerce, Bureau of the Census, *1980 Census of Population, Vol. 1 General Population Characteristics* (United States Government Printing Office, 1982).

base in government and education, grew steadily over the two decades. Between 1970 and 1980 New York State's population declined by 3.7 percent, from 18.2 to 17.6 million. The trend in the St. Lawrence River Basin counties was upward, with St. Lawrence County registered at 1.7 percent gain to 114,254 and Franklin County rising 2.3 percent to 44,929.[1]

While St. Lawrence County rose by 2.7 percent over two decades, centers with healthy economic bases grew while others languished. Note the dramatic decline in Ogdensburg, Massena, and Gouverneur. This is especially true for incorporated villages rather than townships, indicating suburban development even in very small urban places.

ECONOMIC AND INDUSTRIAL PROFILE

The two-county region has one of the lowest per capita incomes in the State of New York, with Franklin County possessing the lowest income average among the 52 upstate counties. Median family income as a percent of New York State's stood at 74 percent and 82 percent for Franklin and St. Lawrence Counties. The population is nearly all white, with most of the minority group composed of American Indians on or near the St. Regis Reservation. The unemployment rate in recent years has substantially exceeded the statewide average. This rate has been especially high in Franklin County, in excess of 10 percent for each of the last ten years. In 1982, Franklin County's rate was 46.5 percent above the State's, while St. Lawrence County stood at 20 percent above New York's. High out-migration, especially among the 18 to 21 age group reflects lack of job opportunity within the region.

Despite the decline in manufacturing, it remains a significant part of the region's economy, especially in St. Lawrence County. Table 3 provides information about manufacturing and total employment as well as payroll. Only Franklin County approximates the national average of 25 percent while the figures are higher for St. Lawrence and Lewis Counties. Even more striking is the contribution of manufacturing employment to total payrolls in the region, 50 percent and 66 percent for St. Lawrence and Lewis Counties, respectively. The figure for Franklin County's payroll is about the same as the manufacturing share of total employment, suggesting the existence of small scale nonunionized firms. This is confirmed in Table 4 where 30 of Franklin County's 47 manufacturing establishments, or 64 percent, have less than ten workers. By contrast, St. Lawrence County has only one-third of its 81 firms in this size classification and records five companies with 500 or more employees. Franklin County has none. In the four-county region only seven firms of this size are recorded.

We would expect the existence of large-scale manufacturing to have an upward impact on average total wages (which is confirmed in Tables 3 to 5). St. Lawrence County records the highest average level of manufacturing wages at $23,961 while Franklin County, with its small firms, has the lowest at $10,116. For non-manufacturing employment the high-low range is relatively narrow, with Jefferson County on top at $12,284 and Franklin County at the bottom at $9,781.

The picture emerging from these data is the vital importance of manufacturing to the economic health of the region. Despite declines from earlier levels, manufacturing is still more important to the region

Table 3. Four-County Employment Profile, 1981

	Number of Employees	Annual Payroll ($1,000s)	% of Total	% of Total
St. Lawrence County				
Manufacturing	7,209	$172,737	32	50
Total	22,482	343,863		
Franklin County				
Manufacturing	1,785	18,057	25	26
Total	7,071	69,762		
Lewis County				
Manufacturing	1,796	31,236	54	66
Total	3,324	47,097		
Jefferson County				
Manufacturing	5,839	107,191	30	39
Total	19,642	276,744		

SOURCE: U.S. Department of Commerce, Bureau of the Census, *County Business Patterns, 1981, New York* (United States Government Printing Office, 1982).

Table 4. Number of Manufacturing Firms by Employment Size Class

County	Total	1 to 4	5 to 9	10 to 19	20 to 49	50 to 99	100 to 249	250 to 299	500 to 999	1000 or more
St. Lawrence	81	17	10	19	16	4	10		3	2
Franklin	47	25	5	3	5	2	6	1		
Lewis	34	12	3	5	5	2	4	3		
Jefferson	78	21	11	13	7	14	7	3	1	1

SOURCE: U.S. Department of Commerce, Bureau of Census, *County Business Patterns, 1981, New York* (United States Government Printing Office, 1982).

Table 5. Average Annual Compensation

	County			
	St. Lawrence	Franklin	Lewis	Jefferson
Manufacturing	$23,961	$10,116	$17,392	$18,358
Non-Manufacturing	11,204	9,781	10,380	12,284
Total	15,295	9,866	14,168	14,089

SOURCE: Derived from U.S. Department of Commerce, Bureau of Census, *County Business Patterns, 1981, New York* (United States Government Printing Office, 1982).

than to the United States as a whole. Efforts to strengthen the region's manufacturing base must be a major part of economic revitalization efforts, if the region hopes to emerge from the doldrums of the last several decades. Given the region's small population size and geographic isolation, export-based manufacturing activity is vital. Through its colleges and universities the region also has substantial export-based service activity, but the rapid growth in this area during the 1960s and 1970s will not be duplicated in the near future.

A frequently stated view within the business community in the two-county area is that the region is relatively unaffected by nation-wide fluctuations in the business cycle. Bryon Gale, Executive Director of the St. Lawrence County Chamber of Commerce, emphasized the region's diversified economic base when he said it seems to "be weathering the economic downturn better than most areas."[2] He cited strength in agriculture, education, and tourism. This observation is substantiated further by two additional types of forces determining the region's fortunes. The first class of forces are the long-term factors, described earlier in the historical overview, which serve to insulate the region from both upturns and troughs in the business cycle. The second set of factors is more likely to create regional fluctuations of an order of magnitude greater than those generated by the current state of the national economy. The most important of these regional destabilizers are those that affect the largest segments of the region's economy. Labor disputes, demand fluctuation, and import competition in aluminum, autos, and footwear industries have an immediate effect upon employment and subsequently operate through the regional economic multiplier to the commercial and service sectors. As higher education has expanded in the region, factors affecting enrollment and financing of the area colleges, such as state budget support levels for the two State University campuses or national trends favoring computer science and engineering degrees offered at Potsdam and Clarkson, have an immediate and secondary impact on the local economy. Federal and state support and subsidy program changes toward the dairy industry also have an unusually powerful impact upon this region, because of the predominance of marginal dairy farms and cheese processors. Finally, changes in federal and state programs, such as the mainstreaming of psychiatric patients in the Ogdensburg Psychiatric Center, forcing its virtual shutdown, in urban restoration and water treatment grants and the termination of the CETA program, all have dramatic affects on a region where a quarter of the work force is employed in government jobs.

ECONOMIC DEVELOPMENT AND PLANNING AGENCIES

The economic development and planning function is highly fractionated in terms of both charge and jurisdiction. There are agencies at the village, county, and regional levels as well as special bodies to oversee the Ogdensburg bridge and port, the Seaway trail, and various industrial park developments. Each of the major villages has a chamber of commerce and an industrial park to promote economic development. St. Lawrence County not only has its own Chamber of Commerce but also has the Economic Development Council and the Office of Economic Development. Franklin County operates under a single county Industrial Development Agency. Finally, there is the Black River-St. Lawrence Regional Planning Board, whose jurisdiction also includes neighboring Jefferson and Lewis counties to the southwest.

Although the number and diversity of these agencies reflect the strong attention devoted to economic redevelopment and planning, they also indicate shortcomings in coordination, cooperation, and a sense of common purpose for working towards these goals. These latter aspects sometimes have manifested themselves in redundant data gathering efforts, the temptation to bad-mouth neighboring villages, failure to develop a region-wide Fact Book to attract new firms, an inadequate success record in applying for available government development grants, and a less than unified approach to the state government bureaucracy.

A recognition of many of these deficiencies recently has led to restructuring and a new spirit of cooperation. In 1982, the Black River-St. Lawrence Economic Development Commission was merged into the Regional Planning Board to improve cost efficiency and enhance coordination. This merged agency has operated to disseminate information, educate village officials on the availability of and strategies for obtaining government grants, and bring economic development representatives together in monthly meetings to improve coordination.

However, reduced federal support for the Economic Development Administration (EDA), an agency the Reagan Administration wanted to eliminate entirely, has begun to take its toll. The Commission has been forced to cut back staff and services to the four-county area. In the two years since the merger, the board was kept solvent through in-kind, rather than cash, support from the county legislatures. The federal ruling this year against such non-cash forms of payment, the additional contribution required by the board's attempt to set up a regional revolving fund, and the declining number of EDA grants available were all reasons cited by the St. Lawrence and Franklin county legislatures to opt for withdrawal of their memberships on the board in 1984. The very existence of the board was endangered because less than the 75 percent (required by EDA) of the counties in the Economic Development District were still members, although the two remaining counties contain a majority of the population and firms in the District. The board has petitioned the EDA to reconstitute the District to include only Lewis and Jefferson counties. In 1981, the two counties employed 29,868 employees, or 50 percent of the four-county total.

There are several types of tactics employed by development agencies to bring new business into the region and retain existing jobs. One strategy involved publicity and contact. A brochure proclaiming the strong points of the region is published and distributed via mailing lists to potentially interested corporations. In addition, agency representatives attend industrial development fairs and pursue follow-up conversations to their brochure contacts.

Any enumeration of a region's locational advantages, of course, is apt to include the cooperative nature of the local government. This second class of tactics may include tax breaks, rezoning, and exemption from existing regulations. Alternatively, public service subsidies may be packaged into the deal, where access roads are built or widened or municipal sewage service extended. A pervasive approach is the use of the "industrial park," where choice property is declared an island of low-tax, industrially-zoned land use. Firms may be offered long-term leases in either abandoned plants bought up and renovated by the local government or in "shell" structures built and financed with government funding.

A third class of efforts, information gathering and secondary data source compilation, is a crucial complement to the first two. The Regional Planning Board has combined U.S. Census data with public service and private business surveys from the county agencies to conduct needs assessments of support services necessary to attract new firms and also to indicate particular industry groups susceptible to departure. In addition to its function as an aid in signaling vulnerability to firm retention, this information has been included in brochures and fact books to promote the region's strong points. It is then used to direct strategies and negotiations with prospective entrant firms. Inventories of vacant plant sites, production facilities, and mines are utilized to target intermediation efforts with potential new tenants.

Special attention has been addressed with considerable success to the development of the Canadian connection. This effort has taken two forms. The first involves direct soliciting to encourage firm relocation to the U.S. side. Without loss of locational access to their established supply sources and markets, Canadian firms employing domestic labor enhance their legitimacy in competing for a share of the U.S. market. In addition, a vacuum effect occurs which draws business from the relatively higher income and more densely populated northern side of the St. Lawrence River where property values and wages are considerably lower. Tax and regulation advantages likewise may exist, especially if firms are shrewd enough to play off nations, states, and localities against each other to derive the most subsidized and least constraining option for their stockholders or owners. In the last couple of years, several high-technology Canadian-based firms have located in the Ogdensburg area. The second form of the Canadian connection relates to using access to the population centers across the border as a drawing card for retail and service firm location. The most successful instance of this strategy has been the sale last year of the abandoned Ogdensburg Mall to the operators of the Charlestown factory outlet group in Utica.

Ogdensburg, in fact, provides a successful example of the use of economic revitalization strategies. Once the seventh largest port in the United States, Ogdensburg has made a substantial comeback in recent years. The city experienced a dramatic decline in its commercial and industrial base in the 1950s, a common occurrence in New York State, the Northeast, and Midwest. This forced the community to recognize the need for new direction and a unified commitment to change. Without the public support for redevelopment, many of the achievements of the past two decades could not have occurred.

Ogdensburg has been quite successful in securing federal support from the U.S. Department of Housing and Urban Development (HUD). Six Urban Development Grants (UDAGs) have been awarded.[3] UDAGs, the principal urban initiative of President Carter, use limited public funds to leverage private investment. Private-public dollar ratios usually fall in the 2.5 to 5.0 range. In Ogdensburg, a 200,000 dollar UDAG facilitated transfer of the abandoned Ogdensburg Mall to Utica-based developers who have begun to replicate the successful discount outlet mall in Utica. Another UDAG furnished 125,000 dollars to leverage 400,000 dollars of private investment for expansion of a hardware business in the city. The purchase and subsequent reopening of the former St. Lawrence Paper Mill by Ponderosa Fiber and its conversion to a deinking plant was accomplished with a 400,000 dollar UDAG grant. The City of Ogdensburg also uses UDAG funds for venture capital by lending them to the Ogdensburg Bridge and Port Authority (OBPA) for its own industrial development projects. These low cost loans, at about 8 percent, permit a revolving source of future project monies to the city. In addition to the UDAGs, a regional bank (Oneida National) and the New York Job Development Authority have provided substantial loans for the financing of shell buildings and Commerce Park.

The OBPA has provided Ogdensburg with an advantage over other towns in the St. Lawrence River Basin. The OBPA is an autonomous creation of the State of New York and is responsible for operating the port, international bridge, city airport, and St. Lawrence Railroad. It owns a great deal of land along the riverfront and to the east of Ogdensburg as well as Riverside Park in the nearby Village of Waddington. This land may be leased out as it sees fit. The OBPA has used its independence and authority to set up a thriving industrial park for light industry, and to construct additional shell buildings for medium-heavy industry financed with the UDAG loan from the city. OBPA collects revenue from leasing space in the buildings at Commerce Park to support its operations and to finance other development projects. The symbiotic relationship between Ogdensburg and OBPA has attracted several high technology and electronics firms from Canada, providing over 600 jobs, into Commerce Park. These firms include Mitel (telecommunications), C-Tech, Inc. (sonar equipment), Compas, Filtran, and Epitek (electronics).

Another effort initiated by the OBPA has been its application for a Foreign Trade Zone (FTZ) at Commerce Park.[4] Should FTZ status be granted by the federal government, raw materials and semi-finished products could be imported duty free into the industrial park at Ogdensburg, substantially enhancing the locational advantages of the area. The primary client for utilizing this FTZ would be the Ottawa area. Clinton County, with the city of Plattsburgh, has made a similar application for an FTZ to recruit from the Montreal region.

Ottawa is a major focus for industrial development in Ogdensburg. The St. Lawrence River Basin provides significant advantages for Canadian firms. A domestic bridgehead for penetrating the enormous U.S. market, which would be enhanced upon the approval of an FTZ, exists only 50 minutes away. A U.S. production site offers an expanding Ottawa firm a base for growth beyond Canada and minimizes the uncertainty associated with currency volatility, tariff, "voluntary" quotas, and domestic content legislation. In addition, the low level of economic development on the U.S. side of the St. Lawrence River translates into low land values, rents, taxes, and wages. Consequently, the highly unionized, heavily taxed and regulated Canadian firm may view this rural area of northern New York State as a favorable site for capital exports. Ogdensburg has successfully realized these potential advantages through an active program of recruiting, community support, and cooperation between the City and the Bridge and Port Authority. Ogdensburg has effectively taken advantage of its proximity to Ottawa. The ability of middle- and upper-level management to commute from the Ottawa areas means that only production line workers need to be recruited locally. Such workers have been readily available in St. Lawrence County where unemployment rates historically have been high.

There is one final area in which Ogdensburg has enjoyed a mild advantage over other towns in St. Lawrence and Franklin Counties. Ogdensburg is the only State chartered city in the region; that affords some flexibility over expenditure accounting and land-use procedures, whereas other villages and towns in the region must operate under standardized practices. Moreover, because Ogdensburg possesses the only non-volunteer fire department in the two-county area, the city offers the opportunity for lower insurance rates to business locating there.

Even with the aid of development bodies the process of reindustrialization can be frustrated, as illustrated by the attempts in the Canton region to bring its abandoned iron ore and paper mills back into operation. In 1980, the St. Lawrence County Industrial Development Agency contracted with an Ohio-based firm that intermediates transfers to shut down industrial sites. The Park Corporation was to renovate and market the former Jones and Laughlin iron ore mine at Star Lake. Four years later, the County IDA exercised the default clause of the contract that Park purchase the mine. Park attempted to purchase and continued efforts to sell the mine to Canadian interests.

Massena, in comparison with Ogdensburg, has not enjoyed new economic development in recent years. Massena possesses an industrial park and an Industrial Development Corporation (IDC) that owns and administers it, but only two tenants have been found. Six years after start-up, 19 of the lots remain vacant. There are several plausible contributing causes for the differential performance between these two

St. Lawrence River towns' reindustrialization efforts. One of the most frequently cited reasons for the inability of the Massena area to attract new firms is the lack of cooperation between the village, town, and the IDC. The Village and Town of Massena have been unable to convene a joint meeting to discuss these issues, and the IDC itself has not met since 1981. In addition, the IDC lacks the leadership and expertise of a full-time industrial developer. The town and village have budgeted 50,000 dollars to the IDC for salary and expenses for such an individual, but the IDC argues that this amount is insufficient. These administrative difficulties stand in sharp contrast to the Bridge and Port Authority of Ogdensburg with its autonomy, professional staffing, revenue sources, and choice land holdings which have successfully brought industry to Ogdensburg. A less tangible reason for Massena's economic problems may be that the town and village have not yet been faced with serious deindustrialization. Despite periodic layoffs and occasional fears of imminent shutdowns of major plants, the Massena area did not experience the economic collapse felt by Ogdensburg. Ogdensburg, traumatized by deindustrialization, quickly cut across traditional local political barriers to encourage economic development. Its back was against the proverbial wall. The catalyst was shared recognition that a crisis existed which dissolved years of factional bickering among local power groups. Let us hope that Massena will not require the strong shock of a plant closing before cooperation towards economic development becomes a reality.

CONCLUSIONS

The St. Lawrence River Basin possesses several factors favorable to economic development. The two international bridges spanning the St. Lawrence Seaway represent assets for the region. This has had striking effects on Ogdensburg where several high-technology firms from Ottawa, Ontario have set up American beachheads. Another benefit of the Canadian connection just occurred when financing was arranged to modernize and reopen a grain elevator which had been closed for decades. The elevator will handle grain from Canada brought in by truck.

Low-cost energy has been the mainstay for Massena. Bauxite is shipped in from Jamaica, Louisiana and elsewhere for reduction in the ALCOA and Reynolds plants, owing to the availability of economical hydro power. In fact, the region generates an enormous surplus of "clean" energy which Niagara Mohawk sells to other parts of the State.

Water and wood are other resources with which the region is richly endowed. Of course, many other areas in the Northeast and Middle-Atlantic states have abundant water supplies, so it would be difficult to sell this factor to prospective firms. Wood, on the other hand, may have potential as an energy source. Wood-chip-fired generating and heating plants are economical only within a 25 mile radius of a raw material site, a classic case of a weight-loss economic activity.

Land and labor are two other factors representing regional strength. Good land is available throughout the region at very low prices, sometimes no more than a few hundred dollars an acre. The region has a pool of well trained labor and a higher education system that usually will respond to training needs expressed by large employers.

The region has several economic disadvantages. Its location is its biggest liability, isolated from large American markets. This problem is compounded by a totally inadequate transportation infrastructure. Large trucks are often too high to pass under existing bridges, the highway system is two-lane, with travel time increased by passing through numerous towns and villages. The region is bordered on the west by Interstate 81, while Interstate 87 passes to its east. When the interstate highway system originally was planned, a "rooftop highway" was envisaged, connecting I-81 and I-87, passing through the region. If this is no longer a possibility, given the economics and politics of the system, improvement in the road network is called for. First of all, the State of New York should review the region's underpasses and designate some for upgrading. Second, a limited access highway should be built, connecting I-87 with the Ogdensburg international bridge. This will open up the entire region to better development prospects.

Improved access and transportation infrastructure are crucial to the economic prospects for the region. This is an area where the State of New York has a major role to play. Slowly, high-technology activity is developing in the region, especially in Ogdensburg, owing largely to Canadian access. But a review of high-technology centers nationally in places like Boston or the Golden Triangle of North Carolina teaches the lesson that a region's institutions of higher education are a powerful resource. In this regard, the St. Lawrence Region is truly favored with four excellent colleges and universities. The colleges, working together through the Associated Colleges of the St. Lawrence Valley, can help to facilitate economic development in the region. Again, the State of New York has a significant role to play to the extent that it supports higher education. Adequate venture capital and risk-taking entrepreneurs can be nurtured under the blanket of higher education in the region.

SEVEN

Local Economic Development and the State

Lawrence Southwick, Jr.

Economic development activities carried on by the local government are affected in a number of ways by the regulations and policies of the state. In New York, especially, local government has to be given authority directly by the State before it can act and its actions are circumscribed by State regulations. Consequently, in the area of economic development it is important to explore the impact that New York has on local government and to ask whether State policies in this area can be improved. For even if policy at both the state and local levels is to promote industry, state and local governments have other objectives too, so a straightforward prescription for increased industrial development alone will not necessarily be acceptable to either.

In this essay I want to explore the impact of the State on local economic development. I will begin with the regulation of the local government by the State and then move to a consideration of the effects of a broader range of State policies and their direct and indirect impact on business. Third, I will examine a variety of economic development policy options available to local communities and the ways in which policy choices shape community behavior. Next, a review of factors within a state which are important to industry will lead to a cross-state empirical analysis of how their impact on industrial development changes in relation to state policies and characteristics. Finally, I will evaluate the performance of New York State economic development-related policies in light of these factors and the public's perception of its performance, and I will consider ways in which State performance can be improved.

REGULATORY IMPACTS OF STATE INTERVENTION

Like most states, New York State imposes restrictions on what local governments may do. Generally these restrictions are intended either to assure that all citizens are treated equitably or that the locality does not act in a way contrary to State purposes or which harms people in neighboring communities. Several instances of such regulations can be cited.

Environmental regulations imposed by the State typically are intended to preserve and protect the environment. Often, however, such regulations, regardless of how well intended, actually reduce the well-being of the people they were meant to serve. State-imposed regulations must be applicable to all areas of the State. Further, they must be written with sufficient rigidity to limit local options.

As a case in point, consider the State Environmental Quality Review Act (SEQR). The purpose of this law was to ensure that economic development would take place only after due consideration of significant environmental factors. However laudable that purpose, the result has turned out quite differently. The SEQR rules and regulations are now often used by the opponents of particular developments as a delaying tactic. The more a project is delayed, the less feasible it becomes economically and the less likely it is to be implemented. The unintended consequence of SEQR is that it is used as a tool to obstruct development rather than enhance its quality.[1] Other consequences follow. Local government must follow State established procedures in its zoning and planning activities. For the most part, these restrictions are designed to ensure that all persons are given due process and are treated equitably. Yet, those procedures which are established with equity and fairness may not actually work to that end if delays are induced. Such delays disadvantage the person who wishes to introduce change and, in effect, may be a denial of due process and equity. More to our point, though, is the outcome that development is rendered more costly and less likely to succeed.

There also are regulations applicable to local government's attempts to attract industry. One of the methods used to attract industry is to issue industrial revenue bonds. While these are not backed by the full faith and credit of the municipality, there is likely to be an effect on credit-worthiness since there is an implicit promise by the municipality to repay them. Both state and local governments are now using industrial revenue bonds to help new firms get started or existing firms to expand. Since officials entrusted with managing the public's funds in this way often are fiscally conservative, firms most likely to receive funds are those least in need of them. This is not necessarily dysfunctional, though, since such firms frequently are stable employers and taxpayers, as well.

It is important to note that both state and local governments are restricted in the use of industrial revenue funds to help existing firms to replace obsolete or worn out capital stock. A firm which moves from one locality to another, whether within the state or from one state to another, can receive such aid.[2] This generates a bias toward the migration of firms and contributes, in turn, to economic instability. It would seem reasonable, particularly in New York and other states which have a good deal of older industry, that some consideration be given to assisting long established employers as well as new firms. If the State lobbied the federal government for equal treatment for established firms, it would take a decisive step toward industrial conservation.

Another consideration for local government is the particular type of firm which may receive such assistance. It has been assumed, in most cases, that gains may be had only through assistance to the industrial type. Housing follows jobs, for example, and need not be subsidized. And commercial endeavors directly serving the local public follow housing. There is a type of commercial enterprise, however, which has the same freedom of location as the industrial organization. Here I refer to the commercial service enterprise which attracts customers from other areas or which provides services to customers in other areas. It is sometimes difficult to distinguish between the commercial service enterprise and an industrial organization in the benefits they provide to the local economy. It should be possible to develop guidelines so that industrial revenue bonds could support such enterprises as well as traditional heavy industry. This is even more important today as the economy is devoted increasingly to the service firm.

Much of what has been said above regarding industrial revenue bonds also can apply to tax abatement schemes. There are two major tax abatement programs currently being used by local governments in New York State which are related to economic development. These programs are for industrial and commercial development. The former is relatively straightforward with the possibility for total abatement of local general taxes for a period of up to 20 years. The degree of abatement is negotiated by the firm and the local government. The State permits the locality substantial freedom to negotiate abatements. The abatement applies only to the increase in the property's value.

For commercial property, the abatement program is somewhat more restricted. It amounts to a 50 percent initial reduction in the increased amount of general taxes. This amount is reduced in subsequent years until, after a decade, it is phased out. The local government can choose to give this abatement either to all commercial developments or to none. It has no latitude to negotiate such reductions for only those firms which otherwise would not locate there. The local government granting such abatements consequently provides reductions to such firms as the neighborhood hamburger stand, which would have located there even without the abatement. It would be better to increase the minimum investment required before this abatement comes into play.[3]

Overall, New York offers local governments considerable leeway in their efforts to develop industry. In fact, it is unlikely that further autonomy is necessary or desirable. Tax incentives and finance aids already are quite adequate. It is only in the types of restrictions which can be invoked to cause delays, such as those on zoning and land use, that the State sends negative signals to industry.

DIRECT STATE INTERVENTION

In addition to the regulation of activities of local governments, the State also is involved directly in the development of commerce. In New York most of the state activities of this sort are carried on by the Commerce Department. A second and obvious area in which the State affects industry is taxes.

It is difficult for a firm which is not accustomed to marketing its products in other countries to acquire the knowledge to do so. New York's Commerce Department policies aimed at helping firms enter new markets clearly can be helpful.[4] It may be, however, that such aids are used mostly by firms which would otherwise develop new or utilize existing foreign markets on their own. Moreover, it is by no means clear that these aids are an attractive feature for firms not already in the State. Typically, a firm will have its markets in mind before selecting its location and will be preoccupied with serving those customers before considering new markets. Firms already situated in New York, however, may be helped to expand or to remain solvent through such support mechanisms.

New York has engaged in national advertising in an effort to attract both tourism and industry. The best known example of this is the "I Love New York" campaign. While such campaigns attract notice and attract comment, their ability to effectively attract industry is questionable. A firm is concerned about a specific location, not a whole state. Its decision makers will not be interested in general image advertising, but with the specific characteristics of the particular location. Accordingly, local government is much more likely than the State to be successful in advertising an area's merits because it can be much more pointed. It also can tailor its appeal to the industries which would benefit the most from that location, while the State has to employ a broader appeal. While the State's advertising probably is not completely useless, in that it may help to counter general image problems, it should not be relied upon for much more.

Another form of direct economic development is offered by New York's Job Development Authority, which provides loans for the expansion of existing firms and for new businesses. Generally, these have been used more for expansion than for the creation of new firms, and ventures often have been in cooperation with local development agencies. Only about half of the states provide such direct loans, so in this area New York has somewhat of a competitive advantage. When these loans have been made cooperatively with local development authorities, their success rate in the creation and expansion of business is improved considerably as a result of the increased efficiency with which the programs are administered.

A number of states impose taxes on personal property in addition to real estate taxes. New York does not. This offers the state a competitive advantage in attracting those firms which have a good deal of machinery and equipment or large inventories. Even though the tax rates on personal property usually are small, such taxes can be a real nuisance. It is necessary to keep track of the amounts of property on hand at various times during the year and its valuation in order to be able to compute the amount owed. The necessary bookkeeping may be more expensive than the tax revenue and hence not cost effective. At the same time, New York has a more complex structure of sales taxes than most states. The required bookkeeping for firms which do business in various parts of the State can be quite tedious as well as costly. This is less important to industry, though, than to major wholesaling firms.

LOCAL COMMUNITY PREFERENCES

Communities have different preferences with regard to attracting industry. As a result, it is difficult to make state policies fit all cases. For instance, local governments have considerable incentive to attract industry in that it generally costs less to provide services to that industry than the firm pays in taxes. Simply put, industry is profitable to local government. On the other hand, few people want to live next to industrial firms, because it is commonly believed that there are damaging effects to one's property value. The result is that a firm has to be capable of generating sufficient profits to overcome its undesirable side effects before the local government will be willing to invest much effort in attracting it.

In attracting industry, local government must be able to show that it behaves responsibly with its funds. Otherwise, the firm will be justified in believing that there will have to be an additional tax burden to pay for government inefficiency and excesses. Fortunately, it is generally the case that the citizens who, along with industry, will have to bear the burden of excesses also are concerned about taxes. As a result, the public has an incentive to elect responsible government. It is important that there be regular audits of local governments, either by outside auditors or by New York State's Department of Audit and Control, to guarantee responsible behavior. Lenders, of course, will insist on this.

If it is permitted by the State, there is an incentive for the local government to impose higher taxes on industrial and commercial property than on residential property. The incentive, simply, is that all of the property is essentially captive and cannot escape the tax. Residents, of course, can more effectively influence tax structure in this direction through their vote than the owners of industrial and commercial property, and local officials, particularly if they are short-sightedly looking only to the next election, may place as much of the tax burden on industry as they can. Clearly, that would be poor policy for a municipality wishing to attract industry. If a business can be assured in advance that it will pay property taxes at the same rate on true property value as homeowners pay, it will be confident that the citizens will not levy excessive taxes. If, on the other hand, local government can levy taxes at a higher rate on business and industry, there is no assurance that a locality will not spend excessively and place the burden on industry. New York has not enforced adequately such equality of property tax rates and is even considering institutionalizing differences in rates. That would be an important error which would harm the ability of New York municipalities to attract industry.

According to a longstanding principle, people choose the community in which they will live according to the mix of amenities and disamenities present.[5] Among the amenities are services provided by government. These amenities will, of course, have different values to different people. Among the disamenities are the taxes to be paid. Usually, the greater the services, the higher the taxes. It is certainly true that local government services and taxes are not the only criteria by which people make choices about where to live. They are concerned about the quality of housing and the neighborhood. They are likely to prefer to live at a convenient distance from their work. They may have concerns about climate or topography. Given all that, however, if there are a number of alternatives available, local government services and taxes may be a deciding factor.

An interesting aspect of this argument is the way in which the amount of commercial and industrial property which is in a community affects property taxes. Local governments find that services to business and industry generally cost less to supply than those businesses and industries pay in taxes. Housing, on the contrary, almost always costs more to service than it pays in taxes. Most often, therefore, the more industry the lower the taxes will be for a given service level.

Because different communities located within a particular geographical area may have different preferences regarding the amount of industry in their communities, they will invest varying degrees of effort to attract business. A township preferring to be a bedroom community will not be concerned about seeking industry or, indeed, about the efforts of other communities to attract industry. A village, township, city, or county actively working to attract industry could well find, however, that a neighboring community seeks the same type of industry. In this event, neighbors may certainly attempt to outbid each other in providing incentives for firms to locate within their borders.[6]

At first glance it would seem that such competition between neighbors will be counterproductive because, in the effort to outbid the other, each will offer excessive inducements. It seems further that the State ought to intervene in order to prevent these excesses and their fiscal consequences. When we consider, though, that other communities outside of New York also are bidding for the same types of industries found attractive in New York, it should be expected that other states will not observe the same kind of restrictions New York might impose on its communities and therefore would be competitive. In fact, it is the case generally that competition among states forces either the state or the localities to grant the same incentives that they might if intercommunity competition within the state were allowed freely. Put simply, the ultimate results of intrastate competition differ little from the results of interstate competition. In addition, competition among states and among localities may be quite healthy, for if states and localities are overtaxing industry, as frequently claimed, a competitively reduced general tax level might well remove an inhibiting factor for the growth of industry.

Clearly, it will not matter a great deal to the community specializing in housing what is done by the community more interested in commerce and industry. These interests are regional in nature. If there is insufficient commerce and industry around to support the demand for housing, the bedroom community will lose out, too. A community usually seeks to attract industry so that it will be financially better off. The greater revenue from increased property taxes outweighs both the added costs of increasing services and the disutility of having industry. It is important that the community that attracts industry be allowed to profit from doing so, for if the tax benefits must be shared across a wider area, as is often proposed, the incentive for communities to offer tax breaks will be reduced. Certainly, it is sufficiently difficult to attract industry that those who make special efforts to do so ought to be encouraged.

FACTORS OF IMPORTANCE TO INDUSTRY

Typically, labor represents the greatest amount of total expenditure by a firm. It is important to the firm that a sufficient quantity of adequately trained workers be available at reasonable cost. If labor costs are too high, through excessive wages, frequent work stoppage, or inadequately trained workers, a locality will be less attractive. Other quite basic factors are as significant. Adequate sources of capital and raw materials must be available and necessary public services must be provided. Since these can be found in a number of states, New York cannot claim significant competitive advantages.

Taxes paid directly by a firm are not usually of such magnitude to make the difference between success and failure. State and local taxes paid are likely to be less than 5 percent of revenues. In addition they are deductible in computing federal taxes, which reduces their effective rate substantially. It is true, however, that differences in tax rates among competing locations will be given consideration in the location choice. Therefore, higher taxes will be a disincentive to the attraction of industry. Vaughan argues that taxes have very little impact on such decisions.[7] However, the fact that such taxes are very similar in magnitude to net profits makes his assertion of their unimportance questionable.

In choosing a location for a firm it is important to avoid risks; the firm will want to know what to expect from government in the future. It has enough to be concerned about in the ordinary course of conducting business and does not want to be surprised and thwarted by sudden shifts in government policies. And the individual making the choice does not want such unanticipated events on his or her record.

The agencies responsible for local industrial development generally have found that firms are attracted more by the services they provide than by tax breaks. The most important of these services are those in which the firm is helped to contend with governmental regulation. The firm wishes to comply with the rules but does not know what they are, how they are to be interpreted, or who enforces them. This is particularly the case when a firm is locating a plant in a new community or a new state. Because of the wide variation in both the rules and the agencies which enforce them, a firm faces a substantial information cost in just finding out to which rules it is subject. Firms seeking a new location can benefit considerably by the provision of information on regulations and how to cope with them. Reductions in property taxes are probably useful to assure the firm that it is wanted; guiding the firm as it proceeds through the regulatory process is more important. This is especially the case in New York where there are a very substantial number of very complex regulations. Although these regulations are necessary to protect the health, safety, and well-being of the citizens of the State, they do raise the cost of starting a plant as well as doing business in the State.

Another factor of significance to the firm considering an industrial location is the level of personal taxation. Typically, the individual who makes the decision about moving a small firm is its owner or a major stockholder who will take expected personal as well as business taxes into account. What about the effect of personal taxes on the larger firm? Again, the level of taxation affects the desirability of a state or locality. The moving decision, however, is more likely to be made by a committee than by an individual. Those who make the decision will not necessarily be the major stockholders and may not be the most highly paid individuals in the firm. Still, they must take into account the effects of the move on the firm's employees. In order to make continued employment with the firm attractive, wages must be paid which compete favorably. If one state has higher personal taxes than another, it is likely that the firm will be forced to pay higher wages.

THE IMPACT OF VARIOUS FACTORS ON INDUSTRY

In order to determine whether the factors discussed in the previous section are as significant as they appear to be, tests were performed on cross-state data to evaluate the impact of these factors in relation

155

to state policies and characteristics. Although preliminary, these tests suggest a fruitful avenue for further research.

The first step identifies measures of the success of a state in attracting industry. There are four which seem to be partial indicators and which are readily available. The first is the ratio of manufacturing employment in 1980 to manufacturing employment in 1970. The second is the ratio of the number of industrial and commercial firms in 1980 to the number in 1970. Each of these measures a change over time which, of course, fails to take into account a state's initial position. It may be, in other words, that those states in good initial positions find it difficult to continue to generate increases by the same percentage. As a result of this problem two additional measures were introduced. The first is the number of small firms (fewer than 20 employees) per capita. This measures the group of industries from which the greatest future growth in jobs can come. Birch places particular emphasis on small firms as generators of desired growth.[8] The second of these measures is the number of foreign-owned firms per capita. This indicates the attractiveness of the state to firms in other countries. Table 1 defines these as follows.

Table 1. Measure of Success in Attracting Industry

CHM = *Manufacturing Employment 1980/Manufacturing Employment 1970*
CIC = *Industrial & Commercial Firms 1980/Industrial & Commercial Firms 1970*
SPP = *Small Firms Per Capita, 1980*
FPC = *Foreign Firms Per Capita, 1980*

Source: U.S. Bureau of the Census, *State and Metropolitan Area Data Book, 1982* (U.S. Government Printing Office, 1982), pages 448, 500, 501, 519, 520.

The variables which could affect these outcomes are, of course, extremely numerous and it is necessary to be selective in choosing among them. The ones selected here are the tax rate faced by a person with an income of 100,000 dollars per year, the proportion of state and local government expenditures which go for welfare, the proportion of the workforce which is unionized, the proportion of the population over age 25 which has not completed high school, the violent crime rate, and the state and local per capita spending. Table 2 lists the definitions of these variables.

Table 2. Independent Variables Affecting Industrialization

TAX = *Marginal State Tax Rate at Income of 100,000 dollars*
WGE = *Welfare Expenses/All Expenses, State and Local Government*
UNZ = *Percent of Workforce Unionized*

Table 2. *Independent Variables Affecting Industrialization—Continued*

CRM = *Violent Crimes per 100,000 population*
LED = *Percent of Population over 25 without High School Education*
SSP = *State Per Capita Expenditures*
LSP = *Local Per Capita Expenditures*

Source: Tax data, U.S. Bureau of the Census, *Statistical Abstract of the United States 1981* (Washington, D.C. 1981), Table 491. Other data from U.S. Bureau of the Census, *State and Metropolitan Area Data Book, 1982* (U.S. Government Printing Office, 1982), pages 448, 484, 486, 502, 513, 515.

The reasons for selecting these variables must be made clear. A hypothesis is that a high tax rate applicable to top management will induce firms to locate away from states and localities levying it. Welfare expenses are nonproductive as far as industry is concerned. Unionization has been indicted as a factor driving industry away, either through excessive wages or through more difficult labor relations processes. Crime is unattractive to anybody and may well induce all workers to wish to avoid such locations. Lack of education and training is a detriment to industry since the workers will not be sufficiently capable. Per capita expenditures were added to determine if there is an effect. To the extent that taxes are levied to cover the costs and governments choose the appropriate level of services, it should have no net effect since gains due to the services will just be balanced by the losses due to the taxes.

The results of the regressions using all 7 independent variables are presented in Table 3. The t-statistics are given below the estimated

Table 3. Regression Results Dependent Variable

Independent Variable	CHM	CIC	SPP	FPC
TAX/1000	− 9.0	− 3.0	.079	.43
	(1.8)	(.6)	(1.1)	(1.1)
WGE	− 8.8	− 1.31	− .004	− .008
	(1.1)	(1.8)	(.4)	(.1)
UNZ/1000	− 15.0	− 9.0	− .092	− .084
	(3.8)	(3.0)	(2.0)	(.3)
CRM/10,000	.39	4.0	− .035	− .240
	(.4)	(3.4)	(2.5)	(3.0)
LED/100	− 1.3	− 1.9	− .020	− .089
	(4.3)	(6.3)	(4.6)	(3.7)
SSP/100	5.9	2.5	− .032	2.6
	(1.1)	(.5)	(.5)	(6.5)
LSP/100	9.7	− 21.6	.100	− 2.2
	(.9)	(2.0)	(1.0)	(2.8)
Const	1.931	2.177	.027	.058
r²/ADJ	.549	.562	.476	.582
F	9.496	9.983	7.359	9.671

coefficients. Some of the independent variables are scaled down to give more readable coefficients.

While all of the equations are significant, the same cannot be said of all of the independent variables. The most strongly consistent among these is the proportion of uneducated people, which exerts a downward pressure on attracting industry. Also, a negative factor in general is unionization. Apparently, the crime rate acts negatively on small and foreign firms but is positively related to increases in the total number of firms (obviously a result of the number of firms rather than being a feature responsible for attracting business).

Because we are less interested in predicting the results for some time into the future than we are in finding correlative effects, the regressions were simplified to eliminate all non-significant effects. This provides a single regression result for each of the industrial attraction measures. First, look at the result for the change in manufacturing employment, CHM (t-statistics are in parentheses).

$$1. \text{ CHM} = 2.15 - .014 \text{ TAX} - .014 \text{ UNZ} - .017 \text{ LED}$$
$$\phantom{1. \text{ CHM} = 2.15} (2.8) (4.7) (5.7)$$
$$r^2/\text{ADJ} = .518$$
$$F = 18.496$$

Equation 1 is strongly significant and indicates negative effects for marginal tax rates, unionization, and lack of education on the change of manufacturing employment. The elasticity of the tax effect is -.5, which means that a 10 percent increase in maximum personal tax rates will reduce the percentage change in manufacturing employment by 5 percent. For New York, a reduction in the rate from 14 to 10 percent would, as a best estimate, have saved 21 percent of the manufacturing jobs which were lost during the ten year period.

Unionization is also a substantial negative force. The elasticity is −.8, so a 10 percent increase in the proportion unionized results in an 18 percent drop in the change in manufacturing jobs. Education, too, is important with an elasticity of −3.2. A 10 percent reduction in the proportion without a high school education would have resulted in a 32 percent improvement in the change in manufacturing jobs.

The second equation deals with the change in the number of industrial and commercial firms. The result

$$2. \text{ CIC} = 2.159 - 1.51 \text{ WGE} - .009 \text{ UNZ} - .338 \text{ CRM}/100$$
$$\phantom{2. \text{ CIC} = 2.159} (2.3) (3.0) (3.6)$$
$$-.018 \text{ LED} - .187 \text{ LSP}$$
$$(6.0) (2.0)$$
$$r^2/\text{ADJ} = .577$$
$$F = 14.359$$

The effect of the proportion of spending which goes for welfare is negative, with an elasticity of $-.9$. To the extent that increases in welfare imply reductions in services for business, there should be such a negative effect. The change elasticity with respect to unionization is -1.1, again showing a substantial effect. It is less, however, than in the previous equation. Apparently, the larger firms are more affected. The elasticity with respect to crime is $-.8$. The elasticity with respect to the lack of education is -3.1, which is similar to the result from the first equation. Finally, the elasticity with respect to local per capita spending is $-.9$. It is difficult to draw any meaningful conclusion from this unless it is that local spending is paid for by business but does not result in commensurate benefits.

The third equation gives the number of small firms per capita. In order to make the equation readable, we will restate it as the number of small firms per 10,000 population. This provides

$$3.\ \text{SPP} * 10^4 = 290 - .864\ \text{UNZ} - .030\ \text{CRM} - 2.275\ \text{LED}$$
$$(2.4) \qquad\qquad (2.6) \qquad\qquad (6.5)$$
$$r^2/\text{ADJ} = .495$$
$$F = 17.006$$

This is also a highly significant equation. The elasticity with respect to unionization is -1.1. This effect is about the same as in the case of the number of firms. The elasticity with respect to the violent crime rate is $-.7$, close to the earlier result. The elasticity with respect to the lack of education is -4.1, again confirming the strong effect from the prior equations.

The final equation deals with the number of foreign owned firms per capita. To make the equation more readable, it is expressed in terms of the number per 1000 of population. The result is

$$4.\ \text{FPC} * 10^3 = 61 + .023\ \text{CRM} - .921\ \text{LED} + 25.0\ \text{SSP}$$
$$(3.0) \qquad\qquad (4.0) \qquad\qquad (6.3)$$
$$- 23.0\ \text{LSP}$$
$$(2.9)$$
$$r^2/\text{ADJ} = .597$$
$$F = 20.056$$

While equation 4 is highly significant, the results are somewhat strange. The crime rate has an elasticity of $+.25$, which indicates that there will be more foreign firms if there is a higher crime rate. The causality does, of course, run in the opposite direction with a large number of such firms being attractive to criminals. The elasticity with respect to education is $-.8$, a smaller effect than found in the other equations, though it is still substantial. The elasticities with respect to state and local per capita spending are, respectively $+.5$ and $-.5$. Since

159

the typical state spending is for services which benefit both businesses and households while local governments, especially schools, benefit households more, this result may be plausible.

We can summarize these elasticities in tabular form. This summary is presented in Table 4. Only significant results are included.

NEW YORK STATE: PERFORMANCE AND PUBLIC PERCEPTION

In the foregoing we have looked at a number of factors which appear to affect industrial development. It is now appropriate to evaluate New York State policies in light of those factors which have important developmental influences. Let us first consider taxes.

In 1980 New York State raised 724 dollars per capita in taxes. The average for the entire United States was 607 dollars. With New York raising 20 percent more in per capita taxes than the national average, the State must suffer from a competitive disadvantage. The taxes on business, however, are not particularly onerous. New York raises only 9.7 percent of its taxes from the corporate income tax. Nationally, the average is the same 9.7 percent. Because New York exceeds the national average number of corporations, this implies that the burden on the firm does not give New York any substantial disadvantage.

Table 4. Elasticities of Desired Outcomes With Respect to State Variables

| | Elasticities Of | | | |
With Respect to	Change in Mfg. Employ- ment	Change in No. Ind. & Comm. Firms	Small Firms Per Capita	Foreign Firms Per Capita
Max. Pers. Tax Rate	− .5			
Unionization	−1.8	−1.1	−1.1	
Lack of Education	−3.2	−3.1	−4.1	−.8
Prop. Spending on Welfare		− .9		
Crime		− .8	− .7	+.3
State Per Capita Spending				+.5
Local Per Capita Spending		− .9		−.5

Just how does New York State rank in a comparison of personal taxes across states? The answer is that New York is the least desirable state on this dimension. It has what must be rated the highest level of personal income taxation. At the lower income levels, which are relevant to the people least likely to make interstate moves in response to tax incentives, New York has personal tax rates which are not greatly different from other states. At the higher income levels, though, New York taxes more heavily. The highest tax bracket in New York starts at an income of 23,000 dollars and pays at a 14 percent rate. The only other state with a higher bracket is Minnesota which has a 16 percent bracket. That does not take effect until the income reaches 32,800 dollars. It is true that New York has a maximum tax rate of 10 percent on "earned income" with the higher rate only on "unearned income." The people who are most mobile, however, either because they own the firm or because various firms are competing for their services, are the ones who will have savings and earnings from those savings. They will consequently be taxed most heavily on those savings and will be most affected by the tax.

What about some of the neighboring states with which New York competes for firms? Pennsylvania has a ceiling rate of 2.2 percent, Ohio's ceiling is 3.5 percent for income over 40,000 dollars, Connecticut has a maximum rate of 9 percent for income over 100,000 dollars, and Michigan has a 4.6 percent flat rate. New York is disadvantaged equally in this regard with respect to the southern states. North Carolina has a 7 percent maximum rate, Georgia has a 6 percent maximum, Virginia's is 5.75 percent, and Kentucky has a 6 percent maximum rate. The national average is 6.6 percent.

It is interesting to compare the progressivity of the actual tax burden on similar families in different communities. In New York City the state and local taxes paid rose from 10.4 percent of income at the 7,500 dollar income level to 15.9 percent of income at the 50,000 dollar level. In Chicago, by comparison, the rates are 9.6 and 7.1 percent respectively. That is an 8 percent disadvantage for New York at the lower income level, but a 124 percent disadvantage at the higher income level. No other of the 30 largest cities has as high a tax level at the higher income level. The average for the 30 cities is 8.3 percent, or only 52 percent of the New York City level. The difference of some 3,815 dollars on a 50,000 dollar income is not insubstantial.

How does New York compare with other states regarding the capability of the labor force? There has been some tendency for New York to lose its lead here. In 1970, we find that some 47.3 percent of New Yorkers over the age of 25 had not completed high school, compared to a national average of 47.7 percent. In the South, the average was 54.9 percent. By 1980, only 33.8 percent of New Yorkers over age 25 had not completed high school. The national average, however, had fallen to 33.7 percent, lower, instead of higher, than New York. And in the South the average dropped to 39.9 percent, whereas in the West the average stood at 25.6 percent. Clearly, New York's literacy rate no longer leads the nation.

A more favorable result can be found in the proportions of college graduates. From 1970 to 1980, the percentage of people who are college graduates in New York increased from 11.9 to 18.7 percent. In the United States as a whole, the corresponding percentage increased from 10.7 to 16.3 percent. In the South, the percentage rose from 9.8 to 14.8 percent. This also means, however, that the numbers of college graduates in the competing states have increased sufficiently so that adequate managerial capacity is present. Furthermore, the competing communities have sufficient numbers of college graduates so that their cohorts from other areas are willing to move there. There clearly are fewer educationally unattractive areas in the U.S. today.

What about the actual costs of labor? At 38.8 percent, New York has a higher percentage of its non-agricultural labor force unionized than any other state. This compares with a national average of 22.5 percent. While this is not translated into higher earnings for New York manufacturing production workers, it may well have an adverse effect on costs. New York production workers earned an average of 283 dollars per week in 1980 compared to a national average of 289 dollars per week. However, union work rules have an adverse effect on productivity and, to the extent that New Yorkers are more heavily unionized, this factor translates into higher costs to business and disadvantages New York relative to other states.

An extremely important aspect of industrial location is the capacity to move goods to market. New York traditionally has had a good transportation system and major markets still remain closer in transportation terms to New York industries than to those in most other states. Moreover, its road network has been better than that of other states. Although that is still true, New York's lead has been reduced. With the substantial aid provided by the federal road programs, other states have received more help than New York and have been able to reduce New York's competitive edge. There seems little more that New York can do in this area to increase its competitive advantage other than seeking more federal aid. Its state gasoline taxes have remained approximately at the national average and so are not uncompetitive. During the decade of the 1970s, the railroad mileage in New York decreased by 18.5 percent compared to a national decrease of 8.5 percent. But because rail transport has been declining in importance nationally, this should not be overstressed even though it certainly does reduce New York's competitiveness for some industries.

Of what significance is the crime rate? Of no surprise, crime had an adverse influence. In 1980 New York had the highest rate of violent crime of any state in the nation at 1,026 crimes per 100,000 population. The national average was 446. Nearby states include New Jersey at 602, Pennsylvania at 362, Vermont at 178, Massachusetts at 600, Michigan at 638 and Ohio at 497. Only Florida, Nevada, and California approximate New York.

New York is often perceived as inhospitable to business and industry. We often see studies of the attractiveness of various states in terms of their quality of life and other preferred features. These studies select various factors which their authors feel are relevant and proceed to classify the states according to these factors. Quite often the studies rank New York toward the bottom of the list. While we may quarrel with particular studies in terms of the bias of the authors or the choice of factors, the result is repeated too frequently to be accidental. It is unlikely to be the case that all these studies contain biases against New York.

Most perceptions people have are based to some extent on reality. If New York is perceived to be hostile to business and industry, there are likely to be grounds for that belief. In order to alter perceptions, it is necessary to alter their underlying reality. Consider the view that New York is more hospitable to nonproducers than to producers. It is a fact that New York has a higher proportion of its population on public assistance than do all but three other states. In addition, the average payment to a public assistance family exceeds the amount in all but three other states. New York's predicament is perceived accurately throughout the U.S. and no amount of advertising can alter that perception. If we do wish to change that perception, we must do better to develop policies which create in New York a favorable and sympathetic disposition toward business interests.

In this regard, New York does try to help the firm locate in the State. Consider, for example, the question of financing the firm. There are four major ways in which the state or local government conceivably could help to provide the required capital. It could provide direct loans. New York State already does so in one way through the Job Development Authority. As another option, state and local governments could provide loan guarantees, which improves security and thus increases the inducement for a private lender to make loans. Again, New York does this. State government could guarantee a firm's bonds in order to provide for longer term financing. New York does this as well. Finally, government could take a direct ownership participation in the firm through the provision of venture capital. It is only recently that New York State has entered this aspect of financing through the Corporation for Innovative Development and, as yet, its financing is limited. It must be noted, too, that by using their Community Development funds from the federal government, some local governments have already acted in this way. Therefore, New York provides capital in all four ways, although to a limited extent in certain cases. In a report in the October 1982 issue of *INC,* it was reported that only seven other states provided as many as three of these forms of capital and only 30 others provided financing through any of these mechanisms.[9] This, too, is a reality which will become well known eventually, all the more quickly through a concerted advertising campaign.

In my estimation, it appears that the State has done all it should to either offer direct aid to the firm or to allow the local government to provide aid. The problems which remain stem from decisions by the state on its other spending and taxing issues. These high tax levels and the concentration of spending on nonproductive activities also cause difficulties for the local government which wishes to attract industry. Until the State solves its problems in these other areas, the difficulties confronting local governments will not be alleviated.

IV

State Revitalization in International Context

EIGHT

The Changing Impact of International Trade
On the Economy of New York State

Walter Goldstein

It is sad to note that New York passed its peak wealth in the 1930s and that a generation later it conceded its preeminent place to California. For the last fifty years the economy of New York has grown in absolute size but it has continued to decline in terms of per capita GNP when compared to the rest of the United States. It is true that the State economy, in total wealth, is the ninth or tenth richest in the world. Producing over 200 billion dollars a year in goods and services, it is richer than 150 of the nations represented in the United Nations. But there is no cause to boast about the wealth of the Empire State when the local economy lost half a million jobs in manufacturing in ten years and unemployment afflicts more than 7 percent of the workforce. In the 1970s New York was one of only two states that lost population, and all too many labor-intensive industries either filed for bankruptcy or fled from New York. In the 1990s, it will be overtaken in size first by Texas and then by Florida, and there is little assurance that it will create sufficient new industry to regain the dynamic growth that it once had enjoyed.

Admittedly, most of the Northeast and the Midwestern states have suffered as badly as New York. In many cases their prospects for arresting the course of industrial decline are not encouraging, while the chance remains that New York might yet reverse its poor performance. Unfortunately, it is so preoccupied with the struggle to balance the state budget each year, to fund necessary social services, and to repair the aging infrastructure of the economy, that it has lost sight of a fundamental reality. Unless it succeeds in halting the decline, the economy of New York will not be able to maintain the high standards of living and employment that 17.6 million citizens have come to expect. It can provide lucrative marketing opportunities and service support for other states' activity, but it will no longer manufacture the primary wealth for which the Empire State was once renowned.

Looking forward into the 1980s, this paper will focus on three critical factors of development in the local economy. Each of the three hinges upon the greater involvement of New York in the rapidly expanding markets of world trade.

1. *As a "mature" economy,* New York has had to phase out many of its manufacturing and blue-collar industries. As a result, 400,000 jobs in manufacturing industries were lost between 1967 and 1982, especially in the steel, automobile, and textile industries. An exodus of goods-producing firms moved work to cheaper wage economies, first to the Sunbelt and then to the less developed countries (LDCs).[1] The flight was frequently engineered by multinational corporations (MNCs) with production plant, headquarters offices, and their financial base in New York State. Many of them pulled their parent headquarters out of New York, too.[2]

2. *The strongest growth* in the last twenty years has been accomplished in many cases by New York companies involved in world trade: (a) foreign MNCs have entered New York State in ever increasing numbers; (b) local firms engaged in export trade have contributed an astounding stimulus to local employment and GNP; and (c) home-based MNCs have built new plant in New York to service the export platforms and subsidiaries that they extended overseas.[3] Local expansion was most marked in the banking and business service sectors, and in the manufacturing industries that concentrate upon capital-intensive production. These export-oriented sectors will continue to offer the best prospects for growth in the 1980s as the State economy phases out more and more of labor-intensive industries that had been built in the first half of the century.

3. *A new form of industrial policy* will be required if New York is to attract incoming direct foreign investment (DFI). New York must learn to adjust to the highly competitive conditions in the world market and to encourage the local activities of U.S. based MNCs and exporting firms. The global market today offers the single most promising boost to local GNP but there is a scramble among states, and countries, to take advantage of the opportunities provided by world trade. New York can gain richly from its growing involvement in world trade and is well positioned to move upward with the fastest growing sectors of the American economy—the highly successful industries that can compete in world trade.

The argument presented here can be stated simply though it will be difficult to weave its three central themes together. Given the "mature," the fully developed or "post-industrial" character of the economy, New York must adjust its capital formation, its skilled workforce, and its structure of government to the exigencies of the world trade system. If it is to expand its economic strength and modernize its productivity base in the 1980s, New York must compete more aggressively in the international order. Adequate capital and market stimuli cannot be drawn from the domestic U.S. economy alone. Nor will federal funds be sufficient to finance welfare needs and industrial subsidies. Even if the U.S. economy were to surge forward into a long wave cycle of growth in the 1980s, New York will find more benefit by increasing its role in foreign trade than by relying on a nationwide upturn of business activity. But in order to do so a number of radical changes must be made. Business conditions must be made attractive to incoming DFI. Labor must be retrained to staff new knowledge-intensive industries and exporting firms. Tax law must be modified. The headquarters of American MNCs and their operating plant must be encouraged to expand at home. Export credits and financing subsidies must be provided and support services must be improved—including mass transit facilities and telecommunications—in order to accelerate the process of modernization and growth. It is by no means certain that these goals will be achieved in the remaining months in this decade. But there is a good chance that New York will benefit appreciably from the mounting expansion of foreign trade and investment. But if it should fail it will find no other stimuli on which it can so profitably rely.

THE NEW YORK ECONOMY IN THE 1980s

According to the U.S. Census Bureau, New York lost both people and wealth in the last decade.[4] Since 1970, the New York population decreased by nearly 4 percent to 17.6 million while the U.S. population rose over the decade by 11.4 percent to 230 million people. A more significant figure appears in the decline of per capita wealth. In 1960 the per capita income of New York exceeded the national average by 22.7 percent but by 1980 it was only ahead by 8.2 percent.

When the 1980–82 recession came to an end, the number of non-agricultural jobs in New York moved up to 7.4 million in 1983, a record high for the State. Most of the increase occurred in nonman-ufacturing industries, with the service sectors providing the greatest impetus and maintaining their position as the largest employer in the State. Finance, insurance, and real estate (the so-called FIRE group), and construction contributed to the improvement, while losses were registered in government, trade, transportation, and manufacturing. In the latter category, New York's share of all U.S. manufacturing fell from 13 to 7 percent between 1960 and 1980. Most of the loss in government was attributed to constant-dollar reductions in federal and State spending.[5]

Approximately 43 percent of the State's unemployed residents in 1981 were aged 16 to 24, and about the same percentage were females. Blacks and other minorities accounted for about one-quarter of the jobless total, but their unemployment rate was more than twice as high as the rate for whites. Of those receiving unemployment benefits during the year, over half were blue-collar workers who had last worked in non-manufacturing establishments. These were the most conspicuous casualties of the business cycle. Not many of them had actually worked for the steel mills or automobile plants that had closed down. Most of them had worked in the trades and services that had relied on the survival of manufacturing plant. When neighboring plant closed, their livelihood was lost too. The hardship suffered by depressed communities and population groups has increased since 1981, but no reliable data is yet published.

Projections indicate that major job gains will occur in the 1980s in the State's clerical, professional, technical, and service occupations, thus continuing a long-run trend away from blue-collar employment. More than 330,000 job openings due to growth or replacement needs and about 430,000 job openings due to geographic and occupational transfers were projected annually through 1985.[6] It is open to question whether these positions will still be filled after the next downturn in the business cycle begins to run its course.

From 1970 to 1981 the State's labor force increased by 7.9 percent, but in contrast the U.S. labor force expanded by 31.3 percent as the "baby boom" added young adults to the work force. In the five years from 1976 to 1981, the State's labor force climbed by 4.4 percent compared with a national growth rate of 13.0 percent. As a result, the New York share of the U.S. labor force dwindled from 9.0 percent in 1970 to 7.4 percent in 1981, as did its share of the nation's value of manufacturing.

The manufacturing industry slipped from its historic place as the State's largest employer to the third largest, lagging behind services and trade. By 1982, the manufacturing job count at 1.4 million was lower by 400,000 than it had been in 1967, but a greater number of new jobs had been created in service industries. This job switch brought unfortunate consequences. Manufacturing workers are paid well and they need considerable support work. For every 100 new factory jobs, 35 service positions are created, while employment in service industries is poorly paid and does not generate work in secondary or tertiary sectors. But some good did come from the change. With nearly 2 million workers in services, New York became less susceptible to national economic recessions than the heavy industries states in the Midwest.

Unfortunately, the decline in factory employment is not likely to be reversed in the 1980s and this will lead eventually to serious consequences. To a lesser extent so will cutbacks in jobs in wholesale and retail trade. Once these jobs are phased out there is little chance that they will ever again be restored to the semi-skilled workers who had once depended on them. (Jobs in trade actually increased to 1.5 million in 1982 but the figure was only marginally greater than it had been ten years earlier.) Like all other states, New York does not know how to arrest the spread of plant closings and job liquidation. Little has or can be done to stem the flight of capital or high-paying jobs. Indeed, as economic forces restructure the distribution of work across the nation, New York might come to learn more about a novel and inequitable phenomenon—"jobless prosperity."[7]

As Figures 1 and 2 show, the workforce of 8 million in New York can be divided into five or six specific groups. Roughly 1.5 million jobs *each* appear in manufacturing, trade, and government, 2.5 million in services (plus finance, insurance and real estate), and nearly 1 million people who were unable to find work or who were no longer fit to apply.

Growth Industries and Industries in Decline

Industries shown in Table 1 can be classified as "long-term" growth industries because they showed substantial net employment increases during the 1970s. From 1971 to 1981, these industries added over half a million new jobs to the State's economy, with nearly three-quarters of the new job growth occurring from 1976 to 1981. In 1981, these industries accounted for 2,600,000 jobs, or 36 percent of all non-agricultural employment in the State. Some 47.4 percent of "growth industry" jobs were in the services category, 16.8 percent were in retail trade, 14.6 percent were in finance, insurance and real estate, and 11.7 percent were in manufacturing. The industries listed in Table 2 experienced substantial job declines during the last decade.

While it is apparent from Table 1 that the largest employment increases (in absolute and in percentage terms) appeared in health,

Figure 1. Nonagricultural Wage and Salary Employment by Industry
New York State 1970 and 1980
(percent distribution)

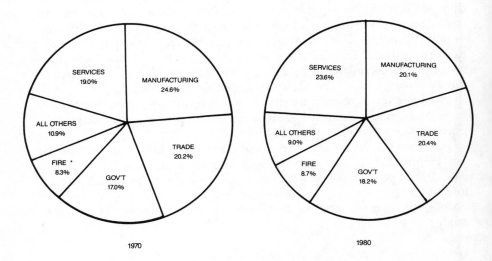

1970

1980

* Finance, Insurance and Real Estate

Source: *Building From Strength: A Program for Economic Growth and Opportunity*   (Albany: Office of the Governor, January, 1982)

Figure 2. Composition of New York State Employment

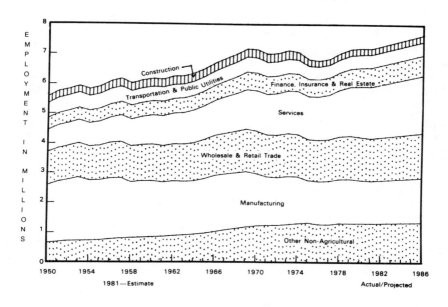

Source: *Building From Strength: A Program for Economic Growth and Opportunity* (Albany: Office of the Governor, January, 1982)

business, and food services, these jobs pay minimum wages to low-skilled people, many of them women, who are not unionized and who receive only 60 percent of the wages paid to men. Employment also mounted in education, social service agencies, banking, and state or local government. Put together, these secondary and tertiary jobs are low in productivity and income. They compare poorly with the blue-collar employment in manufacturing, construction, and goods-making that used to pay wages plus benefits of 20 dollars an hour or 40,000 dollars a year. The notable exceptions, of course, were the garment workers who were largely recruited from women, ethnic minorities, and unskilled transients.[8]

The inference drawn from Tables 1, 2, and 3 is that New York is witnessing a structural change in its workforce and a loss of blue-collar employment that largely paid middle-class wages. The down-grading of income has fueled the suspicion that the local economy is

173

Table 1. Growth Industries

	Annual average employment change 1971–1981 Net	
	(000's)	Percent
Health services	+131.0	+40.7
Business services	+123.9	+49.1
Eating and drinking places	+ 71.4	+31.2
Banking	+ 48.5	+26.9
State government	+ 47.5	+23.3
Legal services	+ 27.1	+64.7
Instruments manufacturing	+ 17.3	+14.9
Miscellaneous retail stores	+ 16.7	+13.6
Amusement and recreation services, except motion pictures	+ 16.3	+31.2
Educational services	+ 15.4	+ 9.6
Security and commodity brokers	+ 12.5	+13.9
Miscellaneous services	+ 11.4	+12.6
Insurance agents and brokers	+ 11.1	+28.2
Machinery (except electrical) manufacturing	+ 11.1	+ 6.9

SOURCE: New York State Department of Labor, *Annual Planning Statement, 1983*

engulfed in a process of "deindustrialization."[9] As a result of these changes, New York has been left with a lopsided economic structure, sagging in the production of goods and increasingly dependent on low-income service employment.

It has become fashionable to suggest that a solution to basic economic problems can be found in the development of high-technology industries and industrial research parks. Unfortunately, the suggestion is inaccurate and misleading. A strategy for reindustrialization in New York must emphasize aggregate employment as well as the modernizing of a few select industries. Semi-conductor firms, bio-tech labs, fine chemicals, laser engineering, and telecommunications are not labor-intensive. Though they provide spin-off employment for supplier and customer firms, and also for support activities, they generate few new jobs. Nor have the job retraining and the vocational skill programs that have been financed—with strictly limited appropriations—by public agencies succeeded in halting job losses.[10] The figures for high-tech employment have never been defined firmly. According to one estimate in the *Wall Street Journal,* New York City managed to add 156,000 jobs in all categories between 1977 and 1983 (to arrive at a total employment of 3.3 million), but not many of them were in high technology; there were, in fact, fewer positions in 1983 than there had been in 1977.[11]

Table 2. Industries in Decline

	Annual average employment change 1971–1981 Net	
	(000's)	Percent
Apparel manufacturing	−66.5	−28.6
General merchandise stores	−33.3	−17.5
Food and kindred products manufacturing	−31.4	−26.1
Miscellaneous manufacturing	−23.9	−30.0
Federal government	−20.7	−11.7
Textile mill products manufacturing	−17.9	−33.9
Primary metals manufacturing	−15.5	−23.3
Auto dealers and service stations	−14.9	−16.1
Leather and leather products manufacturing	−11.8	−29.9
Chemicals and allied products manufacturing	−10.8	−13.1
Railroad transportation	−10.2	−35.8
Apparel sales	−10.0	−10.5
Transportation equipment manufacturing	− 9.7	−11.9

SOURCE: New York State Department of Labor, *Annual Planning Statement, 1983*

Nationally, one job in seven is in high technology but in New York City it is one in 15. City workers still are drawn more heavily into the obsolescing jobs left in manufacturing than into better paying and knowledge-intensive sectors.

A report on statewide industries counting only the 52 SIC categories of high technology gave no greater cause for optimism. It found that New York has more than 10 percent of the nation's jobs in these categories and that 407,000 employees, earning 9 billion dollars a year, currently account for 10 percent of the State's payrolls in the private sector.[12] One in five civilian workers in Rochester, Poughkeepsie, and Binghamton are employed by firms such as IBM, GE, Xerox, and Kodak. But the report added that employment had failed to keep pace with the national average for growth in these industries since 1975. It is significant that one-half of the jobs in high technology are located in only six industries, and that all six industries are dominated by one or two MNC enterprises. New York has caught up with the trend to modernize and internationalize its most capital-intensive firms, but in doing so it also has discovered a crippling liability. Jobs and

175

Table 3. Income from Nonagricultural Employment in New York State and the United States, by Industry (1982) (dollar amount in billions)

Industry Group	Percentage Composition of Employment (1982)[1]		U.S.		State	
	U.S.	State	Amount	Percent	Amount	Percent
Construction	4.4%	3.0%	$ 96.7	5.4%	$ 5.3	3.4%
Finance, Insurance and Real Estate	6.0	9.3	112.7	6.2	17.3	11.1
Government	17.6	17.8	306.2	17.0	24.2	15.5
Manufacturing and Mining	22.3	18.9	486.4	27.0	34.7	22.2
Services and Other	21.2	25.1	359.8	19.9	37.3	23.9
Transportation, Communication and Other Utilities	5.6	5.8	141.9	7.9	13.4	8.6
Wholesale and Retail	22.9	20.1	299.9	16.6	23.8	15.2
	100.0%	100.0%	$1,803.6	100.0%	$156.1	100.0%

SOURCE: United States Department of Labor and United States and State Departments of Commerce; material compiled by New York State Division of Budget.
[1] Detail may not add to total due to rounding.

capital are mobile. People are not. Job creation in the 1980s might therefore spread to states with lower rates of mobility and actually remove key positions from New York.

Given the scarcity of good new jobs, and the trend among MNCs to ship much of their manufacturing operations overseas, it is not surprising that workers striking against General Electric plant closings in upstate New York targeted their protests against the high-tech and the MNC companies. Their picketing placards read "Automate, Emigrate, or Evaporate." Those were, indeed, the strategic options offered by many of the MNCs and the rapidly expanding high-tech industries based in New York. The companies enjoying a high mobility in deploying production facilities and capital investment could choose (a) to rationalize their labor costs by closing old plant, installing robots, or pruning their assembly lines; (b) to shift labor-intensive component assemblies to cheaper wage economies—either in the South, in Mexico or Taiwan; or (c) to gradually phase out plant that were too costly or too unionized to be reformed quickly. Similar choices had been pursued in past years by the steel, automobile, engineering, and textile firms. They once had given strength to New York's goods-producing economy but they closed down instead of modernizing their equipment and labor relations. As a result, New York lost ground in its race to match the industrial expansion achieved by states with a broadly based manufacturing capability (see Table 4).

THE ROLE OF INTERNATIONAL TRADE AND INVESTMENT

The economic history of the United States in the 1970s was measured with depressing indicators and distressful data. The U.S. economy had lost nearly one-half of its commanding lead in the world manufacturing and export markets that it had built up in the years following World War II. Competitors in Japan and Europe had seized control of many of its valuable markets overseas and at home, too. America's trade rivals had rebuilt their industrial plant with modern equipment and they had spent their research and development (R&D) funds in industrial rather than military projects. While the level of industrial productivity remained almost flat in the "mature" economy of the United States, it climbed from year to year in the industrial workplace of its dynamic competitors. The once mighty dollar declined sharply in value after 1971, as the Vietnam war ground to a halt, and no one was confident that the "American century"—proclaimed twenty years before in the chauvinist rhetoric of Henry Luce—would long survive.

Following the disasters of Vietnam and Watergate, and the sudden fall of the dollar, came the two "oil shocks" that helped swing the world order in the 1970s from growth to inflation and recession. Strangely, it went almost without notice that the U.S. economy has scored two significant successes even while it seemed to stagger in retreat. First, it increased the value of export trade five-fold between 1970 and 1980, and it doubled the share of GNP that was derived from foreign exports; with only 5 percent of the world's population it produced 24 percent of global industrial product. If import values are added, international trade amounted to more than 20 percent of GNP and one job in six in U.S. manufacture is derived from export-related business.[13] Second, the U.S. played the leading role in developing a relatively new form of off-shore, international business, the MNC. America's largest MNCs began to deploy considerable sums of direct foreign investment (DFI) in the fast growing economies of its industrial rivals and in the Third World. Many of the MNCs came to manufacture anywhere from one-quarter to one-half of their products or to reap half their net profits overseas. In 1970 the value of American DFI placed overseas was 75 billion dollars but by 1982 it had trebled to 221 billion dollars. While industrial expansion at home remained

Table 4. Leading Industrial States

	Population 1980 (000)	Total 8,000,000 (billions)	Per Capita (dollars)	Nonagricultural Employment 1980 (000)	Manufacturing Employment 1980 (000)	Estimated Retail Sales 1980 8,000,000 (billions)
New York State	17,557	177,658	10,143	7,205	1,451	68,382
United States	226,505	2,133,827	9,458	90,657	20,361	956,655
United States, Exc. N.Y.S.	208,948	1,956,169	9,362	83,452	18,910	888,273
California	23,669	255,647	10,856	9,838	2,001	108,113
Illinois	11,418	121,039	10,658	4,892	1,222	48,052
Indiana	5,490	49,030	8,978	2,137	658	21,535
Massachusetts	5,737	57,243	9,992	2,648	673	25,189
Michigan	9,258	90,976	9,847	3,354	1,007	40,123
Missouri	4,917	43,402	8,846	1,969	436	20,749
New Jersey	7,364	79,051	10,755	3,054	783	31,762
North Carolina	5,874	45,919	7,852	2,385	824	21,562
Ohio	10,797	101,237	9,398	4,399	1,268	44,741
Pennsylvania	11,867	109,942	9,294	4,753	1,328	46,617
Texas	14,228	134,846	9,513	5,862	1,049	70,030
Wisconsin	4,705	43,444	9,254	1,945	560	18,946

SOURCE: *New York State Business Fact Book, 1983* (Albany: New York State Department of Commerce).

178

sluggish during the recessions of the 1970s, the MNCs based in New York (such as GE, GM, IBM, Xerox, and the Wall Street banks) realized significant margins of profit from their plant and operations abroad. Coming late to a realization of the benefits that DFI could secure by internationalizing business methods, the Europeans and Japanese hastened to deploy their own DFI in the U.S. market. Beginning with only a few billion dollars of investment in the U.S.—mostly owned by the U.K. and Canada—they expanded aggressively as the value of the dollar slumped in the 1970s. Incoming DFI passed the 100 billion dollar mark in 1982 as European firms bought out or created several thousand subsidiary firms across the U.S.[14]

New York was one of the first states to appreciate that three sets of benefits could be won by adjusting to the new order of international trade and investment. While domestic GNP grew by only 2 or 3 percent a year (in real or non-inflated values), the world market expanded between the recessions of 1975 and 1980 at a rate of 8 percent a year. The stimuli of international trade and investment stemmed from three sources—the flow of incoming DFI, the expansion of U.S.-based export industries, and the global stretch of American MNCs with considerable capital located in New York. There was little that the domestic economy could offer to match the golden opportunities afforded by the rising magnitude of the world market. By 1980, the value of goods and services sold in world trade was almost 2,000 billion dollars, and 10 percent of it was earned by U.S. companies.[15]

Giant firms swelled in size as they enlarged their market share across the world. Some built 50 or 100 affiliates each overseas. Others stepped up their export sales drives by constructing new plant at home to manufacture components for markets or affiliates overseas. The greatest success was scored by the MNC oil companies, most of them American in ownership, and by the determined export campaigns waged by Japanese manufacturing firms. But in no way was New York a late starter. Local companies like GE and IBM had created thriving subsidiaries or joint venture operations in the 1920s and sixty years later they had become global giants. In addition, there were the New York banks. They competed in international finance in the Euro-dollar market centered in London and their syndicated loans earned sizeable premiums from the OPEC, Third World, and communist clients. By 1980, 12 percent of New York's workforce and manufacturing output was engaged in export trade; and a greater number of incoming MNCs had placed their investment in New York than in any other state. As a consequence of these export and foreign investment successes, employment and GNP were enlarged significantly.[16]

By 1981 New York had become the sixth largest exporter among U.S. states. Its exports were valued at 10.2 billion dollars. They had increased 75 percent over 1977, at more than twice the industrial growth rate of all industrial production. Ninety-eight thousand jobs were directly related to industrial exports and another 74,000 (for a total of 172,000) were indirectly related and 12.7 percent of manufacturing revenues derived from export trade. Another 200,000 people were employed in non-manufacturing industries involved in export activity.

The central argument of this paper is that a continuation of these trends is vital to the expansion of the State's economy. New York already has established itself as one of the leading States in attracting overseas companies. If it is to avoid the steady decline in jobs and revenues that have been forecast for the 1970s and 1980s, it must continue to widen its role in international business. It cannot compete effectively with the Sunbelt industries in manufacturing mass-produced goods for the U.S. market. And it will never undercut the cheap imports with which low-wage economies in Europe and Asia have seized a major share of U.S. consumer markets. One of the few development opportunities available in New York, as more of its high-wage plant close down and its citizens turn to low-paying service employment, is to strengthen its participation in international trade. If it succeeds, it need not resign itself to gloomy predictions of GNP decline and progressive deindustrialization. There are numerous opportunities that can be exploited by adopting a global rather than a regional or national strategy of development. New York already enjoys a strong position to promote its export industries, its home-based MNCs, and its attraction for incoming DFI. But it is uncertain whether these advantages can be exploited aggressively in the rest of the 1980s.[17]

A warning note must be sounded, however, if the enthusiasm for international trade and investment is not to be exaggerated. The golden axiom of "export led growth," that has been pursued so successfully by the Japanese, easily can lead to mistaken industrial and social policies. New York cannot boost its exports or assist its MNC firms while at the same time ignoring the 90 percent of local companies and citizens who are not directly involved in the race, as the British put it, to "export or perish." The needs of the whole community must be considered and adequately funded, too. We cannot impose the ruthless mode of Social Darwinism, rewarding the few who can struggle and prosper while ignoring the claims of everyone else. A policy of encouraging "winning" industries and killing off "losers" would be neither efficient nor just. Moreover, the benefits offered by MNCs—

whether American or foreign in their parent management—are often tempered with the threat of future pain. If an MNC can move easily into New York, it can just as easily move out. Similarly, when an American MNC shifts its labor-intensive production to a cheap wage economy, it can always threaten to relocate the remaining segments of its operations from New York to a more favorable environment elsewhere. They have done so before and they might intensify their free-booting movements in the future. It must be realized that there is a grave risk in relying too heavily on the MNCs or the export industries, for all their vigor and dynamism. A downturn in world trade or an upturn in factor costs in the local economy, could wreak havoc on New York in the years to come. But by the same token, the involvement in foreign trade and investment could realize gains of unsurpassed advantage to the State's economy.[18]

FOREIGN INVESTMENT IN NEW YORK

Over the three years 1977–1980 New York was selected more often than any other state as the location for new, foreign manufacturing facilities. New York acquired 90 new facilities, easily surpassing the next leading states, Texas (55), California (53), Georgia (51), and North Carolina (42). Ten states accounted for 61 percent of new foreign investments in manufacturing, seven of them in the Sunbelt, but New York received the largest number of incoming foreign companies and banks. A large number of them came from Canada, especially when the U.S. dollar rose steeply against the Canadian.[19]

Although New York remains the most favored site for income companies, the Tidewater states and the Sunbelt have shown the steepest rate of relative increase in attracting DFI in manufacturing. Virginia, the Carolinas, Tenessee, Texas, and other states hostile to union shop legislation have attracted DFI from Western Europe, Canada, and Japan. Calculations of DFI are difficult to measure. If the yardstick used is the book value of property, plant, and equipment, New York's record is not impressive. Of the total book value of DFI invested in the United States in 1980 of 100 billion dollars, New York received only 2 billion dollars. In comparison, Texas attracted 4.5 billion dollars, California 3.8 billion dollars, New Jersey 3 billion dollars, and South Carolina 2.5 billion dollars. Different measures must be used, however, to assess the job and GNP creation generated by DFI.[20]

An estimate compiled (in June 1983) by the Port Authority of New York and New Jersey (PANY/NJ) showed the building or

181

acquisiton of U.S. manufacturing plant by foreign firms in the following locations (see Table 5).[21] The same estimate found that 374 manufacturing plant had been built or bought by foreign investment in the NY-NJ metropolitan region. Sixty-six were in New York City, 89 in the outlying suburbs, and 219 in northern New Jersey. The number had grown in the region by 32 percent during the recession of 1981–82 while in the U.S. as a whole it had declined by 22 percent. A year later it was estimated that 5.3 billion dollars in DFI had been invested in New York, of which 3.4 billion had come from Western Europe, 1.1 billion from Canada, and 200 million from Japan and Latin America. Of that total, 2 billion had been invested in manufacturing, fabricated metals, chemicals, and food processing industries. Two hundred thousand people were employed as a result of DFI placements in these industries; their numbers had increased by 80 percent between 1977–1983, while total employment in New York manufacturing over the period had declined by 1.8 percent to 1,433,000. As distinct from employment, there were 3200 foreign firms operating in New York, though only a quarter of them were established outside New York City.[22]

It is worth noting that most of the DFI was invested in capital and not labor-intensive industries. The largest share went to food, metals, chemicals, electrical machinery, instruments, and other high-tech industries. A representative sampling of them includes Siemens, Agfa-Gevaert, Unilever, Beecham Products, Rhone-Poulenc, Philips, Hitachi, Minolta, Ciba-Geigy, and Solvay. In addition, it should be noted that 285 foreign banks have opened or taken over facilities in New York, some of them of considerable size. They employ 38,000 people and account for 75 percent of all foreign banks in the U.S. Real estate purchases have been even more extensive. British banks built three skyscraper towers near Wall Street, a Canadian firm has built over 6 million square feet of office space in Battery Park, and the Japanese built a Park Avenue hotel. To round out the list, British companies

Table 5. Foreign Acquisition of U.S. Manufacturing Plant

New York State	508
California	322
New Jersey	300
Pennsylvania	262
North Carolina	226
Texas	216

SOURCE: Port Authority of New York and New Jersey, *Foreign Investment and Trade Patterns, 1983.*

bought out Saks, Gimbels, Howard Johnson's, Christies, and several major hotels. Most of the foreign companies built impressive HQ office blocks in New York or its suburbs, and many of them bought sales showrooms or dealers' outlets, too. It is still too early to determine exactly how much these investments have added to local employment and GNP, especially if the uncounted value of trade and business services is added to the net total of incoming investments.

Table 6 shows that DFI fell sharply in 1982 (as the value of the dollar rose steeply) and that investment in manufacturing plant declined, though the trends began to reverse in 1984–85. The large sum of DFI in petroleum accounts for the leading position of Texas—as measured in book value—while the flow of money into California and the Midwest came largely from Asia and Canada. In manufacturing industries, investment was concentrated in electronics, machinery, capital goods, processing industries, chemicals, and foods. Automobile investments came from Toyota (for its joint California venture with GM), Volvo, Saab, and Nikon. The food industry and chemicals accounted for capital inflow from Canadian and European firms, while the Japanese concentrated on the finished assembly of automobiles and electronics products. All of them feared that a protectionist enthusiasm might one day sweep through the U.S. Congress and that they should therefore concentrate on creating new U.S. subsidiaries. Access to the U.S. market led many of them to choose location sites in New York even though it sustained higher tax and labor costs than competing states.[23]

The aggregate figures for incoming and outgoing DFI in 1982 are worth comparing—221 billion dollars (out-going) of American DFI overseas earned a repatriable income of 25 billion dollars and a 10 percent return on investment. Foreign investment (incoming) in the U.S. amounted to 100 billion dollars, an earned income of 5 billion dollars, and a rate of return of 5 percent.[24] The managers of MNCs, whether American or not in their parent corporation, obviously were attracted to different states for different reasons. New York capitalized on its closeness to Canada—as the Midwest did in the U.S.-Canadian automobile agreement—and the facilities of New York Harbor. To Japanese and European firms it offered a pool of skilled manpower, access to the U.S. national market, and a business environment (including hotels and business services) appropriate to international trade. The growth of DFI in the New York economy has been rapid and persistent, but it will be dangerous to rely too heavily on it if the turmoil of currency exchange and interest rates should continue to disturb the world trading system. In fact, a closer study of incoming DFI reveals two or three unsettling patterns.

Table 6. U.S. Affiliates of Foreign Companies
(in billions of dollars)

Gross book value of DFI	1980	New Investment	1981	1982
Land	$12.6	Plant bought by acquisition	462	271
Manufacturing		Plant newly established	870	517
plant & equipment,	$115.3B	Total	1332	788
including:				
Petroleum	$37.3B	Investment outlay	$23.2B	$8.6B
Manufacturing	$44.7	including:		
Chemicals	$17.7	Manufacturing	29.3	4.0
Wholesale trade	$ 6.6	Banking	21.4	5.2
Retail trade	$ 4.9	Finance	14.1	N/A
Real estate	$10.2			
Employment	2 million jobs	Employment	429,000	206,000
Payroll	$40 each year	Sales	76.3B	$22.1B
Merchandise				
Sales	$412.7			
Exports	$ 52.2			
Imports	$ 75.8			

SOURCE: *Statistical Abstract of the U.S., 1984* (Washington, D.C.), pp. 822–23.

The first, already noted, is that foreign based MNCs tend to locate their labor-intensive manufacturing in states where tax incentives are advantageous. For example, a "tax holiday" for 15 years was offered by Pennsylvania, along with several subsidized services, to bring in a new Volkswagen plant. MNCs also move to areas where labor is tractable and tax rates are lower. The foreign subsidiaries lured into New York are numerous but they employ fewer people than in other states. Research staffs and marketing specialists have been recruited to look for new product developments, financing opportunities, or takeover possibilities. They report back by satellite to parent HQ in London, Frankfurt, or Tokyo, thus reducing the lead time required to make strategic adjustments to U.S. market conditions. Local technical staff were hired by the 285 foreign banks to service the financial and investment needs of incoming MNCs, along with foreign insurance and non-banking services to support foreign investors.

A few subsidiaries have undertaken the final assembly of expensive products or the manufacture of capital-intensive equipment. They include Zeiss optical instruments, Hitachi machine tools, Nestle food products, and Ronson Metals. Other companies have tapped into chemical processes or feedstocks that are cheaply available in the U.S., such as Solvay and Shiseido chemicals, Hoffmann-LaRoche pharmaceuticals,

British Oxygen, and Air Liquide. Some of them were incorporated on a minority ownership basis or as joint-venture partners. A few preferred to take over established American firms, while others created new subsidiaries to import semi-finished components or to assemble final products. In most cases, subsidiaries were only formed in the last few years and it is too early to determine whether they will follow the rule set by many American MNCs—when the market got rough, the rough "got going." The record of U.S. firms in closing subsidiaries has been troubling in recent years and many "host" nations protested against their runaway behavior. There is a high probability that foreign companies in the United States will also pack up—possibly in haste—if they become disenchanted with their market prospects.[25]

A second problem might intensify as American MNCs flourish. New York could be affected adversely if many of the American-based MNCs listed in the *Fortune* "Top 500" chose to relocate their HQ or plant operations out of the State. The companies have brought prestige and benefit to New York but they could one day threaten to shift production and work schedules to off-shore subsidiaries. Some, in fact, already have relocated to Canada and Europe. Many others have shifted operations to Mexico, Brazil or to the LDCs in Southeast Asia (such as Singapore, Taiwan, South Korea, and Hong Kong) which are known as the NICs—the newly industrialized countries. New York long has been known as the corporate base for many MNCs, such as AT&T, IBM, ITT, Exxon, Union Carbide, GM, Colgate Palmolive, Sperry, RCA, and General Foods, to name but a few. Many of these MNCs do more of their business or earn more of their revenues overseas than at home. It is difficult for New York to reverse the trend when interest or labor rates move upward—or when marketing opportunities become less profitable—at home than overseas. The laws of comparative advantage cannot be disregarded, the directors of the MNCs insist. They cannot allow a sentiment for the parent company's traditional home to replace the fabled "bottom line" on the profit-and-loss account. Global companies are not charitable or welfare organizations. International managers argue that they only can act as "good citizens" in their home or host countries if both parent and subsidiary firms faithfully follow the dictates of the market. If wage demands or inflation rates should rise in one country but fall in another, if exchange rates should be devalued at home while a subsidiary's market share is expanding overseas, it is logical—if not imperative—that MNCs immediately should revise their strategic planning. But the misfortune remains that State officials in New York are rarely forewarned of the MNCs' change in plans and, even if they are, there is little that they can do to change them. To some extent New York could begin to share the unenviable fate of *dependencia* known to many "banana" republics. Feeling grateful to the MNC that brought capital, as well as patented R&D and high-paying jobs into its economy, it may begin to fear the hasty departure that MNCs and other runaway industries have pulled off smartly in many parts of the world.[26]

American DFI has been deployed overseas by small, medium-sized, and a few giant MNCs. At a recent count, 3,500 U.S. parent firms held significant equity shares—the best definition of DFI—in 25,000 affiliates outside the U.S. About one-third were parent firms holding less than 50 million dollars in assets worldwide, but 62 others (with assets exceeding 5 billion dollars) accounted for half of the worldwide investment of U.S. manufacturing industries. Two-hundred and eighty-one non-bank companies enjoyed one billion dollars or more in asset worth in 1977. The total book value of DFI in American hands was only 150 billion dollars in 1977. By 1982 the total value had grown to 221 billion dollars. The phenomenal rate of the MNCs' growth was matched only by the escalation of U.S. export earnings in overseas markets. Exports leaped from 120 to 212 billion dollars in the same period, and largely because the MNCs had become major contributors to the U.S. export drive. In 1980–81, 31 billion dollars in transfer income was received from DFI abroad and 56 of the leading MNCs sold 105 billion dollars worth of exports overseas. At that time the U.S. trade deficit was 28 billion dollars, but it would have been twice as large if American MNCs had not repatriated sizeable earnings and licensing fees from subsidiaries across the world.[27] Three years later the trade deficit reached 120 billion dollars and the contributions earned by the MNCs were even more vital to the U.S. position. The nation had become a net debtor on its external account and it threatened to become a larger borrower of external funds than Brazil and Mexico *combined* by the end of the 1980s.

It has long been apparent that nearly 90 percent of export revenues were earned by a small number of the largest U.S. firms in the *Fortune 500*. By 1980 the MNCs were making formidable contributions to the U.S. balance of payments both in export revenues and in repatriated dividends. To an ever greater extent, economists and trade specialists noted, world commerce was conducted through intracompany transfers. The transactions within the MNC, between its subsidiaries and its home base, had begun to account for somewhere between one-third and one-half of international payments. Clearly, in an economic order where foreign trade offered one of the brightest prospects for industrial growth and innovation, New York had to move ahead on all three levels simultaneously. It had to promote foreign as well as home based MNCs, and the export companies that had built up production in the State.[28]

Attention must now be given to the third factor in world trade, New York's export industries. They are globally competitive, spend more on R&D than most companies, and are found in the fastest growing sectors of the U.S. economy. In 1980 exports directly accounted on a nation-wide basis for 4.8 million jobs, or 5 percent of the total U.S. work force (and 6 percent of jobs in the private sector). A total of 2.8 million jobs were located in manufacturing plant and another 1.9 million in firms supplying the plant with materials, business services, transportation, and trade. In the manufacturing sector and its support industries combined, exports accounted for 14.1 percent of total shipments and 14.7 percent of total employment.

New York came close to matching these ratios. With export-related jobs numbering 388,100, New York stood second to the 518,000 jobs in California. To a large extent these workers were employed in manufacturing, machinery, electric and electronic equipment, power generating and transporting equipment, chemicals and aerospace products. These industries accounted for 75 percent of New York's export earnings and jobs, and managed to expand in the most aggressive and competitive markets in world trade. They did not need to shelter behind protective tariffs, trade quotas, or government subsidies. They had raised their own capital, mainly in New York, had carved out an international market share, and had defended it strongly against foreign competition and rival product innovations. The export industries in New York achieved a high return on their business investment and they earned 10 billion a year in hard foreign currency. Growing by 72 percent in dollar values between 1977 and 1981, the export manufacturing firms were regarded as the strongest and the most valued contributors to the State's economy. Even if they employed only 1 percent in 9 in manufacturing, and 1 in 20 in the civilian workforce, they recorded annual growth and profit rates no other sector of the State economy could match.[29]

INTERNATIONAL BANKING, SERVICES, SHIPPING AND TOURISM

Three other sectors must be included in this review of the contribution that foreign trade makes toward local GNP: international banking, international services, and international shipping and tourism. New York excels in all categories.

It has been noted that 285 foreign banks had established subsidiaries by 1982 in New York. With a dozen new entries in 1983 the total came to 300 foreign branches. Together they employ 38,000 people, largely as computer technicians and backroom staff, and their combined asset worth reached 157 billion dollars. In addition to the 62 nations represented by these 300 banks, 6 of the 9 largest U.S. banks maintain extensive HQ operations as well as numerous branch banks in New York, and nearly every other national bank of any size maintains an office in New York, too. The dominance of the city of London, especially in forming off-shore market or Euro-dollar syndications, has been challenged by New York. By 1983, there were 391 foreign banks with 35,000 employees in London but New York was growing at a faster pace.[30] An International Banking Facility (IBF) was created by New York to ease the regulation of international credit transfers and to evade tight federal restrictions on reserve requirements. In 1983 the Federal Reserve Bank reported that 151 of the nation's 283 IBF establishments were in New York. At a value of 144 billion dollars, this came to 70 percent of total IBF assets of 197 billion dollars. It appears that the deregulation of international financial and banking services has succeeded in only a few years in generating considerable new business.[31]

The benefits derived from international banking must be defined carefully, however, since many negative consequences emerged once the boom years of the 1970s had ended. The banks had built skyscraper offices, mainly in New York City, and they had helped boost both employment and capital formation. But the good they did for the local economy was strictly limited. They had put little of their capital or their voluminous trust funds into industrial or commercial investments in New York. On the contrary, they had gathered billions of dollars in customers' deposits and stockholders' equity from across the state and used them to finance projects in the Sunbelt or the LDCs which directly competed with New York business. Instead of funding minority or small businesses launched at home, they syndicated loans in billion dollar multiples to poorly secured debtors in the Third World. In the 1970s they had earned rich premiums on these high risk loans, and somewhere between 50 and 70 percent of their profit margins had been earned in foreign lending. But in 1985 their loans stand in dire peril, and the banks are particularly anxious about the 800 billion dollars owed by debtor LDCs. Indeed, it has become tempting for some of the LDCs to consider a possible default in paying interest and debt service to the banks or, worse still, to threaten to repudiate the loans outright. No radical action yet has been taken by debtor nations, but there is a strong possibility that one or two of them will try to act rashly in the near future.[32]

Table 7 shows how vulnerable in 1982 were the 9 major banks that had lent sizeable sums to only five of the illiquid debtors, all in Latin America. At that time the five owed 184 billion dollars to syndicates of Western and Japanese banks, but 60 percent of the sum had been borrowed from U.S. banks—mainly in New York. Today their debt exceeds 300 billion dollars, and another 500 billion dollars is owed by communist countries in Eastern Europe or by LDCs in the Third World. Leaving aside the bulk of LDC and communist borrowers, Table 7 shows that Manufacturers Hanover lent 263 percent more than its capital worth to the five countries in Latin America; Citibank exceeded its capital assets by 175 percent, Chase by 154 percent, and Chemical by 168 percent. Fortunately, it is not likely that any one of the five countries will declare a moratorium on debt servicing or on the rescheduling of principal. But if they should ever do so, even for one year, the flagship banks of New York would have to write off their net earnings and one-third of their capital for years to come. They would also have to plead for a massive rescue operation by the Federal Reserve that would make its bail-out of the Continental Illinois Bank in Chicago (at 8.5 billion dollars) look puny in comparison. A ripple wave of failures in international banking could bring acute hardship to New York. Happily, it has not yet occurred and it may never do so. Thus, though the banks have brought prestige and jobs to New York, their financial peril should not be underestimated.[33]

The record in international services is equally impressive in symbolism and short on achievement. New York has developed a range of service sector facilities that surpass any other in the nation. A giant Teleport on Staten Island beams enormous flows of computer data and electronic mail via orbiting satellite traffic across the world. The publishing, television, and communications empires have lent extraordinary glamor to New York and profit to its international commerce. So, too, have the thousands of partnerships of lawyers, accountants, brokers, and consultants who have made the city the hub of the nation's professions. Thousands of their staff work on international as well as on national accounts, earning enormous fees and overhead. Many of them have moved their office activity to the suburbs or the smaller cities. By using integrated-chip technologies, sophisticated data processing, and electronic communications they have multiplied and dispersed the stock of skilled jobs and managerial talent. New York has gained equally

Table 7. Exposure as Percentage of Capital, Major Banks, end-1982

	Argentina	Brazil	Mexico	Venezuela	Chile	Percent Total	Capital (million dollars)
Citibank	18.2	73.5	54.6	18.2	10.0	174.5	5,989
Bank of America	10.2	47.9	52.1	41.7	6.3	158.2	4,799
Chase Manhattan	21.3	56.9	40.0	24.0	11.8	154.0	4,211
Morgan Guaranty	24.4	54.3	34.8	17.5	9.7	140.7	3,107
Manufacturers Hanover	47.5	77.7	66.7	42.4	28.4	262.8	1,592
Chemical	14.9	52.0	60.0	28.0	14.8	169.7	2,499
Continental Illinois	17.8	22.9	32.4	21.6	12.8	107.5	2,143
Bankers Trust	13.2	46.2	46.2	25.1	10.6	141.2	1,895
First National Chicago	14.5	40.6	50.1	17.4	11.6	134.2	1,725
Security Pacific	10.4	29.1	31.2	4.5	7.4	82.5	1,684
Wells Fargo	8.3	40.7	51.0	20.4	6.2	126.6	1,201
Crocker National	38.1	57.3	51.2	22.8	26.5	196.0	1,151
First Interstate	6.9	43.9	63.0	18.5	3.7	136.0	1,080
Marine Midland	n.a.	47.8	28.3	29.2	n.a.	n.a.	1,074
Mellon	n.a.	35.3	41.1	17.6	n.a.	n.a.	1,024
Irving Trust	21.6	38.7	34.1	50.2	n.a.	n.a.	966
First National Boston	n.a.	23.1	28.1	n.a.	n.a.	n.a.	800
Interfirst Dallas	5.1	10.2	30.1	1.3	2.5	49.2	787

SOURCE: William R. Cline, *International Debt and the Stability of the World Economy* (Washington, D.C.: Institute for International Economics, 1983), p. 34.

from its numerous educational and research institutions. They enroll one million full or part time students, and help train the skilled workforce that New York urgently needs. Its 300 universities and colleges have initiated information services for clients in the public and private sectors and added 25,000 students from overseas to the one million enrolled in public and private colleges.[34]

Leading service firms in accounting, leisure industries, brokerage, engineering, and leasing partnerships have begun to play an important role in U.S. foreign trade. As the deficit in U.S. merchandise trade continued to widen, from 6 billion dollars in 1972 to 130 billion dollars in 1984, income from services had to compensate for the deterioration in the U.S. balance of payments. In one estimate for 1980, that excluded the repatriation of investment income and DFI dividends, revenues from foreign services contributed 60 billion dollars to the U.S. current account position. Worldwide trade in services now exceeds 500 billion dollars and the U.S. has exercised a profitable leadership in stimulating its expansion. Some of this leadership capacity was lost when U.S. interest rates and the value of the dollar began to soar as the powerful economic recovery took hold in 1983–84. Nonetheless, America's advantage—like that of New York—has been strong enough to retain its leading position in the so-called third-wave industries of technological and business service delivery. As Figures 3 and 4 demonstrate, service industries have come to fill extensive needs in the domestic economy and in the U.S. balance of payments. Moreover, their role is likely to dramatically expand in future years.[35]

The third sector of foreign trade includes international shipping and tourism. They are conventionally included in the category of services but a change has been needed in recent years. Transportation of people and goods by air and sea, along with tourist facilities and hotels, should be put in a different category than high value-added services in telecommunications, business, law, consulting, and the FIRE industries. Airports, container warehouses, shipping docks, and hotels employ a different (and more numerous) category of workers than the professional and skilled staff hired by professional groups involved in foreign trade. Officials working for the the Port Authority of New York and New Jersey noted that a 500 percent increase in exports and a 600 percent rise in imports materialized in the last decade. Hence they began to replace the outmoded cargo facilities on the New York waterfront and to build huge container ports on what used to be New Jersey marsh land. In addition, the three airports serving New York were expanded considerably. It is estimated that 375,000 jobs in New

Figure 3. U.S. Balance of Payments Trades in Goods and Services

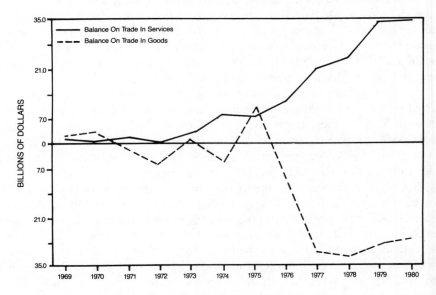

Source: U.S. Dept. of Commerce, Bureau of Economic Analysis

York and 175,000 in New Jersey are linked directly to the region's burgeoning role in international trade and shipping.[36]

Growth statistics for international trade activities are impressive. Segregated according to regions of the U.S. Customs (for 1972–82), New York increased the value of its export trade from 10 to 31 billion dollars, and of its import handling from 13 to 41 billion dollars. In the ten-year period New York widened its lead over all other Customs regions. By 1982, its foreign trade handling amounted to 72 billion dollars. This compared favorably with other U.S. regional values (Baltimore at 46 billion dollars, Boston at 38 billion dollars, New Orleans at 42 billion dollars, Houston at 58 billion dollars, San Francisco at 53 billion dollars, Chicago at 56 billion dollars, and Los Angeles at 42 billion dollars).[37]

Though the United States recorded an ever greater deficit in its merchandise and current account, the value of foreign trade amounted to 500 billion dollars and this provided a significant stimulus to export-related employment. The actual tonnage shipped through PANY/NJ fell from 52 billion long tons in 1974 to 46 billion in 1983, but the value of ocean-borne trade rose from 28 billion dollars to 43 billion

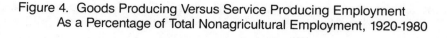

Figure 4. Goods Producing Versus Service Producing Employment
As a Percentage of Total Nonagricultural Employment, 1920-1980

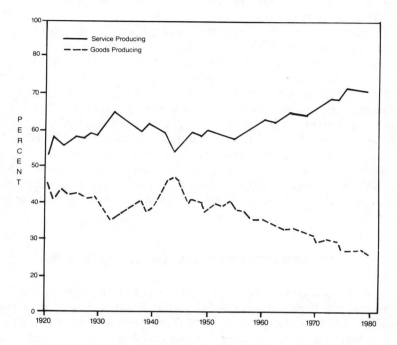

Source: U.S. Department of Labor, Bureau of Labor Statistics

dollars; the latter figure exceeded the cargo value of the second port, Los Angeles, by 7.5 billion dollars and it represented 16 percent of the nation's ocean-borne commerce. A notable increase was also registered in the ports at Albany and the Great Lakes; and at the Canadian frontier foreign trade values added a further 9.5 billion dollars in exports and 13 billion dollars in imports.[38]

The destinations of the PANY/NJ exports were principally the United Kingdom, Saudi Arabia, West Germany, Japan, and 5 other nations in the EEC. The commodities exported were chiefly machinery, photo supplies, gas engines and diesels, motor vehicles, office and electrical machinery, wheat, plastics, and scientific instruments. Roughly one million tons of the more expensive consignments went through the New York airports, where airborne cargo handling doubled over

193

the ten-year period to a value of 37 billion dollars. The fastest increase was recorded in the three New York airports that handled 42 million passengers in 1972 but 64 million in 1983—15 million of whom travelled on international airlines.[39]

Tourism accounts for important income and employment in New York, and the State leads most others in generating tourist revenues. Foreign travel tends to vary inversely with the value of the dollar, but a considerable increase was recorded in the last ten years. As a result, numerous hotels were built in New York City (and a few other locations) and employment in restaurants, entertainment and tourist industries was expanded greatly. To cite just one example, a report on *The Arts as an Industry* found that more tourists came to New York because of the arts and entertainment offerings than for any other purpose. In 1982 the arts accounted for an input of 5.6 billion dollars, 117,000 jobs, and 2 billion dollars in personal spending. This exceeds the figures for advertising, hotel operations, consulting and computer services.[40]

INTERNATIONAL TRADE IN THE 1980s

A sharp change emerged in the international economy in the 1970s. U.S. real GNP growth declined, but the dollar worth of U.S. exports steadily climbed—along with New York's—until the appreciation of the dollar halted the upswing. Japan and a few of the EEC nations took advantage of the dollar's increased worth to widen their penetration of the U.S. market and a new threat came from the subsidized exports of steel, electronics, and consumer durables that were dumped by the NICs on the U.S. market at artificially cheap prices.[41] American industry lost its leadership to Japan and West Germany in automobiles, fabricated steel, machine tools, and engineering products. Light manufacturing, shoes, clothes, toys, and electronics became the preserve of Taiwan and Hong Kong. For its part, the U.S. concentrated on high technology, agriculture, military production, computers, and health sciences. These were the export commodities in which the U.S. and New York could best compete in the emerging division of labor that had seized hold in the international economy.[42]

By 1980, 18 percent of American finished goods were sold overseas and 22 percent of America's consumption goods were imported. Most important, 70 percent of all the goods manufactured in the U.S. had to compete in price and quality with foreign imports. Imports had claimed 26 percent of the automobile market, 25 percent of steel, 60 percent of consumer electronics, and 53 percent of machine tools. The United States enjoyed one of the lowest rates of inflation and one of the lowest ratios of overall government deficit to GNP. Nonetheless, it began to surrender the 20 percent of world manufacturing markets that it had painfully built up, especially in the capital-intensive and mass-production industries, like steel, autos, and textiles, on which its wealth had been built. The United States had been successful in expanding export earnings in the 1970s and they rose by 500 percent between 1970 and 1982. But imports increased at a faster rate, by 600 percent. It was calculated that the volume of imports into the U.S. had diminished domestic employment by at least 3 million jobs and that the U.S. economic recovery would have restored millions of lost jobs if import competition had been more effectively resisted.[43]

Though the strength of the U.S. economic recovery created widespread surprise and an upward movement in the dollar, U.S. export revenues managed to grow at a rate considerably faster than the overall volume of world trade. It now appears that close to one-fifth of the U.S. output of goods production (and 30 percent of its agricultural product) is marketed overseas. That is a remarkable achievement for an economy which barely concerned itself with foreign trade 30 years ago when exports came to only 4 percent of GNP.[44]

It appears, therefore, that U.S. industry is still price-competitive in world markets. Nearly one-fifth of the workforce is employed in some way in foreign trade and U.S. agriculture sells one-third of its embarrassingly rich product overseas. The problem with this success record is that it has come in the wrong industries. It has enriched the successful and competitive firms rather than the ailing and the labor-intensive. The steel mills and the mass production industries, including autos and engineering, lagged into obsolescence as modernizing investments were withheld. As a result, the NICs supplied the United States— usually through its MNCs—with cheap electronic components or steel

Table 8. United States: Exports as Percent of Goods GNP

Year	Total Exports	Manufactured Exports
1955	6.6%	4.7%
1960	7.7%	5.0%
1965	7.8%	5.2%
1970	9.2%	6.4%
1975	15.5%	10.3%
1980	20.0%	13.5%

SOURCE: See footnote 22.

products, and many U.S. plant are now idle. In the 1970s the world became a single structure market. High volume production and standardized production lines were taken over by NIC's or industrialized countries facing cheaper wage rates and manufacturing costs than those burdening American companies. Productivity and hourly output in these countries began to catch up with the U.S. and many of them introduced automated machinery and cost cutting procedures. In theory this was wrong. The poor countries were supposed to supply cheap and unskilled work at a low level of capitalization. But theory led to error. In fact, a major structural shift appeared in the world economy and the U.S. lagged in adjusting to it. The exigencies of comparative cost required a specialization in value-added work. In too many industries American firms were undercut in their own export markets while surrendering low value-added markets to cheap imports at home. Neither the U.S. nor its highly industrialized rivals in OECD were willing or able to program a radical change in their investment policy and they failed to retrain or to reequip millions of workers.

The consequences of structural unemployment and industrial obsolescence are now clearly visible, and they are likely to persist in the Northeast and the Midwest for years to come. The aging steel foundries of Lackawanna County and the non-automated car assembly lines of New York and Michigan are built poorly and they are too costly to be modernized. It is doubtful whether they will ever be replaced *in situ*. The same patterns are to be seen in many other OECD industries. They point to the fact that the old base of industry is aging beyond repair and that the living standards of millions of Americans will decline unless fundamental changes in industrial policy are implemented to stop the rot.[45]

The problem is compounded by the success of the MNCs. Bent on manufacturing a "world car," the auto companies prefer to strike out for new production locations overseas rather than to revive outmoded component or assembly plant at home. Chrysler and General Motors built dozens of plant in Mexico, Ford moved heavily into S.E. Asia, and GM joined a non-union venture in California with its arch rival, Toyota. These initiatives spared the MNCs the difficulty of negotiating with strike-ridden or union shop plants in Westchester and Rockland Counties, let alone in Michigan or Ohio. Similar exercises in cost saving and production standardization were achieved by global companies, such as RCA or ITT, which built component plant or mechanized assembly lines in Singapore or Taiwan where wages are 20 percent of the rates prevailing in New York. General Electric, Zenith, Burlington Mills, Dow Chemical—and their MNC rivals in Europe and Japan—

insist that they cannot compete in any market, at home or abroad, if they have to contend with the hundreds of cheap-wage plant in Malaysia, Brazil or Spain that were planned as joint ventures with host countries or rival MNCs. Those plant pay no pension, medical, or unemployment insurance, and many of their operating or tax costs are paid by the host country's government. Steel workers in New York had received a total compensation package of 26 dollars an hour, or 50,000 dollars a year. In the Philippines or Jamaica a worker makes less in a 48-hour week than his U.S. counterpart, working in an obsolescent plant, receives in one hour. Adolescent workers in Texas Instrument plants in the Philippines earn 20 cents an hour. Those working in the apparel sweat shops of Shanghai probably earn less. It is difficult to contend with the law of comparative advantage when the MNCs, appreciating the magnitude of these cost differentials, begin to redeploy their production schedules and plant investment to the newly emerging centers of cheap manpower.[46]

New York tried to insure itself against a further erosion of its manufacturing industry by giving help to a few growing industries and by luring in foreign investment. But the magnitude of its assistance is tightly limited. Furthermore, the investments of incoming MNCs are invariably sector specific. Too much capital flows into the acquisition of New York real estate, marketing firms, R&D labs, and HQ offices. Too little goes into manufacturing and job-creating ventures. The same can be said of the *Fortune 500* plant at home that tend to dominate the successful export industries. A recent study showed that the largest 100 hold 67 percent of the group's capital assets, 77 percent of its net income, and 68 percent of all sales. Strikingly, the second '500' command roughly 5 percent of this massive wealth.[47] More important, the largest companies in the top 500 are those that have built a global operating base as fully extended MNCs. But at the same time they also play a dominant role in generating export sales from the United States. Their two-pronged advantage provides powerful strength. From their off-shore subsidiaries they draw cheap labor products or, alternatively, build a launching platform to boost their overseas marketing. From their home base the MNCs can weed out all labor-intensive work, preserving only management functions at corporate HQ along with skilled work at R&D labs. Their export sales are successful because they can ship assembly parts from one country to another, or because they can substitute imports for expensive components made at home. As recent studies have shown, the MNCs contribute heavily to U.S. export successes because they are big, vertically integrated, global entities that can redeploy their capital and production schedules freely in the world economic order. By contrast, the political authority of national—let alone state—governments is parochial, landlocked, and financially immobile.[48]

There is ample room for conflict between national or state authorities and the management of the MNCs, but only rarely does it surface. Though their power base is not symmetrical or equal, each side tries its best to work well with the other. A few sensational clashes have occurred, but in the last resort there is little that state or federal authorities can do to force an international firm to change its behavior. They cannot force it to pay the full tax rate, as Exxon and Citicorp recently demonstrated, nor can they force it to rescind a decision to close a local plant.[49] Occasionally, the MNC has had to solicit aid from public agencies, as International Harvester, Chrysler, and Lockheed have done. In other cases, MNCs in the petroleum industry have lobbied for tax exemptions, and in the steel industry for quotas and countervailing tariff charges. But in most instances, it is the political authority that must plead with the MNCs and the successful exporting firms to construct new plant or to maintain existing jobs. It can do so by offering waivers of local taxes or zoning ordinances, and by relaxing state regulations that protect the environment or labor interests. Considering how few are the concessions that New York is either able or willing to offer to its most successful companies, it has been fortunate to hold its place as the fifth largest state in terms of export-related income and employment. In that category, New York has been surpassed only by California, which commands a unique geographical position in trans-Pacific trade, and by the Midwestern states that survive on the U.S.-Canadian automobile agreement of long standing. Texas comes in second place because of its proximity to Mexico and its heavy involvement in agricultural and petro-chemical exports, and Pennsylvania exports a considerable amount of coal. On most counts, therefore, New York has done well to export 13.5 percent of its manufacturers and to maintain 12.2 percent of its manufacturing employment in export-related business. But the question remains to be answered: how can New York improve its future performance and capitalize on this fast growing activity in the world economy?

PROGRAMMING FUTURE CHANGE

A wide range of solutions has been offered to the question of what New York should do in the near to medium-term future. Solutions advocated at a level of macroeconomic planning are generally not feasible since there is little influence that the State can wield, nor can it change the monetary or fiscal priorities set by federal authorities. There are few options available to radically modify tax or regulatory policies within the State, to offer job or export financing, or to persuade footloose companies to turn away from possible locations in the Northeast and enter New York. There is little hope of increasing the development funds, industrial inducements, job training partnerships, and tax incentives that state government can offer. In most years it can barely raise enough tax revenue to fund the social and municipal service requirements of its 17.6 million citizens or to balance the state budget. Moreover, it is doubtful that new companies would relocate to New York because marginal changes had been made in state laws and tax levels. Business managers often urge changes in tax and regulatory law to improve the business climate, but they seem to forget that the cash value of such incentives or exemptions would be slight in comparison to changes in current wage rates, which account for the largest factor cost in running industrial enterprises. And changes in wage rates, too, lie outside the competence of state government.

Putting these reservations aside, it is useful to look at the policy recommendations that various schools of economic planning and industrial policy have advocated. The first, which is possibly the most popular and the least effective, is to extend the numerous devices of trade protection to shut out cheap and competitive imports. Non-tariff barriers, countervailing duties, and import quotas already have been imposed to curb steel, automobiles, machine tools, and apparel imports. Many more have been called for, though none of them have succeeded in boosting U.S. industries by sheltering them from the winds of foreign competition. The appreciation of the dollar and of U.S. interest rates, in any case, cut severely into U.S. export sales and cost the nation roughly 3 million jobs between 1980 and 1983. A worse setback was engineered by the American MNCs that constructed 600 *maquiladoras* (or "golden mills") in the tariff-free zones of Mexico adjacent to the U.S. border. In some of these zones Chrysler builds its K-cars with local labor that costs 1 dollar an hour. In others, U.S. pharmaceutical firms manufacture standard consumer products and ship them without tariff across the border. To compound the problem of cheap imports, it is calculated that millions of office computers and 100,000 robots will displace a considerable number of workers within the decade. Hence an appeal has been made by labor unions—short sighted as it might appear—to protect the jobs that exist today, even if they cost too much and produce too little in comparison to countries with lower factor costs.

A second recommendation has been to subsidize U.S. exports and services in the pattern set by competitors in Japan and Western Europe. Steel works receive extensive government support in the EEC, Japan, and all of the NICs. So too do many other industries, ranging from aeróspace to shipbuilding, computers to basic engineering. Agriculture in the United States has long enjoyed federal aid and farm price supports amounting to 28 billion dollars a year, and it employs only 2 percent of the workforce. Why should industrial workers not be supported too? it is asked. Financing by the U.S. Export-Import Bank and tax exemptions awarded (in the DISC program) have encouraged domestic international sales companies. Why should assistance not also be granted to workers who want to buy plant on the verge of closing or to communities that aim to refurbish local industry? The question raises intriguing possibilities but in the last resort they are also dismissed. Only the federal government could afford to fund such programs; and the free market thinking of the president and the congress regards them with horror.

A third set of recommendations came from Alvin Toffler and other enthusiasts of a "third wave reindustrialization." They have written passionately about the need to finance and modernize the data processing industries, micro-electronics, computerized communications, bio-genetics, industrial robotization, and sophisticated environmental technologies. The new industries will supposedly raise the productivity of labor and capital, enlarge GNP, and revive U.S. export fortunes. But if only half these good tidings materialize, however, these new industries will provide work, including secondary and tertiary employment, for less than 10 percent of the workforce. Unfortunately, it will not be for the same 10 percent that is now without permanent work. The hard core unemployed today number roughly 11 million people and they lack both the vocational skills and the geographical mobility needed to make them useful. Many are too old or sick to move, too uneducated to learn new skills, and too beaten down by poverty and insecurity to start life again in a new climate or a new industry. The subsidizing of high-tech industries appeals to political futurists and systems engineers but, for at least two reasons, will provide few real solutions. First, the high-tech market is extremely volatile, as the ambitious start-up companies in Silicon Valley found to their cost, and it is likely that the subsidies proffered by public agencies will go down the drain, as they did in the synthetic fuels industry.[50] Second, the State does not have the resources to make more than a token investment in new ventures. And even if it did, there might be a better return if funds were invested for the public good, in health, education, housing, or mass transit, so that all industries and communities might gain.

A fourth recommendation points to the legislating of a comprehensive form of industrial policy. It has beeen widely criticized by a number of supply-side economists, free market enthusiasts, and doubting entrepreneurs. They see it as a concealed plea for selective socialism, high government spending, a New Deal form of state-capitalism, Keynesian demand management, overblown social planning, or collectivist intervention in free market economies. To put it mildly, industrial planning has lost most of its popular appeal in an era of Reaganomics. Alternative formulations have been offered by less radical schools of industrial planning. As a leading banker and social market theorist, Felix Rohatyn has urged the revival of a Reconstruction Finance Corporation. It would deflect a portion of the proceeds from immediately productive enterprises to longer term investment in promising but risky enterprises and it would help build a "national alliance" of business, labor, and political parties to redefine economic priorities. Among the many critics who have rejected his scheme, Robert Lawrence of the Brookings Institution argues that the market alone can determine which sunset industries should be allowed to die and which sunrise firms deserve a long-term mode of support.[51]

Conservative critics have been equally outspoken in repudiating the demands of the AFL-CIO for stern reciprocity clauses, if not outright protectionism, to tilt the balance against America's trade rivals who flout GATT rules of free trade. Unions have appealed for action to shut out subsidized imports, especially South Korean or European steel, to impose trade quotas, as in the Multi-Fiber Agreement, or to impose a 90 percent domestic-content requirement for all goods, such as Japanese cars or machine tools, that are sold in large numbers in the United States. It is worth noting that a rising tide of protectionist and mercantilist thinking has been traced in many countries. In the United States, the House of Representatives already has endorsed a domestic-content proposal, and the debate over trade quotas and off-setting duties was argued noisily during the presidential elections in 1984.[52]

Regardless of what happens to any of these proposals, none can help the New York economy in the short term. The level of factor endowment costs in New York surely will remain high. It cannot be lowered by marginal tinkering with new styles of government intervention, business subsidies or protectionist alliances. There are a few other measures that might be taken. They include initiatives to spur the growth of new industries, to underwrite business loans, provide tax relief, extend assistance to export marketing and to R&D labs, and to make the State more attractive to capital investment coming from both American and foreign sources. None of them are dramatic but over time these *ad hoc* initiatives could make a significant impact. Among the most important are the following.

Infrastructure: the upgrading of transport facilities, container docks at the upstate and downstate ports, the modernization of rail links and urban mass transit, and the development of cheaper energy sources. These improvements would be of immediate and direct assistance in boosting foreign trade and the entry of new industry.

Job creation and job training: Even if budgetary limitations remain tight, offers can be made of limited tax incentives or tax abatements for new industrial plant that help to recruit and retrain workers. With revenues drawn from an industrial bond issue, the State could help fund programs through the multilayered educational facilities in New York that develop its most valuable resource—a pool of one million educated young people, nearly 40 percent of whom register for college or post-secondary training.

Industrial assistance programs: Local and federal agencies could begin to fulfill tasks that now go by virtually in neglect. A regional planning model should be developed to help determine which industries show the greatest (or the least) signs of promise, where new capital formation should be encouraged, and what support services could best be supplied by government.[53] The export advisory and promotional services at the state and the federal level have long given useful aid but they need to be expanded. Market-sensitive assistance should be furnished by the tax and equalization agencies, the educational system, and the departments of labor, transportation and environmental protection. There is no way in which the public sector can replace the capital or the business decisions of industry in a market driven society, but there are numerous ancillary services that it can provide in order to accelerate economic development.

Short of changing the nation's monetarist or trade protection policies, there are no sweeping reforms that any state can pursue at the level of macroeconomic planning. And even at a micro-level, change must be handled cautiously if the delicate balance is to be maintained between the interests of capital and labor, of rich and poor, of high and low technology sectors.[54] To cite just one example, if the proposal were ever adopted to pay rates below minimum wage for young workers, managers might be tempted to fire older workers (especially in aging plant) who had accumulated seniority benefits or who refused to move into newly designated "enterprise zones."[55] Another case must also be cited. At the present time, the educational system emphasizes training for 3.5 million school children and one million college students for jobs that are not likely to survive the 1980s. Spending 10 billion dollars a year on public schools, at $2,700 per student a year, the State has failed to determine what children need to learn and how the education budget can be better spent. This deficiency must be repaired decisively.[56]

In the end, New York must attune its economic development to the competitive and the sensitively shifting trends in international trade. To put it starkly, that's where the money is. Some growth will come through providing support and services to the manufacturing workers who remain productively employed in the Northeast, and some will come from the expansion of secondary employment, trade, and the FIRE services. At present 1.5 million people in manufacturing jobs are supported by roughly 5.5 million in trade, construction, transportation, services, finance and government. This ratio is parasitic, though it conforms to the norm prevailing in the U.S. economy. It can be reduced either by slashing the levels of public and private sector support for the goods making economy, which is unwise, or a change can be effected by raising the productivity of capital and labor during the last years of the 1980s. Obviously, the potential of New York to cope with the swelling volume of international trade and investment is considerable. The conclusion is therefore warranted that the modernizing of the economic base will help realize the full potential of local manufacturing and business services by harnessing its growth to that of foreign trade.

NINE

Foreign Direct Investment and Regional Development:

The Case of Canadian Investment in New York State

Prem Gandhi

During the past decade and a half regional economic development has acquired new significance in the United States as its competitive position in the world economy has been eroded by Western Europe, Japan, and the newly industrialized countries in Asia and South America.[1] The declining position of the United States in world trade has been dramatic in the matured industries such as steel, automobiles, textiles and apparel, footwear, television, and electrical appliances. At the same time, in the Northeast and Midwest a sense of urgency has arisen as these regions have witnessed a deterioration of their relative position by the out-migration of population and business.

Although the regional decline of the Northeast and Midwest can be traced back to the 1940s, economic conditions worsened in the 1960s as business tried to find less hostile environments away from the high wages, union pressures, and overregulated economies of these parts and gravitated toward markets emerging in the South and Southwestern United States. Soaring energy costs in the 1970s and their devastating effects on the costs of production hastened this out-migration away from the Northeast. In addition, the macroeconomic problems of stagflation and America's declining competitive position in the world economy exacerbated the regional and structural shifts of the United States economy. This was inevitable since the lagging Northeast and Midwest possessed a major share of the matured industries that had borne the brunt of import competition. Efforts to revitalize the economies of these regions in the 1980s have renewed interest not only in reshaping their existing structure, but also in seeking new strategies to maintain and upgrade regional competitive positions in the United States. These strategies are designed to provide shares in the increasing employment opportunities in industries that are new and unrelated to matured industries in regions with high unemployment.

For New York, the task of economic revitalization demands a series of concerted steps to attract and retain private investment. Much has been done in the past 5–6 years to change the investment climate in the State by easing the over-regulation of business, reducing personal and corporate taxes, and providing investment incentives such as tax-holidays and job-training rebates. The goal has been to maintain a competitive edge over other states in attracting new investment. The success of such steps can be measured by the fact that compared to the rest of the United States, New York was better able to weather the Reagan recession. In 1983 it also improved its ranking in personal income from 11th to 5th position in the country. A good deal more needs to be done, however, especially when one considers that New York State still is perceived to be hostile to business interests, as evidenced by its recent ranking as 39th among business' locational preferences. Even more alarming is the continuation of intolerably high unemployment rates in the once prosperous Buffalo-Niagara region and, even in the best of economic times, in regions such as northern New York. Equally important, potentially high growth regions such as Rochester need a breathing space to adjust their economic structure to compete effectively in the world market. Because of the diversity of the economic base in New York, macropolicies at the state level have to be supplemented by micropolicies at the regional level for all regions in New York State to achieve their growth potentials and participate effectively in the revitalization process.

Attracting foreign investment, especially from Canada, is one such strategy that analysis strongly recommends as a means for New York to supplement domestic investments in regional development.[2] Putting aside more complex arguments, this strategy is favored for two basic reasons. New York is located along the rich Canadian industrial axis, which stretches from Quebec City-Montreal to Ottawa-Toronto-St. Catherine and beyond to London and Windsor, and it possesses nearly 70 percent of the Canadian market.[3] With these points in mind I want to examine the locational preferences of Canadian investment in New York as a first step in redirecting public policy discussion in this area. I also intend to redress partially the imbalance of literature on United States-Canadian economic relations. Studies have focused rather exclusively on the impact of United States trade and investment on the Canadian economy.

BACKGROUND AND SURVEY QUESTIONNAIRES

Traditionally, though the United States has invested heavily in Canada, Canada has invested twice as much in the United States on a per-capita basis. In the past 7–8 years the flow of Canadian investment has increased further. Canadian multinationals have raised their stakes in the United States economy partially in response to the political and economic uncertainty in Canada since 1976 and, more importantly, to overcome the limitation of small markets in Canada by taking advantage of the relatively high-growth market potential in this country. Similarly, while the literature on international capital flows abound with studies of the incentives for multinational enterprises (MNE) to move across political boundaries, little is known about the impact of small companies' locational preferences on regional economies in the United States and Canada. What motivates the hundreds of small Canadian companies that leave their protected market in Canada to enter the competitive jungle supposedly dominated by corporate gains in the United States?

The flow of Canadian investment to New York, though part of the broader picture of capital inflow into this country, is unique in many respects. The bulk of Canadian investment in recent years has gone into such sectors as real estate, oil and petroleum, mining chemicals, and primary metals. These are sectors in which New York finds itself at a distinct disadvantage relative to such states as Texas, California, Utah, Florida, and others. Similarly, in 1981 when Canada ranked first among foreign countries investing in the United States, the largest investment went into acquiring a 20 percent share in a chemical corporation headquartered in Delaware. Though Canadians also invest heavily in the manufacturing sector, the industrial and product composition of their investment preference is inconsistent with the industrial base of New York State. Yet, New York State continues to attract large amounts of foreign investment, including Canadian, which provided manufacturing employment to 179,000 New Yorkers in 1980 and disbursed about $3.5 billion in wages and salaries in the State's economy.[4] Moreover, New York's international exposure offers a distinct advantage. Its location along the United States-Canadian border, access to international trade routes, historical importance as an entry point for millions of immigrants to the United States, its location as the financial capital of the world and as the single most important location for multinational corporation headquarters, all provide New York with opportunities to enhance its comparative advantage. From the perspective of public policy, an effective case can be made for foreign investment to fill the gap between the investment New York requires to revitalize its economic base and its available domestic savings. Though New York State was late to recognize the potential benefits of foreign-capital inflow, beginning with Governor Carey's second administration it undertook aggressive initiatives to attract foreign investments. Two such initiatives were the governor's trips to Western Europe and Japan and his appointment of a Council on International Business.[5]

Furthermore, all private investment, especially foreign, is very concerned about the attitudes and the business environment in the community where it locates. Supportive attitudes and the corresponding efforts of regional development groups and community organizations are important in attracting, retaining, and helping new business prosper in their communities. Though the kinds of business can provide clues to the overall business environment, in many ways community attitudes toward business, particularly foreign, are more often reflected in the type of advertising strategies communities undertake to market themselves, the organizational structure of development agencies, in the interaction between development agencies and other community groups, and by the ways in which foreign business is integrated into the community. Unfortunately, such concerns have been a neglected field of inquiry in the literature on international business.

Consequently, two major issues must be investigated. First, what factors determine the decision of Canadian companies to locate in New York State generally and in the particular region of their choice? Second, what kind of attitudes do communities display toward business, especially Canadian business, and what efforts do they make to attract, retain, and nurture new businesses? By pursuing these questions the investigation departs from the traditional studies of foreign direct investment by concentrating on the decision factors of small and medium size, rather than multinational, corporations, and by quantifying the attitudes of the various communities in New York State toward Canadian business.

For the purposes of analysis New York is divided into ten economic regions similar to the regional profile designed by the State Department of Commerce. A comprehensive listing of 235 Canadian companies was prepared from lists obtained from Commerce, regional development agencies, and the Canadian Consulate in Buffalo. Companies were identified in terms of their location in ten economic regions.[6] Each of them was sent a questionnaire with questions covering four major areas—the profile of the company, factors responsible for its location, its assessment of the community, and the company's assessment of the future of international trade and of investment opportunities between the United States, New York, and Canada.

Similarly, for every county in the ten economic regions of the State, its industrial development agency and Chamber of Commerce were taken as representatives of the community. Each of 121 agencies, derived from a list provided by the State Department of Commerce, was sent a questionnaire designed to assess the extent of a community's involvement and success in attracting new business generally and Canadian business in particular, its promotional strategies to attract new investment to its area, its attitude toward Canadian companies and the efforts made by community agencies to retain business. (Though both questionnaires were computer-oriented, open-ended responses were invited as they cast additional light on economic policy issues pertinent to the area under study.)

The list of 235 Canadian companies included those that had ceased operations, were unreachable at recorded addresses, or had changed ownership since the lists were prepared by head agencies. It also included Canadian operations such as banks, investment and brokerage houses, life insurance, trucking and packing companies, and others whose location in the New York City area rested primarily on the importance of the city as the financial and commercial center of the world. After eliminating these companies from consideration the final 165 names were used, of which 73 companies responded to the questionnaire yielding an overall return rate of 44 percent. From the list of community agencies, only 110 were considered usable since in many counties the IDA and the Chamber of Commerce worked together. The responses from the agencies numbered 51, representing 46 percent of the total.[7]

THE CASE FOR FOREIGN INVESTMENT

In many ways, the flow of international investment is tied to the concerns of the political economy at home and abroad. International economists always have argued for an unrestricted flow of trade and productive resources, especially labor, capital, and management. Since universally free trade is not politically possible among trading partners with unequal economic power, however, the relocation of resources, especially capital, is the easiest, safest, and cheapest way to overcome this problem. Because of the uncertain economic policies of governments, including tariffs, it is cheaper to move a unit of capital across political boundaries then to export and continue to bear the transportation and tariff costs.

While since 1945 tariffs have continued to decline among the indusrialized countries of the world, international flow of investment has increased at a fantastic rate. At the same time, starting in the mid 1950s the composition of international investment changed from portfolio capital to direct investment. This change in the type of capital flows between the countries also was accompanied by the organizational and institutional changes through which such flows occur. The emergence of multinational enterprises since 1950 and the accompanying development of international production has been a fascinating phenomenon of international economic relations. In the past, various attempts to explain the impressive growth of MNE, with their emphasis on foreign direct investment, and to relate it to the theory of capital flow and trade theory have not been satisfactory. All flows within the MNE, e.g., goods, services, and capital between parent and subsidiaries and between the subsidiaries themselves, can never be considered unidirectional as such theories suggest. Among earlier explanations for such capital flows by MNE in the industrialized countries were the increasing size of the market, relative growth rates of the markets in these countries, increasing trade and interdependence due to rising specialization, economies of scale, role of transportation, tariff, and marketing costs in merchandise trade, stability of the economic and political institutions in these countries, and the availability of surplus investment funds. To this list recently has been added the increasing importance of information and the need to internalize activities within the MNE.

In any event, the history of international investment to and from the Unitea States is the history of the changing importance of each of these factors both here and abroad. As long as the economies of Western Europe were rapidly expanding and the United States could provide the investment funds, it did so. The increasing balance of payments deficit in the United States since 1957 caused a surplus of dollars abroad and depressed the value of dollars in the foreign exchange markets, thus increasing the inflationary pressure at home. Starting from the position of dominance after World War II, in the ensuing period the United States has found its economic and political power being challenged and its willingness to maintain that power being tested. Once the oil crisis hit the industrialized countries, the United States, beset with the problems of high inflation and lagging growth (stagflation) in the 1970s, undertook corrective measures that made this country an attractive place to invest surplus dollars accumulated abroad by other industrialized countries. The United States benefitted from a huge inflow of investment funds, though by the end of the 1970s it reversed its international payments position from a creditor to a debtor nation. In short, as the dominance of the United States declined in the world economy, it found itself becoming more internationalized.

Prepared from the data provided by the United States Department of Commerce, Table 1 conveys the essentials of these flow. For example, starting from a modest inflow of foreign direct investment of 1.5 billion dollars in 1970, the United States attracted a huge capital inflow of 22 billion dollars in 1981, and 10.4 billion in 1982. Though the United States continues to invest abroad, the bulk of such investment is financed more out of reinvested earnings of incorporated affiliates abroad and less by the direct outflow from the United States. Net capital inflows to the United States in 1981 and 1982 far outstripped the outflow of 9.7 billion dollars and a negative flow of 3 billion dollars, respectively. Similarly, as is clear from Table 2, taken from a benchmark study of foreign direct investment in the United States in 1980, the value of assets of non-bank United States affiliates of foreign investors stood at 292 billion dollars, with manufacturing ranked first with 82 billion dollars in assets. Needless to say, New York is among the top three states in this country to benefit from such an inflow of international investment.

Table 1. Foreign Direct Investment Position in the United States, 1977–82 (millions of dollars)

Direct Investment Position	1977	1978	1979	1980	1981	1982
All areas	34,595	42,471	54,462	68,351	90,421	101,844
Manufacturing	14,030	17,202	20,876	25,159	29,976	32,186
Canada[1]	5,650	6,180	7,154	10,074	9,883	9,823
Manufacturing	3,077	3,213	3,615	5,199	3,519	3,617
Net Capital Inflows						
Outflows (−)	3,728	7,897	11,877	13,666	21,998	10,390
Manufacturing	1,414	3,197	3,672	4,275	4,788	2,169
Canada	294	680	931	2,811	1,493	−1,067
Manufacturing	244	278	402	1,583	478	152

1. Figures include the position of unincorporated affiliates which in 1981 and 1982 stand at 756 and 764 million dollars, respectively.

SOURCE: United States Department of Commerce, *Survey of Current Business,* (August 1983), pp. 31–41.

Table 2. Selected Data for Non-Bank United States' Affiliates, 1980–1981. Total and Canada's Share

All Industries	1980 Total	1980 Canada's Share	1981 Total	1981 Canada's Share
Assets (million $)	292,033	47,879	395,032	78,518
Sales (million $)	412,705	35,456	503,745	60,944
Gross Book Value of Property, Plant Equipment (million $)	127,838	23,141	180,005	46,311
Expenditures for New Plant & Equipment (million $)	16,891	3,868	25,018	7,755
Net Income (million $)	8,917	1,068	11,463	2,810
No. of Employees	2,033,932	290,018	2,343,115	423,938
Employee Compensation (million $)	40,047	5,997	52,916	11,008
U.S. Exports Shipped by Affiliates (million $)	52,199	1,792	64,060	4,435
U.S. Imports Shipped to Affiliates	75,803	5,553	81,599	8,221
Manufacturing				
Assets (million $)	81,684	13,140	120,523	38,368
No. of Employees	1,102,804	150,613	1,280,835	280,573
New York				
No. of Employees	179,292	21,456	204,393	23,224
Gross Book Value of Property, Plant and Equipment (million $)	5,329	——	7,113	——

SOURCE: United States Department of Commerce, *Survey of Current Business,* (November 1983), pp. 19–34.

CANADIAN INVESTMENT IN NEW YORK

Based on data collected by the International Trade Administration of the United States Department of Commerce, in 1981 and 1982 Canada invested approximately 538 million dollars and 96 million dollars, respectively, in New York State. The bulk of the investment in 1981 went into real property and for acquiring a wholesale trade distributorship in 1982. As Tables 3 and 4 reveal, investment in manufacturing facilities was negligible in both years though between 1977 and 1980 manufacturing was the foremost important sector in terms of the number of completed transactions by foreign investors in the United States. Part of the reason for the recent slowdown in manufacturing investment is attributed to the worsening economic conditions in the United States.[8]

Table 3. Canadian Investment in New York State, 1981
1981 Value (millions of dollars)[1]

	Total Inflow From All Countries	Total Inflow From Canada	Total Inflow In New York	Canadian Investment In New York State
Grand Total	27,247.00	10,145.30	2,900.00	538.00
Manufacturing	7,103.70	3,572.70	779.00	1.00
Transportation Communication Public Utilities	328.00	154.00	161.00	154.00
Wholesale Trade	273.00	3.00	83.00	—
Retail Trade	659.00	184.00	113.00	—
Finance and Insurance	1,201.40	—	96.00	—
Services	1,073.70	134.00	607.00	15.00
Real Property	7,446.30	5,300.80	1,028.70	336.00
Unclassified	—	—	—	—
Agriculture, Forestry Fisheries	5.00	—	—	—
Mining	9,150.20	790.00	334.00	2.00

1. Value of investment is based on figures provided by the investors, not all of whom have reported the value of transactions. The number of cases where value was known for the total inflow in 1981 was 571 out of the total number of cases in that year, 1,203. These figures need not correspond with the figures reported elsewhere or in the New York State Survey.
SOURCE: Calculated from United States Department of Commerce, Foreign Direct Investment in the United States (International Trade Administration, Washington, D.C., December 1982).

Canadian investment grew in value from 2.5 billion dollars in 1960 to 13.4 billion dollars in 1977, of which 52.3 percent was located in the United States. In comparison to the world trade, though, Canadian investment is quite small (3.9 percent). Yet in relation to its economic base, Canada ranks very high among the most active investors in the world. Since 1976, the overflow of Canadian investment has stirred quite a debate in Canada, especially in view of the economic and political uncertainty surrounding that country. To date, there is little written explaining why Canadians invest abroad. One study has suggested that Canadian investment is prompted by domestic market saturation, drive for growth, relative scarcity of production factors, access to foreign markets, need for certain raw materials, and tax and other financial advantages.[9] The same study goes on to argue that while in the 1960s Canadian resource-based firms invested abroad to overcome the barrier of small markets in Canada and to diversify, in the 1970s the usual reasons for investing abroad have been supplemented by Canadian concerns about high inflation, profits, labor-management

Table 4. Canadian Investment in New York State, 1982
1982 Value (millions of dollars)[1]

	Total Inflow From All Countries	Total Inflow From Canada	Total Inflow In New York	Canadian Ivestment In New York State
Grand Total	13,912.70	3,940.00	1,900.00	95.70
Manufacturing	2,700.00	432.00	601.00	8.00
Transportation	24.00	–	–	–
Communication				
Public Utilities				
Wholesale Trade	162.00	75.00	77.00	75.00
Retail Trade	540.00	63.00	65.00	13.00
Finance and Insurance	1,290.00	40.00	783.00	–
Services	665.00	176.00	148.00	–
Real Property	6,080.00	3,055.00	119.00	–
Unclassified	2,430.00	97.00	–	–
Agriculture, Forestry, Fisheries	–	–	–	–
Mining	–	–	–	–

SOURCE: Calculated from United States Department of Commerce, *Foreign Direct Investment in the United States* (International Trade Administration, Washington, D.C., Feburary 1984).
[1] Value of investment is based on figures provided by the investors, not all of whom have reported the value of transactions. The number of cases where value was known for the total inflow in 1982 was 370, out of the total number of cases in that year, 913. These figures need not correspond with the figures reported elsewhere or in the New York State Survey.

relations, frequent strikes, union militancy and fear of expropriation, and general economic and political uncertainties surrounding Quebec. In 1978, Litvak and Maule studied 25 small and medium size Canadian companies to examine their decisions to locate in the United States.[10] They discovered a variety of reasons for the U.S. investments. Among the most central were market considerations (including such factors as high growth potential in the United States, concern for tariffs, and export development from the United States), United States production cost factors (availability of advanced technology, stable labor force, managerial talent, and so forth), the United States political-economic environment (such as freedom from regulatory burdens and federal/state incentives), Canadian corporate resources and capabilities, and Canadian economic-political concerns. While such studies must be regarded seriously in any discussion of Canadian investment in the U.S., rather than further inquire into these types of factors influencing Canadian decisions to settle in this country the present survey results offer a somewhat different explanation for the attraction of New York as a location for Canadian firms' United States operations.

Tables 3 and 4 provide figures for the flow of foreign and Canadian investment in New York State in 1981 and 1982. Table 5, constructed from the questionnaires sent to Canadian businesses, gives an overview of the Canadian companies which I surveyed. If a general profile of a typical Canadian business in New York is drawn, the company tends to be small with total assets valued at less than 1.5 million dollars. It would be in operation in New York for 15 years and in its current location for 9 years. Its preferred location would be either in Erie County in the west or Clinton County in the northern part of the State. In all probability, it has a Canadian parent (93 percent) most likely to be in Ontario (60 percent). The decision to locate in New York State was made after a careful evaluation of alternative sites outside the State (62 percent), usually in the Southeast (42 percent) or Northeast other than New York (38 percent). It started with eight employees in manufacturing and the assembling sector (57 percent) producing a product classified as an instrument or equipment. Since its establishment the company has increased employment by over 900 percent to 73 employees, who are at present virtually all full time (97 percent). In addition, it currently employs 23 additional employees in supervisory/management positions, 80 percent of which are United States citizens. Because of the length of time it has operated here, it is in New York State without regard to the economic and political uncertainty created by the election of Parti-Quebecois in 1976 and the fear of Quebec separation in Canada (86 percent). Though the New York State representatives in Canada played a part in the company's decision to locate in New York (31 percent considered them extremely important), the proximity of the area in New York State closest to the parent's location in Canada and the top executives' personal knowledge of the locational area played the most crucial part in the decision process.

In finer detail, the picture that emerges from this survey shows that though a typical Canadian company in New York is small, 15 percent of the respondents indicated their assets to be valued in excess of 9 million dollars and another 21 percent placed them between 1.5–2.0 million dollars. Of those responding, 29 percent of the Canadian companies in New York State were from Quebec and another 1.4 percent from British Columbia. Among the other principle type of activities in which Canadians are involved in the State are processing (packaging, etc.) and warehousing (14 percent), trade, both wholesale and retail (11 percent), research, engineering and consultancy (11.4

Table 5. Profile of Canadian Companies in New York, 1983

Manufacturing	(37)	Less than 100,000	(4)	0–10	(20)
Assembling	(4)	100,001–500,000	(18)	11–20	(14)
Processing	(4)	500,001–1,000,000	(7)	21–40	(12)
Warehousing	(6)	1,000,001–1,500,000	(8)	41–60	(8)
Servicing	(6)	1,500,001–3,000,000	(14)	61–100	(5)
Wholesaling	(6)	3,000,001–6,000,000	(3)	101–150	(6)
Retailing	(2)	6,000,001–9,000,000	(2)	151–250	(1)
Research	(1)	over 9,000,000	(10)	251–500	(2)
Others	(7)	No response	(7)	over 500	(3)
			No Response		(2)

SOURCE: Questionnaires

percent), and servicing (8 percent). Of all the Canadian firms that evaluated alternative locations outside the State, 9 percent evaluated all the major regions in the United States before deciding on New York. With the exception of the Binghamton region, Canadian companies are located throughout the State with secondary concentrations in Niagara County, New York City, Jefferson, St. Lawrence, and Genesee counties.

What attracted Canadian companies to New York? Table 6 summarizes the locational attraction of New York State. There are a number of specific points, however, that require a closer look.

First, in aggregation, it seems that the decision to locate in New York State was dictated by two major concerns, nearness to the parent company in Canada (81 percent) and the potential for growth in the United States relative to the Canadian market (79 percent). Thus, Canadian companies consider New York as a gateway to the United States market and their primary concern—nearness to the Canadian parent—influenced the importance they attached to regional location (77 percent). The significance of being near the parent organization is rather unique in international locational analysis. Although several reasons can be advanced for this preference, it is quite natural for companies that are small, family owned and managed, since the nearness of their offspring in New York makes it easier for management to commute to and from the Canadian parent for better supervision and control. The importance of "nearness to the Canadian parent" also was confirmed by the survey of the community agencies, both those who use the location of their area near Canada to attract Canadian companies as well as those communities who view their location away from Canada as a distinct disadvantage in their efforts to attract such companies.

Table 6. Importance of Locational Factors for Canadian Firms in New York[1]

Extremely Important (over 60 percent)		Moderately Important (30–59 percent)		Somewhat Important (less than 30 percent)	
Nearness to		Nearness to Customers		Community	
Parent Company	81%	in United States	39%	Attitude	29%
Potential for					
Growth in U.S.	79%	Trainable Labor	39%	Airways	24%
Location of		U.S.-Canadian		New York State	
the Area	77%	Tariff	34%	Incentives	24%
Transportation				Existing Indus.	
Highways	64%	Skilled Labor	32%	Base	22%
				Local	
				Incentives	20%
				Public Infra-	
				structure	18%
				Banking Res.	16%
				Low Electric	
				Rates	15%
				Potential for	
				Exports from	
				U.S.	15%
				Railways	9%
				Raw Materials	8%
				Special Facil-	
				ities for	
				Foreign Trade	5%
				Cultural	
				Amenities	3.3%
				Seaways	2%

SOURCE: Questionnaires.

[1] *Rating Scale.* Companies settling in New York were asked to rate the importance of each factor in their locational decision on a scale of one to five (Five = Extremely Important; Four = Very Important; Three = Moderately Important; Two = Somewhat Important; One = Not Important). The table refers to the percentage of companies that considered these factors as Extremely or Very Important, e.g., Access to Railways was considered as Extremely to Very Important by only 9 percent of the respondents. The rest checked that factor as Somewhat or Not Important. Non-respondents were adjusted in calculating the percentages.

Second, a large percentage of respondents (64 percent) indicated that access to transportation-highway networks was a factor of significance. With the exception of airways (24 percent), other modes of transportation seemed unimportant for Canadian business operations. It is not surprising to see highways among the extremely important locational factors cited by Canadian firms. In the literature on regional economics, access to highway networks is considered a locational advantage because of the economical freight rates in transporting goods over distances of 500 miles or less. The advantage of interstate highways linking New York State with the rest of the country and with Canadian highways also is important in this context because of the companies' requirements to commute between their headquarters in Canada and their subsidiaries in New York.[11] Airways received relatively solid marks because of the large percentage of servicing, research, and consultancy firms which responded to the survey and because of their obvious importance to Canadian business as an efficient means of transporting high-valued goods to distant U.S. markets.

Third, the moderate importance of the labor (32 and 39 percent) factor influencing Canadian decisions to locate in New York is surprising. Two possible explanations are either that New York has a readily available pool of labor or that the companies are not labor-intensive, an explanation confirmed by the small number of employees. In practically every region of the State, including the northern area with traditionally high unemployment, Canadians mentioned labor as secondary to highway transportation. It is reasonable to assume that the high percentage of processors, distributors, wholesale and retail traders who responded to the survey could have contributed to these results.

Fourth, the other set of considerations in the moderately important category was nearness to customers in the United States and the United States-Canadian tariff conditions. This is precisely what should have been expected. Since the firms have had contacts with the United States' market before establishing full-fledged facilities here, the move to the U.S. made it easier for the Canadian companies to provide better services to their customers. At the same time, the decision to invest in the United States had more to do with the Canadian concern for growth potential in the United States beyond a given stage of simply exporting from Canada. It should be noted that "Buy American" attitudes displayed among Americans may also have contributed to the Canadian decision to set-up subsidiaries in the United States.[12]

Fifth, among the least important considerations were a diverse group of locational factors that included those which often generate heated public policy debate—state and local incentives to attract new industries, adequate public infrastructure, low electric and power rates, and so forth. From the survey none of these were considered important enough in aggregate. In fact, when companies were asked whether or not they would have moved into New York in the absence of state and/or local incentives, the reply was affirmative (74 percent and 66 percent, respectively). Our own feeling, however, is that once the decision to invest in the United States was made, companies looked at those locations that satisfied their most important consideration—"nearness to Canadian parent." After that, other locational advantages, such as state and local incentives and low cost electric power, were simply considered sweeteners.[13]

Sixth, how helpful or receptive was the New York community to the Canadian companies? The two types of community agencies to receive the highest rating for the support they gave to the Canadian companies were the local development agencies (43 percent) and the local Chamber of Commerce (31 percent). The lowest rating went to the labor unions (6 percent) and local civic organizations (7 percent). Local government, public media, and the business organizations received moderate ratings (16–21 percent). All in all, 76 percent of the companies rated the business environment in their community as highly favorable to their business operations. Almost three-quarters of the companies were satisfied with their decision to locate in New York State and their respective community and were willing to support local agency efforts to attract other Canadian companies to the area. Their satisfaction with the decision was based on the fact that 59 percent of the Canadians had expanded since locating, while 26 percent had multiplied by opening branches elsewhere and were optimistic of future profits and growth (75 percent).

At the same time, almost one-quarter of the companies would have preferred that the community agencies better understand and appreciate the problems of beginning a new business, and also would have liked to see more fanfare for their company in the public media. Among that which the companies missed most in the community's initial reception was the opportunity to get acquainted with local civic and community groups and a somewhat warmer reception by the public officials.

Finally, with regard to the Canadian business community's assessment of future United States-New York-Canadian trade, investment, and free-trade options between the two countries, responses from the companies were as expected. More liberal trade and investment policies between the two countries were favored. In the literature of international economics, movement toward economic integration by two political entities consists of several steps, ranging from a preferential treatment of each other's imports to a large overall tariff reduction, sectoral free trade, and free-trade area to a common market. At the extremes lies tariff-ridden trade between the trading partners and political integration. Adjacent to this hierarchy lies a half-way house or foreign trade zone designed to overcome the disadvantage of imports cutting into the production and employment opportunities in the community. A foreign trade zone encourages importers to assemble and store their products in the zone without paying duty until goods actually are imported into the United States. While less than one-third (30 percent) favored the establishment of free-trade zones in their communities, almost three-quarters (71 percent) of the respondents favored a large overall tariff reduction between the United States and Canada. Further steps toward the establishment of a common market between the two countries received lower ratings (sectoral free-trade, 65 percent; complete free-trade, 55 percent; and a common market, 53 percent). The surprising element in the survey, however, came from the 24 percent of the respondents who favored a political integration between the two countries!

Although the factors which decisively influence Canadian locational decisions already have been highlighted, three additional concerns deserve mention. The survey of Canadian business indicates clearly that tax rates did not *discourage* companies from moving into New York, but were a major disincentive for further expansion. The complexity of tax laws and the lack of proper explanation also drew complaints from management because this obscured the opportunities for easing tax burdens. Regulatory policies were not coordinated well by agencies, companies often remarked, thus creating considerable uncertainty within businesses potentially subject to regulatory constraints. And together with tax rates and regulatory policies, United States immigration and customs laws are a source of difficulty. Canadian businesses object to the frequent limitations these laws impose on the free movement of personnel and goods between Canada and the U.S. In each of these three areas Canadian business must contend with rules and regulations which, it believes, unnecessarily jeopardize cost effective and efficient operations.

COMMUNITY SURVEY

The community questionnaire was designed to evaluate the extent of a community's involvement and success in attracting new businesses in general and Canadian business in particular. The survey examined community promotional strategies, including regional information offered to help attract new investment into its area, community attitudes toward Canadian companies, and community efforts to retain business in its region. The findings of the survey were instructive.

While most of the communities surveyed actively sought new business regardless of its national origin (49 percent), many agencies did report that they were too small and lacked the necessary budgetary resources and personnel to undertake any kind of promotional activity. In addition, they expressed the feeling that economic development was not their priority. They already were too busy helping existing business to be involved with attracting new investments.

Though it is extremely difficult to determine precisely the number of new businesses that located in New York as a result of a community's promotional efforts, it appears that roughly 68 percent of all new Canadian firms settled as a consequence of community efforts as compared to 52 percent of other foreign business (European and Japanese) and 25 percent of new American companies. Overall, the majority of the agencies (57 percent) considered their promotional activities as moderately successful, while 10 percent marked them as particularly unsuccessful approaches to attracting new business.

With regard to the success of particular marketing strategies, the techniques for attracting Canadian business most frequently mentioned by the agency were personal visitations and follow-up contacts with prospective clients (72 percent). Almost 55 percent of the agencies used direct mailing and 45 percent involved the regional representatives of the New York State Department of Commerce in their marketing strategies. So far as advertisement in the Canadian media was concerned, 33 percent used trade journals to solicit new business, followed by Canadian newspapers (17 percent), television, and radio. It is interesting to note that only 63 percent of the agencies used a similar set of strategies to attract United States companies. Table 7 gives the breakdown of regional strengths as promoted by community agencies to attract new investment, both domestic and Canadian. A majority of the agencies (56 percent) viewed the contribution of Canadian investment in their community as a significant source of income, employment, and new skills. In their estimation, Canadian companies did act as responsible corporate citizens (42 percent).

What efforts did the community make to retain Canadian companies in their area? Community responses to this inquiry are very sketchy and only crude insight is provided. In order to appreciate properly the significance of their efforts, however, it first would be important to understand the reasons for business leaving a community. In the absence of such data it nevertheless is clear from community responses that they believe that the main reasons companies left both their area and New York State were the availability of better alternatives in other parts of the country (75 percent) and rising taxes in New York (66 percent).

Our survey of community agencies also uncovered beliefs communities held about why they did not succeed in attracting Canadian companies. These reasons can be sorted into three distinct categories.

221

Table 7. Importance of Regional Strengths as Attractions for Canadian Investment[1]

Extremely Important (over 60 percent)		Moderately Important (30–59 percent)		Somewhat Important (less than 30 percent)	
Location of Area	92%	New York State Incentives	58%	Potential for Export From U.S.	18%
				Special Facilities for Foreign Trade	14%
Access to Highways	86%	Access to Banking	56%	Seaways	14%
Potential for Growth in U.S.	83%	Public Infrastructure	54%		
Community Attitudes	76%	Existing Industrial Base	48%		
Trainable Labor	72%	Airways	41%		
Local Incentives	70%	Railways	40%		
Nearness to Present Customers	66%	Tariffs	37%		
Availability of Skilled Labor	65%	Cultural Amenities	37%		
Nearness to Parent Company	60%	Raw Materials	35%		
Low Electric Rates	60%				

SOURCE: Questionnaires.

[1] *Rating Scale:* As in the case of the business questionnaire, Community agencies were asked to rate, on a scale of one to five, the importance of each factor in their region that they use to attract new companies. The table refers to the percentage of agencies that considered these factors as Extremely or Very Important, e.g., Special Facilities for Foreign Trade was considered as Extremely or Very Important by 14 percent of the respondents. The rest checked that factor as Somewhat or Not Important. Nonrespondents were adjusted in calculating the percentages.

Budgetary Problems

Perhaps the most compelling reasons for failure to attract Canadian business, and the most frequently cited (30 percent), are budgetary and personnel limitations. One respondent commented, for example, that "research, development, and production of a promotional package targeted to Canadian firms in particular is too expensive for our current budget, and our agency has only two on staff and a very limited access to funds to promote our attractiveness." Budget restrictions have prevented agencies from spending large amounts of money on direct mail advertising, promotion of their areas to interested Canadian businesses, or from sending representatives to the United States or New

York State organized trade shows. Lack of budget for such agencies may also limit their promotional activities to attract *any* new businesses, including American.

Yet, if budgetary problems were to be resolved by New York State through outright grants to the communities, how would the agencies use such funds? Their responses indicated that funds would be used to

1. Produce advertising and promotional material specifically directed to the Canadian market and to invest in direct sales contacts with those empowered to make relocation decisions.

2. Hire an industrial development staff to contact Canadian industries, publish brochures and kits.

3. Establish offices in Quebec and Toronto and canvas the major businesses, offering to assist them in locating sites in New York State.

4. Follow-up leads from the New York State Department of Commerce by personal visits and encourage and pay for business prospects to visit the community.

5. Provide better services and/or incentives to businesses, i.e., low cost loans.

Location of Area Away from Canada

At least 14 percent of the community agencies spoke of the disadvantage of their area of being located at too great a distance from Canada. For such agencies the reasons for undertaking little promotional activity to attract Canadian companies has been because they "are not located close enough to the United States/Canadian border and, historically, Canadian companies do not appear to be interested in locating this far south in the State." This comparative disadvantage in location gives such agencies a feeling that "our location could not compete with the Erie-Buffalo-Niagara-Batavia-Clinton county area." In fact, locationally disadvantaged agencies which invested in some promotional activity to attract Canadian companies have felt frustrated because "after several attempts to attract Canadian firms it has become apparent that these firms prefer United States locations *immediately* near the border, such as Buffalo. Businesses view the added miles [70] to travel east to Rochester a burden." Consequently, these agencies have indicated that given the additional budgetary support they would prefer to "expend funds to call on firms in the Canadian mid and far west." One agency went so far as to suggest that besides setting up offices in Montreal, Ottawa, and Toronto one office should be set up "in the far western side of Canada toward Vancouver."

Lack of A Formal Strategy

Among the responses received from community agencies were those where "currently, there is no formalized strategy to actively attract new industry." The reasons for such an absence are either that they are "too busy" or that "promotions usually do not pay positively for the expense involved." We also discovered that the absence of a promotional effort to aggressively recruit Canadian firms is due to either "not being aware of the economic potential" or "being unaware of Canadian interest in coming to New York State."

PUBLIC POLICY ISSUES

The main objective of the narrative has been to report the findings of the business and community surveys and to explore the strategic dimensions of the decision-making process of Canadian businesses locating operations in New York State and of those involved in attracting business to their communities. The statistics on the scale of foreign investments in New York should convey the importance of such investments to the State as well as the relative position of the State in the United States (Tables 1 through 4). Given the preferences of large Canadian companies to invest in areas such as real property, mining, petroleum, and chemicals (which in New York State is at a relative disadvantage in the United States), one is struck by the fact that in any given year there are *scores* of small Canadian firms that do move into this State for their own peculiar reasons. The question is whether New York State should leave this inflow of investment alone and let the chips fall where they may, or whether it should develop a strategy to increase investment from Canada by removing hurdles in its path or by alleviating the problems that affect such an inflow. One answer to this question already seems to have been provided. Measures required to enhance investment have surfaced clearly in the course of this paper, while others must be drawn out of the analysis. The concern here is twofold—to promote an awareness in New York of the significance of Canadian investment and to encourage a discussion of the public policy issues which it raises. The following items are recommended for consideration.[14]

In order to attract foreign business, New York State must show a solid government commitment by a more visible presence outside of the United States. Several agencies have suggested that the State of New York should have at least two offices in Canada fully staffed to work with industrial teams and community representatives when they go to Canada. Currently, the State regional representatives in Canada do provide some support to the community agencies. There is general agreement, however, that under the conditions which now define New York State's presence in Canada—one representative with very little administrative and staff support—there is no guarantee at any time that the necessary support will be available to the community representatives.

Besides devoting additional State resources to Canadian recruitment, there is also a need for closer cooperation on recruitment efforts between local agencies and the New York State Department of Commerce. Minimally, such cooperation should encompass research on specific locational advantages which would accrue to Canadian firms locating in New York State, sharing of promotional and advertising costs, better referral systems between the State's representatives in Canada and community agencies, and more up-to-date regional industrial and business directories.

Concerned as we are in this study with the issue of economic development, it seems from the survey that that is not the precise concern for many communities. Many agencies have remarked that they are preoccupied with retaining business and that their marketing is directed to that end. Part of the reason for this preoccupation has to do with the size of the agency and the lack of budgetary support by the community. The challenge for the community, on the other hand, is to continue to maintain a viable economic base to make it attractive to domestic and foreign business. Consequently, it is important that communities design long range strategic economic development programs directed at enhancing economic opportunity and provide the financial resources necessary to ensure implementation of the plan. Additional support and resources should be available at the State level to place economic development efforts on a level competitive with other states.

New York should continue to improve the business climate in the state. The business posture is one problem that drives away investment despite excellent labor, good transportation, fine recreation, culture, and so on, that this state possesses. In the words of one agency, "The State of New York is anti-business regardless of what the current administration says. We overregulate business and have the highest personal income tax in the United States. We give the utilities license to steal from the consumers and we have a public service commission that the utilities own."

New York State must make every effort to reform its tax laws, including personal and corporate taxes. At the same time, it should reevaluate its incentive programs and better coordinate them with local incentives. If incentives do not play a significant part in attracting Canadian or other businesses, a cost-effective program should be undertaken to spend greater resources on developing campaigns, local development and demonstration programs, etc. In addition, it is conceivable that many companies may be either unaware of the State's incentives or need a better explanation of them.

Numerous complaints about customs and immigration laws by business and community agencies were registered. In the words of one agency, "One of the major problems that faces most companies coming into the United States from Canada, especially if they are bringing employees, is immigration. It does appear that because most of these companies which are new also specialize in high technology, and are abundant in the Canadian provinces, a more liberal attitude by the Immigration Department would assist in building our economy in the United States." In the same vein, a better management of customs regulations, particularly as they affect Canadian parent-companies and their United States subsidiaries, should be a high priority. It is recommended strongly that New York take a leadership role in this country by modifying these rules and regulations and by eliminating a lot of bureaucratic red tape and the accompanying frustrations for new corporate entrants into the United States.

One of the chronic complaints heard from community agencies has been their dissatisfaction with high interest rates attached to business loans made by local banks. Since 80–90 percent of the investment funds are borrowed locally, agencies have suggested that additional sources of low interest financing are needed desperately. Canadian companies, while successful in marketing their products in Canada, are treated in New York as new business ventures. Hence, they experience difficulty in obtaining conventional financing. Some look for low interest financing as a reward for generating jobs in the United States.

CONCLUDING REMARKS

Given the nature and the scope of foreign investment in this country, inflow is a decisive means to internationalize productive resources, especially capital. Inflows of foreign direct-investment accompanied by the inflow of technology and management and marketing techniques can prove useful to the United States' industrial structure. With its long history of international exposure, New York can benefit a good deal in its economic revitalization efforts by competing for an increasing share of such an inflow of investment funds. This study has examined the attraction of New York to Canadian investors. If a single overall conclusion is to be drawn, it is captured in the words of one agency surveyed: "The market is there and there are companies waiting to be invited to the United States. But they require more than the assistance we now offer on a limited scale."

V

Partners:
The Government, Business,
and Academic Communities

TEN

Building the Twentieth-Century Public Works Machine:

Robert Moses and the Public Authority*

Jon J. Lines, Ellen L. Parker, David C. Perry

> The State's Infrastructure is the cornerstone
> of New York's economy. Our economic
> growth and industrial development are
> dependent upon massive investments that
> the State has wisely made in the past, and
> must continue to make in the future.
>
> Governor Mario Cuomo
> *Annual Budget Message 1984*

N o politician or academic would quarrel with Governor Cuomo's assessment of the importance of public infrastructure to the economic viability and political stability of the State. Indeed, the argument is scarcely new. Urban scholars have produced libraries of studies on the impact of infrastructure on suburbanization, changes in the population and the economic base, the growth and development of urban politics, and regional and interregional relationships between cities.

New studies of uneven regional economic development and urban fiscal crisis simply underscore Cuomo's assessment pointing to the poor condition of physical infrastructure as one of the critical roadblocks to economic and social growth and stability, not only in older areas such as New York State, but in the growth centers of Texas and California

* Research conducted for this paper was supported, in part, by the Office of the President, SUNY at Buffalo, and by a grant from the National Endowment for the Arts.

231

as well.[1] Where economic renewal in the Frostbelt cities is impeded by crumbling and outdated public works, economic growth in the Sunbelt is constrained by overburdened sewers, roads, water systems, and other public works.[2] This body of literature is replete with an almost technologically deterministic adherence to the importance of public infrastructure for urban development. Yet, it lacks an understanding of the *process* through which public policy and public works evolve. While public infrastructure has substantial effects on the economic, political and social formation of the city, it does not just appear on the landscape. Public works are products of complex and sophisticated political decision making, the dynamics of which form the topic of this paper.

The intent here is to provide a historical analysis of one of the major institutional ingredients of this decision-making process—the statutory public authority. In New York State, more and more of what Governor Cuomo calls the "wise investment of the past" has been funneled through these public authorities. Today there are forty-one such bodies with a combined bonded indebtedness of twenty-four billion dollars, nearly seven times that of the State itself.[3] The public authority complex has become so important that it is now referred to as "the fourth branch of government."[4]

This "branch of government" appears to be a most unpopular one for many legislators. Responding to the fiscal crisis which shook the Urban Development Corporation, one of the largest of these authorities, the Moreland Committee reported that the power and authority of this type of "government" was substantially overextended.

Public authorities in New York have been allowed to create debt obligations without adequate coordination, supervision or control by the Executive and Legislative branches of government.[5]

A more recent confidential report to the State legislature describes the authority process as one which "has changed in profound and threatening ways."[6] The governor and the legislature are faced with a difficult dilemma. The widely recognized need to make massive investments in the State's infrastructure has led the executive and legislative branches of State government to consider an increased role for the public authority. At the same time, however, the State's law makers have become increasingly critical of the role and efficacy of the public authority as an agency of infrastructure development and its appropriateness in a democratic society.

The premise of our argument is that the statutory public authority has been a singularly innovative tool for meeting and solving the exigencies of twentieth-century infrastructure development. The very autonomy of the public authority, now under debate, has allowed it historically to generate substantial amounts of capital through bonds rather than taxes. This autonomy also has made the public authority network substantially unresponsive to political control and oversight. Before engaging in another round of infrastructure development through the use of the public authority, we need to analyze this institution further.

Just as the authority has escaped substantial legislative control and oversight, however, so has it rarely been the subject of scholarly analysis.[7] We want to begin the task of developing this body of scholarship in three ways. First, a general introduction and review of the basic characteristics of the public authority will be offered and, second, we will detail the events surrounding the inauguration and evolution of one of the most powerful and effective public authorities in the United States, the Triborough Bridge Authority (TBA). Finally, to study the TBA means to study the administrative practices of its founder, Robert Moses. In large part, the characteristics of public authorities as autonomous agencies of public works policy were set in place during the formative years of the TBA. Using the complete files of the TBA and Robert Moses, which never before have been opened to researchers, we hope to contribute a new measure of insight into the formation of decision-making processes of public infrastructure.[8] Along the way, this case study will supply a new glimpse into the world of these "government owned businesses," where the most important actors are appointed administrators, bond underwriters, attorneys, and construction operatives.[9] These groups exist in a world substantially removed by law, administrative privilege, and the confidentiality of attorney-client relations from legislative oversight, political control, and citizen input, much less scholarly inquiry and study.

In the course of investigation we also discover a somewhat different view of Robert Moses. Moses ceases to appear as the all-knowing, comprehensive planner who used the public authority in ways to suit his own ends.[10] To the contrary, he emerges as a pragmatic administrator without any more complete understanding of the potential utility of the authority than anyone else. While it is clear that Moses must be credited with the design of this agency of public works policy, it is also clear that he learned of the authority's potential only through a protracted and fitful process of legislative and administrative experience.

THE PUBLIC AUTHORITY

The importance of the public authority lies in the fact that it became the institutional tool which most easily facilitated the development of public infrastructure. Its success was rooted in its ability to raise funds through the sale of bonds secured against the revenues of the projects the authority built. This represented a "new" source of funds which freed the public agencies from a reliance on taxes for its fiscal base. This capacity to generate revenues independent of the politics of taxation allowed the public authority substantial autonomy from conventional governmental control and oversight. Consequently, the authority is a double-edged sword. The very autonomy which enables the authority to generate huge sums of revenues and build massive amounts of public infrastructure can pose a threat to those who advocate strong legislative and executive oversight and control over agencies of the State.

Austin Tobin, the legendary Executive Director of the Port of New York Authority (PNYA), argued that

the true public authority is a public corporation set up outside the regular framework of federal, state or local government, and freed from the procedures and restrictions of routine government operations, in order that it may bring the best techniques of private management to the operation of self supporting or revenue producing public enterprise.[11]

As a result, early on public officials were more than willing to give up governmental control over the authority and its practices to benefit from the revenue generating capacity of the autonomous authority. In 1938, Harvard University political scientist Lincoln Gordon observed that "no feature in recent thought in applied economics is more striking than the rapidity with which [authorities have] gained favor among almost all sections of opinion."[12]

Evolution of the Public Authority

The popularity of the modern public authority evolved within the context of historical forces which influenced the larger evolution of political structures designed to meet the needs of the American economy and society. Political demands in the context of the "post-industrial" and "bureaucratic" state required a new mode of public administration employing corporate organizational structures of the private sector designed to overcome the limitations of conventional governmental processes.[13]

The historical roots of the public authority can be traced to eighteenth-century relationships between government and colonial and post-colonial economic interests. The modern twentieth-century authority, or "public benefit corporation," as it is constitutionally designated in New York State, generally is seen to have originated in the creation of the Port of New York Authority (PNYA) in 1921. This agency, the first to actually use the term "authority" in its title in this country, was created to coordinate the use of bi-state port facilities in the New York-New Jersey region and to mitigate the potentially ruinous competition between these states. By the mid 1930s, the New York Port Authority was hailed as a model that was so "successful [at] its work in the construction and operation of terminal and transportation facilities within the port district that a pattern was set up in this state and other states."[14] Its success was attributed in no small way to the fact that the Port Authority was an entity independent of both state governments. It was, in fact, an autonomous corporation. The two states maintained some control in the form of appointments to the governing board, financial review by the state comptrollers, and gubernatorial veto power over the Authority's governing board's minutes. The Port Authority, however, was substantially free of any real control over its administrative practices, policy decisions, project selection, and day-to-day operations.

In the 1930s, with the depression and Roosevelt's New Deal, the public authority took on a very different function from the one applied to the Port Authority. It would be used as a short-term economic generator of jobs through its management of new public works projects. Cities were confronted with the need for economic revitalization, the rapid creation of jobs for millions of displaced workers, and the building of physical infrastructure to accomodate the new development patterns created by metropolitanization. Local governments, though, also were faced with declining revenues. Tax and debt limitations structured into state constitutions had made it impossible to borrow funds or raise revenues through traditional sources to finance depression era demands. Roosevelt entered office with a commitment to use the powers of the federal government to address the exigencies of the depression. Opposed to providing direct federal grants to local governments to assist them with their fiscal problems, Roosevelt's administration turned to public works as one expedient way of creating jobs.

Two federal agencies were to have considerable influence in the creation of public authorities in urban areas, the Reconstruction Finance Corporation (RFC) and the Public Works Administration (PWA). The RFC was created in 1932, the last year of the Hoover Administration. While the RFC was used primarily to provide capital to failing banks and large industries, it also was authorized to make capital available for self-liquidating public works projects. The PWA was created under Title II of the National Industrial Recovery Act of 1933 (NIRA). Under the NIRA provisions creating the agency, the PWA could loan money to finance public works considered to be of significant public benefit.

Because of constitutionally imposed municipal debt and tax limitations, it was unclear whether the federal government legally could loan money directly to local governments. Both the RFC and the PWA, however, were empowered to loan funds to municipal public authorities. A number of authorities had been established even before Roosevelt took office and utilized RFC and PWA financing.[15] Under Roosevelt's Administration local public authorities proliferated.

Perhaps the most important stimulus to the creation of public authorities was a letter Roosevelt wrote to the 48 state governors in 1934.[16] This letter explicitly urged the states to adopt legislation allowing for the creation of "revenue-financed special governments," or public authorities.[17] His five recommendations for revising the "procedure relative to municipal finance . . . at least for the duration of the existing emergency" were

1. Simplification of the procedure for the authorization and financing by municipalities of public works projects, and conferring of additional powers upon municipalities to undertake such projects and issue bonds to finance the same.

2. Creation of municipal improvement authorities without the power to tax but with power to issue bonds payable solely from the income of revenue-producing improvements, such as water, sewer, and electric light and power systems.

3. Authorizing municipalities to engage in slum clearance including condemnation of necessary lands, and the construction, operation and maintenance of low-cost housing, to make contributions therefore, and to enter into contracts with the federal government in connection therewith.

4. Providing for the creation of non-profit benefit corporations or agencies to provide for the electrification of rural communities with the assistance of the federal government.

5. Validation of bonds or other obligations heretofore issued by municipalities for public works projects and sold to the federal government.[18]

In short, Roosevelt envisioned the creation of public authorities which would be "clothed with the power of Government but possessed of the flexibility and initiative of a private enterprise."[19] The public authority was enthusiastically adopted by many states between 1933 and 1939.[20]

Roosevelt saw the public authority as a short-term, expedient solution to the problems of creating jobs by building needed public works in an era of economic depression. The federal government's role was simply that of a banker. It would purchase bonds issued by the public authority to finance a single revenue-producing project. The public authority would maintain and operate that project until the bonds were retired, at which time the authority would go out of existence and its assets would revert to the local government. But the public authority proved to be more resilient than Roosevelt, or even Moses, originally intended. It had two major advantages over conventional government, fiscal flexibility and political and administrative autonomy. These characteristics of the public authority, as exemplified by the TBA, enabled the authority eventually to sell its bonds on the *private* bond market, perpetuate its existence, and emerge as a major actor in the development of public infrastructure.

Financially, the public authority was seen as a way of financing public works without the levy of additional taxes or increasing the indebtedness of conventional government. The primary revenue source of the public authority was user-fees on the facilities it built and operated, e.g., tolls, sewer rents, water charges, etc. Revenue bonds sold by the authority were secured against these fees. Since the authority was perceived as being "self-supporting," these charges had to be adequate to cover debt service and operating expenses.

Administratively, the public authority was granted considerable autonomy and flexibility. In general, authorities are governed by appointed boards of directors who have considerable freedom in choosing high level administrators. The authority boards and administrators virtually have complete autonomy in administrative matters including employment and promotion practices, purchasing policy, bidding procedures, accounting practices, and setting fees for the use of the facilities they control. While basic policy decisions, such as the placement of a bridge or alignment of a highway, are subject to political review, this oversight is indirect, at best.[21] Provided the authority stays within the mandate granted in the Public Authorities Law, it has virtually unlimited control over its administrative practices.

These characteristics of the public authority found their articulation in the establishment and practices of the TBA. Under the guidance of Robert Moses, the TBA evolved from a single purpose authority created to finance and build a single bridge, the Triborough Bridge, to a multi-purpose agency of infrastructure development. By the end of the 1930s it became one of the most important and influential public works agencies in New York City. It was armed with the administrative independence and the financial power to successfully direct public works investments of the magnitude envisioned by the politicians of the past and the governor of the present. The case study which follows examines the first stage of this evolution from the TBA's creation in 1933 to 1937, when it first gained access to the private bond market.

ROBERT MOSES AND THE TRIBOROUGH BRIDGE AUTHORITY

In 1938 Robert Moses declared:

From the beginning it has been our conception that the function of the Authority is not merely to build and maintain certain water crossings within the city, but to help solve metropolitan arterial and recreational problems.

If I may be permitted a personal note, I would say it has long been a cherished ambition of mine to weave together the frayed edges of New York's metropolitan arterial tapestry. We have never lacked plans, sound and unsound, practical and fantastic. What we have lacked has been unified execution. . . . The Triborough Bridge Authority has provided the warp on the loom, the heavier threads across which the light ones are woven. . . . The best use for its surplus, from both business and civic points of view, is for improvement of approaches and connections, to open up new territory and improve surrounding property.[22]

While these words were written for the fifth anniversary of the opening of the Triborough Bridge, it was the design and organization of the Authority and not the bridge that Robert Moses was commemorating. In the space of a few years, the Triborough had evolved from the traditional temporary, single purpose authority envisioned by Roosevelt into a diversified, self-perpetuating multi-purpose agency. The solidification of the TBA's political and administrative autonomy turned the authority into what one observer called a classical "borrowing machine."[23]

As "the warp on the metropolitan loom," the TBA was, or would become, involved in the long range and coordinated planning of bridges, arterials, parks, parkways, tunnels, sports facilities, and numerous other projects in the New York City area. Moses' comment, however, was made with the benefit of hindsight. Moses had "never lacked plans," but he did not immediately recognize the potential of the TBA as the agency to realize his dreams. Indeed, we will suggest that, contrary to the highly deterministic "great-man" thesis of Robert Caro[24] and other critics, Moses did not immediately grasp the broader significance of the public authority.

The process by which the TBA achieved its expanded mandate and the autonomy and flexibility required to implement its larger purposes was incremental. It took over three years and three separate State amendments to the original TBA Act for the internal evolution of the Authority to be completed. As late as the 1936 amendment empowering the TBA to build the Bronx-Whitestone Bridge, Moses still had not realized the full potential of the Authority. It was not until early 1937 that the Triborough's relationship with the private bond market matured sufficiently to afford the Authority the fiscal flexibility and political autonomy which ultimately would make it such a powerful agency.

The Triborough Bridge Authority was created originally as a solution to a specific problem. The city of New York had initiated the Triborough Bridge project in 1925.[25] By 1927, general plans had been drawn up and the Bureau of Estimate and Apportionment allocated 150,000 dollars for surveys and test borings. In 1929, New York City passed legislation designating the Triborough Bridge as a self-liquidating toll bridge to be financed by city corporate stock and revenue bonds. Three million dollars were appropriated for the project.[26] The groundbreaking ceremony for the bridge was held on October 25, 1929, the day after "Black Thursday," the day the stock market crashed.[27]

It soon became evident that the city would be unable to complete the project. With 5,380,377 dollars invested in the project, the city was forced to halt progress when, on March 23, 1933, local bankers informed Mayor O'Brien that they were "not willing or able to finance the Triborough Bridge."[28] With the city unable to sell bonds to raise funds for the project, another means of completing the bridge had to be found. One solution rested with federal funds becoming available for public works projects. In the same letter in which they denied financing, James J. Hoey, a principal in the underwriting firms of Hoey and Ellison and a member of the New York State Emergency Public Works Commission, advised the mayor that "this improvement [the Triborough Bridge] ought to be started and I am confident that the Reconstruction Finance Corporation will supply the money. . . ."[29] He recommended passing a law in the State legislature creating the Triborough Bridge Authority as a public benefit corporation specifically charged with the responsibility for completing the Triborough Bridge. The Authority would raise funds for the bridge by issuing bonds which would be purchased by the federal Reconstruction Finance Corporation (RFC).

Moses, as Chairman of the New York State Emergency Public Works Commission, was instrumental from the outset in the formation of the TBA, although he was not actually to become a member of the Authority until 1934. The day after fellow Commission member Hoey suggested the creation of the TBA, Moses outlined a detailed procedure to follow "in order to avoid future difficulties and to assure immediate progress on the Triborough Bridge."[30] The Emergency Public Works Commission assumed responsibility for the formation of the Authority, including its organizational design, the writing of the necessary legislation, lobbying for passage of the Triborough Bridge Act, and coordinating the implementation of the project at all levels of government.

From the beginning, intergovernmental cooperation was the key to the creation of the Authority and the successful completion of the Triborough Bridge project. According to New York State law, the State Legislature had to pass the necessary enabling legislation creating the TBA. The cooperation of the city was essential. Its Department of Plant and Structures had control over all the plans, maps, contracts and papers connected with the project which were necessary if the TBA was to assume responsibility for the building of the bridge. The federal government's support was required to finance the bridge since the city, and by implication the TBA, was effectively closed out of the private bond market. If the RFC refused to purchase Triborough bonds, the project would be no more feasible under the Authority's control than it had been under the city's.

The expanded role the TBA was to assume was not explicitly contemplated at the time of its formation. The original legislation drafted under the supervision of Moses and the Emergency Public Works Board provided for a three member public benefit corporation of limited duration. As the legislation read, "Said board and its corporate existence shall continue only for a period of five years and thereafter until all its liabilities have been met and its bonds have been paid in full."[31]

In spite of the fact that the TBA was conceived as a short-term corporate entity, the members of the Authority always were eager to establish its independence from the city. The city was seen as the major threat to the Authority's autonomy, especially since the Department of Plant and Structures, which had initiated the Triborough Bridge project four years earlier, had retained control over the project until the creation of the Authority. A great deal of discussion was devoted to clarifying the legal relationship between the TBA and the city of New York, including such issues as responsibility for land acquisition, for alignment and construction of the approaches to the bridge and even for the printing of TBA stationery.[32]

The relationship with the federal government was not perceived to be as problematic. The federal government was regarded merely as a source of funds, a "banker" who would purchase the 35 million dollars in bonds the TBA was authorized to issue. Moses commented in a draft of a letter to Albert Goldman, Commissioner of the Department of Plant and Structures, that the TBA "is a municipal corporation which must borrow from bankers on no security other than the bridge undertaking itself. It is immaterial whether the bankers are in Wall Street or in Washington."[33] The Reconstruction Finance Corporation, the federal agency which was the TBA's expected source of financing, encouraged this interpretation. It unequivocally represented itself as "a banking organization" more concerned with return on investment than with substantive issues of policy and control.[34]

It was in this context that the TBA sought federal financing. On May 26, 1933, George Gordon Battle, Chairman of the Triborough Bridge Authority, wrote Moses for assistance in applying to the RFC.[35] Moses had negotiated successfully with Jesse Jones, the head of the RFC, in the past, and Battle hoped Moses would be able to convince the RFC to fund the approaches to the Triborough in addition to the bridge itself.

While negotiations between the TBA and the RFC were underway, Congress passed the National Industrial Recovery Act (NIRA). Title II of the bill, "Public Works and Construction Projects," created the Federal Emergency Administration of Public Works to administer "a comprehensive program of public works." The Act included extensive provisions for "emergency construction of public highways." It also allowed the Administrator of the Public Works Administration to authorize grants of up to 30 percent of the cost of labor and materials on acceptable projects.[36]

Moses recognized the possibilities of the new Federal Emergency Public Works Administration, and recommended that the TBA apply to the new agency instead of the RFC for financing. In a memo dated May 29, 1933, he pointed to provisions of the act that made the TBA eligible for a grant of up to 30 percent of labor and material costs in addition to the loan. In addition, the provisions for highway aid could be used to supplement financing for the approaches to the bridge. "Under these circumstances," he stated, "it would be sheer folly to attempt to jam through an inadequate financing scheme for the Triborough Bridge under the expiring and inadequate public works powers of the R.F.C."[37]

With the 30 percent subsidy and the highway aid, more adequate approaches could be planned without raising tolls to cover the extra costs. Another provision in the NIRA enabled cities like New York to use these PWA funds to finance complementary projects, especially roads. It was feasible to design "a plan which will produce a completed bridge project properly integrated with streets, highways, and parkways."[38]

In less than a month, on June 21, 1933, the Triborough Bridge Authority filed an application with the Federal Emergency Administration of Public Works for a loan and grant.[39] By August 22, the application had been accepted and 44,200,000 dollars was budgeted for the Triborough Bridge, including 37 million dollars in Authority bonds to be purchased by the PWA and an estimated 7 million dollars minimum in a direct grant to subsidize 30 percent of the cost of labor and materials.

Moses still doubted the viability of the TBA without federal assistance. The young and unproven authority was merely the means for extending and unifying the parkway system. Moses was unsure whether a toll bridge could successfully compete against other bridges and bring in enough tolls to cover the expenses to retire the bonds, make the interest payments, and maintain the bridge. He also did not have much confidence in the members and employees of the Authority.[40] Although still not formally a member of the TBA, Moses played a very direct role in its activities. He drafted letters for Battle and loaned the assistance of his employees in the State and Long Island Parks Commissions. Battle, grateful for the support, reported to Moses "how much the members of the Authority and our Counsel appreciate the splendid assistance of yourself, Mr. Taylor, Mr. Andres, Mr. McNulty and your other Associates who have been of such inestimable help to us."[41]

The early days of the TBA only could have confirmed Moses' doubts. In the span of three months, the entire leadership of the Authority was overturned. Battle resigned at the end of November for health reasons,[42] and the other members of the board were forced out by newly elected Mayor Fiorello LaGuardia for political reasons stemming from charges of corruption.[43]

Nathan Burkan was appointed to the Board as Chairman and George McLaughlin filled one of the two remaining seats on the Board. On February 4, 1934, Robert Moses gained effective control of the Authority when he was appointed to the Board as Secretary and Chief Executive

Officer.[44] Moses, now directly responsible for the activities of the Authority, moved quickly "to get rid of the old staff and to engage reputable consultants."[45] He retained O.H. Ammann, then engineer of the Port of New York Authority, as part-time engineer and hired retired Army Brigadier General Paul Loeser as the Director of the Authority. The latter was a non-political, no-nonsense office manager, who, according to Moses, aggravated just about everyone he knew, but was as loyal as he was efficient. Moses previously had employed Loeser to reorganize the Long Island Parks Commission and now he would use him as part of his team to rebuild the TBA.

Moses considered the staff of the TBA to be incapable of "designing and completing an undertaking of this magnitude" and authorized Loeser to hire new men. Studies by Ammann confirmed Moses' fears. There was a 9 million dollar discrepancy between the cost of what was planned and the total funds available. There were also technical errors in the design of the bridge. The original plan called for two roadways each thirty-six feet wide to accommodate eight lanes of traffic. In actuality, only six lanes would fit in this space. The plan rather grandiosely provided that an upper deck be added, and the piers were designed to handle the extra load. Also, the entire bridge was to be faced with expensive granite.

In the interest of economy and efficiency, the new Triborough Bridge plan abandoned the granite facing and the second deck. The roadways were widened to forty-two feet in order to easily serve eight lanes of traffic. The money saved by these adjustments was used to improve the approaches, the access to Ward's and Randall's Island, and the toll collection facilities.[46] More extensive provisions for the park facilities were added, as well.

With these changes, the conception of the Triborough Bridge was altered. It was no longer simply a river crossing, but a "modern Metropolitan Traffic Artery" incorporating parks, parkways, and recreational facilities into the construction of the bridge itself. Under Moses' leadership, the Authority would emerge as a tool for coordinating and implementing a much larger agenda.

At the same time as internal reorganization of the Authority offered opportunities for coordination of disparate public projects, the Triborough's relations with the Public Works Administration threatened to impede these possibilities. No one associated with the Triborough had anticipated the magnitude of restrictions, rules, and regulations the PWA required. Harold Ickes, the Administrator of the Public Works Administration, was a meticulous and organized public official who sought to review and clear every aspect of expenditure of federal funds.

Sensitive to the historic legacy of graft which had accompanied past "pork barrel" public works projects, Ickes headed a PWA bureaucracy which demanded strict accounting of all expenses.

There was another source of difficulty between the TBA and PWA. As a result of a longstanding feud between President Roosevelt and Moses, the TBA became the target of a bitter attack. Roosevelt ordered Ickes to issue PWA Order No. 129, which stated that "no funds shall be advanced to any authority . . wholly within the confines of a municipality, any of the members of the governing body of which authority . . . holds any public office under said municipality." This order was a transparent effort to remove Moses, who was also City Parks Commissioner, from the head of the Triborough. Although the attempt failed, it left a legacy of TBA mistrust of the PWA.[47]

The officials of the TBA now realized that the real threat to their agential independence was not the financially destitute city of New York but the federal government. There were numerous federal controls over the Authority, including regulations governing the disbursement of revenues, construction contracts, labor conditions, and wages and the keeping of accounts and records, among others. All plans and expenditures of the Authority were subject to the approval of the Public Works Administration's Residential Project Engineer and Resident Project Auditor. The procedure for the requisitioning of money was exceptionally involved. Over twenty-two separate documents could be required before the government would approve a requisition.[48]

These restrictions became even more aggravating and confining when Moses sought to use the TBA as the agency through which to build a bridge linking the Bronx to Long Island. This Bronx-Whitestone bridge had been a part of his dream for a Belt Parkway system as early as 1930.[49] If the Triborough Act could be amended to include the construction of the new bridge, another section of this Belt Parkway would be in place. This amendment, however, could not be passed without the permission of the PWA.

On February 26, 1935, Moses received a memo from the Triborough Bridge Authority's counsel, Edward G. Griffin, forwarding a first draft of the amendment to the Triborough Bridge Act. Griffin discussed the difficulties he and Louis Delafield, Triborough bonding counsel, believed would arise in instituting the Whitestone Bridge project. Specifically, he doubted the PWA would allow the TBA to issue any new bonds to finance the new bridge.

It is unlikely that the federal government would consent to our making the obligations of the Whitestone Bridge a lien upon any earnings of the Triborough

Bridge. . . . Our Loan Agreement provides in Paragrah 22—"The Borrower agrees that so long as any of the bonds are outstanding . . . it will not issue any [additional] bonds or obligations."[50]

In the same memo, Griffin suggested that they simply ignore the provisions of the Loan Agreement for the time being. "When and if we issue Whitestone bonds," Griffin suggested, "we can ask the PWA for a waiver under paragraph 22 of the Loan Agreement." The PWA, however, was becoming increasingly difficult to deal with. Consequently, the enthusiasm for the Industrial Recovery Act's public works funding exhibited by the Authority in 1933 was replaced by resentment at what seemed to the TBA to be increasingly arbitrary and restrictive controls. Significantly, however, there was as yet no mention of refunding the original Triborough Bridge bonds. The discussion revolved around locating a suitable funding source for the new Bronx-Whitestone Bridge. The Triborough Bridge was an entirely separate project, and the Triborough Bridge bonds were to remain in the hands of the PWA.

Moses needed to evaluate the funding sources available. Assuming private financing to be unfeasible, he requested Loeser to compare the methods of the PWA and the RFC. On February 25, 1935, he received a copy of Ammann's analysis entitled "Triborough Bridge—Effect of Control of Project by P.W.A."[51] In this analysis, Ammann concluded that private financing clearly was preferable. Yet the conditions of the bond market still made private financing impossible. The federal government was the only reliable bond buyer available, and the RFC offered distinct advantages over the PWA. Instead of the complete and complicated control over all phases of the project demanded by the PWA, the RFC required only general financial oversight, occasional inspection of construction work and a monthly project report. At the same time, Ammann was highly critical of the PWA's "intricacy of procedure and the multitude of detailed influences" that led to extra costs and delay. In all, the PWA's regulations and strict supervision seriously hindered the TBA's potential for flexibility and autonomy.

Concurrent with Moses' evaluation of possible funding sources, a sharp internal debate emerged within the TBA over the form the new Whitestone Bridge Bonds should take. There were two points of view. Either the bonds for the Whitestone should be entirely independent of the Triborough issue, or they should be considered junior securities, claimable by Triborough Bridge bond holders. Griffin felt strongly that the bonds "issued for the building of the Triborough Bridge must be confined to the single project it [the TBA] was authorized to build and liquidate." The Whitestone Bridge bonds, therefore, had to be entirely distinct from the original Triborough bonds even though they were issued by the same public benefit corporation. "The tolls of the Whitestone," Griffin insisted, "shall be devoted exclusively to the retirement of Whitestone bonds."[52] In the same way, the revenue from the Triborough Bridge had to be applied solely to retiring the Triborough Bridge bonds. Delafield, on the other hand, was of the opinion that all revenues of the Authority, from whatever source, had been pledged to the holders of Triborough Bridge bonds. In a letter to Griffin, he claimed that "when the bonds were issued it was intended that the bonds should be general obligations of this particular corporation and not obligations payable only out of revenue in existence at the time they were issued. . . . Therefore revenues not then contemplated were included in the pledge for the security of the bondholders."[53] In effect, Whitestone bonds had to be junior to the original Triborough Bridge Bonds. They were still entirely separate issues, however, and not a refinancing of the Authority's assets.

Moses viewed Delafield's position as seditious. He felt that issuing the Whitestone bonds as second liens would be disastrous to their bond rating. The Triborough Bridge had not yet opened. Whether its toll revenues could actually cover debt service and operating expenses as yet was unproven. If the Whitestone Bridge bonds were made second liens on the revenues from the Triborough Bridge, investors in the Triborough Bridge bonds would have first lien on the Whitestone revenues in the event of default of either bridge. Moses felt this would make the Whitestone bonds impossible to sell, even to the federal government. "No Whitestone bonds could be sold under any such conditions," Moses argued, and "if the Washington lawyers press these points, the Triborough bonds also would be unsalable."[54] Moses' position was pragmatic. For the Whitestone bonds to be marketable, particularly on the private market, they had to be safe and very secure. According to Moses, "the amendment to the [Triborough] law authorizing the Whitestone Bridge set it up as an entirely independent financial entity, placed under the Triborough Authority for convenience and economy in administration only."[55]

In one sense, Griffin's interpretation limited the Authority's internal flexibility in that it specified the way in which toll revenues had to be allocated. But more important was the fact that an authority, originally created for a single purpose, now was given control over two distinct revenue-producing projects. Griffin recognized that this changed the nature of the Authority. "The Authority," he indicated, "will not then be [after the Whitestone amendment is passed] an authority, board or commission constituting an independent corporation or entity *created for a specific project.*"[56]

During negotiations with the RFC for the sale of Whitestone bonds, the PWA sold some of its Triborough Bridge bonds to the RFC. To the federal government, this transaction was routine. The members of the TBA, already suspicious of the PWA and concerned about the Whitestone Bond issue, were alarmed. The TBA's concern was magnified by the fact that its discovery of the sale was accidental.

The Authority hurriedly sought legal counsel on the matter.[57] The loan agreement between the TBA and the PWA was a contract between the Authority and the United States Government. It was uncertain whether it applied to the Reconstruction Finance Corporation as an instrumentality of the federal government. Even if this were legally the case, evidence suggested that the RFC would contest such an interpretation since that corporation considered itself distinct from the federal bureaucracy. The TBA's rights under the terms of the loan agreement were thrown into question. The most critical issue arising from this ambiguity concerned the Triborough's right to recapture its bonds under Paragraph 22 of the loan agreement. This was an important issue because the Authority was considering selling its bonds on the private market.[58] If the RFC refused to honor the loan agreement, the TBA could be prevented from repurchasing the bonds the Corporation held for resale on the private bond market.

These developments put the TBA in a more tenuous situation. The negotiation of a bond sale is always complex, even under the best of conditions. The ambiguities and uncertainties seriously jeopardized the sale of the Whitestone bonds. Moses commented,

We are not in a position to make an agreement [with the private underwriters] independently of the federal authorities. We still have to deal with the PWA—at least until the construction is done and the full grant [on the Triborough Bridge] has been paid. Then we must deal with the RFC and the sale of bonds must be by negotiation.[59]

Given such a fragile political environment, Moses and his staff were more committed than ever to presenting a conservative and non-controversial alteration of the State Act authorizing the Triborough's management of both bridge projects. In the 1936 amendment to the Triborough Bridge Act, the Whitestone and the Triborough projects were explicitly kept separate.[60] For example, in the paragraph specifying the amount of bonds authorized for the project, two distinct bond issues were identified. Thirty-five million dollars was authorized for the Triborough Bridge and 15 million dollars for the Whitestone.

Every mention of either bridge project very carefully distinguished between them. The clause discussing the termination of the Authority stated that once the Triborough's bonds had been paid in full and the liabilities of the Authority incurred in connection with the Triborough Bridge had been met, then that Bridge would pass to the city of New York. The statement was repeated for the case of the Whitestone Bridge. The implication was that the projects would pass to the city separately once their respective bonds and liabilities no longer existed. If it were necessary for a receiver to take possession of one bridge because of default, the TBA would retain control of the other bridge.

Soon after the passage of the May, 1936, amendment authorizing the separate financing of both bridges, the staff of the TBA set about designing yet another amendment which would provide a significantly different and unprecedented change in this fiscal practice. Spurred, apparently, by the surprising success of the Triborough Bridge, which generated, from its opening in 1936, substantially more revenues than Moses or any other official had anticipated, the TBA began to consider seriously recapitalizing these highly collateralized bonds. A strategy was evolving to refinance the Triborough and Whitestone bonds, consolidating them in one bond issue covering both bridges. In so doing, the recapitalized Triborough bonds would give the Authority a new and expanded source of revenues. Although refinancing put the Authority deeper in debt, this was to its advantage. Once the TBA no longer held any liabilities, it would cease to exist. At the rate that the Triborough Bridge was generating revenue, this could mean a short life for the Authority.[61] Refinancing, therefore, not only provided the Authority with extra capital, it prolonged its corporate existence!

The process for accomplishing the full import of this amendment was as complex as it was revolutionary. Not only did Moses and the Triborough need to convince the legislature to pass a new amendment within months of the Bronx-Whitestone amendment, but they also had to convince the major holder of Triborough Bridge bonds, the RFC, of the logic of this refinancing strategy. In essence, gaining the acceptance of both the legislature and the RFC for this amendment was tantamount to asking the legislature to give up political control and the RFC to surrender fiscal control of the Authority.

For the TBA, therefore, there was much at stake. The Authority could escape nettlesome government regulations and, more importantly, it could totally restructure its financing mechanisms. No longer dependent on government support, the Authority would have greater autonomy over when and how to access its funds because of its relationship with the private money market, as well as how and where to spend these monies. While the benefits of such a strategy were considerable, the risks also were apparent. Therefore, alternative strategies were considered, including selling all 50 million dollars of bonds on the private market or selling only the 15 million dollar Whitestone issue to private investors.[62]

The first written evidence of Moses' intention to carry forward with the refinancing plan appears in an undated draft of a letter from Moses to Jesse Jones of the RFC. Moses couched his arguments in conservative bankers terminology. While this proposal would revolutionize the nature of the public authority, Moses presented it as the most rational response to the current situation.

It is obvious . . . that the sensible thing to do is ultimately to have one bond covering both structures, and have the revenues pooled to meet the common obligation. . . . It is assumed that the R.F.C. plans to dispose of its holdings in bonds of municipalities and municipal corporations at the earliest convenient time, and as nearly as possible on the basis of one hundred cents on the dollar. It seems to us that all interests will be best served by a new issue sold to private investors covering both structures, and we are sure that by this means the federal authorities can recapture their entire loan.[63]

Negotiations with private underwriters emphasized the need to convince Jones to agree to the refinancing plan. The private market was only able to absorb between 25 and 27 million dollars in bonds. The TBA wanted to refund the 35 million dollars of Triborough Bridge bonds held by the RFC and issue an additional 15 million dollars of Whitestone Bridge bonds. This left a 23 million dollar discrepancy between what the market would absorb and what the TBA wished to sell. Even if the refinancing amendment were to pass, the TBA would need the RFC to retain possession of 23 million dollars of Triborough bonds, at least until the market could absorb another installment of bonds.[64]

Moses had little confidence Jones would agree to the deal. In an effort to convince Jones, Moses wrote that "the Triborough will gain enormously by being pooled with the new structure if we can work out such an agreement with you." In the same letter, Moses, emphasizing the advantages to the RFC of this arrangement, pointed out that "twenty-five million of the new [Triborough Bridge] bonds in your possession . . . could be sold later at a substantial premium when the first issue is absorbed."[65]

249

The refinancing amendment passed the State legislature in January of 1937.[66] Of all the amendments to the Triborough Act this one was the most important. Although the Act still provided for the dissolution of the Authority and the passage of its holdings to the city of New York, this amendment made the provision meaningless.

When all liabilities incurred by the authority *of every kind and character* have been met and all its bonds have been paid in full . . . all rights and properties of the authority shall pass to the City of New York. The authority shall retain *full* jurisdiction and control over *all* its projects, with the right and duty to charge tolls and collect revenues therefrom, for the benefit of the holders of *any* of its bonds or other liabilities *even if not issued or incurred in connection with the project.*[67]

So long as the Authority continued to issue bonds, it would retain full jurisdiction over all its projects. This represented a substantial change from all earlier versions of the act. Even in the 1936 amendment authorizing the Whitestone, it had been clear that the holdings of the Authority were eventually to pass to the city.

The amendment also removed all distinctions between the revenues of the two projects.

All tolls and other revenues derived from either project shall be applied to the . . . payment of interest or principle of bonds . . . whether issued in connection with such project or any other project . . . surplus funds from either project remaining after providing for all contract provisions with respect to any bonds, shall be used to meet obligations incurred for the other project.[68]

But the most significant alteration of the Act was Subdivision 9, "Bonds of the Authority." Under this paragraph, the TBA was given the power to issue bonds for *any corporate purpose.* The authorized bonded indebtedness limit was raised 3 million dollars to a total of 53 million dollars. Most importantly, the paragraph stated that "the Authority shall have power from time to time to refund any bonds by the issuance of new bonds, whether the bonds to be refunded have or have not matured, and may issue bonds partly to refund bonds then outstanding and partly *for any other corporate purposes.*"[69] With this clause, the TBA was given the right to issue bonds when it chose, affording the Authority a perpetual source of funds. Further, the TBA could refund bonds for any corporate purpose whatever, giving the Authority financial and operational autonomy. Any project consistent with its general mandate of enhancing its Triborough and Whitestone projects could be planned and paid for by issuing new securities.

Finally, to insure Triborough autonomy from legislative interference, the amendment provided that all the powers given to the TBA in this amendment would be contained in any and all bonds. Tolls and revenues of both projects were pledged to secure the payment of the bonds "or of any issue of the bonds." Since bond resolutions were considered to be contracts between the Authority and its bond holders, representative government had no right to impair these resolutions.[70] In short, the only parties who could not revoke the powers of the Authority were the Authority itself or the bondholders. The legislature had, with the passage of this amendment, foreclosed on the issue of future city or State oversight.

The municipal bond market improved considerably after a January 1937 Treasury Department ruling which granted tax-exempt status to the bonds of municipal corporations. Moses' bankers indicated that the market could absorb the entire 53 million dollar issue, which included 18 million dollars for the Whitestone and 35 million dollars to refund the outstanding Triborough Bridge bonds held by the RFC.[71]

Moses wanted to move quickly while market conditions were favorable. He sent notice to Jones that the TBA wished to repurchase its bonds under Section 23 of the 1933 Loan Agreement. On February 3, 1937, Moses requested a firm offer from Dillon Read and Company, the major bond underwriting firm, which he needed to negotiate the repurchase of the bonds held by the RFC. Moses wrote that he "had several unfortunate experiences in the past, as a public official, in prolonged negotiation, leading finally to an absurd offer which necessitated starting over again. . . . It will be necessary for us to receive a definitive offer from you by the end of the week."[72]

The underwriters, while definitely interested, were unwilling to make a firm commitment until a specific ruling on the tax-exempt status of the TBA bonds was made. Jones also stalled, disputing which bonds the RFC would purchase and the price and yield of those bonds. He also urged PWA financing for the new bridge. Moses adamantly refused to have anything to do with the PWA, "not only because of the rules and regulations governing P.W.A. contracts which are wholly unfavorable to efficient and economic work, but also because of our past relations with this organization."[73] Moses stressed that he had no such objections to the RFC, and "repeatedly stated [that] we have had no . . . trouble on any of the State authority projects financed by the R.F.C. and that if this were a question of dealing with you [the RFC] . . . the situation would be entirely different."[74]

Market conditions continued to improve in the Spring of 1937 and Moses was anxious to close the deal. On April 16, Moses wrote to

Jones with a firm offer. Twenty-five million dollars of bonds would be sold by the underwriting group led by Dillan Read and Company on the private bond market, 7 million dollars of which would be to retire Triborough Bridge bonds held by the RFC and 18 million dollars for the Whitestone project. The TBA would pay the RFC a total of 7,210,000 dollars for the 7 million dollars in bonds held by the RFC. The RFC would agree not to sell the remaining 28 million dollars in bonds that it held for 90 days, or for 30 days after the bonds being marketed by the underwriting group had been sold, whichever was earlier.[75]

On April 20, 1937, a letter of agreement was signed by the TBA and the RFC. The TBA board passed a resolution covering the new bond issue on April 23, and the exchange was made on April 27. Thirty-five million dollars in Sinking Fund Revenue bonds and 18 million dollars in Serial Revenue Bonds were issued. Twenty-five million in bonds was sold on the private market through the underwriters. The RFC received 28 million dollars in bonds in exchange for the outstanding Triborough Bridge bonds they held.

By the first week in May, the underwriters had sold the 25 million dollars in bonds on the private market, and announced their sales were closed.[76] On August 2, the TBA received notice from their bond counsel, Hawkins, Delafield and Longfellow, that the RFC had sold the 28 million dollars in Triborough bonds it held to Dillon Read and Company. With this transaction, the TBA was finally free from federal involvement, and had established the close relationship with the private bond market which exists to this day.

This completed the process of transforming the TBA from a single project authority dependent upon government financing to a multipurpose agency with an independent source of revenues and capital funds. The Authority was now able to sell *general* revenue bonds secured against income from any Authority asset rather than bonds secured against a *specific* project. This gave the Authority considerable latitude in planning and executing projects in the future since the revenue from financially successful projects could be used to subsidize new or marginal projects.

CONCLUSION

The period of the Authority's birth and early development, which has been the focus of this essay, provides us with new insight into both the power and effectiveness of the Authority and the decision-making process of its chief architect, Robert Moses. The evidence found in the TBTA papers presents a somewhat different Robert Moses than the one described in other studies. While there is no doubt that Moses was at the center of the process wherein the Authority was created, neither he nor any of those around him were prescient enough at the outset to see how powerful and effective the independent authority could become. The picture that emerges from our study is one of expedient incrementalism with Moses and his contemporaries drafting and redrafting laws, and forming political strategies and intergovernmental alliances to pragmatically fit the exigencies of the moment as they strove to build the Triborough Bridge.

At first, Moses saw the authority concept as a means whereby the Triborough Bridge could be financed through the PWA. The independence of the authority was not viewed as an ideological necessity so much as a way to keep the project financially free of the fiscally burdened city. All the while, the TBA was considered to be no more than a single purpose agency, designed to go out of business once the Triborough Bridge was completed.

Later, Moses began to see the value of using authority-based bonds to fund other projects, namely the Bronx-Whitestone Bridge, and he used the TBA as the funding instrument for this project. There was still no clear evidence that Moses favored creating the TBA as a permanent agency of public works. Rather, he argued vehemently that the bonds for each project would be tied to each bridge and retired separately, thus leading to the ultimate dissolution of the Authority.

In late 1936, the financial success of the Triborough Bridge was evident, giving the Authority a stable source of revenues. At the same time the increasing political interference of governmental actors, especially those in the PWA, led Moses to question the dependencies that had developed. This seemed to have been enough to push Moses to initiate state laws which would result ultimately in the effective corporate and political independence of the Authority.

This transformation of the nature of the TBA was an incremental process. While Moses saw the value of the public authority as an agential tool for building public infrastructure, he did not realize its full potential until 1936 when he began the process of achieving consolidated bond financing for the TBA. This fact, however, does not diminish the significance of its contribution, as evidenced by the fact that the TBA evolved into the institution Moses used to realize his transportation plans for the New York–New Jersey Region. Over the next three decades, the TBA was consolidated with four other New York City authorities, giving the renamed Triborough Bridge and

Tunnel Authority (TBTA) a greatly expanded financial base and expanded control over major public works projects.[77] By the mid 1960s, the TBTA was responsible for capital expenditures of over one-half billion dollars for the construction and operation of nine bridges.[78] The agency also was involved in the building of numerous expressways, parkways and other municipal projects. All of this amounted to a legacy which placed the TBTA at the center of the process of urban development in the New York City area.[79]

The importance of understanding the role of the public authority as a tool for public infrastructure development is underscored by the 1975 Temporary State Commission Report on state and local financing in New York which argued that if public authorities "are to proliferate, then they will undoubtedly increasingly affect the citizens of the State; and if they affect the citizenry, there should be an increased understanding of their presence."[80]

The alarm sounded by the Commission, by any stretch of the imagination, comes too late. What Robert Moses learned by trial and error in the 1930s has long been a fact of public policy life. In the present era of fiscal as well as infrastructural decline, the public authority remains a singularly important agency for generating investment capital and developing and managing public works. Nationwide, there are over "six thousand local and regional authorities and one thousand state and interstate authorities" with expenditures of "more than 14 billion dollars per year on operations, including interest payments, and some 10 billion dollars per year in new capital facilities."[81]

In New York State, as we indicated earlier, the authorities of the State now have a combined indebtedness which is nearly seven times that of the State itself. This increased dependence upon the authority for the building of public works under conditions of growing debt and growing demand for new and renewed public works raises a very real issue. Are public authorities so functionally overburdened and financially impacted that they are no longer a politically viable or financially attractive agency for new public works policy? Indeed, heightened dependency on the public authority to meet the need for refurbishing existing infrastructure as well as the construction of new public works may well force fiscal crisis in a heretofore unexpected arena—the public authorities themselves. If this is the case, we cannot assume that the public authority can be expected to bear the full weight of policy making, financing and execution.

Now, as in the 1930s, there is no prescient seer who has designed a new instrument of public works policy. If Moses' experience with the TBA provides a history which can inform the future, the most important lessons lie not with a replication of Moses' past policies but with the initiation of a new round of political-economic pragmatism. The success of "Moses the pragmatist," not "Moses the omniscient power broker," is most instructive for those prepared to design and utilize innovative institutions of governance to address the problems of public infrastructure.

ELEVEN

The Center for Industrial Innovation at RPI:

Critical Reflections on New York's Economic Recovery

Michael Black and Richard Worthington

It is certainly true that many contemporary problems stem from past technological successes. The ubiquitous phenomenon of technology now reaches into the deepest interiors of our lives, affecting our physical, social, and political environments. Responses to the social significance of technology have ranged from technocratic and politically moderate undertakings such as technology assessment to radical critiques grounded in an assessment of the Western scientific mode of thought.[1] Notwithstanding the costs of past technological successes, current technology policy discussions are dominated by a concern for the "Reindustrialization of America." Implicit within the notion of reindustrialization is a nascent technological optimism that largely ignores social assessments of technology, whether moderate or radical. Instead, technology is largely assumed in such discussions to be the key factor in resolving current economic and political dilemmas.

A fruitful avenue for understanding these developments is suggested by Murray Edelman's work on the role of symbols in politics.[2] In this case the symbol is clean, productive, high technology. Its role for elites and citizens alike is a diffuse promise for good times to come. We pursue this study with concern about the use of this symbol and its bearing on our reindustrialization strategy. Several decisive issues underlie our effort. Is the high-technology symbol laden with possibilities for myopia and self-delusion? How may we debate the merits of the technological and social paths which lie ahead? How may we best anticipate the effects of rapid reindustrialization? Is there a role for enlightened social intervention in achieving desirable values and goals while minimizing unwanted consequences?

To confront these issues in an attempt to understand the technological dimensions of the reindustrialization debate we have selected a case study. The Center for Industrial Innovation (CII) at Rensselaer Polytechnic Institute is a crucial element of New York State's high-technology strategy. We intend to examine the process by which CII came into existence while assessing its likely contributions and shortcomings. In the latter sections of the paper we will examine the symbolic role of high technology in the politics of reindustrialization and comment on technology policy in New York State in light of this discussion.

ATARI DEMOCRACY

In a recent influential contribution to the current discussion on reindustrialization, Ira Magaziner and Robert Reich map out two broad approaches to economic development and their implications for technology policy.[3] Although divergent in strategy and scope, the two approaches also have basic similarities. After highlighting the authors' rendering of the "supply side" strategy for economic recovery we will consider their discussion of a more interventionist counterpart which political observers have associated with "Atari Democrats," Democrats who see a key role for high technology in economic recovery.

The supply-side model of economic health stresses unrestrained capital accumulation. Technology is a *result* of capital agglomeration. Jobs accrue in direct proportion to the success with which entrepreneurs are able to achieve their ends. Business is insulated as effectively as possible from regulatory interference in the private marketplace although supportive governmental policies, such as military contracts or sponsorship of research and development, are welcome. This growth strategy is liberal in ideology and elite-dominated and technocratic in practice. Social policy emerges through corporate default when the unaddressed consequences of growth cause sufficient disruptions for society to demand restitution.

Atari Democracy resembles the supply-side perspective in an interesting way. It, too, stresses direct accumulation while jobs are the secondary consequence of technological growth. But within this model technology assumes greater significance as a tool of economic policy. The overall strategy is, like its Republican counterpart, trickle-down in nature, with the important proviso that the state must rationally intervene to guide and stimulate growth within the private sector. Even though social policy is a more explicit concern for Atari Democrats, it arises within the context of an elite-dominated technocratic order. Phrases like "production enhancement" are leavened by assurances about jobs and unions being important to economic and political policy. This model—as far as labor goes—is basically conciliatory in nature, taking into account the likely externalities produced by the growth process and then trying to lessen their negative impacts. The greater significance of social welfare in this model is indicated by the fact that an early chapter in the Reich and Magaziner book is devoted entirely to demonstrating that, compared to the United States, the superior social welfare performance of Western Europe and Japan helps explain their superior productivity performance in recent years.[4] But this concern for redistribution is not allowed to interfere with an implicit pattern of transnational, class-based economic planning.

These two models share the objective of growth through accumulation and the belief that high technology is an important means for attaining it. Both models presuppose existing patterns of elite domination in the political economy. As a consequence, policy becomes the exclusive domain of specialists, representing the necessary balance between inputs and outputs for the attainment of instrumental ends. In both models, public discussion and debate are counterproductive as the political domain resembles an arena of instrumentalities divorced from a critical evaluation of policy alternatives. We will return to this theme of instrumental politics after examining the policy process and analytical rationale which lead to the formation of CII.

THE CENTER FOR INDUSTRIAL INNOVATION

The issue of economic stagnation in America and what to do about it has been a principal policy concern not only at the national level, but at the regional, state, and local levels as well. "Sunbelt vs. Snowbelt," the "Second War Between the States," and other slogans have emerged in recent years as symbolic indicators of the conflict among geographically designated economies. This conflict arose within the context of stagnation. Several important political decision makers in New York have identified increased productivity through technological innovation as a key both to national economic recovery and to renewed growth and competitiveness within the State. According to a contract study undertaken by Battelle-Columbus Laboratories for the New York State Science and Technology Foundation, New York is well-situated to compete with other states in high-technology industries because many already are located here.[5] The State is well-integrated into markets for and suppliers of high-technology industries. An outstanding educational infrastructure exists, firms in the State have good access to financial services since New York City is the financial center of the country, and the labor force is highly and diversely skilled.[6]

In the late 1970s, policy planners in the governor's office and in the office of Assembly Speaker Stanley Fink began to look systematically at state policy on technology and economic development. The first results of these efforts were seven bills passed by the legislature and signed into law in 1981. These bills included tax credits for high technology investments and the reorganization of the Science and Technology Foundation, which in recent years virtually had been inactive. They also included measures which might be considered "enabling legislation" in the sense that they made possible or enhanced subsequent legislation directed toward the same policy goals.

One milestone of the State's efforts in technology policy was the passage in 1982 of a bill to incur 30 million dollars in bonded indebtedness for loans to assist in the creation of a Center for Industrial Innovation (CII) at RPI. At the same time, the legislature allocated 5 million dollars for the creation of Centers for Advanced Technology (CATs) at five locations around the State to be determined by a process of competitive proposals. We will examine the provisions of and rationale for the CII bill, the planning contexts in the universities, state government, and corporations out of which it grew, its legislative history, and its significance in light of these factors.

The basic rationale provided for CII from its earliest planning stages to final legislation consisted of several essential points. The business argument in favor of the Center is that research and development plays a key role in the development of new products and processes that will increase the productivity and competitiveness of enterprises within the State. The educational argument is that students and faculty will benefit from access to the research and development environment, and that their experience will benefit the economy by supplying highly skilled personnel. Finally, "the rapid expansion of employment opportunities" in the industries benefitting through CII was cited consistently as a justification for it.[7] Intimately related to these claims for CII are those factors, already noted, which make New York an appropriate choice for a high-technology path to economic recovery.[8] Finally, there was a contestable finding by the legislature that RPI was sufficiently in the lead in key program areas to make it the best location for CII. Yet, regardless of sections in the CII legislation asserting the virtues of educational-industrial-government partnerships, it is interesting to note that none of CII's advocates provided direct arguments explaining why existing market mechanisms and corporate-university linkages are unable to generate technological growth adequate to the needs of industry. In our estimation, in high-technology areas existing arrangements are adequate, but the temptation of socialized costs and more direct control over university-based research are strong attractions for the corporate sector.

The provisions of the legislation can be divided into those which concern its financing and those pertaining to the Center's functions. The financing provisions call upon the State's Urban Development Corporation to let 30 million dollars in bonds and lend the proceeds to RPI for construction of a facility against which the State will have a lien. When the Center is completed, the State will lease it from RPI and lease it back for 600,000 dollars per year until the principal is retired. The State will pay the interest, while RPI is obligated to pay the remaining cost of equipping the Center, estimated to be 35 million dollars.

The provisions stipulate three basic program areas for CII, microelectronics, manufacturing productivity, and interactive computer graphics, as well as the development of programs to involve other educational institutions, technical assistance to small businesses, and continuing educational programs. Both financing and program plans are subject to approval by the State Budget Director and must be filed with the Senate Finance and the Assembly Ways and Means Committees.

The process by which CII came into existence perhaps is more illuminating for technology policy and economic recovery. The idea for New York State subsidized industrial research centers at university locations first emerged from an economic planning group (the High Technology Opportunities Task Force, created in August 1978) in Governor Hugh Carey's office. As the Task Force's title and location indicate, the assumptions motivating the governor were that high technology presented opportunities for economic initiatives and that State policy could favorably affect these opportunities.[9] While policy ideas began to issue from the executive branch, another group was formed in the Program Office of State Assembly Speaker Stanley Fink to coordinate technology policy. As of late 1981 the major legislative proposal to come out of these planning processes, aside from the seven bills passed in 1981, was for a program to establish the Centers for Advanced Technology. The CATs concept had been an item of discussion in the Governor's office since 1978 but had required more development and political support than provided by the 1981 bills.

At the same time that State policy was developing in these areas, RPI was making strides in the area of applied industrial research. Under the new presidency of George Low, an RPI graduate who had risen to prominence as manager of NASA's Apollo program, new life was breathed into the oldest technological university in the country. With substantial assistance from corporate sources, Centers for Interactive Computer Graphics, Manufacturing Productivity, and Integrated Electronics had been established at RPI under Low's leadership. Concurrently, a portion of the Institute's endowment was allocated for the development of a Technology Park on Institute property in neighboring North Greenbush. The idea here was that RPI would invest in the development of infrastructure (roads, sewers, etc.) on a 400-acre site, and rent space to high-technology firms for research and development or light manufacturing facilities that would benefit from proximity to one another and to RPI's highly trained faculty and students. A final project undertaken by RPI during this period was to provide incubator space for small, new high-technology firms needing space and an environment in which to turn promising ideas into commercially viable enterprises.

For the most part the activities in the State government and those at RPI evolved without formal linkages, although Governor Carey's positive image of the RPI efforts was symbolized by his planned attendance at the Rensselaer Technology Park groundbreaking ceremonies in September, 1981. These separate-but-parallel trajectories converged on November 16, 1981, when Low and the chief executive officers of four major global corporations met with Governor Carey and members of his staff in Albany. (The four corporate heads were Walter A. Fallon of Eastman-Kodak, John R. Opel of International Business Machines, George A. Strichman of Colt Industries, and John F. Welch, Jr., of General Electric. Strichman is also chair of the RPI Board of Trustees.) At the meeting, Low and his colleagues proposed CII to Governor Carey who, according to aides and legislative observers, became an enthusiastic partisan and included it in his *State of the State Message* and budget for 1982.

A number of factors seem to have combined to make Carey such an enthusiastic and dedicated lobbyist for what was a relatively small item in a 30 billion dollar budget. First, the RPI proposal differed from the CATs program. CII overtook CATs as the cornerstone of the governor's policy planning because it specified a location, was of larger scale, was based on three programs that were already in place, and had garnered pledges of corporate support in the amount of 10 million dollars. Second, according to a Carey aide present at the meeting, the governor was impressed by Low's ability to bring together such a prestigious cast from the corporate sector for the meeting. In comparison to the atmosphere of crisis in which Governor Carey had dealt with corporate leadership throughout his political career, the opportunity to work cooperatively with the corporations toward goals for which he had a strong preference understandably was attractive. Finally, Carey was entering his last year in office. It is likely that he believed it important not to pass up an opportunity to move aggressively in an area about which he felt strongly, particularly when he could not rely on similar support for the project from a possible successor.

Given the appeal of high technology in American culture, the close fit between the CII proposal and State policy planning, the prestigious and financially significant corporate backing it enjoyed, and the enthusiastic support of a governor entering his last legislative session, it is not surprising that the CII bill moved through the legislature with relative ease. Indeed, it is not an exaggeration to say that there was no debate concerning the bill on either the Senate or Assembly floors, and committee and staff work in both houses was minimal. Nonetheless, there was negotiation among the offices of the leaders of the legislature, the governor, and RPI, the principal items of which are important to our case study.

In the office of Assembly Speaker Stanley Fink (a Democrat from Brooklyn), program planning on technology policy had been underway since 1979 and was crucial in the passage of the 1981 bills. When first presented with the CII proposal by Low and representatives from the governor's office in early 1982, Fink's response was favorable on the particulars, but he told them he wanted to see a more comprehensive plan on the role of technology in the State's economic development. When a reply from the governor's office to Fink was provided shortly thereafter, the remaining items of negotiation were sections of the legislation itself.[10] The principal inputs from Fink's office became the sections of the legislation requiring CII linkages with other colleges and universities in the State, educational and technical services outreach to smaller enterprises located throughout the State, and a detailed plan from RPI to be approved by the State Budget Director showing how the financing and program provisions of the legislation were to be met. Fink also required Low and his subordinates to present evidence justifying the location of CII at RPI before giving his full support to the bill.

In the other legislative chamber, Senate Majority Leader Warren Anderson (a Republican from Binghamton) went along with the CII bill, although less enthusiastically. Furthermore, Anderson maintained his opposition to the CATs bill until the last day of the session. On that day a conservative Democratic Assemblyman managed to penetrate the defense perimeter of Anderson's legislative aides and, in a personal meeting, persuaded him to vote for the bill.

Anderson and his staff had a number of objections which applied to both the CATs and CII bills. One objection was that there should be more detailed planning of precisely what educational and technical services were required by which businesses in various localities *prior* to allocating State funds. Related to this was a sense that inadequate staff work was being accorded these issues. Finally, one legislative aide we interviewed wondered why the Democrats were in such a rush to establish CATs and CII if State technology policy was of the central and enduring importance to economic development that its proponents were claiming it to be.

The financing provisions of the CII bill were probably the most controversial aspect from the Republican side. Under the lease-back arrangement described earlier, the State essentially becomes dependent on unproven revenues from CII to pay off the bonds without having a piece of property that can readily be used for other purposes should CII fail. Also, since none of the bonding authorities available to the State was clearly the most appropriate for this new type of venture, political friction inevitably arose over whether the Republican controlled Dormitory Authority or the Democrat controlled Urban Development Corporation should be used (the Democrats won).

Other political actors hardly became involved in the CII legislation. The State University of New York system (the largest university system in the world) might have been expected to present a formidable barrier to the allocation of State funds for establishment of a research center at a private university. It appears to have been taken by storm. Its involvement was limited to a resolution by the system's Faculty Senate protesting the CII bill. The private universities in the State seem to have been persuaded that they had more to gain from a united front for continued state subsidies, an expectation unambiguously stated by Cornell President Frank H. T. Rhodes in his speech at the CII convocation in October of 1982. Organized labor might also have been expected to influence legislation of significance to the economy in general and employment in particular. It was not heard from, however, until the bill reached the Assembly floor, and then only to argue for letting separate contracts on CII construction.

One very clear conclusion that can be drawn from an examination of CII's legislative history is that very little effort was put into establishing the validity of the basic arguments for the bill. Most of the conflict over it, in fact, pertained to its details rather than essential objectives. As we note in the next section, the major independent study on the high-technology path for New York State, the Battelle study, makes a much better case for the business rationale than for the employment and educational claims. Given the strong influence of the corporate sector in bringing CII into existence, the focus of a critical examination of CII and the high-technology path to economic development becomes apparent.

HIGH TECHNOLOGY AND ECONOMIC POLICY

At this point it will be useful to look closely at the arguments made for CII in light of the high-technology economic development strategy of which it is a key part. The purpose of this analysis will be to determine whether or not this strategy has positive employment and other public welfare benefits that would make it appealing to the public at large. Another public benefit claimed for CII and CATs, for example, is that of educational and research opportunities. But there is good reason to believe that these did not appear to be significant considerations for the key decision makers. It may be that the principal beneficiaries of the strategy are indeed a relatively small number of large corporations, such as those headed by the four CEO's who accompanied Mr. Low to Governor Carey's office in November of 1981, and whose agendas are the ones most clearly served by the high-technology strategy. To the extent that there are public benefits, and there unquestionably are, they trickle down through the matrix of needs of the global corporations.

Education

Viewed from an academic perspective, the most controversial aspect of CII is whether or not the increased integration of educational institutions with industry impairs the open and creative pursuit of knowledge that is the principal purpose of the university.[11] Although there is nothing new in industrial-university linkages, CII certainly gives the linkage a more programmatic character than is the case under arrangements of contract research with individual faculty members or departments. And the presence of profit-making enterprises on campus under the incubator program is a new step in industrial-university linkage.

Yet the substantive educational issues involved in the formation of such linkages in New York State were never more than a secondary concern of the principal organizations involved. In the legislature, neither the Assembly nor the Senate referred the CII bill to committees which have a responsibility for State educational policy. In the governor's office, the volume of documentation dealing with the educational features of CII and CATs was minimal, especially by comparison to documentation of the economic dimensions of the bills. One principal actor in the governor's office told us that the various "findings" of the legislature concerning the educational virtues of CII were included in the legislation strictly to protect RPI's tax exempt status, which might otherwise be called into question by its entry into the business of industrial research. At RPI, the principal long-term planning document (*Rensselaer 2000*, published in 1977) briefly suggested the concept of a technology park. While a committee including faculty members was formed by the administration in 1979 to examine the implications of the technology park idea, and Mr. Low gave the elected Faculty Council a report on the outlines of the project in September of 1979, the faculty never initiated a sustained, autonomous review of the project concept from the standpoint of educational goals. The faculty was first informed of the CII project in February 1982, and again it made no effort to examine the project from its position as guardian of academic values. Finally, the volume of the Battelle report examining higher education in relation to the development of New York's high-technology industry does so entirely from the perspective of business needs.

To recognize this is not to conclude that traditional academic values of autonomy are impaired by CII. It does mean that this new organizational venture was entered into with no serious examination of the issue. In particular, the RPI faculty, who were most directly connected with this issue, have done virtually nothing. If faculty are clear in their commitment to educational goals, one would expect at least that the elected Faculty Council would appoint a committee to investigate and report on the details of the Institute's responsibilities to the State. Nothing resembling such action has occurred. Since other actors are motivated principally by business rather than educational goals, it is not surprising that they have taken a business perspective. However, even if CII and CATs are compatible with academic values, there remains the issue that many of the Centers are located at private institutions accessible mostly to elite groupings rather than at public universities which also are accessible to the taxpayers and students who subsidize these high-technology programs. These issues no doubt will receive greater attention as both CII and CATs bills move from legislation to implementation. It is important to note, though, that the fundamental decisions concerning how industry and the universities are to interact with regard to high-technology research already have been made.

Employment

One of the most critical dimensions of the reindustrialization debate is the issue of job creation. Work as an intrinsically rewarding and meaningful social activity is also a key indicator of the relative health of society. In creating CII, jobs were of secondary importance to the primary goal of economic growth. Little attention was paid to qualitative or quantitative aspects of employment. This may well be a significant oversight.

In assessing the historical shift from a goods economy characterized by industrial production to the service-and-information society, several indicators stand out. One study examining income distribution in the traditional industrial society found 34 percent of the available industrial jobs offering subsistence pay, 40 percent in middle income earnings, and 26 percent in the highest pay brackets. By sharp contrast, the service-and-information economy offers subsistence wages to 56 percent of its laborers, while 27 percent are middle income recipients, and 17 percent remain in the highest income group.[12]

What one observes here is evidence of an evolving dual economy, where few high paying technical-managerial positions stand in contrast to the low wage often associated with the retail trade and the service sectors.[13] Middle income recipients find their once secure position eroded through a steady de-skilling process of scientific management which rationalizes the workplace in the name of efficiency and productivity enhancement.[14] Economically, politically, and culturally, the dual economy threatens to widen the gap between the haves and the have-nots.

For relating these general trends to high-technology economies in particular, the best available data appears to be provided by Bluestone and Harrison. They have used a wide variety of economic and social indicators to analyze the consequences of New England reindustrialization. Bluestone and Harrison report that by 1977, "over half of all New England jobs were in the high-technology field."[15] They go on to argue that despite the substantial boom in computer software and other high-technology sales and development, "three jobs were created in other sectors of the Massachusetts' economy for every one job created in the high-tech area."[16] In conjunction with this late seventies economic boom, several unsettling trends in employment were revealed. The authors found that five basic tendencies accompanied the shift away from the old-fashioned, New England industrial economic model. Summarizing the results of their work, the following trends are indicated.

1. Despite substantial job creation, net adjusted incomes actually fell relative to other national employment regions.

2. The type of economic development occurring tends to increase income inequality.

3. Employment under the new productive model was becoming more unstable, with a growing incidence of part-time, part-year work, a very high rate of employee turnover, and a sharp rise in the creation of certain boom-bust industries such as aircraft engines.

4. Barriers to upward mobility among workers seem to be greater in the new productive model.

5. There is a tendency among the fastest growing industries to continue a pattern of geographical restructuring—continuing an accelerating pattern of dispersal of production on a global basis.

Underlying all of these trends is a de-skilling dynamic which eliminates the most capricious and costly article in the productive process—labor. As one executive summarized the corporate perspective on plant location, "Labor costs are the big thing, far and away. Nine out of ten times you can hang it on labor costs and unionization."[17]

The increasing autonomy of the productive process from labor is achieved through the creation of technical forms which effectively neutralize skilled labor's traditional hold over production. Because this fully automated "global supermarket" complex is capital intensive, it naturally deepens the advantage of highly capitalized firms in the struggle to find outlets for production surpluses.[18] The resulting polarization within various industrial sectors is often expressed as uneven development among social classes and geographical areas, leaving public policy makers to deal with the wreckage. Paradoxically, the policy response often takes the form of publicly underwritten guarantees of union- and tax-free environments to lure corporate investors. As such, it increases the power of capital over labor and local communities, and it is the power of capital which underlies polarization and uneven development in the first place.

What must be clarified, then, is that the crucial issues for public policy makers do not concern efficient management of industrial decline. Nor do they concern aggressive competition against other localities and countries similarly suffering from subordination to the interests of capital. Instead, they revolve around the normative dimensions of choice. Central to this is the matter of an equitable and stable relationship between capital and labor. In the prevailing political environment, however, a long-term strategy of full employment is antithetical to the beliefs and assumptions which enter into policy options comprising the high-technology strategy.

This becomes even clearer when we attempt to measure accurately the impact of high technology within a service-and-information society. Research on unemployment indicates that the official government figures are understated. In a society beset with 7 to 11 percent officially acknowledged unemployment, in actuality between 25 and 35 percent of its potential working population are structurally—which in part means technologically—unemployed.[19] To make matters worse, unemployment is unequally dispersed within the populace. Among black American males, roughly 40 percent of the adults remain unemployed while 60 percent of the teenagers have no real work prospects. And cities like Detroit now feature what in essence amounts to a demilitarized zone between ethnic communities which makes them resemble warring social factions.

The roots of this indifference were described succinctly by Margaret Mead when she declared that "the unadorned truth is that we do not need now, and will not need later, much of the marginal labor—the very young, the very old, the very uneducated and the very stupid."[20] Anthropologist Marvin Harris discerns direct links between the evolution of the service and information society, high marginal employment of women in the workforce, and rising black unemployment.[21]

The demands for education posed by high-technology jobs are also of significant interest. High tech, science-based industrial sectors, including aerospace and biotechnology, computers and semiconductors, share a rapid pace of technological change which leads to rapid obsolescence in the labor force. In one example, Lucas Aerospace, the average half-life of an aerospace job is 1.6 years.[22] What kind of educational process will it take to develop people who can conceptually retool every 3.2 years? If it takes years to master the complex technical and conceptual information necessary to perform certain prescribed tasks, who is going to foot the bill for reeducating the workforce every four years or so? What will the psychological costs be for workers who constantly must shift concentrated tasks to satisfy the new industrial means?

Growth

The Battelle report is the major public document on high-tech policy and economic growth produced for New York State to date. Before examining it, two preliminary points should be made. First, the report bears many of the markings of having been compiled hastily. For the most part, this affects the report's polish rather than its substance. A typical example is a sentence reading "over 70 major companies are funding major research in monoclonal antibodies compared to less than 10 percent 2 years ago," in which a raw number is compared to a percentage with no additional information.[23] Sloppiness characterizes the report's conceptual underpinnings, as well. Second, the report is a reasonably good document for the limited purposes of identifying possible areas of high-technology growth in the State and identifying some of the related issues (such as the educational issues already discussed). In our opinion, it is an inadequate document from which to assess the desirability of these areas of high-tech development or formulate a strategy for economic growth which incorporates them.

The core of the report is *Special Report IV,* which is devoted largely to describing a computer model used in identifying high-technology activities from among the State's 411 industrial manufacturing activities and ranking them according to their desirability.[24] The first task of its analysis was to describe New York's manufacturing activities in terms of employment growth, linkages to suppliers and markets, attraction of foreign investment, and export potentials. This process helped the researchers to develop criteria for identifying high-technology activities. The first computer screen assigned scores for the 411 activities on the basis of wages (higher wages—high score), educational attainment of the workforce (higher education—high score), and occupational structure of the workforce (high proportion of professional and technical categories—high score). Variables given less weight in the model are distance to markets (less distance—high score), energy consumption (low consumption—high score) and land requirements for manufacturing facilities (low requirements—high score). This screening reduced the number of potentially desirable manufacturing activities to 135. On the basis of sensitivity analyses and technical criteria, this list was expanded to 140 activities, to which were added 18 activities identified on the basis of literature and reports prepared for various locales within New York State. These industries then were scored for 7 broad criteria represented by 25 specific variables (see Appendix I). The factors include projected long-term growth, employment trends, number of new establishments, changes in the value of shipments, research and development expenditures, market size, and energy and land requirements. The narrative indicates that, with the exception of energy and land requirements, higher numbers were considered to be positive indicators, though no specific scoring methodology is discussed. Although there is certainly great value in familiarizing oneself with an issue through the kind of complex modelling process used by Battelle, drawing conclusions from such models is more an art than a science. Many factors relevant to this model lead us to question the conclusion drawn by the Battelle researchers.

The basic flaw in the report is the conception of economic development implicit in Battelle's operational definition of high technology. Criteria used in defining high-technology industries include significant reliance on new scientific/technological breakthroughs (such as genetic engineering), a high (15 percent or more) proportion of technical and professional workers, high growth rates, average wage rates higher than in two thirds of all manufacturing activities, capital intensity (per employee investment above the national average), and educational levels in the workforce above the national average. By using these indicators of high technology, the computer model excludes a number of high employment-generating industrial activities because they do not fit the criteria. For example, in terms of employment, 8 of the top 50 industrial activities in New York State not included in the final 158 activities analyzed accounted for 44,855 new jobs from 1970 to 1978, a 53 percent increase! Consequently, although Battelle originally included employment growth among those manufacturing activities which were used as a basis for its high-technology concept, in the final analysis the report's criteria for high technology excludes industrial activity that generates high employment. It is clear, therefore, that the Battelle report's perspective on high technology does not yield an adequate notion of economic development because it does not permit some industries which generate high employment to become a focus of New York State's technology policy. According to this logic, technology ceases to be a means serving human ends, such as employment and all that is entailed by it, and becomes an end in itself.

Related to this displacement of ends by means is the absence, noted earlier in connection with executive and legislative deliberation, of an explicit justification for State subsidies to high technology. Assuming, as we have not, that its definition of high-technology growth is sound, the Battelle report then becomes preoccupied with a strategy for promoting it while failing to address the basic rationale for public sector promotion. Further on we will show that the report does contain such a rationale, but as its political underpinnings are controversial and arguably in contradiction to the broad purposes Battelle claimed for the high-technology strategy, the report avoids spelling it out clearly. It should be noted, as well, that a reasoned defense of the State's involvement in technological development only could highlight high technology as one of many conceivable alternatives for strategic economic development.

The work of Bluestone and Harrison also calls attention to several other weaknesses in the Battelle report. For one, the evidence in the report indicates that there is a slight disadvantage for average weekly earnings in New York's high-technology areas compared to overall manufacturing wages in the State (the former as a percentage of the latter equals 98.7 percent for the 31 most desirable industries, and 99 percent for the list of 158 activities). The computer model also compares New York high-technology earnings to all manufacturing earnings in the United States, but the 14 percent advantage for New York is about the same as the advantage obtained when all New York manufacturing earnings are compared with U.S. earnings. In other words, the presence of higher wages in New York manufacturing cannot be explained by the presence of high-technology activities. It is important, too, to mention that the Battelle report contains no analysis of the distribution of earnings within high-technology industries. It is thus impossible to determine if income distribution is more or less equitable than in other manufacturing activities.

Another deficiency in the Battelle report is its failure to model the interaction of high-technology activities with the New York, U.S., and global economies. Even if it could be shown that the socioeconomic trends within high-technology industries were favorable, it would be important to know if overall polarization, such as has taken place in New England, would be likely to result. Probably the most critical issue in this regard is unemployment, which has shown a clear rising trend since the 1960s and is related to a variety of social ills. Technological change always has eliminated jobs, but generally speaking economic growth has been adequate to compensate for this dislocation through the generation of new jobs.

Two of the three major areas of high-technology growth for New York State identified by Governor Carey are medical/biological technologies, and information/manufacturing productivity technologies.[25] Job growth in the medical/biological area has been high for New York State, and is projected to continue. The aggregate significance of medical-biological industry, however, is indicated by the fact that only one of the specific activities in this area rank among the State's top 50 manufacturing activities in terms of jobs.

The employment picture in the information/manufacturing productivity area is less clear. While industrial activities such as the manufacture of electronic computing equipment and semiconductors already account for a substantial volume of jobs in New York and are very likely to continue to expand, the total employment impact is very likely to be negative. At the core of the information, communications, and manufacturing productivity growth areas is the microprocessor, whether the industry in question is actually manufacturing microprocessing equipment, or using it for robotics, computer aided design, and so forth. As a recent Worldwatch Institute report argues, it is the pervasiveness of microelectronic technology that threatens the conventional way in which jobs lost in old industries are replaced by jobs created in new areas.[26] Microelectronic technology is reducing the need for labor in industries ranging from banking to steelworks. At the same time, the process of manufacturing products which now incorporates microelectronic technology is typically less labor intensive than the process used previously. An excellent example is an electronic telex machine manufactured by Standard Electric Lorenz, which has replaced 936 moving parts with one microprocessor. Work hours involved in manufacturing one machine are cut by nearly four-fifths.[27] Viewed historically, the loss of agricultural jobs in the United States was compensated for by new jobs in industry, while industrial job loss in the last 30 years has been compensated for by new employment in the service and government sectors of the economy. Microprocessing technology is historically unique in that it is now affecting the employment picture in all these areas simultaneously.

It is difficult to move from these general observations to precise predictions because of the problems associated with economic modelling and the fact that we are only entering upon the microelectronic revolution. A recent survey by the General Accounting Office of studies on the short and long-term employment impact of automation concluded that short-term displacement definitely will occur, but that predictions about long-term impacts vary according to assumptions built into predictive models.[28] At the same time, the Battelle report clearly establishes the significance of information/manufacturing productivity industries in New York and the State's outstanding comparative advantages in these areas. Regardless of the employment impacts of the new technologies, there is virtually unanimous agreement that those countries (or states) that lag behind technologically will lose more jobs than those which take the lead because of their inability to compete in national and international markets.[29] This parallels the Tragedy of the Commons, where the rational strategy for the individual is irrational for the collectivity. Our basic objection to the Battelle report and to the public sector of New York State which shares its rationale is that the technology policy they uncritically embrace fails to consider the consequences for other economic sectors and for the populations employed within them.

273

FROM AGRICULTURE TO INDUSTRY?

We want to conclude this analysis of high technology and economic policy by briefly considering whether or not past government-industry-university partnerships in technological and economic development are as unambiguous in their public benefits as present rhetoric would have us believe. Our reflections are prompted by interviews where numerous advocates of CII cited the agricultural extension system as their model for New York's current technology policy. Here, according to respondents, was one example where government, universities, and industry contributed to enhanced productivity.

Taking the case of the tomato industry in California as an example of industrial progress through government-industry-university collaboration, output per acre in 1940 was 8 tons. In 1960 the same acre yielded 17 tons, and by 1980 the figure had grown to 24 tons.[30] Green revolution technologies contributed to growth in this industry as few applied scientific and technological achievements had in others. As with many such tales, however, this one has a soft underbelly.

One prominent individual to have taken a critical look at American agribusiness is former Secretary of Agriculture Bob Bergland, who served in the Carter cabinet. Bergland was the first small farmer in forty years to hold such an esteemed managerial role and consequently took uncommon stands on such issues as farm mechanization.

I find it difficult, if not impossible to justify the use of federal funds to finance research leading to the development of machines or other technologies that may increase production or processing efficiency but at the same time damage the soil, pollute the environment, displace willing workers, and reduce or eliminate competition. I do not believe a federally financed research effort ought to benefit a small number of individuals, corporations or narrow interest groups to such an extent and in such a way as to make it possible, in time, for the beneficiaries to gain control of the farm-to-market structure, monopolize the sources of finance at every step, and increase their profits by selling what may well be an inferior product at a price that is insulated from competition.[31]

With the disappearance of 36,000 small farmers across America each year, a pattern of increasing energy inefficiency, and a chronic surplus of agricultural commodities one must wonder about a publicly underwritten productivity enhancement strategy. In California alone, the state-subsidized invention of the mechanical tomato harvester "replaced two-thirds of the peak time harvest jobs while eliminating four-fifths of the farmers," translating into the loss of 35,000 agricultural jobs while the average acreage per farm has risen from 45 to 350 acres.[32]

Our point is that uncritical advocacy of technological efficiency and productivity amounts to a tacit belief in technology more than an appreciation of its actual consequence. Why not stress that if agricultural extension is our model for technology policy in reindustrialization, then historical experience instructs us to be cautious about social dislocation? For policy makers, the lesson is to make informed choices among a myriad of experimental possibilities while using historical precedent as a critical guide.

CII: THE SYMBOLIC USE OF POLITICS

We turn now from a substantive critique of technology policy to an analysis of its political roots. In a recent study of American politics since World War II, Alan Wolfe demonstrates that the American system of conflict resolution is based on a compact of growth maximization, rather than an accommodation of substantive differences among contending political constituencies. In the absence of growth, political actors are required to negotiate substantive political differences in the formation of public policy, whether these differences take place along class, race, geographic, or other dimensions. As Wolfe argues, growth has made possible the maintenance of social peace without confronting potentially divisive political issues in the policy arena. He refers to this as "change without change."[33] The current concern for reindustrialization derives from the fact that the growth boom underpinning this fragile consensus is over. The instrumental and technocratic mode of politics inherent in the growth scenario is thus confronted by a more substantive and less controllable form of political development threatening the interests of elites. In order to examine elite responses to this political opening, a few aspects of technocratic politics should be brought into the foreground.

In order to reestablish this managerial-technocratic prerogative in an economic context of stagnation, elites are forced to deliver symbolic packages as substitutes for the substantive ones which can no longer be guaranteed by the productive apparatus. At a time of fiscal and policy impasse, the need for the political system to respond visibly to problems besetting an anxious citizenry is crucial. High technology— however one defines it—provides policy makers with a flashy focal point from which to plan the reconstruction of an ailing economy. High-tech reindustrialization provides an identifiable symbol which assures citizens that answers to persistent and deepening problems such as unemployment and stagflation do exist. That such issues as CII are not debated in the New York State Assembly and Senate strikes us as revealing. What it suggests, as we have claimed, is both an underlying consensus and, perhaps more significantly, a pervasive sense that identifiable policy alternatives to the current impasse must be *sought*. In the face of complexity, legislators and their party leaders feel compelled to embrace symbolic packages which look good to constituencies at home (even though one may not understand what one is supporting). The CII case study offers us an elegant example where economic anomie coupled with shaky public confidence helped turn decision makers toward symbolic action.

There is nothing wrong with symbolic action *per se*. Good intentions, as Thomas Dye points out, are sometimes better conveyers of vitality and social confidence than tangible policy accomplishments.

The policies of government may tell us more about the aspirations of a society and its leadership than about actual conditions. Policies do more than effect change in societal conditions; they also help hold men together and maintain an orderly state.[34]

People need something powerful to believe in and toward which to strive. Thus, the implicit but illusory consensus which underpins "society's central project" remains every bit as significant as objective performance. In a sense, therefore, the degree to which policy makers are able to project political ideals overshadows measurable consequences of success. And if we take the case of CII in a society where progress-as-productivity is a universal ideal, how might policy makers modify long existing industrial practices while avoiding fundamental political and economic change? In such a society the answer is clear. The task for policy makers, in the generation of dramatically new economic and political imperatives, becomes that of grafting new images of possibility onto well-established patterns of practice. Policy makers sometimes work intuitively, guided by informed hunches, in the creation of new responses to old problems. When faced with political and economic transition, they must be able to generate believable symbolic bridges to untestable futures in a manner somehow continuous with the past. At stake here are the issues of cultural continuity and social change central to any society in transition. With regard to CII, which symbolic threads can be disclosed which articulate a future that solves the problems and preserves the values of the present and the past?

Talk of reindustrialization which now fills the air waves of popular culture can be interpreted as part of a pervasive culture-wide desire for social and economic recovery. Judging from the frequency with which the term "high tech" is heard in the media, one is hard pressed to disagree with Aaron Gurwitz that high tech is "the latest development fad to hit the streets of America."[35] Implicit within both reindustrialization and high tech is a doctrine which holds that traditional ends and means of production remain unqualifiably "good." What underlies this position is a several centuries old belief that science and technology are the principal determinants of human purpose and other social goods. The accompanying set of assumptions and normative beliefs which underlie the reindustrialization position seems to have changed little in symbolic content. We can think of no clearer example of this than the uncritical adoption of the Center for Industrial Innovation for the development of industrial technology. Would not resisting such a concept as high technology amount to a repudiation of centuries of cumulative progress? Who among policy makers would challenge the imposing quartet of progress, reindustrialization, high technology and economic growth while remaining in political office?

So new policy objectives and instrumental directives are cast within a hybridized trio of existing political, economic and technological beliefs. Technocratic idealism—in keeping with Herman Kahn's "technology and growth enthusiasts"—beckons applied science to yet again unlock unrealized futures.[36] Yet the rationale which pervades "single-issue" technological policy is itself a derivation of this brand of science. Science as a "neutral" symbol, from acid rain studies to Battelle Reports supporting the Center for Industrial Innovation, justifies the policy strategies whose good it is supposed to advance. Policy makers have learned to rely upon independent scientific review processes to "take off the political heat."[37] Instead of confronting the value laden content of policy formulation, political managers create autonomous scientific commissions to invent criteria justifying preordained courses of action, thereby removing discussion from the public domain. Instead of clarifying policy objectives, science becomes a technocratic instrument which mystifies the public by creating a language package inaccessible to journalist and citizen alike. The result is frustrated intervention by outsiders in the actual policy process coupled with a real fall in democratic, participatory practice.

If science is invoked by policy makers as a primary justification for pursuing a newly articulated social ideal, one is left wondering about the actual role of politics in the process. The truth, we have suggested, lies somewhere outside of the realm of tangible results and nearer to metaphysics. As Murray Edelman argues, the use of myths, rites, and other symbolic forms in public policy formation is far from accidental.

Not only does systematic research suggest that the most cherished forms of popular participation in government are largely symbolic, but also that many of the public programs universally taught and believed to benefit a mass public in fact benefit relatively small groups.[38]

This is most assuredly the case when one examines the likely long-term consequences of Atari Democracy, especially when the costs and benefits are tallied on an international scale. Of great significance, however, is the degree to which stated pursuits such as CII "demonstrably maintain quiescence," that is to say, where policy assumes a form of "symbolic assurance that can be expected to satisfy a symbolic goal."[39] The explicit objective is less significant than its overall psychic impact where the citizenry may rest assured that policy makers are doing *something* in the wake of social and economic anomie. It is precisely at a time when economic conditions threaten the security of large groups, or when they are characterized by an absence of organization furthering the common interest, that symbolically reassuring activities are likely to come into play.[40] What concerns us about this process is the extent to which, and the reasons why, society—with little or no debate or dialogue—blithely follows the trained instincts of the few. The effective consequence of isolating policy from the public, of its "scientization" by an elite, and of the symbolic assurances policy provides, is that social policy happens not out of a genuine discourse on stated goals but through default of those who are excluded from the debate.

POLICY ALTERNATIVES

In light of the foregoing analysis, the issue of policy alternatives for New York's reindustrialization presents something of a dilemma. The crux of our analysis is that in defining the role of technology in reindustrialization, the State's decision makers have scarcely raised the most important questions, much less examined them adequately to formulate policies to resolve serious problems. We do not want to suggest that these failures have to do with professional shortcomings of the principal decision makers involved. On the contrary, our investigation has convinced us that by and large these decision makers have acted with greater public spiritedness and idealism, and far less parochialism and pork-barrel politicking, than one typically encounters when public authorities are asked to subsidize private enterprise. Yet this idealism is squarely within the worldview of scientific rationalism, which is systematically blind to the political content of technology.

If, in dealing with the issue of economic policy for New York State one must operate within the framework of technocratic policy making, then the kind of policy solution represented by CII is elegant. Not only does it hold the prospect for improved productivity and competitiveness, it also decentralizes the instruments of public policy. This is a brilliant way of addressing the need for planning in a society which is ideologically ill-disposed toward it. At an operational level, the shared private/public sector funding feature of CII allows for a close articulation of activities, gives industry leverage in the formation and implementation of state policy, and when dealing with their political constituencies provides both sides with the rationale that the other is subsidizing its activities. In short, within the existing political economy, decentralized rationalization of technological development and productivity improvement is an important strategic development. It surely makes better economic sense than attempts to restore productivity by accumulating greater wealth in the hands of the rich or through weak attempts to promote "appropriate technology" and cultural change through tax credits, demonstration projects, and the like. But if we are correct in our belief that the high-technology path will bring with it intensified problems of dislocation, unemployment, environmental entropy, a dual economy, and social breakdown, the elegance of its fit with the existing political economy offers small solace.

In our estimation an appropriate policy for New York State would be to make the issue of technology a more central feature of legislative affairs. The decisive issue to be confronted by the State's examination of technology is to reconcile the high-technology scenario, which is already unfolding, with the legitimate claims of working people and local communities concerning employment and community stability. Is there a means by which high-technology developments can be incorporated into a State policy guided by these broader concerns? We do not believe that anyone knows, since we see no evidence that anyone has attempted to address this problem outside the trickle-down assumptions of social welfare already discussed in this paper. If there is such a means, if high technology can be harnessed to a progressive political agenda, it would surely entail a balance with the development of labor-intensive industries. State policy must be formulated in such a manner as to promote the integration of high technology into a broader technology and economic policy. To accomplish this, however, there first must be a political thrust that propels a genuinely critical examination of technology into the center of the policy arena.

TWELVE

Reindustrialization in New York:

The Role of the State University

John W. Kalas

I t has been half a century since our nation last devoted the amount of energy it is expending today to the exploration of its economic structure and to the search for a responsive industrial policy. Economic conditions have dominated the media for the past few years and doubts about our country's economic viability have been an issue for more than a decade. Similarities certainly exist between the great depression of the 30s and the stagnation of the early 80s. Yet the differences are most instructive. Fifty years ago the national goal was to resurrect the industrial base of the 20s—reignite the blast furnaces, turn on the assembly lines, and increase demand for long accepted products. Today's dilemma is much more complex; we are not only contending with a sluggish economy but simultaneously wrestling with the questions of what and how to produce. Reducing unemployment and increasing national productivity are no longer matters of returning men and women to the factories, offices, and stores where they once worked. What is needed is to develop new means of production, new products, new crafts, and the skills and knowledge of an advanced society.

Central economic facts today are industry's growing dependence on science and technology and the developing links between the nation's laboratories and its factories and marketplaces. Ubiquitous digital technology is perhaps the first cause of this union between research center and production facility, but is not the only cause. Research in molecular biology is finding a crucial place in pharmaceuticals, industrial chemicals, food, and drink. Lasers and fiber optics are finding applications in metalworking, microphotography, printing, and visual and auditory entertainment. Whatever the specifics, the general theme is well established. To ensure growth and renewal, American industry must tie itself ever more closely to the latest efforts of scientists and engineers. Industry does invest in its own laboratories and private research. But industry can and does rely on the work being conducted in colleges and universities. This reliance should be cultivated, for higher education can serve the scientific needs of commerce and also provide industry with the human resources upon which advancement depends.

Universities across the country are involving themselves with industry in a number of ways. Four are worth noting:

The first, universally accepted and time-honored, is that of "education for employment." The university prepares students at all levels, from office worker to technician to graduate engineer, to be productive. Education for employment takes place in the regular college curriculum, the continuing education model and contract courses, and through special manpower programs that retrain workers.

A second approach is "technological participation." Economic growth, it is argued, is a function of technological advancement. University involvement in key fields such as engineering and biotechnology is a critical factor in keeping pace with world competition in technical fields. Universities and industries, therefore, must continue to establish new forms of collaboration to enable research findings to be quickly and effectively assimilated. The inventions of university faculty are part of the formal commercialization process through patenting and licensing. Industrially supported contract research is growing. Research centers in areas of industrial interest, such as robotics, are being developed. And through university-based technology transfer offices, technological partnerships between industry and the academic community are becoming increasingly important.

A third method is "extension." As the Morrill Act of the nineteenth century established the land-grant concept that revolutionized American agriculture, universities now may participate in a new "Morrill Act" by providing management skills, technology, and technical assistance to large and small businesses modernizing to become more competitive.

Finally, there is "strategic planning." The United States requires significant adjustments in its economic and political institutions if it is to remain competitive in the emerging world economy. An outline of the necessary changes are coming into focus. Industry must diminish its reliance on inflexible mass production and pursue flexible specialized production. Capital must be patient, reinvesting in plant, innovation, and research and development. The workforce must be provided with opportunities for continual retraining and upgrading. Tax structures and political support mechanisms must be revised to be responsive to global economic realities. Such a major reconfiguration of American economic life has implications for the entire social and economic fabric of the country. Considering education in this light, the university must mobilize those persons who have the intellectual resources to interpret the economic and political implications of what society faces and the social, psychological, moral, and humanistic implications as well. The university's involvement in economic development must include the political scientist as surely as it does the engineer, the moral philosopher along with the accountant.

The methods described here are by no means mutually exclusive, and one would be hard-pressed to point to an example of a pure case of any one of these types; but they do represent the areas of emphasis which different universities stress. In the case of the State University of New York, all four methods can be followed. The equal diversity of the State University and the economy of New York State allows for such an approach.

THE STATE UNIVERSITY OF NEW YORK: EDUCATION FOR EMPLOYMENT

The State University of New York now has almost 1,000,000 alumni, the vast majority of whom are living and working in New York State. Each year the University awards roughly 55,000 degrees, about evenly divided between the State supported campuses and the community colleges. Because most of these graduates enter the work force, one could truly say that all of the University's degree-granting curricula are relevant to the economic well-being of the State. In this section, however, those programs that bear more directly upon rein-dustrialization in the State will be singled out. Recently, SUNY has placed new emphasis upon those programs which directly affect rein-dustrialization; most important are the programs in engineering, computer science, and biotechnology.

Engineering Programs

Recent reports document the role that engineering sciences play in contemporary industrial development, the need for engineering graduates at all levels, and the opportunity for university and industry collaboration in research and industrial innovation.[1] Engineering and engineering technology programs of the State University of New York were the subject of a comprehensive report issued by the University in January, 1982, entitled, *Investment Needs: Engineering and the Engineering Technologies*.[2] That report presented an agenda for the University to strengthen and expand its investments in this area commensurate with the growing need by New York State industry for educated and trained personnel and for research resources in engineering and related fields.

Associate degrees or certificates in engineering technology fields are offered in 21 of the University's 30 community colleges and the six Agricultural and Technical Colleges. Specialties are offered in such widely varied technical fields as aeronautics, engineering graphics, architectural technology, chemical technology, electromechanics, industrial technology, textiles, instrumentation and construction technology. In 1980, over 21,000 students were enrolled in these programs and over 5,000 degrees were awarded. Ninety-five percent of these graduates remained in New York State and either were directly employed in their fields of interest or continued their education.

State University campuses awarded 1,349 bachelor of technology degrees in 1980, a large number though still far below the need of the State's technically-oriented industry. To bridge this gap, the University has mapped out a selective expansion effort in baccalaureate-level technology programs. On Long Island, where the needs of technologically-oriented industry are particularly great, the Agricultural and Technical College at Farmingdale plans to augment its lower-division programs in aerospace technology and electrical and mechanical technology by offering bachelor of technology degrees in these areas. The Agricultural and Technical Colleges at Alfred and Cobleskill also are planning an addition of programs at the bachelor of technology level in order to address specific needs. At Cobleskill, an upper-division program in agriculture is being developed and, at Alfred, upper-division programs in civil technology (surveying), electrical technology, electromechanical technology, and mechanical technology are being planned. In addition, the College of Technology at Utica/Rome is strengthening its bachelor of technology programs in mechanical and electrical engineering. State University College at Buffalo's existing programs in engineering technology and its program in industrial technology will be strengthened, and the College is implementing a plan to significantly increase its investment in equipment.

Also included in the University's plan are efforts to strengthen and expand its existing baccalaureate programs at the University Centers at Buffalo and Stony Brook and to continue the specialized undergraduate programs at the College of Environmental Science and Forestry and the Maritime College, and at the Statutory Colleges of Ceramics and Agriculture and Life Sciences. Using its considerable investment in science and technology curricula as a base, the University Center at Binghamton was authorized in the fall of 1982 to offer bachelor of science degrees in electrical, mechanical, and industrial engineering. Binghamton offered its first courses in these programs in the fall 1983 semester. In June, 1982, the Board of Trustees of the State University approved new upper-division programs in computer and electrical engineering to be offered by the State University College at New Paltz. The focus on upper-division programs is based on present and planned industrial and technological expansion in the mid-Hudson region and on the need for further study by graduates of community colleges in the area.

At the post-baccalaureate level, there is a nationwide concern about the decline in doctoral degrees in engineering granted by American universities—from a high of 3,774 in 1972 to 2,751 in 1980, a decline of 27 percent.[3] National organizations, such as the National Association of State Universities and Land-Grant Colleges (NASULGC) and the National Academy of Engineering, have called for expansion and increased support of graduate programs in engineering in order to prevent deterioration of both the academic and industrial engineering base in this country. NASULGC recently issued a *Report on the Quality of Engineering Education* which urged that, to maintain quality in engineering education, the number of Ph.D. graduates should increase by 1,000 per year and the overall number of engineering graduates should increase proportionately.[4] In response to these needs the State University is strengthening its doctoral engineering programs at the University Centers at Stony Brook and Buffalo. In addition, the University will maintain its strong specialized graduate engineering programs at the College of Environmental Science and Forestry, the College of Agriculture and Life Sciences, and the College of Ceramics.

The equipment problems in engineering education are also directly related to quality. The NASULGC report cites Dean Daniel Drucker of the University of Illinois, who estimates that "it would cost the Nation 1 billion dollars to overcome the current equipment problems in engineering education."[5] This issue is of particular importance to the State University as it implements its plans to strengthen and expand its programs. The new federal interest in scientific equipment will prove helpful.

A recent NSF-supported study conducted by New York University indicated that engineering faculties account for half of the university/

industry interaction reported by universities. Chemistry and computer science account for 10 percent each, medicine and business for 7 percent, with all other disciplines accounting for the remainder.[6] This strong relationship with industry characterizes the University's experience in two distinctive ways. First, many of SUNY's undergraduate and master's level engineering programs are essentially regional in character. The planning for these programs was designed to meet regional student and industry needs. The "investment needs" configuration of programs, both in strengthening and in expanding offerings, took shape as a result of the recognition of regional economic needs, as well as State needs. Program plans are being made in consultation with regional industrial leadership. Likewise, industry is turning increasingly to regional SUNY campuses for assistance, a fact that is reflected in contract research support to faculty. IBM's Endicott plant supports Binghamton research, for example, and Bethlehem Steel supports work in the School of Engineering at Buffalo.

The search for engineering faculty, although highly competitive, in fact is drawing the campuses and engineering related industries closer together. SUNY campuses are undertaking joint hiring with industry or hiring full-time faculty with assurances from industry that faculty will be offered summer opportunities. Similarly, joint research relationships with local industry are being arranged. The result is the emergence of stronger collegial and cooperative relationships that are beneficial to both the State University and the industrial community.

Computer Science Programs

The pervasiveness and speed with which computer technology has been introduced into our society demand an unprecedented response from educational institutions. A rapidly growing proportion of the U.S. labor force is currently involved in information and computer-related jobs, and the demand for people educated and trained in these areas is expected to accelerate. Higher education is faced with the dual responsibilities of providing computer literate students and educating the technicians, programmers, analysts, and the future teachers and researchers of computer and information sciences. The State University's institutions continue to respond to these needs. Short courses (credit and non-credit), workshops, and seminars on computers and their technology are offered on every campus to registered students as well as to members of the local community through continuing education programs. Individual courses in computer science are offered whenever possible to all students. But many of the University's campuses are experiencing a level of student demand that is difficult to satisfy fully.

The growth that has taken place in computer science and related programs within the University has been almost entirely at the associate and baccalaureate degree levels. The number of associate degree programs increased from 25 to 45, while the number of baccalaureate programs increased from 8 to 18. Additionally, since the fall of 1981 13 new associate degree programs have been approved. Even more indicative of the student demand for these programs is the increase in enrollments—at the associate level there has been an enrollment increase of 234 percent, and at the baccalaureate level the increase was 305 percent. Some examples of the majors offered at the associate level include computer technology, computer science, data processing-programming and systems, and computing graphics technology. Majors offered at the baccalaureate level include computer and information sciences, computer science and applied mathematics, and information systems management.

The situation at the graduate level presents a far different picture. There has been no increase in the number of programs, and the number of doctoral level students actually has declined. Since the fall of 1981, however, the State University has approved a new Ph.D. program at Albany and an M.S. program in computer science at New Paltz.

Comparing the total number of degrees awarded in the computer sciences in New York State with those granted by the State University yields some additional insights. Again, the University appears to be making a significant contribution via the number of degrees at the associate and baccalaureate level. The statistics at the graduate level, however, indicate that the University should consider expanding its efforts. The statistics at the doctoral level are most startling—three graduates out of only 23 statewide. The most recent data available from the U.S. Department of Education, National Center for Education Statistics, indicate 240 doctoral degrees granted nationally in 1979–80. The national shortage of doctoral trained computer scientists already is well documented. In order to respond to this dramatic shortage, the University must strengthen and expand its three doctoral programs.

Biotechnology Programs

In the brief thirty years since James D. Watson and Francis H. C. Crick described the structure of genetic material, the biotechnological field has grown immensely, both as a pure science and in terms of commercial interest. On the commercial side, there are estimates which suggest that medical, agricultural, and biochemical applications of

Table 1. Comparison of Number of Programs and Enrollment in Computer and Information Sciences and Data Processing Technologies, Fall 1975 and Fall 1981, and Total Degrees Granted in These Programs Between 1975–76 and 1981–82 at the State University of New York*

Degree Level	Fall 1975		Fall 1981		Percent Change Fall '75 to Fall '81		Total Degrees 1975–76 1981–82
	Number of Programs	Enroll-ment	Number of Programs	Enroll-ment	Number of Programs	Enroll-ment	
Certificate	12	342	14	314	+ 16.7	− 8.2	510
Associate	25	2784	45	9304	+ 80.0	+234.2	5341
Bachelor	8	878	18	3559	+125.0	+305.4	2899
Master's	2	83	2	84	–	+ 1.2	442
Doctoral	2	174	2	159	–	− 8.6	46
Total	49	4261	81	13,420	+ 63.5	+215.3	9238

SOURCE: Office of Institutional Research and Planning, APIS (HEGIS Categories (07 and 51)
* Includes only those programs indicating enrollment in fall terms.

Table 2. Degrees Granted in Computer and Information Sciences and Data Processing Technologies New York State and SUNY 1980–81

Degree Level	Total State	SUNY	Percent SUNY
Associate	1723	966	56.1
Bachelor	1728	602	34.8
Master's	518	71	13.7
Doctoral	23	3	13.0

SOURCE: College and University Degrees Conferred, New York State 1980–81, The State Education Department

biotechnology could become a 100 billion dollar industry within the next decade.[7] The State University's research activities are of major interest to the biotechnological industry, partly because universities spawn most of the basic research in the field, and partly because the gap between pure science and commercial application is far narrower in biotechnology than in most other scientific fields. The State University of New York is no exception. A great deal of interest is presently being expressed by pharmaceutical companies in the work conducted, particularly at the basic sciences divisions of the University's four medical centers. Each of these centers has a high level of supported research from companies such as Merck, Pfizer, Upjohn, and Lilly, to name but a few, and the centers are producing substances and refining techniques with a wide variety of medical applications. In addition to

SUNY's medical centers, there are a number of specialized research centers advancing basic understanding in the biotechnological field. Included among these are the Center for Somatic-Cell Genetics and Biochemistry at Binghamton and the newly-designated Center for Biotechnology at Stony Brook.

Research and instruction in biotechnology also are taking place under the auspices of departments of biological sciences at all of the University Centers, the Colleges of Environmental Science and Forestry, and many of the Arts and Science Colleges. All of these campuses are preparing students who will conduct research and carry through the techniques that will enable the biotechnological industry to grow within the State. Within the Arts and Science Colleges, the In Vitro Cell Science Center at the SUNY College at Plattsburgh offers a unique program. Fifteen students a semester participate in an immersion program, spending full time developing laboratory techniques and conducting experiments in cell science. The College at Fredonia now offers one of the few baccalaureate majors in recombinant gene technology. Students are learning the basic techniques of gene and cell cloning, protoplast fusion, nucleic acid hybridization, and DNA sequencing. At a symposium on Monoclonal Antibodies and Hybridoma Technology that was held in May of 1982 in Albany, University faculty from five campuses presented papers on their current research to an audience that included industrial and governmental representatives as well as colleagues from other SUNY campuses.

In addition to curricular reconfiguration, the reindustrialization effort is aided through the avenue of what is traditionally called continuing education. The role the State University is playing in the training and retraining mode as related to reindustrialization is also of growing importance and may be discussed under several headings.

Job Maintenance

The loss of jobs in the smokestack industries has continued with what seems like inexorability. Yet there is ample evidence that many industries, even old industries, can be transformed by the adoption of newer technologies and management practices. Recognition that change is possible has become an important redevelopment strategy in New York. Clearly, one key to retaining manufacturing jobs and halting attrition is to train the workforce in these industries for the technologies and methodologies that will keep the plants open and the jobs secure. An example is the training program provided jointly by the SUNY College at Buffalo and Erie Community College at the Tonawanda

289

Chevrolet plant. Workers are being trained to understand and use automated equipment in the assembly of the L–4 engine. At the same time, as a means of improving quality control, both workers and management attend seminars on workers' motivation and explore alternative work formats such as quality groups. Similarly, Jamestown Community College assisted the wood furniture industry, which several years ago was threatened with extinction, by providing training not only in the wood crafts themselves, but in marketing, finance, and inventory maintenance. That industry once again provides stable employment within the Jamestown community.

Further, the State of New York has made available funds to support company-specific training programs that are designed to stabilize existing industries. These funds are available on a project basis to community colleges through a program known as "contract courses." In 1981, the first year of the project, courses were conducted for over 100 different businesses, providing nearly 200 courses to over 40,000 persons. In its second year, the program expanded and reached as many as 70,000 persons.

Training for Unemployed Workers

State University campuses have been involved in Federal programs that are providing support for the training and retraining of unemployed workers. Since the fall of 1983, the principal manpower training program in the country has been the Job Training Partnership Act (JTPA), with federal funds flowing through the State to localities. The State University has two representatives on the statewide policy body as well as representation on most of the local Private Industry Councils (PICs) which service regional Service Delivery Areas (SDAs). The campuses also are responsible for a relatively high level of training. A survey completed in March of 1984 indicated that within the community colleges alone, JTPA funds in excess of 2.2 million dollars have been awarded to 23 campuses to provide direct vocational training or supportive basic skills. Approximately 2600 persons will benefit from the training. Several of the State-operated campuses are providing similar training.

In addition to the JTPA, the State of New York has provided funds targeted to assist unemployed workers, particularly those who have been displaced as a result of structural unemployment. Eleven SUNY community colleges were awarded 420,000 dollars in State appropriated funds in January of 1984 for the purpose of providing specialized training for displaced workers. SUNY campuses have been much involved as well in training programs for workers living in areas of acute unemployment. In the particularly hard hit areas of Western New York, the SUNY campuses (the Buffalo Center, the College at Buffalo, Erie Community College, and Niagara Community College) have cooperated to provide training for the large numbers of displaced steel workers.

Workforce Upgrading

Much of the training provided by State University campuses comes in the form of upgrading skills. This takes two forms, one measurable and one not. Literally thousands of continuing education students are taking courses through individual enrollment at an employer's request or with the support, including financial, of an employer. There is no way to determine how many of the thousands of students who are taking accounting, computer programming, management, industrial psychology, business English, or hundreds of other such offerings are doing so as a direct attempt to make themselves more useful to their employers, but the number is large. In addition, and much more measurable, are the courses that are arranged directly between continuing education departments and employers. Even here the courses being offered at any one time are too numerous to list, but an indication of the kinds of offerings for which there is greatest demand will give a measure of the importance of this area.

Many campuses periodically provide seminars for small businessmen on a number of basic topics such as finance, marketing and sales, legal problems, personnel evaluation, and management. Also, companies are turning to the University to provide workers with training and understanding of computers. This training runs the range from an employer seeking to provide general level employees with computer literacy to a highly technical company like Grumman contracting for seminars on VLSI to be offered to its engineers.

The University provides training which introduces new technologies to employees. A number of SUNY campuses, for example, provide basic instruction in CAD/CAM operation, including, in some cases, the specific applications related to a particular plant. Management training is particularly useful to a number of companies, particularly those that are adapting management styles commensurate with technological change. Smokestack industries such as specialty steel companies or banks, where management as well as staff must adjust to the rapidity of introduction of new technologies, have called upon University resources for management training. Word processing training is another good example of the ways SUNY colleges introduce large numbers of employees to newer, more efficient patterns of work.

The University, as can easily be determined from these examples, is a natural and obvious locus of training for employment. Will this role continue as it has in recent years and, correspondingly, should the University continue to assume this role?

That the rapid growth of knowledge and the continuing pattern of career migration require continuous updating in knowledge and skills is beginning to gain acceptance. Despite a persistent belief in some university circles that the learning process is somehow debased if it occurs after 4:00 p.m., with individuals over 25 years of age, or in the months of June, July, or August, universities are providing learning opportunities for wide segments of the public. But it is difficult for colleges and universities to do what they are currently being asked to do, namely to provide quick solutions to the problems of unemployment, especially as faced by displaced workers and youth with low skill development. The University is not at its best when called upon to provide quick, short-term, and often remedial training to alleviate an immediate need. The University accepts the task, but the positive results are likely to be modest.

The University will not be able to escape the more remedial role so long as there are people with immediate training needs and the basic federal manpower programs stress only short-term training for unemployed workers. Training provided by universities is more effective among workers who already are employed, for whom motivation is provided by potential upward mobility in employment, where an ongoing base of skill levels can be presumed, and where a longer term approach rather than a quick fix offers greatest value to the economy. Available funding should begin to shift in the direction of those already working, drawing the unemployed into the orbit of work as the employed, by virtue of training, vacate entry level work for more skilled positions. That is a process more easily conceived than achieved, but until it is accomplished the maximum utility of the university capacity will not be exploited.

At least two SUNY campuses are undertaking training and development programs under the guise of the older apprenticeship model which provided for continuous skill upgrading. The SUNY Agricultural and Technical College at Farmingdale is providing training in tool and die making with the American Tool and Die Association. Also, the SUNY College at Oneonta is employing the apprenticeship concept with workers in a local Bendix plant. In both cases skill development is understood to be continuous, permitting workers both accessible entry to jobs and a continuous challenge. The University is in a position to be useful on a continuing basis in such instances. Training of this kind, shielded from the immediacies and pressures of income maintenance, ensures the greatest long-term benefit.

TECHNOLOGICAL PARTICIPATION

When one thinks of university involvement in reindustrialization, first thought is given to university resources in science and technology. Momentarily setting aside its validity, the claim has become nearly axiomatic that reindustrialization will be a movement from the smoke-stack industries of the old industrial regime to a new high-tech industrial order. The new regime would emphsize the computer and rapid information flow, biotechnical developments, continuing discoveries of even more useful materials to replace those drawn from the earth and sea, and innovative manufacturing techniques drawing upon some of these resources as characterized by the development of robotics.

While the rhetoric that commits the nation's basic industrial core to the junk heap is hyperbolic, it is true that the newer technologies represent an important growth area of the economy and that universities are now—as never before—a major knowledge resource for the development of new technologies. The telephone, the transistor, and the laser grew up in industrial laboratories or their informal precursors. The digital computer and monoclonal antibodies have emerged from the university laboratory. As a result of this change, the relationship between the university and industry has grown considerably closer in the past five years. Industry wants access to the intellectual resources necessary to maintain competitiveness in world markets and the university needs financial support in order to fuel its ever more expensive research enterprise. Within the State University of New York, this new set of relationships is assuming several forms.

Contract Research

In the year ending June 30, 1983, the Research Foundation of SUNY reported active research supports from companies just in excess of 7 million dollars. Although this amount represents less than 5 percent of the total of external funds committed for research within the University, it does reflect a slow and steady growth trend from previous years. During the 1984 fiscal year, SUNY campuses worked on research contracts with 170 different companies. The dollar volume of work is dominated by the leading pharmaceutical companies and a number of other major companies located in New York (such as GE and IBM), but 565 different companies have contracted for research of one kind or another since 1980.[8] Every indication is that growth of this type of research support is continuing.

The contract research relationship grows out of an industry's concern to solve a highly particular problem that is inhibiting corporate growth or to develop a specific product that will serve as the basis of corporate growth. The contract is generally with one researcher to deal with a discrete issue and is concluded when the issue is resolved or the product is developed.

Conferences and Seminars

In addition to specific research assistance, companies seek state-of-the-art knowledge in fields that impinge upon their industrial development. SUNY, like other universities, provides seminars and conferences in which faculty experts describe current trends and directions in a given field. While the University has not adopted the procedure whereby companies subscribe to a continuing program, as in MIT's Industrial Liaison project, it has provided conferences on such topics as hybridomas and software development.

Research Institutes

SUNY offers a number of opportunities for industry to work closely with faculty in areas of significant economic potential. The Marine Sciences Research Center (MSRC) at Stony Brook is the SUNY-wide center for research, graduate education, and public service in the marine sciences. One distinguishing characteristic of MSRC is its focus on the Coastal Ocean—from approximately the seaward edge of the continental shelf inland to the last measurable traces of sea salt. Another feature that distinguishes the MSRC from other oceanographic institutions, coastal and deep sea, is its use of science to solve complex problems that arise from society's multiple and conflicting uses of the Coastal Ocean, many of which have important economic consequences. For example, Long Island's power plants alone draw more than one million gallons of water from New York's coastal waters every minute and return them at an elevated temperature. If the power plants in the Metropolitan New York City area and those along the Hudson are included, the number increases manyfold. Once-through cooling systems are the most economical cooling systems possible, but they can have adverse impacts on aquatic resources, particularly fish eggs and larvae that are entrained. MSRC scientists developed models to show how mortalities of entrained organisms can be reduced greatly by adjusting flow rates and temperature elevations. The savings have been enormous.

MSRC research is valuable to entire industries, such as hard clam fishing. New York's Great South Bay historically has produced more than 50 percent of the nation's total harvest of hard clams. Employing more than 6,000 people and having an aggregate value, when all the multipliers are applied, of more than 100 million dollars per year, the hard clam fishery is one of Long Island's major industries. It is also an industry in trouble, one that could collapse if steps are not taken promptly. With support from the New York Sea Grant Institute, MSRC designed and implemented a comprehensive three-year study of the Great South Bay and its clam resources. Although the practical results of the study are yet to be evaluated, there is every expectation that the research will yield a comprehensive management plan for the hard clam fishery. Similar MSRC assistance is provided to the oyster industry, and to those concerned with waste disposal and energy production.

The New York Sea Grant Institute is a cooperative activity of the State University of New York and Cornell University. The Institute's program of research, training, and extension activities is intended to foster the efficient development of New York's abundant coastal resources. In this regard, New York's Great Lakes coast is a prime recreational resource. While traditional tourist attractions such as Niagara Falls and the Thousand Islands region remain popular, much of the new tourism centers on sport fishery. Spurred by the salmonoid stocking program of the Department of Environmental Conservation, the Lake Ontario recreational fishery has been estimated to contribute over 100 million dollars annually to the regional economy, with perhaps 25 percent of this accounted for by salmon and trout fishing. Sea Grant has had a central role in increasing public awareness of the development opportunities represented by the new fishery. It helps coastal communities assess their service infrastructure to meet the expected influx of fishermen, and its assistance enables marine trade industries to capitalize on the increased demand for their services and products. The Sea Grant Institute was involved in founding the Empire State Lake Ontario Trout & Salmon Derby (ESLO), the largest sportfishing tournament in the world. In 1982, ESLO's estimated eonomic impact in the seven Lake Ontario counties was 2.9 million dollars. In addition, Sea Grant helped develop the Lake Ontario charter boat business. This new business has brought over 2 million dollars of new funds into the Lake Ontario coastal economy.

Sea Grant's role in the revitalization of New York's fishing industries has increased commercial fishing interest in gaining support for private investment in new shore-side facilities and improved state-of-the-art harvesting for squid, a species not previously taken by New York fishermen but which has excellent export potential. In 1982, this new catch taken by New York fishermen and sold to Japanese firms had a value of 600,000 dollars. The Sea Grant Institute has assisted New York City and the Port Authority of New York and New Jersey in developing a seafood industrial complex in Brooklyn which will expand the fishery potential for export markets; the planned development will create over 2,000 new jobs.

Of all New York's coastal opportunities, aquaculture may have the greatest potential for expansion. Sea Grant involvement with the Marine Sciences Research Center in Long Island's shellfish industry has been described. But aquaculture goes beyond food production. Sea Grant is evaluating the feasibility of culturing seaweeds in enormous quantities as a feedstock for energy production and as a replacement for petro-chemical feedstocks. This replenishable source of important chemicals could provide a new dimension to New York's important chemical industries.

The Department of Paper Science and Engineering at the College of Environmental Science and Forestry in Syracuse supports studies in the physical sciences and chemical engineering, with specific emphasis on those aspects which relate to the manufacture of pulp and paper. Studies in chemical engineering include unit operations basic to the pulp and paper industry, as well as specialized activities in water and air pollution engineering. The sponsored research program of the Department is coordinated through the Empire State Research Institute. The Institute conducts a broad research program to generate new information regarding the fundamentals, the science, the engineering, and the technology of the papermaking process. Recent work has concentrated on a number of areas of potential importance for future development of the industry—improvements in high-yield pulps, new chemical pulping and bleaching processes, retention, drainage, and sheet formation, water removal and drying, characterization and treatment of effluents, and paper as a basic material. In addition to a large number of special purpose laboratories, the Institute enjoys the use of an experimental pulp and paper mill equipped with one 12-inch and one 48-inch Fourdrinier paper machine, thermomechanical refining equipment, and a number of pulp digesters. The major paper producing companies are part of the Institute and support its continuing program.

The Atmospheric Sciences Research Center (ASRC) at Albany was established in 1961 to promote programs of research in the basic and applied sciences, especially as they relate to man's environment, to encourage the fullest participation in these research activities by faculty and students of all units of the State University and by all appropriate industrial, governmental and educational groups, and in all other respects to develop the Center in the best interests of the people of New York State. Since its early days, the ASRC has embraced the tradition of fostering mutually beneficial programs with the private sector. Scientists in industry are appointed as Visiting Research Associates and work jointly with the ASRC staff on a variety of projects. For ASRC these relationships provide not just new sources of support, but they also help the Center to fulfill a fundamental responsibility to disseminate knowledge and, at the same time, to receive new research stimuli. There are also several New York small businesses which the ASRC has aided in their formation, such as W.S. Fleming Associates Inc., Scott-Healey Inc., and Associated Weather Services (AWS). Those companies already have succeeded in attracting national funding for energy, economics, and computer studies.

Much of ASRC's work focuses on the consequences of industrial activities on atmospheric conditions. The much discussed topic of acid rain in the Adirondack region is a case in point. Some of this work is conducted independently of industrial support and, in fact, monitors industrial activity. In some instances, industries support ASRC investigations, such as the stone-cutting company which asked ASRC to test the character of air-borne dust particles resulting from the cutting operation. One of the activities most identified with ASRC is that of cloud physics. The making of rain and the analysis of fog are of commercial interest in fields such as agriculture, transportation, electric power generation, and electronics. Companies like General Electric have supported and collaborated with ASRC scientists in cloud physics research.

ASRC maintains three field stations, one atop a 22-story dormitory on the SUNY Albany campus, one on Whiteface Mountain in the Adirondacks, and one at Blenheim/Gilboa in Schoharie County. From these stations, and with data exchange with similar stations around the country, ASRC provides meteorological information that is utilized by all the media in Northeastern New York and beyond. Although this is not a contracted service with industry, a large number of companies rely heavily on the accuracy of meteorological information for which ASRC is responsible.

More recently, two SUNY campuses have participated in the program initiated by the State of New York to establish Centers for Advanced Technology in areas important to industry. The Stony Brook Center for Biotechnology emphasizes three areas of investigation—genetic engineering, immunodiagnostics, and drug development; applied oral biology; and orthopedic and rehabilitative diagnostics and therapeutics. In addition to the resources of some fifteen academic departments at Stony Brook, the Center draws on such nearby resources as the Cold Spring Harbor Laboratories, Brookhaven National laboratories and the Plum Island Animal Disease Center. The Buffalo Center for Health Instrumentation Devices emphasizes the utilization of modern sensing and electronic information processing devices and techniques for the development and optimal use of new and refined medical instruments and methods for monitoring cardiac, metabolic, sensory, neurological, and neuromuscular functions. Particular emphasis is placed on noninvasive devices and procedures. The Center stresses the development of new devices and their transfer to commercial production, especially to companies located in the economically hard hit areas of Western New York. In addition to the talents of University faculty, the resources of Roswell Park Memorial Institute, the Western New York Technology Development Center, and the Buffalo General Hospital will be available to the Center.

A final example of an institutionalized research relationship is the recently formed Calspan-UB, Inc., where the University Center at Buffalo and a single company, the Arvin Corporation, have developed a collaborative program of research. University research faculty and company scientists have joined together to use the Calspan research facilities in areas such as aerospace, chemical, mechanical, electrical, and computer engineering.

Incubator Space

One current profile of the millionaire is the bearded 27 year old Ph.D. in computer science who does not own a necktie. But the entrepreneur with an idea, whatever his personal style, frequently needs access to technical information and expertise as well as assistance with the nontechnological aspects of the business world. Many universities have provided space at low rent on or adjacent to a campus so that new high-technology companies can draw upon university resources during the formative stages of new research. As a result these facilities have come to be known as incubators. Policy constraints on the use of University facilities have prevented SUNY campuses from providing this kind of service to incipient high-technology companies, though a number of campuses are finding acceptable and permissible alternatives that will soon enable the University to provide assistance in this area.

Technology Transfer

The Research Foundation of SUNY provides a University-wide service of technology transfer, aimed primarily at moving the University's ideas into the marketplace through the process of patenting and licensing. Created in 1979, the Technology Transfer Office is charged with transmitting University inventions from the laboratory to the marketplace. University inventions consist of those made under State support, to which SUNY retains title, and inventions made with external sponsorship, to which the Research Foundation retains title on behalf of SUNY. The steps in the process of technology transfer include:

Disclosure. When a faculty member's idea, process, or device has been judged to be of patent value, the idea is formally disclosed through the campus research office. Assistance is available to the inventor to protect patentable rights. If a SUNY investigator makes a discovery without using University facilities and wholly on his or her own time, the University makes no claim to ownership. SUNY research investigators are free to publish the results of their research. However, patent rights (especially in foreign countries) may be jeopardized by premature disclosure, and a professional judgment is needed about the timing of publication.

Evaluation. Inventions next are evaluated for both patentability and market potential. The first, a very technical matter, is referred to specialized attorneys retained by the Research Foundation. The second is undertaken by the Technology Transfer Office in conjunction with the inventor.

Marketing. Through personal contact, meetings, and publications, the Technology Transfer Office advertises University inventions and finds potential industrial licensees. Direct personal contact with company representatives by prospective licensees is supplemented by participation at technology and industrial development conferences such as those sponsored by the Licensing Executive Society and the American Association of Small Research Companies.

Licensing. Following SUNY Patent Policy and the Guidelines of the Patent Policy Board, the Technology Transfer Office negotiates both exclusive and nonexclusive licenses, option agreements, and research contracts with licensing provisions. For example, a major U.S. company is developing a SUNY invention under an Option/ Licensing Agreement for which it pays the Research Foundation 5,000 dollars annually until commercial sale, whereupon an exclusive license requiring a minimum payment of 5,000 dollars or 5 percent of net sales begins. The company also is supporting a two-year research project in the subject area for the amount of 147,190 dollars, for which it receives a first option to exclusive license on any resulting new inventions. The company will reimburse the Research Foundation for all domestic and foreign patenting expenses.

Patenting. The Technology Transfer Office files patent applications at appropriate times when warranted. The Office also seeks to have application expenses borne by a company as part of a licensing agreement. Because of the relatively high cost of applications, the Technology Transfer Office requires reimbursement from licensing companies for all foreign filings, but is less insistent on assistance for domestic applications.

Royalties. According to SUNY Patent Policy, inventors get 40 percent of gross royalties unless there is a sponsor limitation, which is now uncommon. The inventor's campuses get the bulk of the remaining royalties.

Table 3 indicates the growth of the Technology Transfer Office since its inception in 1979, and the relative activity at several of the stages described above. Table 4 indicates the type of agreements that the Office of Technology Transfer has negotiated, some of the companies involved, and the duration of the agreements. It summarizes an important and growing type of economic development activity.

The wide range of SUNY activities related to technology development and transfer is indicative of similar developments in universities around the country. As with any new and growing relationships, there have been problems. From the university point of view, the problems are twofold—the ownership and disposition of intellectual property and

Table 3. Disclosures and Patent Applications January, 1979 to April, 1983

Disclosures & Applications	Pre 1979	1979	1980	1981	1982	3 mos. of 1983	TOTAL
Invention Disclosures	5	23	18	33	36	10	125
U.S. Patent Applications	—	6	10	13	15	4	48
Foreign Patent Applications	—	—	—	9	35	16	60
U.S. Patents (issued)	—	1	1	7	—	—	9
Foreign Patents (issued)	2	—	—	—	—	—	2

SOURCE: Technology Transfer Office, The Research Foundation of SUNY.

Table 4. Summary of Industrial Agreements

	Exclusive	Non-Exclusive	Option/License
Instruments for Research and Industry	1	—	—
Lever Brothers	1	—	—
Cadema Medical Products, Inc.	1	—	—
Benedict Nuclear Pharmaceutical, Inc.	1	—	—
Frederick Haer	—	1	1
Enzo Biochem	—	1	1
Rowley Biochemicals	—	1	—
Velsicol Chemical Co.	—	—	1
Eli Lilly	—	—	2
Burroughs Wellcome	—	—	2
Bristol Laboratories	—	—	1
Nuclear Genetic Technology, Inc.	—	—	1
Daikin Kogyo Co., Ltd.	—	—	1

Licenses	Date of Agreement	Term of License
Instruments for Research and Industry	January, 1983	5 years
Lever Brothers	March, 1983	8 years
Cadema Medical Products, Inc.	March, 1983	10 years
Benedict Nuclear Pharmaceutical, Inc.	March, 1983	5 years
Frederick Haer	August, 1982	To end of patent life
Enzo Biochem	October, 1982	To end of patent life
Rowley Biochemicals	January, 1982	To end of patent life

SOURCE: Technology Transfer Office, The Research Foundation of SUNY.

the range of potential conflicts of interest on the part of university faculty who participate in industry-related research programs.

The intellectual property issue is sensitive because industry tends to take a proprietary view toward research results which it supports. Non-disclosure of research findings is also essential to industry if patent ownership is an issue. Universities, on the other hand, take the position that research findings must be public because the free dissemination of new information is essential to the nature of the university. Most universities also take the position that patents developed on university facilities belong to them, with both the faculty and the institution having rights to royalty from license income. Generally, if the university and the company come to a specific understanding before the research is conducted, these issues can be settled so that the interests of both parties are served. As time passes and the experience of each with the other grows, expectations and negotiations will become increasingly routine.

The other issue has to do with faculty conflicts of interest, most significantly in cases where a faculty member establishes his own company, has an equity ownership in a company, or otherwise gains from a company that conducts business in the faculty member's area of academic expertise. The faculty member then may be tempted to withhold knowledge from public awareness for the benefit of his company, neglect his own academic appointment, or use students, particularly graduate students, for corporate rather than educational ends. Ira Heyman of the University of California at Berkeley has described these potential problems as conflicts of commitment more than conflicts of interest, because the issue is where the faculty member's loyalty is invested rather than whether a legal line has been crossed. These matters can be resolved, and the university can establish and enforce policies which will protect its vital roles.

Although these issues have caused consternation in recent years, they are unlikely to be the abiding problems of the new relationship between universities and industry. The problems that lie immediately ahead will have to do with the most effective structures within which university-industry relationships can flourish and how best the university can preserve its essential attributes through this period of change. Specifically, this means first that the university must review all of the forms that technological assistance to industry now takes and, as experience dictates, confine itself to those forms that are most efficient and effective. We are currently in a period when many kinds of structural arrangements are being designed, some more effective than others. During the next few years the less effective patterns will fall by the wayside. When that occurs the structural arrangements for the university's involvement with industry will have been established fundamentally. And at that point the effects of these arrangements on the university's essential qualities and attributes can be appraised clearly and the preservation— both of the university's distinctive features and its new linkages with the industrial community—can be confronted squarely. At the least, areas of great commercial interest—engineering, biology, chemistry, computer science, and management—will receive the giant share of the resources from the private sector, potentially resulting in an imbalance of resources between commercially relevant disciplines, on the one hand, and the humanities and some of the social sciences, on the other. In relative terms the progress of the latter group could be retarded and the balance of strength which universities have sought to maintain would be jeopardized.

Some would argue that the marketplace should control the university through an academic natural selection process. Most would take the position that the university has a responsibility to maintain curricular balance independent of immediate student and commercial interests. The issue is not new to universities, except that industrial interests can complicate the problem. The university has the responsibility to ensure that it effectively communicates its need for balance to all its constituencies, including the companies on whom it relies for scientific research support. As the universities and private sector become more closely involved, there is reason to believe that corporations will see the value of supporting the humanities and social sciences as well as research programs in chemistry or engineering. It is in the interest of corporations to operate in a society greatly enriched by the comprehensive character of the university.

TECHNICAL ASSISTANCE

A university is a repository of the expertise that can genuinely assist economic development. The very concept of the land-grant college illustrates the point, and the point is accentuated by the role that land-grant colleges have played in the phenomenal strength of U.S. agriculture. In the latter half of the nineteenth century the Morrill Acts, named after former Vermont Senator Justin Morrill, established land-grant colleges for the sake of agriculture. Many people now are calling for the passage of a set of new Morrill Acts which would stimulate the universities to do for reindustrialization in America what the original acts did for agriculture. Many of the ideas espoused by the proponents of the new Morrill Acts already are being implemented in SUNY and other institutions. But perhaps the genius of the first Morrill Acts was not that agricultural research was conducted in the university setting, but that an extension and public service network was created to ensure that there was a broad delivery system for the new idea that the university produced.

It is very important to turn attention, therefore, to the University's role in public service and technical assistance. This, too, takes several forms.

Consulting

Much of the delivery of knowledge takes place through highly individualized formal and informal consulting. The classical example is that of the engineer who makes his expertise available to a company and is paid for his assistance, or the management faculty member who provides his management skills in the same way. For the most part, as part of their professional responsibility, SUNY faculty are permitted to devote a limited portion of their time to consulting and to retain any compensation. That is the formal side of consulting. In addition, many faculty assist organizations informally when they are called upon and rarely are reimbursed for their efforts. It is impossible to measure the degree to which formal and informal consulting takes place or to determine with any accuracy its effect on the reindustrialization of New York, but it is a significant University contribution which ought not be ignored simply because its impact cannot be guaged precisely. In addition to consulting, however, the University is involved in a number of more formalized relationships that can affect reindustrialization.

Public Service Offices

Fifty-nine Public Service Offices presently are functioning on SUNY campuses as special points of access for business, industry, and local government. Some are able to offer sophisticated services while others only now are beginning to define their responsibilities. With respect to the development of their function, three points seem to be in order. First, most Public Service Offices—those with multiple and other functions—need more staff. Second, campuses need more complete inventories of the resources available within the University to provide specialized research, training, and technical assistance so that Public Service Officers can respond effectively to requests from prospective clients. As a broker, the Public Service Officer should know what resources are available on campus and match those resources with the needs of prospective clients or be able to tap resources within and outside of the system. As soon as a more comprehensive system-wide personnel inventory is in place, ability to search the system will be enhanced. In the meantime, if each campus has a comprehensive resource inventory available to its Public Service Officer, the functioning of the Public Service Network will be strengthened. Third, more campuses need to inform the public that Public Service Officers are a point of access for economic assistance.

Development Centers for Business

The 32 Development Centers for Business perform a distinct role as packagers and deliverers of research, training, and technical assistance which draw in campus-based resources to meet the needs of clients. Located in such diverse economic regions of the State as Buffalo, Plattsburgh, Geneseo, and Farmingdale, the Centers are called upon to deliver assistance designed for their particular clientele. The delivery of such resources requires cooperative working relationships with University departments where experience in research and technical assistance reside, and with Continuing Education Centers, the usual locus for training mechanisms. Cooperation among campus Development Centers for Business is required also to deliver specialized services and for business endeavors involving two or more campuses.

Development Centers for Business perform several functions. They communicate with the public about programs of assistance offered by the State and Federal Governments and provide one-on-one counseling in financial management and planning to small businesses to help them achieve a level where they can afford private, full-service accounting and business consultants. Centers also conduct feasibility studies for small businesses applying for assistance and provide information about international trade and finance. They provide training for prospective minority entrepreneurs and counseling for those needing assistance. Training the existing workforce in new technologies is another of their tasks. The Centers provide access to University technologies and research for development of innovative techniques, and make technical information available through SUNY data bases (eventually to include marketing information from the U.S. Department of Commerce). Finally, the Development Centers advertise the availability of their services through media and other organizations.

There are three points that should be considered in connection with the development of the Development Centers for Business. First, improved organization and increased staffing will enhance the capacity of the Centers to serve more businesses and industries. Second, record keeping that documents the services and achievements of the Centers is worthy of attention from the standpoint of justifying budgets to support this activity. Third, it is desirable that campuses work to derive full benefit from a close involvement with their Advisory Board.

The appointment of the Advisory Boards for the Development Centers for Business is an important part of the program. In response to the Chancellor's invitation, acceptance of membership—drawn largely from the business community and now totaling more than 200 for the 32

DCB's—indicates a desire for a closer working relationship between business and the University. Advisory Board members expect that they will have a substantive involvement with the University in programs contributing to economic development. Some Advisory Board members have stressed the seriousness of their intention to help provide DCB efforts.

Technical Assistance Centers

The SUNY system contains five Technical Assistance Centers. In addition to offering technical assistance, the Economic Development and Technical Assistance Center at Plattsburgh and the Urban Research and Development Center at the State University College at Buffalo are simultaneously the bases of the Development Centers for Business. There are also the Trade Adjustment Assistance Center at Binghamton, the Regional Economic Assistance Center at the State University of New York at Buffalo, and the Center for Industrial Cooperation at the State University of New York at Stony Brook. The Economic Development and Technical Assistance Center at Plattsburgh has been acclaimed by both Governors Carey and Cuomo for service to hundreds of companies. In particular, it has been praised for keeping business in New York and attracting foreign corporations. The Trade Adjustment Assistance Center at Binghamton, one of eleven similar Centers in the nation funded by the International Trade Administration, U.S. Department of Commerce, assists businesses that have been adversely affected by foreign imports. The Center has saved businesses from bankruptcy and has realigned their operations so they can compete successfully in the international as well as the domestic marketplace. The service area of the Trade Adjustment Assistance Center is New York State apart from Long Island and New York City. All of the Technical Assistance Centers can be credited with saving jobs and participating in applied research of major consequence to their clients.

International Programs

In 1981, the National Academy of Sciences established a panel on Advanced Technology Competition and the Industrial Allies, consisting of distinguished university and industry representatives and chaired by Howard W. Johnson of M.I.T. The panel announced its findings in March of 1983 in a report entitled, *International Competition in Advanced Technology: Decisions for America*. The major recommendation of the report deserves special mention.

Advanced technology development and trade must be considered as among the highest priorities of the nation. The United States must initiate a two-part strategy: to maintain the nation's capacity for technological innovation and to foster an open healthy trading system.[9]

In addition to the many technically-oriented programs described, the State University also has many activities that foster international trade and understanding.

Foreign Students

The presence of foreign students augments the pluralistic character of the University and establishes a base of international understanding on the part of both American students and students from other countries. There were 6,458 foreign students enrolled on all campuses throughout the system in the fall of 1981. This represented a net increase of 494 over the fall of 1980 figures, or 8.3 percent. Statistics show that since 1977 foreign student enrollment in SUNY has increased by over 65 percent.

Foreign students educated in the United States tend to turn to the United States again when trade considerations arise. A recent study by the Fulbright Commission reveals that more than twenty current heads of state and 250 cabinet ministers in foreign countries were trained in the United States. University records reveal that alumni hold positions such as Deputy Director of the Division of Trade and Agriculture in Sierra Leone, president of an Indonesian import-export firm which has set up offices in New York and which sends its executives to SUNY for training, and director of a company in Kenya which holds franchise rights for a New York company that distributes New York's products.

International Exchange Program

The State University has developed continuing exchange programs with the Provincial Universities in Quebec, Canada, and Moscow State University in the Soviet Union, a small but unique project with the People's Republic of China, an agreement with Yugoslavia relating to the development of the community college concept, mutual exchanges related to graduate education with Swedish universities, and a number of shorter-term exchanges with Third World countries. In addition, SUNY offers American students the opportunity to study abroad in over 100 approved programs. In 1981, about 1,900 students participated in these overseas programs. Program and travel costs continue to rise with overseas programs, making it more difficult for students to avail themselves of the opportunity, but the University continues to stress the value of such exchanges.

Export Programs

By means of SUNY's Public Service Network, information and technical assistance are available to assist New York businesses seeking world markets. New York businesses have access to U.S. Department of Commerce data on world markets in order to determine parts of the world in which there are markets for New York goods. Technical assistance is available to assist with international financing, international tariff regulations, cultural concerns that affect marketing, legal problems, and any special concerns related to trade with particular countries. The Public Service Offices of SUNY also have conducted a series of seminars across the State describing the process of export to interested small businessmen. In addition, several SUNY campuses conduct continuing education programs on exports and export assistance.

International Development Assistance

In January, 1982, the International Development Assistance Service (IDAS) was established in the Office of International Programs in the SUNY Central Administration to facilitate mobilization of international development efforts. Conceptually, SUNY-IDAS is a consortial arrangement whereby the technical assistance capability and training capacity within the SUNY system can be joined to other development assistance opportunities. A primary example of the IDAS concept at work is the current negotiation involving a 25 million dollar contract to be supported by a World Bank loan for a Teacher Training Project with the Government of Indonesia. SUNY Albany will serve as the lead campus for the project which will involve 17 SUNY campuses in all. Projects with other governments including Tunisia, Pakistan, and Kuwait are currently under review. The residents of New York State as well as Third World countries will benefit from the success of IDAS. As SUNY becomes more active in global development, the perspectives necessary to full participation in the world's economy will become integral to the University's thinking and benefit both students and New York State businesses seeking assistance in developing international markets.

These activities raise a major question about the university's role in relationship to industry. To what extent do efforts extended primarily to the business community lead to a loss of impartiality or at least a narrowing of perspective on the part of the university? An example is in order. A group of farm workers has filed suit against the University of California at Davis on the grounds that the Davis agricultural research program is devoted to the interests of agribusiness to the exclusion of the interests of the farm worker. Machinery development through research conducted at Davis has enhanced greatly agricultural efficiency and productivity. The suit contends, however, that the cost has been large-scale unemployment among agricultural workers and the virtual extinction of the family farm in California. The University of California contends that it serves the interests of agriculture generally and that its research has made a tremendous contribution to the economy of the state of California as a result. Its efforts have not been directed to the benefit of one segment of the agricultural community— in this case agribusiness—but to the entire agricultural community.

Quite apart from the merits or demerits of the California case, the potential problem of the university being captured by one set of interests merits continuous attention. If the SUNY campuses are involved in providing large amounts of technical assistance to business, are the interests of organized labor and the ordinary consumer well served? The University has the obvious responsibility to see to it that its activities are in the public interest and not in some sectarian interest only. Further, to the extent that SUNY assists companies in export and participation in the world economy, the University also has a responsibility to maintain objectivity and fairness on an international scale that would include concern for the interests of lesser developed countries, and the concerns of human rights and human need as well as assistance to multinational corporations. It will be the responsibility of the University to maintain the balance of its concerns. This will not be easy in light of the financial inequities supporting its varied activities. Universities will have to work hard to find the funds to maintain the balance.

STRATEGIC PLANNING

There is a final area of importance to the reindustrialization process, an area which, compared to the others, has received considerably less attention. University scholars in fields such as economics, political science, and other social sciences whose studies encompass long-term economic and industrial trends are a significant but largely underutilized resource to both corporate and government strategic planners. Historically, at least, academic scholars have exhibited a predilection for so overburdening judgments with qualifications that planners have found their erudition to be of little use. More recently, however, with the addition of computer-assisted modeling to the arsenal of both the planner and the academic, the increasingly unambiguous formulation of alternatives for planning purposes is now both feasible and academically respectable, as the following examples indicate.

Econometric Modeling

Industry and government have come to rely heavily on econometric models for planning purposes. At least two of the major national econometric modeling services (Wharton and DRI) had their genesis in universities. Other universities are providing econometric models specifically designed to produce data pertinent to a state or region. The State University of New York has not developed such a working model although it has proposed doing so to a number of state agencies in New York. States such as Tennessee do rely on the state university to provide the data that is of use to a variety of public and private agencies.

Special Needs Assessments

There are a number of areas of importance to the economic future of a region and its industries that rely on information produced by university researchers. The following examples will serve as indications of what is meant here. In the area of land use planning, the State University College at Oneonta has developed a capacity for gathering and analyzing data generated by remote sensing through Landsat satellite technology. The data generated through this means provide an inexpensive and accurate way for local government to maintain controlled development and for industry and agriculture to determine such issues as optimal plant sitings and infrastructure needs. Infrastructure needs and use patterns are themselves an important area of University research. SUNY Buffalo researchers played a planning role in the construction of mass transit in Buffalo. Other researchers have studied such important, if undramatic, problems as cost reduction in pothole repair.

Energy availability and environmental protection also have been studied by SUNY faculty. The electric power load demand that would result from the introduction of the electric car has been analyzed by a SUNY Buffalo faculty member for a public utility in Rochester. The SUNY College of Environmental Science and Forestry studied the environmental and economic impacts of opening the St. Lawrence Seaway to year-round commercial shipping. Manpower projections are another area where University research aids local industries and governments to plan for economic growth that will prevent human dislocation.

There are numbers of questions directed primarily at governmental policy formation at the State level that have important implications for industry. For example, a Stony Brook team investigating plant closings within the State has much to say to policy makers who review tax incentives for new business ventures, or who review State supported loan guarantees and venture capital funds. Each of these studies fills a need related to the process of reindustrialization within the State.

Industry-specific Projections

Yet a final type of university input into the planning process is made possible through industry-specific projections. As a case in point, the supply and demand projections of various types of wood available through the Renewable Resources Institute at the State University College of Environmental Science and Forestry are of importance to the timber and paper industries. At the SUNY statutory College of Ceramics at Alfred detailed analyses of properties of various ceramics materials are made. These are of importance to the large number of industries for which the use of ceramic substances is becoming of increasing importance.

Making projections raises the problem of judgments based upon these projections. What should be the role of the university in regard to the provision of this type of information? The most useful distinction for determining the role of the university is that between the *analyst* and the *counselor*. The university's role should be that of the former rather than the latter. In this sense, the university role will differ from that of a corporate strategic planner or of an advisor to a policy maker. This distinction is easy to articulate but difficult to observe in fact. Analysis that is of use to the advisor or the planner will more often than not contain recommendations or options as well as statistical information. The work of the analyst will, as a consequence, contain judgments. At the same time, the advisor will gather analytic data and make judgments on the basis of the data just as the academic does. There seems as a result to be little in the way of a functional difference.

Yet, in the final analysis, there is a difference. While projecting outcomes and making recommendations, analysts will concern themselves with the interests of the policy makers of special interest groups only insofar as their possible actions may affect policy outcomes and therefore must be factored into policy analysis. The advisor, on the other hand, interprets the same factors but recommends courses of action in the interest of whoever is being advised. As a result, the work of the analyst and the advisor are almost synonymous on noncontroversial issues. The two efforts part company as the issue becomes more controversial, and it is just at this point that the university analyst needs to involve analytical strictures.

Once again the university runs a danger of excess, but it cannot avoid problems by seeking isolation from potential conflicts. Rather, it must recognize its vulnerabilities and struggle to maintain its proper role, two tasks which SUNY has integrated into the developmental courses of action it has elected to pursue.

VI

Special Issues

THIRTEEN

Defense Procurement and the Reindustrialization of New York State

James E. Ryan

From the beginning of 1981 to the end of 1982 the nation experienced severe recession followed by the first stirrings of economic recovery. Data for nonagricultural and manufacturing employment indicate that the trough of the recession occurred between the middle and the end of calendar year 1982. While the nation welcomed real signs of recovery during the conclusion of that period, New York State continued to show a decline in employment, particularly blue-collar manufacturing employment. In 1982 and 1983 the State lost a total of 121,000 manufacturing positions, and during 1983, a time of increasing recovery for the rest of the nation, New York lost manufacturing jobs at an accelerating rate and in absolute terms. The average annual loss of manufacturing jobs in the State for 1982 numbered 58,000 and the loss measured for 1983 numbered 63,000. Positions in the nonmanufacturing sector increased by 40,000 in calendar year 1982 and by only 6,000 between the end of that year and the end of 1983, on average. This means that the net loss of jobs over the two-year period numbered 75,000, most of which were lost in 1983 and in the manufacturing sector.[1]

While recent aggregate figures for the State indicate an economy in decline, an examination of individual labor market areas and selected counties indicates that certain parts of the State consistently have enjoyed prosperity and low unemployment.[2] Several quite distinctive characteristics were common to these areas. One or more large, technologically sophisticated manufacturing operations employed at least 15 percent of the manufacturing labor force in the areas in which they were located.[3] These firms performed a large part of their operations on behalf of the Department of Defense and all had received substantial—at least 30 percent—increases in defense procurement contracts from the beginning of FY1982 to the close of FY1983.[4] These facts certainly should lead us to explore the possibility that defense procurement contracts can be used as an aid in the reindustrialization of New York State. But considering the efficacy of defense procurement contracts as an aid to New York's economic revitalization first requires that we examine the economic condition of the State and the relationship of New York to the federal fisc. From such an examination it will be possible to draw some inferences about how the economy of the State may respond to changes in federal procurement policy. The history of the economic behavior of New York over the past ten years provides a starting point.

A STAGNATING ECONOMY

Although the economy of New York State was affected more adversely during the recession of 1974–1975 than the nation as a whole, its unemployment level remained well below the national average during the recent recession. The reasons generally given for this development have to do with a "new equilibrium" that was reached toward the end of the 1970s. The argument entails the hypothesis that service sector jobs replaced those positions that were lost in the manufacturing sector and that an economy based on service employment is more "recession resistant" than a manufacturing economy.[5] While there clearly is some truth to this claim, such an economic foundation is flawed. Economies dominated by the service sector are less vulnerable to economic contractions, but they also tend to become stagnant. During periods of economic recovery, economies without a strong manufacturing base are not likely to participate in a general business boom. Such was the case with New York after 1975. The State's rate of increase in total employment never reached one half of the national average for the period 1975–1981. And its manufacturing sector never again reached 1973 levels.[6]

The loss of manufacturing has lead to loss of population, slow real income growth, and an increasing proportion of dependent citizens. As manufacturing jobs left the State, many managerial, skilled and semi-skilled workers left with them. The State's population declined by 3.8 percent between 1970 and 1980. New York was the only State to lose population during this period except for Rhode Island, which lost .3 percent of its population.[7] At the same time, lower paying service sector employment replaced manufacturing employment, a process that lead to a relatively slow rate of real income growth. New York was the worst performer in this category during the 1970s. The State's real per capita income growth was only 8 percent. The next worst performer was New Jersey with a real per capita income growth of 18 percent. On the other hand, the national average for per capita real income growth was 36 percent.[8] As those productive persons associated with manufacturing fled the State, New York was left with a high proportion of the elderly and the poor, a population requiring more public services which now must be financed from a shrinking tax base.

The loss of manufacturing employment and the resulting economic weakness is one essential part of a dynamic that all older, urban-industrial states have undergone. In general, these states are characterized by high levels of public services for dependent citizens and suffer correspondingly high per capita tax burdens. Wages are generally higher than elsewhere in the country and the labor image is unfavorable from management's point of view. Long-standing problems are aggravated further in large cities as social ills brought on by economic weakness, such as crime and blight, intensify. And once intensified, these problems can create political pressures hostile to programs aimed at ameliorating social ills. At the same time, within such a social and economic context of decline additional political pressures arise to accommodate business interests. The consequence is that elected officials are forced into a position where it is easy to appear indecisive in the face of competing interests.[9] But at the same time New York State has somewhat special problems, too. Nearly two-thirds of all its energy needs are met by expensive, imported petroleum. Unusually strict pollution and environmental controls add considerably to the cost of doing business. Both the general problems of older urban states and the special problems of New York can issue in the loss of business confidence and a further loss of manufacturing employment.

Yanklevich, Skelly, and White found that management perceptions of these problems in New York varied, but the least favorable outlook was given by chief executive officers of large, urban manufacturing firms. It was these same types of firms that were most likely to leave the State.[10] The economic weakness produced by the loss of blue-collar manufacturing has made the State more sensitive to the effects of both the amount of federal funds flowing into the State relative to its federal tax burden and the specific mix of federal expenditures in the State.

ARTIFICIAL INFLOWS, REAL OUTFLOWS

The State paid 47.3 billion dollars in total federal taxes, including all trust funds, in 1981, 48.8 billion dollars in 1982, and 48.4 billion dollars in 1983. This constitutes 8.14 percent, 8.16 percent, and 8.33 percent, respectively, of the nation's total tax burden for each of those fiscal years.[11] Documented federal outlays in New York State for Fiscal Years 1981, 1982 and 1983 amounted to 42.2 billion dollars, 44.43 billion dollars, and 50.1 billion dollars, respectively.[12] Federal outlays do not consider interest payments and when adjustments are made for this omission New York State appears to have received a net inflow of federal expenditures during the past three fiscal years.[13] Due to large deficits, however, most states received more in federal expenditures than they paid in federal taxes and New York did not share in deficit financed expenditures in proportion to its tax payments. When this factor is taken into account, it is estimated that New York State fell short of its share of federal expenditures by between 5 and 7 billion dollars in each of the past three fiscal years (1981–83). While New York does not share equitably in federal expenditures, it bears a higher proportion of the burden of the federal deficit since it pays a higher share of interest payments compared to the national average. This results in a large drain on the State's economy relative to other states.[14] But the size of New York's real outflow of funds is not the only problem.

FEDERAL EXPENDITURES ENCOURAGE ECONOMIC STAGNATION

New York usually has ranked below the national average in per capita federal expenditure amounts with no apparent harm to its economy in the past. However, since the middle of the 1970s, New York also has become sensitive to the mix of federal expenditures that it receives because of its weakened economy. The State is now receiving little of those direct federal expenditures going toward procurement. Expenditures for these purposes have moved steadily to the South and West over the last decade.[15]

Table 1 indicates the percentage of total federal expenditures in New York by selected functional areas and compares them to the State's total tax burden for fiscal years 1981, 1982, and 1983, repectively. The first area, "National Defense," consistently has ranked slightly above 5 percent since the middle of the 1970s. The State has

Table 1. Federal Expenditures in New York as a Percentage of Total Expenditure for Major Functional Areas, Compared with New York's Percentage Share of the Nation's Tax Burden

		FISCAL YEAR		
		1981	1982	1983
TAX BURDEN		8.14	8.18	8.33
FUNCTIONAL AREA				
A.	National Defense	5.07	5.2	5.4
B.	Retirement and Veteran's Benefits			
	1. General Retirement and Disability	8.9	9.0	8.7
	2. Federal Retirement and Disability	3.7	3.7	3.6
	3. Veterans' Benefits and Services	6.3	6.4	6.6
C.	Human Capital			
	1. Health and Health Care Services	9.4	4.7	8.6
	2. Public Assistance and Other Income			
	Supplements	14.9	14.4	14.3
	3. Employment and Training Assistance	9.3	11.6	7.7
	4. Education Programs	7.7	7.3	5.0
	5. Human Development Services	7.3	7.3	9.4
D.	Public Infrastructure			
	1. Highways and Transportation	8.4	8.2	9.0
	2. Pollution Control and Abatement	7.5	8.3	9.7
	3. Community Development	11.4	12.6	11.8
	4. Water Resources	.01	.01	.01
E.	Other Grants to State and Local Governments	7.9	6.4	6.6
F.	Other Programs and Payments to Individuals	6.1	5.5	6.7

SOURCE: U.S. Bureau of the Census, *Federal Expenditures by State,* for Fiscal Years 1981, 1982, 1983.

few military bases, none of which are considered large. Hence, when defense expenditure figures are disaggregated into the subcategories of salaries and procurement, one would see that New York only receives about 1.8 percent of all federal military salaries.[16] In 1981, the State received about 6.7 percent of all DOD procurement funds. This figure rose to 6.8 percent in 1982 and 6.9 percent in 1983.[17] While this increase has been helpful in providing some manufacturing jobs, it was not enough to offset the net loss of jobs which occurred in New York for 1981 and 1982. The calculated effects of the increase in procurement contracts over that period, however, underscores the issue of using such contracts to aid New York's manufacturing sector.

The second major functional area, "Retirement and Veterans' Benefits," represents a mixed picture. New York has a higher proportion of elderly people than most states and thus receives more in federal monies than it pays in federal taxes for the sub area of "General Retirement Payments." The State does not do well, though, in the other sub areas, notably "Federal Retirement and Disability," and "Veteran's

319

Benefits." This is partly a reflection of the few military installations in the State.

Since the State also has a high proportion of persons in need, it does relatively well in the major functional area of "Human Capital," although this varies by program. Most notably, the State collects a high percentage—almost twice its tax burden—in the sub area of "Public Assistance and Other Income Supplements." These programs constitute the largest share of the major functional area of "Human Capital." In the major functional area of "Public Infrastructure," the sub area of "Highways and Transportation" favors New York because of distribution formulae. Most of the federal expenditures in this subcategory come out of the highway trust fund or programs for mass transit. The formulae for distribution of federal funds in the sub area of "Community Development" also favors New York. The sub area of "Pollution Control and Abatement" mostly involves project grants for capital construction and the share of federal receipts therefore demonstrates a lumpiness from year to year. Finally, the sub area of "Water Resources" always has been a problem for New York. Programs classified under this sub area involve projects of the Corps of Engineers whose priority water projects usually are found in the South and West. The last major functional areas, "Other Grants to State and Local Governments" and "Other Programs and Payments to Individuals," are not meaningfully disaggregated in federal data. However, these are not large programs.

Generally speaking, then, we can say that New York does well with regard to transfer payments and many federal grant-in-aid programs. The State does less well with regard to discretionary programs involving salaries and procurement. These latter fields are dominated by the Department of Defense. The largest share of federal expenditures in New York goes toward consumption rather than investment or the encouragement of investment. Distributional formulae guarantee that New York will receive a relatively large federal share of income assistance monies. While such funds help to insure a slightly higher standard of living for the less fortunate, they have little effect in stimulating economic growth. Overall, they help to maintain the status quo in the State. Those programs not directly involved with income assistance, education, employment, and training, but with human capital generally, also tend to be targeted toward the poor. Regardless of the good intentions of the proponents of these programs, the fact is that they do not produce the stimulus necessary for investment, nor do they produce large multiplier effects that will lead to large increases in available employment. Certain programs aimed at infrastructure development and maintenance, such as those supported through trust funds for highway and airport construction, are more useful in providing an attractive environment for investment. Unfortunately, these programs are slow to show effects. In contrast, federal procurement contracts can have an immediate effect on the availability of blue-collar jobs. Moreover, these programs dwarf others which expand federal funds in the states.

GREATEST POTENTIAL IS WITH THE DEPARTMENT OF DEFENSE

Table 2 shows the significance of Department of Defense, Department of Energy, and National Aeronautics and Space Administration federal procurement programs. The size of these procurement programs amounts to roughly 14 percent of the U.S. GNP.[18] The table indicates that all purchases—grants, salaries, procurement—have fallen slightly compared to total outlays. More significantly, however, the types of goods and services purchased between Fiscal Years 1981 and 1983 have shifted gradually toward defense related uses and away from civilian ones.

Most discussion of fiscal federalism centers on the numerous grant-in-aid programs, and much of this discussion tends to be confused since it often includes transfer payments, such as federal "grants" to the states for old age assistance. Those programs designed to assist subnational units of government to purchase goods and services (true grants) constitute only about 25 percent of all government purchases.

Table 2. Outlays Comparing Major Transfer Payments and Major Procurement Expenditures (in billions of dollars)

| | FISCAL YEAR | | |
	1981	1982	1983
TOTAL FEDERAL OUTLAYS	$708.8	$745.0	$773.8
Interest Payments	95.0	117.0	128.0
Other Transfers	259.6	286.0	325.8
OUTLAYS LESS TRANSFERS	354.2	342.0	319.0
Grants to State & Local Governments	94.8	88.2	92.7
Active Military and DOD Civilian Salaries	46.0	51.0	53.0
Procurement for DOD, NASA, and Energy	122.0	137.0	150.0
Other Programs	91.4	65.8	23.3

SOURCE: Estimated from National Tax Foundation and *Federal Expenditures by State,* for Fiscal Years 1981, 1982, 1983.

The lion's share of purchase activity, and of economic influence, lies elsewhere.

The other 75 percent of federal purchases for goods and services are classified under the categories of "Wages and Salaries" and "Procurement." Both categories are dominated by DOD. About 65 percent of all salaries and wages disbursed by the federal government go to DOD active military and civilian personnel. Between 75 and 80 percent of all procurement expenditures are made on behalf of the Department of Defense. This figure increases to 95 percent when purchases by NASA and the Department of Energy are included.[19] Moreover, in the past three years, the rate of federal procurement has grown relative to wages and salaries.

DIFFERENT MIXES PRODUCE DIFFERENT RESULTS

As the distribution of federal procurement expenditures shifts toward the South and the West, the difference in the resulting mix of federal expenditures can be seen when the state of California is compared with New York. In 1983, California received almost 31 billion dollars in procurement contracts or 20 percent of all federal expenditures in this area. New York, on the other hand, received about 9.6 billion dollars or about 6.9 percent of all procurement.[20] A comparison of the resulting mix of expenditures shows that California received about 33 percent more in procurement expenditures than it did in transfer payments. New York received about twice as much in transfers as it did in procurement.[21] Given this difference, and considering the economic condition of both states, the question arises, "What benefits would accrue to New York State if there had been a redistribution of federal defense procurement contracts in previous years?"

DEFENSE SPENDING: BURDEN OR PROP?

Before examining the possible answers to this question, the consequences of the use of defense outlays as part of economic policy should be considered. Defense outlays have a mixed reputation as being both an economic burden and an economic prop.[22] Many believe that the resources used for defense would be better invested in social programs such as education, cleaner streets, and more aid for the unfortunate, to name but a few. Most will concede, however, that defense is a necessary burden and that it ought to be borne as efficiently as possible.

On the other hand, defense production is used as a prop for the economy. It has supplied millions of jobs and has been a singular source of prosperity for different regions of the country. Those who view defense as a burden assume that demand for other goods and services should replace the present one for defense. Those who view defense as a prop fear that no other demands might exist.[23] Along these lines we can recall President Eisenhower's 1953 statement—

The cost of one heavy bomber is this: a modern brick school in more than thirty cities. It is two electric power plants, each serving a town of 60,000 population. It is two fine, fully equipped hospitals. It is some fifty miles of concrete highway.[24]

—as well as the facts that, in the 1980s, across the nation and the State we are closing schools, overbuilding electric power capacity in many regions, closing hospital wings for lack of patients, and desperately repairing and replacing existing infrastructure.

The deindustrialization and reindustrialization of the nation is one of the most discussed and distressing topics of the day. The effects of deindustrialization are known to touch large segments of the population. Widespread capital flight and private disinvestment has been documented.[25] Unemployment and underemployment is a constant threat to those who once depended on U.S. industry as an avenue for upward mobility.[26] Finally, we must consider the effect of deindustrialization in terms of strategic military consequences, since our basic blue-collar industries have been most devastated by the process of deindustrialization.[27]

The experience of New York State since the early 1970s may be considered an example of deindustrialization. Industry left the State. The structure of consumer demand changed as a large proportion of public expenditures in New York consisted increasingly of transfer payments. While New York had not been sensitive to the distribution of defense expenditures prior to the 1970s, defense expenditures might now provide a sorely needed stimulus to the economy.[28]

DEFENSE SPENDING AS REDISTRIBUTION

The notion of defense spending as a form of redistribution is not new. The impact of defense procurement has been recognized since the beginning of the Korean conflict. In 1951 directives from the President and the Secretary of Defense took steps to provide procurement from labor surplus areas.[29] Initially, the mechanism for redistribution allowed that the requirement for acceptance of a low bid be waived under certain circumstances. Congress criticized this system and initiated a "set aside" procedure in 1953. In 1954, however, the Congress consistently barred payment to other than the lowest bidder.[30]

In 1959, Senator Jacob Javits proposed to Congress that

the security of the Nation requires that its economy, and the economy of each section of the country, be maintained at a level which can support its programs for defense and sustain the private economic system. . . . [T]he procuring agency shall consider the strategic and economic desirability of allocating purchases to different geographical areas of the Nation and to eligible suppliers from whom relatively small procurements have been purchased.[31]

Congress did not accept this provision but did eventually enact a measure for the consideration of small business under a "fair share" criterion.[32]

In 1960, policy was amended to provide set asides for persistent labor surplus areas. By 1964 the record indicated that special set asides for these areas were not successful. Less than 1 percent of all DOD procurement had gone to such areas.[33] More recently, the Congressional members of the Northeast-Midwest Coalition led an effort to redistribute some procurement funds to distressed regions. In 1980 Congress established a test program in which the Defense Logistics Agency (DLA) would set aside 3.4 billion dollars to purchase nonstrategic goods from areas of high unemployment. In 1981 this set aside provision was extended and the amount authorized under this provision was increased to 5 billion dollars. An amendment to the 1983 defense procurement authorization bill reduced this amount to 4 billion dollars.[34]

None of the previous efforts to aid regions in distress have been particularly successful. This is because most of the goods and services purchased through federal procurement expenditures, particularly for defense, tend to be products that are produced by businesses that are technologically sophisticated and which make goods to order within tight tolerances.[35] The goods required by the federal government do not lend themselves to the geographic dispersion of purchase orders. Nor are they likely to be produced by firms that have traditionally been disadvantaged. In 1983, total set asides for labor surplus areas and minority- and women-owned business amount to less than 1.5 percent of all federal procurement.[36]

DEFENSE AND REINDUSTRIALIZATION: THE POSSIBILITIES

While measures aimed at redistribution have been designed to relieve acute or chronic unemployment, recent consideration has been given to the use of procurement dollars to aid in the reindustrialization of the nation and to protect those industries that are strategically important.[37] Such a consideration could be of particular importance to the state of New York.

To explore the possibilities it is necessary to see in what areas, given federal procurement policies and trends, New York is likely to do best with its resources. The evidence suggests that the most immediate results, and therefore the results with the most political appeal, are in the area of blue-collar manufacture of sophisticated weaponry and components, along with electronics, for the Department of Defense. New York State is at a disadvantage with regard to the wages and salaries portion of the federal budget since it has few military installations. Moreover, the purchase of standard items from small business is not promising since this part of the procurement budget is too small and must be dispersed too widely across the nation to be of much help to New York State.[38]

Approximately 54 percent of all federal procurement contracts go to the purchase of equipment and supplies. About 13 percent recently has gone to research and development activities.[39]. Eighty-seven percent of all procurement dollars go to large organizations for equipment, supplies, and research and development.[40] The Department of Energy gives the highest proportion—about 20 percent—of its procurement budget to education and non-profit organizations. Recently, however, this sum only has amounted to about 2 billion dollars.[41] The largest amount of federally procured research and development originates with the Department of Defense, which spent 16 billion dollars in 1983 for this purpose. The National Aeronautics and Space Administration spent about 3.4 billion dollars for research and development in Fiscal Year 1983.[42] So, for all practical purposes, the possibilities that *may* yet remain open to New York State appear to be blue-collar manufacturing of weapons systems and components and DOD sponsored research and development activities, including research which is university based.

"R&D" IS NOT PROMISING

The term "research and development" actually covers, in addition to basic scientific and engineering work, the production, testing, and evaluation of prototypes. While it is possible that actions designed to procure more research and development contracts would stimulate an alliance between the academic and business communities, the outlook is not promising. Most defense dollars go to the support of development, production, and testing—not research.

A defense firm may engage in the spectrum of engineering which ranges from the pursuit of basic knowledge to development and production. But very little government support for research is to be found that is involved with the development of basic knowledge or new processes. Government interest only becomes significant after there is both a perceived need for a product and the economic feasibility of production is fairly certain.[43] Nor is the firm likely to be seriously interested in university based basic research. To begin with, basic research as an investment is a luxury that only the largest private organizations can afford. Yet, even these firms have shown a reluctance to become involved with the university in the past twenty years because the process of university basic research is too far removed from a saleable product.[44]

Finally, regardless of the possibilities, this part of the procurement budget is too small to produce an immediate and significant effect on the economy of New York State. For example, although organizations such as Calspan and Sierra Research Corporation in western New York have received contract increases of around 30 percent from the federal government over the past three fiscal years, the total amounts awarded in 1983 are not enough to have a serious impact on unemployment in the region.[45]

BLUE-COLLAR MANUFACTURING: A TRADITIONAL AID

This leaves the possibility of utilizing defense procurement contracts aimed at large, established manufacturing firms in New York as an aid in revitalizing industry. The recent experience of New York State indicates that while many manufacturing positions were lost, some regions of the State did not fare too badly. Aaron Gurwitz has found that some labor market areas performed well relative to the nation and to the rest of the State during the last recession. Large firms involved with the blue-collar manufacturing using technologically sophisticated processes were located in these areas. In particular, Gurwitz identifies the Nassau-Suffolk, Poughkeepsie, and Binghamton areas as those which performed particularly well, not only during the recent recession but also over the period extending from 1974 to 1981.[46] The dominant firms in these areas do a significant amount of defense work. Grumman Corporation is the largest manufacturing firm in the Nassau-Suffolk area and may be classified as a true defense firm in that almost all of its manufacturing is presently done on behalf of the Department of Defense. International Business Machines is the dominant firm in both the Poughkeepsie and Binghamton areas. General Electric also has a large operation in Binghamton. These three firms continually rank in the top twenty federal defense procurement contracting firms in the nation.[47]

The data indicate that while total manufacturing losses in New York State were increasing steadily through the 1981–1983 period, these areas' manufacturing employment either only slightly decreased or actually increased. The performance lead to increases in the number of nonmanufacturing positions available in these labor market areas.[48] These same areas experienced real growth in the dollar amount of DOD procurement contracts and/or had an above average per capita DOD procurement expenditure relative to the State as a whole.[49]

SOME CALCULATIONS: WHAT IF?

It is possible to estimate how much of an increase in DOD procurement contracts would have been necessary in the past three fiscal years in order to halt the decline in the manufacturing sector in New York State. Using past procurement data, we also can make some estimates as to whether the major defense firms in the State could have absorbed such increases. (The details of the estimation procedure are contained in an appendix to this paper.)

Assuming that it would take approximately 60,000 dollars to support one worker in a capital intensive defense firm (see appendix), multiplying this figure by 58,000, the number of manufacturing jobs lost in New York State during 1982, provides a value of 3.5 billion dollars. This is the estimated increase in defense procurement contracts that would have halted the manufacturing decline in Fiscal Year 1982. Applying the same procedure to the job losses for Fiscal Year 1983 (63,000) produces an additional dollar value of about 3.8 billion dollars.

These calculations represent a rough estimate. They do not take into account any multiplier effects that would create other employment. Nor do they estimate the possible loss of positions in either other branches of manufacturing or nonmanufacturing. Finally, such calculations do not address the statewide distribution of a hypothetical increase in

DOD procurement contracts. However, they do give some indication of the economic influence of federal procurement programs.

Hypothetical increases on the order of 3 to 4 billion dollars do not seem to be beyond the capacity of New York firms to absorb. In the Fiscal Years 1982 and 1983, the dollar worth of procurement contracts awarded to companies in New York rose by slightly more than 3 billion dollars.[50] Even if the capacity of large manufacturing firms will not accommodate such increases immediately, given the recent rapid growth in contracts, capacity could be expanded or such firms could rely more on subcontracting. At any rate, this possible limitation does not detract from the apparently large economic influence that federal procurement programs possess.

It is not possible, in view of the lack of data, to accurately estimate the effect of an increase in procurement contracts on other sectors of New York's manufacturing industry. However, two points are worthy of consideration. First, most of these firms have not traditionally participated as prime contractors in defense procurement, so it is not likely that they would be affected. Second, it is possible that these firms may benefit as subcontractors.

Nonmanufacturing employment possibly could suffer if the mix of federal expenditures in New York was changed to reflect more procurement and less of other types of expenditures, particularly in the short run and especially in the public sector. Planned federal cutbacks in employment and training programs for fiscal year 1985, for instance, will result in an estimated loss of two hundred positions to the New York State Department of Labor. The high multiplier effects of additional blue-collar manufacturing positions, however, probably would increase the available number of nonmanufacturing jobs although temporary dislocations would occur. Moreover, the present problem in New York State is manufacturing decline and not the decline of the nonmanufacturing sector.

Finally, the distribution of federal expenditures is concentrated in a few regions of the State, and those parts of the State which have suffered most traditionally have not received many contracts. The special problems of western New York are well known. It probably would be necessary for either the state of New York or the federal government to implement policies involving incentives for major contractors to subcontract to distressed areas.[51]

A MODEST PROPOSAL FOR SUBSTANTIAL BENEFIT

Regardless of whether additional federal procurement contracts were or were not subcontracted, it would take relatively little in the way of additional procurement contracts, given the size of the procurement budget, to greatly aid the manufacturing sector in New York State. In Fiscal Year 1983, California was awarded 26 billion dollars in Department of Defense procurement contracts. New York received 9.6 billion dollars. California's share of the DOD procurement program included 20 percent of that budget. New York's share was 6.9 percent.[52] It is clear that a slight redistribution from states like California would be quite beneficial to New York. The benefit to a weakened economy in the East would probably outweigh any damage to a very strong economy such as that of California.

It might be noted that although some defense dollars would be redistributed under this proposal, had this action taken place in Fiscal Year 1982 or 1983 New York State would still have been a net contributor to the federal treasury. In 1983, New York State fell short of sharing federal expenditures in proportion to its total tax burden by about 6 billion dollars.[53] An increase in that year in federal expenditures in the State of between a suggested 3.5 billion to 4 billion dollars would have still made the State a net loser with regard to the real flow of federal expenditures.

CONCLUSION

The use of defense procurement contracts as an aid to revitalizing New York's manufacturing sector is one policy which should be considered in the discussion about reindustrializing New York State. While the use of defense outlays as prop for the economy may not be a long-term solution, its potential is politically attractive and would require a relatively small redistribution of federal defense expenditures. Such a policy also may give those who wish to pursue longer range solutions more time to fully develop and implement them.

FOURTEEN

Old Federalism and New Federalism
In New York State

Richard H. Silkman

The centerpiece of the Reagan Administration's domestic policy, its New Federalism, has been and continues to be a major effort at reorganizing intergovernmental fiscal relations. This effort consists of many component parts, programs knitted together by a common ideology. At the core is the objective of decentralizing government operations—shifting both provision and funding responsibilities in a wide range of currently provided government services from the federal to state and local levels. By so doing, it is argued, services will be produced more efficiently while dollars will be targeted more effectively to meet local needs. In addition, the Administration has sought to place greater emphasis on the private sector and, in particular, on the not-for-profit sector for the provision of many of those services currently provided by government. It has also encouraged the more extensive use of user charges to raise revenues and simultaneously reduce "unnecessary" demand for those services. However, these explicit objectives must not obscure the implicit agenda of the Reagan Administration—the absolute reduction in the size of government and the scope of government responsibilities at all levels in our federalist system.

In the analysis that follows, I assess these New Federalism initiatives and their short and long-term economic impact on New York State. In order to address this issue, I will characterize briefly the advantages and disadvantages of fiscally centralized governments, examine the role played by intergovernmental aid programs in a federalist system, describe the components of the New Federalism, and provide a general overview of its impact on state and local governments.

CENTRALIZATION, DECENTRALIZATION, AND INTERGOVERNMENTAL GRANTS

Our federalist system today is different from what it was yesterday and from what it will be tomorrow. Indeed, it is a testament to evolution without design, to an attempt to balance politically the advantages and disadvantages from centralized and decentralized forms of government. Over time, but especially since World War II, our federalist system has become increasingly centralized primarily because the mix of services provided by government has shifted to national defense and income maintenance—services for which the federal government enjoys a comparative advantage. Whether this trend will continue is unclear. The Reagan Administration seems intent on reversing it by returning to the state and local governments much of what during the postwar period has been allocated to the federal government. If successful, we will see a new federalist landscape of undoubtedly the same degree of permanence enjoyed by its predecessor. If the history of intergovernmental relations has taught us anything, it is that there is no optimal federalist system. There are only consequences whose normative implications rarely invite political consensus. The fiscal consequences of centralized and decentralized government structures, most notably efficiency, effectiveness, and equity, deserve particular attention.

Benefits of a Fiscally Centralized Government

The case for centralizing the fiscal responsibilities of government rests upon the federal government's comparative advantages in four areas—economic stabilization, income redistribution, externality management, and tax collection. This is not to suggest that other levels of government cannot engage in these activities. After all, all levels of government levy and collect taxes. Rather, the argument usually made is that the central government can perform these tasks more efficiently, more effectively, and more equitably than its state and local counterparts.

Consider economic stabilization. The federal government has at its disposal both monetary and fiscal policy which can be used to fine-tune economic growth. On the other hand, since state and local governments are prohibited from issuing money and are highly open economies, they cannot engage in monetary policy and will find fiscal policy to be far less successful.[1] Or, consider income redistribution. The smallness and openness of state and local economies together with the potential for population mobility limit the extent to which these governments can undertake redistributive endeavors. The state or local government which too vigorously pursues redistributive policies will find itself in a position not unlike that of an insurance company utilizing clients who are not serious risks to subsidize clients who are. In the insurance case, this is the problem of "moral hazard;" in the public sector, it is the "free rider" problem. In both cases a clear economic incentive exists for the subsidizers to exit from either the company or the locality, leaving to those that remain the burden of financing the risky or the poor.

Because the federal government can operate more effectively redistributive programs, it has greater discretion over the type of taxes it can levy to raise revenues. In particular, the federal government can tax income at progressive rates far in excess of those available to states and localities. Accordingly, the federal tax structure is generally thought to be more equitable than state and local tax structures.[2] And when combined with compensatory expenditure schemes the progressiveness of the income tax provides a valuable tool at the federal level for equalizing intra-national wealth or income distribution. At the same time, the size of the tax collection effort at the federal level permits the realization of scale economies which greatly reduce collection costs. Indeed, on a percentage basis, the federal government is generally 10 to 20 times more efficient than states and localities, incurring only a dollar of cost for each thousand dollars collected.

Finally, it is argued that centralization is necessary to ensure the optimal provision of goods and services which possess positive or negative externalities. Goods such as national defense, education, congestion, or pollution require that local levels of government consider the full scope of benefits and costs—not just those germane to local residents—when determining service levels. Without centralization, either in the provision of services, in the determination of property rights, or in the establishment of interdistrict tax and/or subsidy rates, this will not occur. Rather, local governments will have the economic incentive to stop providing the good or service long before (in the case of positive externalities) or long after (in the case of negative externalities) Pareto Optimal output levels for the collective group of local governments have been attained.[3]

Benefits of a Fiscally Decentralized Government

The chief advantage of a fiscally decentralized government is its responsiveness to the different demands of residents in different localities. As long as the within-community variance in the demand for public services is less than the across-community variance, a condition which Tiebout type processes in residential choice behavior will ensure, and so long as there are neither significant externalities nor scale economies in the provision of such services, local provision of varying output levels always will be more efficient than central provision of any uniform level of output across all localities.[4] The presumption here is that local governments know, and have the financial wherewithal to meet, their resident's demands, and are in the best position to provide services in a manner most consistent with their preferences.

A corollary to this argument is that decentralization enhances the choice set available to residents who may select tax burdens they face and public service levels they consume. Where there is such variation across local communities, residents can vote on foot by residing in those communities providing the mix of services and taxes most consistent with their preferences.[5] In this way, economic (allocative) efficiency is increased since the spatial distribution of local government activity will conform more closely to the tastes of the spatially distributed population.

The variation afforded through a decentralized system of small local government units may result in other positive effects, including innovation, increased efficiency, and improved accountability. The fact that many local government units, e.g., local school districts or police and fire departments, are performing the same functions invariably results in a wide range of production processes in use at any one time, many of which are experimental. In theory at least, this variation in production processes presents the opportunity to evaluate different techniques, one against the others, and to select those which are most effective and efficient. Further, as the number of local government units increase, the cost to local residents of moving decreases, making exit a more viable option. We would expect this to enhance the competitiveness among local government units and will, other things remaining constant, impose additional pressures upon communities to adopt the most effective and efficient production techniques and compel them to be more responsive or more accountable to local residents.[6]

Intergovernmental Grants in a Federal System

Intergovernmental grants represent an attempt to obtain the benefits of both centralized and decentralized government structures in the financing and provision of public services.[7] As generally conceived, tax revenues collected by higher levels of government are returned to local governments via intergovernmental grant-in-aid programs. In this way, communities benefit from the equity and efficiency of higher level government tax structures yet are able to preserve local discretion in the selection of public service output levels. In addition, through the judicious use of price and income effects, grants-in-aid programs can induce local governments to increase or decrease output levels of particular public services to counteract the effects of externalities or to encourage redistribution efforts.[8]

It is not surprising that a tool as powerful as intergovernmental grants has become used so widely. Since the early 1950s, federal aid has increased three-fold as a percent of state and local revenues from their own sources. Simultaneously, state aid has become increasingly important at the local level, primarily in response to reform in public school finance, and presently accounts for over half of all local expenditures. Coincident with the growth in the magnitude of intergovernmental aid have been significant and innovative changes in the way such aid is distributed. They range from general revenue sharing to project grants, from block grants to categorical grants, from open-ended matching programs to input reimbursement schemes, all of which—with the possible exception of general revenue sharing—are designed to alter local government behavior.[9] They do this either through pure income supplements or through changing the prices localities face for inputs or outputs, while preserving local government discretion and provision.

The case for intergovernmental grants, however, is not without some debate. While it is agreed generally that intergovernmental grants stimulate local spending, it is by no means clear that the resulting spatial distribution of public service levels is closer to Pareto Optimality.[10] Since it is difficult to estimate quantitatively the magnitude of spillover effects, it is nearly impossible to determine the relative financial burdens for each locality affected by the provision of a public service. Further, if we accept Niskanen's hypothesis that bureaucracies grow too large in and of themselves or Wagner's that voters, suffering from "fiscal illusion," underestimate the price of public services and hence demand too much in the way of government expenditures, intergovernmental grants may succeed only in exacerbating a situation characterized by too much government. They may move the entire system away from, not closer to, Pareto Optimality.[11]

There also is mounting evidence suggesting that intergovernmental aid can result in looser government accountability and lower operating efficiency in the provision of public services.[12] In an important sense, intergovernmental aid is similar to third-party payments wherein neither service providers nor service recipients have the economic incentive to ensure the efficient use of revenues. The result is that, while intergovernmental aid increases local expenditures (the "flypaper effect"), it is by no means clear that it increases service levels. It may serve only to subsidize local inefficiency.

In sum, intergovernmental aid represents either a means of realizing the benefits of both centralized and decentralized government or a route to government that is too large, less accountable, and productively inefficient. After almost three decades of rapid growth and diversification, the intergovernmental aid system, especially federal to state and local government aid programs, recently has undergone a period of critical review and rapid change designed to increase its flexibility by placing more control in the hands of local governments.[13] This process began during the Nixon Administration with the General Revenue Sharing program in 1972 and continued through the Ford and Carter presidencies with the consolidation of categorical grants in three areas—Employment and Training (CETA), Community Development (DCBG), and Social Services (Title XX).[14] The New Federalism initiatives enacted thus far during the Reagan Administration extend and accelerate these consolidation efforts, while those initiatives still pending, if enacted, promise to substantially alter the future relationships among federal, state, and local governments.

THE NEW FEDERALISM: COMPONENTS

The New Federalism, as conceived, proposed, and enacted by the Reagan Administration, contains both tax and expenditure components. On the tax side, the centerpiece of the New Federalism is the Economic Recovery Tax Act of 1981. Its provisions include significant cuts in personal income tax rates, accelerated depreciation schedules, "safe harbor leasing" provisions, and tax indexing to be introduced in 1985. In addition, the Administration elsewhere has proposed roll-backs in certain federal excise taxes to provide "tax room" for states and localities as the proposed federal trust fund is phased out beginning in 1988. On the expenditure side is the Omnibus Budget Reconciliation Act of

1981, a massive piece of legislation which merged 77 categorical grant programs into nine block-grant programs while reducing overall expenditures for these programs by 25.3 percent or 2.061 billion dollars. When added to the expenditure cuts in entitlement programs such as AFDC, Foodstamps, Medicaid, and the School Lunch Program, the total domestic budget was trimmed by 6.4 percent or 31.6 billion dollars in nominal terms.[15] Further, the Administration has advanced a long term proposal to "rebalance" intergovernmental fiscal relations. One component of this proposal calls for the federal government turning over full responsibility for AFDC to the states in return for its assuming the full cost of acute medical services for the eligible poor and the establishment of a block grant to the states for longer-term health care. A second component would establish a temporary trust fund through 1988 earmarked to support a number of federal programs to be turned back to states and localities. Beginning in 1988, this trust fund would be phased out over four years leaving the state and local governments fully responsible for financing this set of services.

The Omnibus Budget Reconciliation Act of 1981

The Reagan Administration wasted no time in presenting the core of its federalism initiative to the Congress. In the spring of 1981, legislation was proposed to consolidate 85 categorical grant programs into seven block grants. In fact, nine block grants were created by the Reconciliation Act, consolidating 77 of the categorical programs. Those escaping consolidation include a number of small programs in Health Services (e.g., family planning, venereal disease control, migrant worker health, black lung disease, and immunization) and certain Title I Elementary-Secondary Education programs. While overall federal funding for services in these nine functional areas was reduced, certain areas fared far worse than others. Employment and training, education, social services, and transportation now face percentage reductions of 63 percent, 42 percent, 23 percent and 16 percent, respectively, when 1986 projected outlays are compared to outlays for 1981. And when inflation is factored in, these losses are substantially greater. Only health stands to gain, in large part due to projected increases in the Medicare and Medicaid entitlement programs. When these two programs are factored out, remaining health care expenditures will increase only slightly through 1986. If those programs not affected by this consolidation legislation are factored out, the four health-related block grants, Preventive Health, Alcohol, Drug Abuse, and Mental Health, Maternal and Child Health, and Primary Care, suffered direct cutbacks of 28 percent in FY82 relative to FY80 spending levels.

The budget figures, though, tell only part of the story. Valuable insight can be gained into the Administration's implicit intent by careful review of the implementation guidelines for each of the block grant areas. For instance, maintenance of effort or nonsubstitution provisions accompany only three of the block grants—Education, Preventive Health, and Alcohol, Drug Abuse and Mental Health—and only as a result of congressional action. In the other six program areas, the signal is unmistakably clear. The federal government will not move to stop states and localities from substituting these federal block grant funds for locally raised revenues.

Similarly, while all nine program areas require annual reports, this requirement clearly is intended to ensure only minimal compliance with the administrative guidelines established by the programs and not to evaluate program effectiveness. In fact, in four of the program areas (Preventive Health, Alcohol, Drug Abuse and Mental Health, Community Services, and Low-Income Energy Assistance) "the secretary may not prescribe the manner in which the States will comply with the provisions of this subsection," here referring to program assurances. In these four program areas as well as in Maternal and Child Health and Primary Care, "in conducting an evaluation or a review of block grant programs, neither the Secretary not the Comptroller General may request information in forms that are not readily available." Yet even here, reporting and evaluation is more prescribed than in the Social Services area where the Title XX program is run as a special revenue sharing program with no formal evaluation requirements. It is only in Education that specific mention is made of program evaluation. The Conference Report states, however, that the specific, objective standards to be used are matters of state and local decision and that national competency testing is not mandated. The federal government is again sending a clear signal to states and localities, this time indicating that it does not intend to impose upon these governments priorities among program objectives nor does it view itself as accountable for program operations nor their consequences.

Economic Recovery Tax Act of 1981

Strictly speaking, the Economic Recovery Tax Act of 1981 (ERTA) is a national tax program. It has only minimal intergovernmental consequences arising from its impact on states and localities where income tax statutes are tied closely to the federal income tax. Yet, it is an integral part of the Reagan Administration's domestic policy and is a key instrument in its quest to reduce the size and scope of government. For this reason and for the sheer size of its dollar impact, ERTA warrants inclusion in this discussion of the New Federalism.

ERTA affects both individuals and corporations through changes in the personal and corporate income tax provisions. For the individual, the most discussed component of this tax package is the 25 percent reduction in marginal tax rates over a three-year period beginning in 1981. Given present and projected inflation rates through 1984, this cut will be sufficiently large to protect the taxpayer from bracket creep, reducing tax burdens as a percent of income. Beginning in 1985, marginal tax rates will be indexed to inflation to prevent those unenacted, automatic tax increases that result from the combination of inflation and a progressive tax structure. Other provisions of ERTA affecting the personal income tax include a reduction in the maximum tax rate on unearned income from 70 percent to 50 percent, a similar reduction in the maximum tax applied to long-term capital gains from 28 percent to 20 percent, a deduction for two wage-earner households, increased child care benefits, and liberalized regulations governing the use and limits placed upon IRA and Keogh retirement plans.

For corporations, two provisions are especially noteworthy. The first is the Accelerated Cost Recovery System which greatly speeds up depreciation schedules for capital assets. Under the 10–5–3 depreciation scheme, effective corporate tax rates are substantially lower, often less than 50 percent of the statutory rates. The second, and perhaps most controversial, provision is safe harbor leasing, a scheme whereby unused tax or depreciation credits can be sold by corporations with no taxable incomes to those better able to take advantage of the new tax benefits.

The total cost to the federal government from these provisions in ERTA is difficult to estimate since they will depend heavily on the rate of inflation, the extent of corporate investment, and the degree to which safe harbor leasing arrangements are negotiated. Nevertheless, those estimates that are available suggest that by 1985, the first year of indexation, the federal government will lose approximately 180 billion dollars or 18.5 percent of total federal revenues. The consequent impact on the states will be substantially smaller and will depend upon the extent to which each state with a personal or corporate tax adopts and/or otherwise modifies these various provisions.[16]

Intergovernmental Realignment

The most far-reaching changes in the federalism structure proposed by the Reagan Administration are those which would be implemented over the longer term. These include the proposed federal-state "swap" of income maintenance and health care programs and the establishment and gradual phaseout of a federal trust fund designed to ease the ultimate turn-back of many federal programs to the states. As originally put forward in President Reagan's State of the Union Address in 1982, the states would take over full control of both the food stamp and AFDC programs. In return, Medicaid would be funded fully by the federal government. Additionally, certain federal revenues from excise taxes and the oil windfall profits tax would be earmarked to an interim trust fund to initially aid the states in financing this swap and a host of other programs being returned to state governments. To further assist states, the federal government would reduce its excise tax levies to create tax room and potential revenue sources for the states and localities.

Since originally proposed, however, some key changes have been made in the broad federalism initiative. First, the food stamp program has been removed from the swap and federal responsiblity for the takeover of the Medicaid program was reduced accordingly to include only acute medical care and a portion of long-term care for the poor, where the poor are defined as only those eligible for Supplemental Social Security and state AFDC. Second, the windfall profits tax revenues are no longer earmarked for inclusion in the trust fund but have been replaced less than dollar for dollar by general revenues. The list of federal programs to be returned to the states has been shortened, though not significantly, through the omission of migrant health, the Urban Development Action Grant (UDAG) program, and Primary Highway Transportation, among others. Finally, large federal deficits have forced the Administration to renege on its promise to lower excise tax rates. In fact, the Tax Equity and Fiscal Responsibility Act of 1982 actually doubles the federal excise tax on cigarettes. This is hardly in keeping with the original spirit of the New Federalism proposals, which called for a return of programs and revenue sources to the state governments.

IMPACT OF THE NEW FEDERALISM ON STATE AND LOCAL GOVERNMENTS

It is still premature to assess the impact of the New Federalism initiatives on state and local governments. Secondary data sources are generally not yet available to quantitatively measure fiscal impacts. Similarly, many states only recently have adjusted legislatively to key aspects of the New Federalism. California, for example, did not accept three of the block grants in FY82 but relied instead on federal administration through the Secretary's office. Nevertheless, certain trends are visible and general conclusions possible, based, in part, on the ongoing monitoring efforts by the Urban Institute of state and local government responses to the New Federalism program.[17] The first general conclusion that can be drawn is that states and localities are not replacing in any substantive amounts revenues lost through federal budget cuts, but are passing these cuts through in the form of service reductions to the service recipients.[18] The Reagan Administration appears to be succeeding in its efforts to reduce the overall size of government. This is especially true for those states facing internal fiscal problems and budgetary woes, such as Michigan, Minnesota, California, Ohio, Indiana, and New York. The resource rich states, on the other hand, such as Oklahoma, Colorado, Alaska, and Montana, have replaced federal dollars though generally on a less than dollar for dollar basis.[19] Interestingly, the net effect of replacement has been to make state spending levels slightly more equal overall. Certain service areas have experienced higher replacement ratios than others. Many more states are replacing some of the federal cuts in social services than are replacing federal cuts in Low-Income Energy Assistance or Alcohol, Drug Abuse, and Mental Health. In fact, the transfer provision of the Low-Income Energy Assistance grant has been used in many states to fund key social services such as day care centers. Both of these observations, however, may change even over the short term as states become more familiar with the new federal programs, as national macroeconomic conditions improve, and as energy rich states begin to feel the full impact of falling energy prices.

The second general conclusion is that neither states nor localities have moved decisively to take advantage of the "tax room" created by ERTA in 1981. Estimates place the size of the federal tax cuts under ERTA in 1982 to be roughly 38 billion dollars and in 1983 to be over 92 billion dollars.[20] Yet, according to an ACIR report, only four states—Ohio, Minnesota, Michigan, and Oregon—raised individual income taxes between January, 1981 and August, 1982, and only eight states enacted sales tax increases during this same period.[21] The states noticeably are reluctant to levy where the federal government has reduced. In fact, those states which could afford to do so followed the lead set by the federal government and *reduced* their tax burdens. Among these states are those rich in natural resources and energy such as Colorado, New Mexico, North Dakota, Montana, and Alaska, all of which have either reduced or eliminated income taxation since 1980.

341

For the most part, however, states appear to be fighting a rear-guard action by turning to higher excise taxes on gasoline and motor fuels, alcohol, and tobacco in the short run in the hope that better national economic conditions will relieve their longer-term fiscal problems.

The third general conclusion is that the New Federalism has served to highlight the differences in taxing capacities of the fifty states and to reduce the differences, if only slightly to date, in state spending levels on key public services. The initial effect of the New Federalism has been for states to become more similar. Generally, those states with the highest spending levels have not replaced federal dollars while those with lower spending levels, more often the *nouveau riche* among the states, have. However, it is unlikely that this trend will continue. Rather, to the extent that federal aid was equalizing, its reduction should result in greater disparity among the states in fiscal efforts. In addition, the federal tax cuts are not neutral in their interstate impacts. For example, Davis has computed the relative benefit to states that results from lower federal taxes and compared this to a state's relative capacity to raise own-source revenues. It is not surprising that states like Nevada, Connecticut, and Delaware, which are not federal tax exporters (i.e., more money flow out of those states to Washington than Washington returns in federal spending), yet relatively well off with high fiscal capacities, will fare better under the New Federalism than will states like Idaho, Utah, Tennessee, and Alabama.[22]

There are other issues of impact which are equally important, yet for which it is simply too early to reach definite conclusions. Three such issues come to mind.

1. Are there significant administrative cost savings associated with consolidating categorical grant programs?

2. Will the targeting of federal dollars to the economically disadvantaged be reduced as states exercise increased discretion over program funding?

3. Will the impoverished central cities lose to the remainder of their states as the control of federal programs is turned over to state governments?

It is possible, of course, to speculate on answers to these questions based upon previous, less ambitious consolidation efforts and on historical spending patterns at the federal, state, and local levels.

With regard to the first question, the answer appears to be "No." According to a GAO study of federal and state experience in past block grant programs, an examination of administrative costs before and after consolidation and general comparisons of administrative costs between block grants and categorical programs have revealed no conclusive evidence to support the claim that the earlier block grants led to sizable reductions in administrative costs—that is, cost savings of 10 percent or more—although they do not eliminate the possibility that some cost savings did emerge. The cost reductions that resulted from consolidating categoricals were relatively small and, in some cases, administrative costs increased after the block grants were created.[23]

Needless to say, estimating administrative costs in even the simplest of cases is never easy. Yet, GAO efforts strongly suggest that the 25 percent cut in federal funding levels for most of the new block grant programs will not be fully or even mostly compensated for by administrative cost savings, as the Reagan Administration originally argued.

The targeting question is answered less easily since each of the nine block grants created by the Omnibus Budget Reconciliation Act have different eligibility requirements, which, as a rule, are less rigid than those for the earlier block grants evaluated by the GAO. Thus, while the GAO was not able to identify a loss in targeting resulting from these consolidation efforts, the conclusion is less applicable in this case. However, the eligibility restrictions accompanying these new block grants are significantly more stringent than those tied to general revenue sharing, suggesting that the lack of targeting will be less of a concern in these nine functional areas than it was under general revenue sharing. Unfortunately, as I argue later, the absence of reporting requirements imposed upon states and localities under the new federalism may make it impossible to measure quantitatively the overall impact of grant consolidation and increased state discretion on the targeting of federal funds to those most in need.

It also will be difficult to assess the extent to which central cities gain or lose at the hands of state governments as states gain control over the allocation of federal dollars. It is often argued that state legislatures are less able politically to focus resources on the needs of relatively few, albeit large, local governments. To some extent that is true, as state aid programs such as aid to public schools invariably have something for everyone, even the wealthiest of the state's local communities. In New York State, however, Albany generally has been as responsive as Washington, and occasionally more responsive, to the needs of New York City. Table 1 illustrates this point quite clearly. The left-hand column lists selected federal aid programs which distribute funds either directly to localities or to localities via state pass-through provisions. These programs were chosen because they have approximate counterparts in New York State (as listed in the right-hand column). The entries in the table represent the percent of funds in each program distributed in New York State and targeted to New York City. Thus, New York City receives 58 percent of all of the New York State general revenue sharing funds allocated to New York State counties, municipalities, and towns. It is difficult to argue, for this program at least, that New York City is receiving better treatment from the federal government than it is from its own state government. Similarly, in housing, transportation, and social services, New York City fares as well and often somewhat better under state versus federal programs. In housing, for example, the city receives roughly 64 percent of HUD Section 8 money distributed in New York State, yet over 75 percent of the annual housing subsidy allowances through the State's Division of Housing and Community Renewal State Aided Public Housing Program. It is only in education, owing in large measure to the Department of Agriculture's School Lunch Program and to Title I of the Elementary and Secondary Education Act (Chapter 1 of the new Education Consolidation and Improvement Act of 1981), which have strict low-income and economically disadvantged eligibility requirements, that the federal government appears more responsive to the needs of New York City. Yet, if we subtract these two federal programs, neither of which have state level counterparts, the city does only somewhat better under the federal umbrella.

While these numbers represent only a weak litmus test in New York State and cannot be used to generalize across other states, they seem to indicate that our nation's central cities will not be raped by their state legislatures as the states assume control of federal grants-in-aid programs.

Evaluating the New Federalism

There remains one subtle but potentially far-reaching aspect of the New Federalism which cuts across all of the consolidation and turnback initiatives to one degree or another. It is the relaxation, or in some cases the omission, of reporting requirements and uniform date collection efforts imposed on state recipients of federal aid under previous intergovernmental grant programs. In a word, the Reagan Administration has moved to restrict severely the opportunity for federal, including congressional, oversight of the state's use of federal aid monies. As the GAO reports, the

Table 1. New York City's Share of Federal and State Aid Support—Selected Program Areas

Federal Aid to New York State		State Aid to New York State	
Program	Share (%)	Program	Share (%)
General Revenue Sharing	59	General Revenue Sharing	58
HUD Programs:		Division of Housing and Community Renewal Programs:	
		State Aided Public Housing	78
CDBG Program	67	Total Loan Funds (to 1982)	77
UDAG Program	54	Annual Housing Subsidy	70
Section 8—Housing Allowances	64	Urban Initiatives Program	68
		Neighborhood Preservation	31
		Urban Renewal Assistance Program	
Transportation Programs		Transportation Programs	
UMTA—Capital Improvement Grants	66	Motor Fuel Tax Revenues Distribution	50
UMTA—Formula Grants Program	82	Motor Vehicle Fee Distribution	50
Highway Planning/Construction	26	Mass Transit Operating Aid (section 18-b)	89
Total Dept. of Transportation	52		
Education Programs		Education Programs	
Education—Disadvantaged Children	64	Aid to Public Schools	29
School Lunch/Breakfast	67		
Remainder—Dept. of Educ. Programs	38		
Social Service Programs		Social Services	
Runaway Youth	37	Runaway and Homeless Youth	25
Older Persons—Opportunities	81	Community Services—Elderly	29
Community Service Admin.—Total	33	Recreation for the Elderly	47

SOURCE: *Geographic Distribution of Federal Funds in New York—1980*, Community Services Administration, Washington, D.C. 1981; *State Aid to Local Governments—1981*, Office of the State Comptroller, State of New York, Albany, 1982; *New York State Statistical Yearbook—1980*, Division of the Budget Albany, 1982.

Congress may never know whether the new block grants enacted under the Omnibus Budget Reconciliation Act of 1981 are successful in social targeting—or in other objectives—because the Federal Government is not requiring uniform data collection.[24]

As indicated above, the legislation for each of the nine block-grant areas substantially lessens the reporting requirements of state governments vis-a-vis the prior categorical aid programs. In fact, in half of the cases the legislation expressly forbids the Secretary from prescribing the manner in which states must comply with the spirit of the legislation and from establishing burdensome reporting requirements.[25] The explicit intent of these provisions is to ensure local discretion in the selection of output levels and program technologies. A consequence may very well be that we will lose the ability to conduct national evaluations of the effectiveness of state and locally provided services. This comes at a particularly inopportune time since, as a nation, we have become increasingly concerned with the efficient and effective use of our tax dollars.

This is not to suggest that evaluation will cease, for certainly states and localities will continue their own evaluation efforts. However, whether or not they will expand upon them to fill the void left by the federal government is problematic. Undoubtedly, in some cases state and local governments will undertake to replace some of the federal evaluation efforts, especially in those areas such as education and mental health where the states traditionally have exercised substantial discretion. On the other hand, it is doubtful that they would support the large scale research efforts undertaken by the federal government. Furthermore, where state and local governments do replace federal evaluation research, the scope is likely to be severely restricted to within-state activities, the duration is likely to be short-term rather than longitudinal, and the quality is, in general, likely to be inferior to that of federal efforts.

It is ironic that, at a time when the encouragement of local discretion is certain to result in increasing the local variation in public service levels and program technologies, evaluation research should be so crippled. What promises to be an exciting time of change in state and local government behavior may come and go without the opportunity for careful scrutiny. And, in the process, we may never know the full impact of this New Federalism on our federalist system, on public service recipients, and on the effectiveness, efficiency, and equity of public service provision and delivery.

THE ECONOMIC IMPACT OF THE NEW FEDERALISM ON NEW YORK STATE

Trying to assess the economic impact of the New Federalism on New York State is undoubtedly somewhat premature at this time. It is premature since the Reagan program has only been in place for a few years and it can be argued that state and local governments have begun only recently to adopt strategies to deal with its immediate effects. Also, many of the key provisions of the New Federalism have yet to be enacted, and Congress has shown a strong reluctance to rubber stamp President Reagan's most recent proposals. It must be noted, as well, that secondary data sources necessary for estimating impacts are weak, frequently only estimates themselves and not observed data, and often inconsistent. Nevertheless, even at this relatively early stage of analysis available data can offer useful insights, especially by initially focusing on the macroeconomic impact of tax policy and subsequently on the impact of funding reductions in Title XX at the program level.

Macroeconomic Impacts

Although the New Federalism has little to recommend it to New York, we can begin the discussion on a positive note with the one rose among the many thorns. New York State residents will realize, through the mid 1980s, substantial tax savings due to the individual income tax provisions of the Economic Recovery Tax Act of 1981. Table 2 offers estimates of this tax savings for the years 1981–1985. This tax savings is based upon the estimated reduction in national individual income tax liabilities (row 1) multiplied by .08, or the fraction of the U.S. individual income tax paid in 1979 by New York State residents.[26] Unfortunately, a similar ratio is not available for business tax liabilities because of the difficulty of geographically placing multifirm and multinational corporations. Consequently, corporate tax savings have not been included. As is evident, as early as 1982, ERTA has had a significant impact on New York State residents, and by 1983 will amount to approximately 22 percent of the total 1982–83 proposed New York State budget.[27] For example, it will become apparent that, by comparison, this reduction will dwarf program cuts in Title XX.

Clearly, Washington has created substantial tax room for New York state should the State elect to increase its taxes. The problem, of course, is that New York State, unlike the federal government, is tightly

347

Table 2. Estimating National Revenue Effects of ERTA and the Implications for New York State Federal Income Tax Payments, 1981–85

	1981	1982	1983	1984	1985
Reductions in National Income Tax Liabilities (millions of dollars)	39	26,929	71,098	114,684	148,237
Reductions in National Business Tax Liabilities (millions of dollars)	1,562	10,657	18,599	28,275	39,269
Total Reductions in National Tax Liabilities* (millions of dollars)	1,565	37,656	92,732	149,963	199,311
Tax Savings in New York State Residents from Reductions in Individual Income Tax Total (millions of dollars)	125	3,012	7,418	11,997	15,945
Total Tax Savings as a Percent of the 1982–83 Proposed New York State Budget	0.4%	8.9%	21.9%	35.4%	47.1%

* This is not the simple sum of the reductions in individual and business tax liabilities due to other provisions of the legislation.
SOURCE: Joint Committee on Taxation (1981), "Summary of H.R. 4242: The Economic Recovery Tax Act of 1981," U.S. Congress, Washington, D.C. and *The Statistical Abstract of the United States,* (1981), U.S. Department of Commerce, Washington, D.C.

constrained regarding unilateral taxing and expenditure decisions. Its actions must be coordinated closely with those of other states that are competitors for residents, industry, and economic activity. And unfortunately, the competitive nature of interstate relations is exacerbated by absolute reductions in federal tax levies since such reductions serve to increase the relative importance of state and local tax rate differentials. It is a somewhat ironic yet very real outcome of ERTA that, rather than create tax room for states and localities, federal tax reductions only further constrain state and local taxing and expenditure discretion while heightening the intensity of interstate tax competition. It is not surprising, then, to find, as the Urban Institute has, that states have not moved to fill the void left by federal tax cuts, and that the burden of such cuts falls almost exclusively on low-income service recipients.[28] Viewed in this light, even the rose in the New Federalism quickly loses its fragrance.

From the perspective of aggregate revenue flows, New York State as a whole neither gains nor loses significantly as a result of balanced federal tax and expenditure policies. In 1979, for instance, the ratio of total federal spending in New York State versus total federal taxes paid by residents of the State was .96 (37.112 billion dollars spent versus 38.853 billion collected). This reflects relatively recent improvements in this ratio, which stood at only .89 as late as 1975. Other states, however, are affected substantially by balanced changes in aggregate federal tax and expenditure policies. For example, New Jersey receives from the federal government considerably less than it pays out in taxes (12.629 billion dollars versus 18.224 billion dollars). Balanced reductions benefit New Jersey residents as a whole more than they do New York State residents and much more than residents of Mississippi, who actually are made worse off. (The comparable ratio for Mississippi in 1979 was 1.58 or 5.036 billion dollars in federal expenditures as against only 3.191 billion dollars in federal taxes collected.)

This is not to suggest that balanced federal reductions do not have serious intrastate distributional consequences. Those who receive federal benefits are generally not the same as those who pay federal taxes. The former are largely economically disadvantaged while the latter are comparatively affluent. Put very directly, federal policy allows taxpayers in New York State to gain completely at the expense of the recipients of federally funded services. Since the federal expenditures-to-taxes ratio is close to 1.00, the total impact of balanced federal reductions can be thought of as remaining within the "family," making it at least mathematically possible to redress this redistribution using state tax policy.

Microeconomic Impacts

At the program level the full impact of the New Federalism can be understood best by examining budgetary and service provision impacts of federal funding cutbacks on the state, county, and local governments. Unfortunately, such information is difficult to obtain since state data is being released in 1984 for FY81–82. FY82–83 data will not be available until the following year, if at all, given changes in state reporting requirements contained in the Omnibus Budget Reconciliation Act (as described earlier). And once obtained, the data available for FY81–82 is difficult to understand since federal, state, and local expenditure categories often do not conform and since states and localities are very adept at treating federal funds as fungible and manipulating federal program guidelines. As a result, the effect of program cuts in Title XX, for example, may be dampened by states as they switch service recipients to open-ended entitlement programs such as AFDC and Medicaid.[29] Nevertheless, such micro-level examination is instructive for the qualitative insight it provides into state and local government response to the New Federalism. Below, I take a detailed look at funding levels and client populations served in New York State under

Title XX of the Social Security Act for the Fiscal Years 79–80, 80–81, and 81–82. This last year is the first year of the New Federalism initiative, so by comparing outcomes across these fiscal years we should acquire some insight into at least the initial impact of the Reagan Administration's federalism policies in New York State. The title XX program was chosen since it funds only social services, that area where the funding cutbacks have seemed to receive the most publicity.

Statewide, Title XX allocations fell from 243.6 million dollars in 1980–81 to only 184.9 million dollars in 1981–82 or by 24.1 percent. Of this total, only 98 percent of 181.2 million dollars was allocated to local districts under the existing allocation formula, which is based upon 1972 populations and service expenditures. An additional 10.0 million dollars was transferred from the Low-Income Energy Assistance block grant in accord with federal guidelines, thus raising the total federal allocation to 191.2 million dollars or 21.5 percent lower than the previous year.[30]

In light of the funding reductions, local social service districts in the State were given priority mandates from Albany and were instructed to maximize, wherever possible, the use of other federal funding programs (such as Title XX Medical Assistance) of the Social Security Act to support overlapping services to the eligible client populations. Based upon the revised *Consolidated Service Plans* submitted to Albany by each county and by New York City, the majority of the local districts anticipated meeting the reduction in funding either by shifting Title XX clients to other programs or reducing the training activities generally undertaken with Title XX funds. Since these other programs require higher local matching ratios than the 12.5 percent local match under Title XX, this shift would necessitate increasing local expenditures and would reduce some of the redistribution elements of the Title XX program.[31] Only New York City, which is in the unenviable position of having to make up 87 percent of the federal cutbacks despite the fact that it only accounts for 68.1 percent of the total allocation, anticipated generating substantial additional local revenues.[32]

In this context Table 3 is illuminating. It reports the total Title XX funds (75 percent federal plus 25 percent state and local) expended in New York State by social services and the total number of service recipients (including those funded through Title XX and other federal and state programs) for each of three fiscal years. The first column indicates the percent of total statewide expenditures for each service derived from Title XX in 1981–82, the only year such data was available. As is evident, certain social service areas are substantially more dependent upon Title XX funding than are others. The bottom line in this table is especially important since it documents the significant drop in total Title XX funds available to New York State (as noted above). Yet, despite this funding reduction, the number of service recipients actually has increased over this three year period according to the estimated data published by the New York State Department of Social Services. On the fact of it, it appears that the State has weathered the first year of the Reagan Administration's budget quite well.

On closer inspection, however, it becomes apparent that services generally fall into one of three categories. The first, which I designate the "impact category," consists of those services which experienced reductions in Title XX funding and in clients served between 1979–80 and 1981–82 (see the last two columns in Table 3 for the percentage changes). For these services, other funding sources (including local) were not used to replace Title XX cutbacks. Day Care, Education, Employment, and to a lesser extent Adoption, are included in this category. The second, which I call the "fungible priority category," includes those services which faced significant funding reductions from the Title XX grant program, but which were able to maintain client populations through either the transfer of clients to other federal programs or the increase in state and/or local support. Family Planning, Foster Care for children, Housing Improvement, and Preventive Services for Children and Adults fall into this category and are characterized by the presence of either alternative funding programs, such as AFDC, Medicaid, or Title XIX, or instances of persons in life threatening situations and situations of substantial or imminent jeopardy. The third category, "non-fungible priority," contains the remaining services wherein funding levels and recipient numbers were pretty much constant or may actually have increased over the three years.

Viewed in this way, two points must be made regarding the impact of Title XX cuts in New York State. First, New York State has been very successful in shifting the financial burden for many social services to open-ended federal grant programs. This, in turn, has allowed the State to meet its funding priorities in these and other key social service areas. Second, the primary impact of the Title XX cuts has been felt in the areas of Employment, Education, and Day Care, with New York City facing the brunt of the cuts in Day Care (2.2 million dollars and 10,400 recipients). What remains to be seen, though, is whether or not the State can continue to so effectively absorb reductions in federal social service programs as the full impact of the Reagan Administration's efforts to trim entitlement programs through tightened eligibility standards is felt. The 1982–83 data should prove especially

Table 3. The Allocation of Title XX funds and the Client Populations Served by Social Service Area in New York State—1979–80 through 1981–82

Service Area		1979–80		1980–81		1981–82		Percent Change 1979 to 1982	
		Dollars*	Clients	Dollars*	Clients	Dollars*	Clients	Dollars	Clients
Adoption	9.1	4.452	11,530	4.042	11,104	2.953	10,558	− 33.7	− 8.4
Day Care	76.1	138.553	104,208	136.055	94,442	134.474	87,701	− 2.9	− 15.8
Education	49.2	.579	8,167	.418	4,610	.183	3,260	− 68.4	− 60.1
Employment	27.2	2.660	13,487	.729	7,644	.325	6,050	− 87.8	− 55.1
Family Planning	29.8	2.291	36,270	2.113	46,839	2.421	62,716	5.7	72.9
Foster Care—Adults	41.4	.750	3,208	.443	3,355	.871	4,576	16.1	42.6
Foster Care—Children	3.0	19.321	57,910	17.948	59,804	10.583	59,967	− 45.2	3.6
Health Related	21.0	3.067	43,923	2.667	80,019	2.704	54,652	− 11.8	24.4
Home Management	93.9	4.238	18,016	3.749	21,368	3.161	12,660	− 25.4	− 29.7
Homemaker	36.7	11.109	15,262	14.841	19,143	12.646	18,782	13.8	23.6
Housekeeper/Chore	10.9	2.271	12,707	3.089	13,877	4.502	18,116	98.2	42.6
Housing Improvement	57.7	3.050	18,188	2.511	16,388	2.204	24,342	− 27.7	33.8
Information/Referral	96.3	8.874	612,833	8.168	633,722	8.645	744,011	− 2.6	21.4
Preventive	35.7	21.314	53,515	16.850	49,725	14.588	62,267	− 31.2	16.4
Protective—Adults	50.5	7.068	15,189	7.078	16,636	6.286	19,217	− 11.1	26.5
Protective—Children	37.2	42.619	102,542	42.790	101,157	18.262	152,881	− 57.2	49.1
Domestic Violence	14.1	.447	2,607	.400	1,763	.456	5,533	2.0	1.1
Senior Citizens	84.0	28.720	181,043	29.221	191,693	29.823	189,410	3.8	4.6
Transportation	2.3	.592	6,569	.493	5,582	.320	13,400	− 45.9	1.0
Unmarried Parents	99.1	1.592	5,321	1.400	8,182	1.628	5,044	2.3	− 5.2
TOTALS		304.022	1,322,495	295.008	1,387,053	258.524	1,555,143	− 15.0	17.6

* Dollar figures are reported in thousands of dollars and have not been adjusted for inflation.
SOURCE: *Consolidated Service Plans* for the New York State Department of Social Services, 1979–80, 1980–81, and 1981–82, Albany, New York.

revealing in this regard, since the opportunity to substitute state and locally raised revenues was limited severely due to New York State's own budgetary woes.

IMPLICATIONS FOR REINDUSTRIALIZATION

The thrust of the Reagan Administration's New Federalism is to reduce the size of government at all levels—federal, state and local. On this point there should be neither doubt nor confusion. The means through which the Administration hopes to accomplish this end is shifting the administrative responsibility and financial support for a wide range of existing federal grant programs to the state governments. In this regard, the Administration is counting on the competitive pressures among the states to keep taxes low and expenditures in check. The experience to date, although limited, suggests that the Administration will be successful.

Whether we believe that government is or is not too large, we only can feel disturbed by the Administration's efforts to thwart research and evaluation in key program areas. As a result of legislative provisions initiated by the Administration and enacted by Congress, we are in serious danger of losing our ability to assess the effectiveness, efficiency, and equity with which government services are provided. While the Reagan Administration may view this as a small price to pay for protecting states and localities from federal intrusion into what it views as essentially their affairs, in a much larger sense these provisions may prove especially costly during this period of national concern over the efficacious use of taxpayer dollars. A few years from now, a new Congress, reviewing the impact of its predecessor's handiwork during the 1981 and 1982 legislative sessions, may be surprised to learn that key questions concerning issues such as performance, targeting, and effectiveness are simply unanswerable for lack of a uniform and consistent national data base.

Closer to home, New York State thus far has been reasonably successful in coping with federal program cuts, primarily by shifting its client population and the services provided to it from those areas experiencing funding reductions to open-ended entitlement programs. It is unlikely that such successes will continue in the future. They will certainly not continue if the Administration's long-term objective of returning AFDC to the states is realized.

What New York will not be able to dodge, however, even over the near term, is the constraining impact the New Federalism will have on economic development and state and local taxation and expenditure decisions. At the macro-level, this Administration's economic policies have contributed to record federal deficits which generally are acknowledged to be the primary cause of record *real* interest rates. These, in turn, serve to stifle the sizeable and long-term investment commitment required for any significant reindustrialization effort.

High real interest rates are a major cause for concern in New York State for two other reasons as well. Internationally, these interest rates are responsible for buoying the price of the dollar and turning the terms of trade against the United States. Our export industries have been especially hard hit at a particularly unfortunate time, when new York State's efforts to nurture international markets were beginning to bear fruit. But also hard hit have been domestic industries which face stiff competition from foreign producers, industries such as textiles and apparel, shoes, and electronics, all of which have been mainstays of the State's economy.

Domestically, high real interest rates exaggerate the cost of borrowing money, which makes it more attractive for firms to seek out opportunities for creatively financing operations. In the recent past, a major financier has been state and local governments through a wide range of initiatives such as Industrial Development (Revenue) Bonds, tax abatements and exemptions, infrastructure construction and renovation, industrial parks, plant renovation, and job training programs, all of which reduce the capital costs of economic development or expansion while representing financial drains on state and local government treasuries. In the absence of federal legislation, e.g., tightened restrictions on the use of Industrial Revenue Bonds, we can expect increased interstate competition for industry and for jobs. To the extent that the New Federalism imposes increased financial burdens on state and local governments as federal programs are returned to the states, it will no doubt hurt the ability of all states and localities to underwrite industrial development. Some states, however, will be hurt far worse than others. The energy rich states such as Texas, Colorado, and Wyoming should weather the federally induced belt tightening considerably better than those states such as New York that are trying to reindustrialize. Their relatively low tax rates and locationally insensitive tax bases offer these states the financial means and discretion to continue to publicly underwrite economic development. Other less fortunate states will have to be very selective in offering incentives for firms and industries and in the process will be forced to make some very difficult choices between established firms and new enterprises, between industrial giants and small business, between mature industries and areas of emerging growth. And their development planning will have to be reassessed and optimized, balancing financial incentives, tax exemptions, training programs and infrastructure needs, all key components of any reindustrialization effort. It is clear that reindustrialization does not occur *de novo*. By definition, it begins from an existing social and economic foundation. The problem confronting most states today, including New York, is that their foundations have been weakened structurally by years of physical deterioration and by rapid technological advances which have rendered much of their physical and human capital stocks obsolete. Any reindustrialization strategy depends upon efforts to rebuild social and economic foundations. Since this is indeed the case, surely the New Federalism is a giant step in the wrong direction.

Whether New York State, or any other state, for that matter, will be capable fiscally of supporting existing public service systems and rebuilding physical plants and social infrastructure while attempting to reindustrialize under the guns of competing states is problematic. The greatest danger of the New Federalism is that its promise of tax room, discretion, and local autonomy will evaporate before economic competition among the states and the reduction in federal dollars. The New Federalism may have the ironic effect of making states and localities more, rather than less, dependent upon the federal government and the success of federal economic policies for their economic development and reindustrialization efforts.

FIFTEEN

Acid Rain:

Public Policy in the Face of Uncertainty

Roman Hedges and Donald J. Reeb

" "A cid rain." The words sound frightful. We can conjure up a number of bad images with no additional prodding. We all know that acid is dangerous. To think that there is something as dangerous as acid in the gentle spring rain! Clearly, government policy must put a stop to this. Anything less would be irresponsible. Or would it?

Acid rain is among the most visible environmental "problems" in the country at the present time. It is an important area for scrutiny for that reason alone. It is important for other reasons as well. The "problem" of acid rain requires governmental intervention if it is to be addressed adequately, because no individual or corporation has the capacity unilaterally to affect the problem fundamentally. Yet, the ability of the government to succeed—in virtually anything—is questioned seriously by many.

Successful public policy requires a clear statement of a problem and a thorough understanding of the processes which generate it. Only then can an assessment of the desirability of a course of action or inaction be made sensibly. In order for a course of action to succeed once it is selected, it must be possible for public officials to manipulate those factors which have been identified as important contributors to the problem. Resources such as popular support, political and administrative skill, and technological capacity are essential.[1] Although at present the elements required for success are not all in place, acid rain policy is being made nevertheless.

It is our intention to examine governmental policy concerning acid rain. Our discussion will include the existing scientific knowledge of acid rain and the views of the business community and the public at large. We also will consider the economic impact of acid rain and current air pollution policy, and conclude by offering policy recommendations. Our attention will be confined to New York State for two reasons. Having recently enacted legislation to limit emissions thought to produce acid rain, New York is in the forefront in this policy area, and within its borders lies one of the regions believed to be affected uniquely by acid rain—the Adirondack Mountains.

ACID RAIN: SOME DEFINITIONS

"Acid rain" refers to the deposition of both wet and dry acidic material in the atmosphere on the natural and man-made surfaces of the earth. Acid deposition is distinguished from local air pollution by virtue of the fact that it has been transported over relatively long distances. It is produced when primary pollutants such as nitrogen and sulfur oxides are released into the atmosphere, usually resulting from the burning of fossil fuels. Once in the air, these primary pollutants are transformed by chemical processes involving water vapor and sunlight into several different acidic substances, including sulfuric, nitric, and hydrochloric acid, and ozone. The specific substances created, as well as the site of deposition, are interdependent with atmospheric conditions. As the acidic substances are deposited on material and biotic surfaces, the acids react with those substances and new chemical substances are released.[2]

Claims abound that acidic deposition damages the environment. Before possible effects can be assessed, however, the scientific basis for such claims must be established. Otherwise, all of the concerns in the list of possible effects remain on the agenda as vague possibilities and unanswerable questions.

THE EFFECTS OF ACID RAIN: THE PHYSICAL SCIENCE

The physical sciences have tackled the question of the effects of acidic deposition on the environment by conducting investigations in several different broad areas, namely, aquatic life, forest productivity, agricultural productivity, materials damage, human health, and the quality of life. Our review of the available evidence will reflect those divisions.

It is well known that as water gets more acidic there is a reduction in the variety of plant and animal species which can be sustained. Many of the fish of greatest interest to sport and commercial fishers (e.g., trout) are particularly sensitive to the acidity of water. Young fish seem to be especially vulnerable. Increased acidification also is associated with a rise in the levels of chemically and biologically available forms of certain, frequently toxic, metals such as aluminum, mercury, cadmium, and zinc, which may play a role in further undermining the fish stock.[3]

The response of a specific body of water to the introduction of a given amount of acid will depend on many factors. A larger volume of water will, other things being equal, show a smaller response simply because the acid will be diluted more. A body of water located in soils containing relatively large amounts of material which can "buffer" the acid will be affected less by the introduction of a given amount of acid. The buffering capacity of the soil is so variable that some areas virtually have an unlimited capacity to absorb acid while others practically have no buffering capacity. In New York, the Adirondack Mountains, portions of the eastern side of the central Hudson Valley, and Long Island all have soils with little buffering capacity.[4]

The New York State Department of Environmental Conservation has provided the basic documentation concerning acidified—"dead"—lakes. One fifth of the lakes in the Adirondack Mountain area now have waters too acidic to support game fish such as trout.[5] This is due to the combined effects of their small size, relatively acidic depositions, and soils with little or no buffering capacity. More recent data has extended the area of damage in New York to include the Western Catskills and the Rensselaer highlands.[6]

While there is little doubt about present conditions in the lakes and streams which have been studied, the direct causes of current acidity levels are far less clear. It appears that the waters of the Adirondacks have become less supportive of fish life over the years in ways which suggest that increased acidification due to acidic deposition could be the cause, but the historic acidity and biological activity levels of those bodies of water are not well documented. The result is scientific uncertainty about the precise factors responsible for acidity levels.

Our knowledge of the effects of acidic deposition on the forests of the State is less substantial. There are both direct effects of acidic deposition upon the trees and indirect effects on the forest plants attributable to the alterations of soil chemistry produced by acidic deposition. For example, highly acidic soils cause naturally present aluminum to be made available for absorption by the trees. Aluminum may decrease the ability of trees to draw water from the soil.[7]

Acid deposition is suspected as a cause in the relative decline in the growth of high altitude red spruce in New York and evidence exists suggesting the deleterious effect of high levels of acid on maple seedlings and seed germination.[8] There is also evidence indicating that forest microbe species diversity is reduced by acid deposition and that the surviving microbes are pathogenic.[9] On the one hand, laboratory evidence has connected increased acidity with enhanced tree growth under some conditions.[10] Scientific uncertainty surrounding the effects of acidic deposition on forest productivity stems from the fact that the effects of acidic deposition on trees, which grow slowly, are species and site specific. This means that certain knowledge also grows rather slowly.

The effects of acidic deposition on agricultural production involves another increment in complexity. The more straightforward effect of acid deposition is largely on soil chemistry. Since soil chemistry is an important and well understood factor in agriculture, it is standard agricultural practice to alter soil conditions through the use of fertilizers, lime, and other common farm chemicals and to change crops and cultivars to match soil conditions. Of course, such practices serve to overwhelm virtually all evidence of the effects of acidic deposition. Thus, the indirect effects of acidity through changes in agricultural practices have the potential for being most significant. A productive farmer either will raise only those crops which match the soil conditions or will alter the soil conditions.

In addition, it is important to note that much of the agricultural activity of the State takes place in those areas which have a large natural buffering capacity and are less vulnerable to acidic deposition. As a consequence, minimal attention is paid to acid deposition and what little is known of the specific effects attributable to acidic deposition is from field station and laboratory studies whose generalizability is questionable.[11]

Deterioration of materials, though ubiquitous, is even more difficult to study. It is widely known that acids damage buildings, bridges, paints, and other man-made articles. The urban setting of most materials, unlike that of fisheries, forestry, and agriculture, makes damage estimates of the effects of acidic deposition significantly more difficult to verify. General air pollution in urban areas undoubtedly overwhelms the effects of acidic deposition. Moreover, the division of scientific labor which keeps local air pollution distinct from acid rain compounds the difficulties. Baer and Berman are undertaking an innovative study of government-provided tombstones of known age and size. Rates of deterioration have been measured for Long Island, Bath, New York City, and several other cemetery sites. Preliminary indications are that 40 percent of the deterioration is from causes other than local air pollution.[12]

The possible negative effects of acidic deposition on human health have not yet been identified completely. There is but one area where acid precipitation is thought to be important. Acid deposition makes aluminum, lead, and other toxic metals available in some water systems at levels in excess of drinking water safety standards. Large scale studies of the presence of such dangerous substances are relatively recent. The results of small scale studies, however, are quite alarming.[13]

The final area of concern centers on issues surrounding the quality of life, such as visible air pollution. The scientific community has simply paid little attention to this dimension. This is undoubtedly because the effects of acid deposition on the quality of life are taken to be derivative from effects in the areas cited above, because they are thought to be overwhelmed by local air pollution sources, and because they are dependent upon the perceptions of people, which are difficult to measure.

This brief sketch of the literature demonstrates that there is considerable research activity. Yet, the state of knowledge regarding the effects of acidic deposition is primitive by the traditional standards of scientific inquiry. In many instances the evidence is circumstantial. Laboratory results are often too constrained to permit us to generalize to real world concerns. Field studies of sufficient duration to detect effects which might not appear for years have just begun. The list of appropriate caveats goes on. Research on the effects of acid rain is akin to that on smoking and lung cancer in the 1920s (40 years before the Surgeon General's report). Cigarettes then were called coffin nails, but there was scant scientific evidence connecting cigarette smoking to lung cancer and other illnesses. There are many reasons why there is little physical science evidence of damage attributable to acidic deposition. We will return to a discussion of these reasons below. Before that, however, we wish to examine the views of the public and of industry in order to make clear the context within which assessments and proposals for actions are cast.

THE EFFECTS OF ACID RAIN: THE PUBLIC VIEW

In order to assess public understanding and opinion, we conducted a telephone survey of New Yorkers concerning acid deposition. The study design permits us to examine perceptions of citizens throughout the State and to enable us to examine separately the perceptions and understanding of acid deposition in the Adirondack region. We designated the Adirondack region of New York for special attention because it seems to be the one place in the State where significant effects of acidic deposition are likely to be observable. In addition, this portion of the State has been the focal point of many newspaper and television stories on acid rain in New York.

The Adirondack region was defined as a separate strata and a probability sample of 300 individuals was drawn. A "rest of the State" strata was allocated 301 interviews. These two representative strata were analyzed separately and, with the application of proper weightings, were combined to produce a representative statewide survey. Each of the two sample strata produced results which were within 6 percent of the true population figures 95 percent of the time. The combined sample has a slightly smaller margin of error. The survey was conducted in March, 1983.[14]

The questions included in the survey instrument were designed to provide information on New Yorkers' levels of awareness, knowledge, and concern about acidic deposition. (To avoid needlessly confusing the respondents we used the term acid rain in the interviews.) The respondents' policy preferences were assessed also. Several additional items were included in the instrument simply to provide context. These items tap the general issue concerns of the citizenry. Two items intended to place the concerns about the environment into a more realistic focus asked the respondents to consider trade-offs between the economy and the environment.

Fully 93 percent of the respondents from the Adirondack region said that they had heard of acid rain and more than three Adirondackers in four said that acid rain is a problem in New York State. Over one-third of the Adirondack respondents believed that acid rain is an extremely serious problem in the State. Three in four residents from elsewhere in the State said that they had heard of acid rain and almost 60 percent said that it was a problem in New York State.

To place these findings into context, "only" one in three indicated that the shortage of oil, gasoline, and other fuels was a cause for "a great deal" of concern. Three in four indicated that we were spending either "too little" or "about the right amount" on improving and protecting the environment in the State. Indeed, environmental protection was of general concern. Acid rain was just one of several specifics. Three-fourths of the respondents indicated that the disposal of hazardous industrial chemical wastes is of "great concern" and two-thirds of those polled expressed a similar level of concern about toxic chemicals such as PCB's and pesticides. The same proportion do not want to relax the current environmental regulations to produce additional electric power. Three in five New York residents believe that we can have strict environmental controls without hurting business. Over 55 percent of those asked said that "severe damage to the [Adirondack] region would affect me personally." To be sure, those who live in the region said this more frequently (65 percent), but this form of concern even outstrips the number who live or have vacationed there in the last five years (42 percent).

The respondents presented us with a sophisticated version of the general argument that the deterioration of the Adirondack region is an issue of personal concern above and beyond narrow self-interest. The creation of a "special place" in the Adirondack mountains for all New York residents was central to the framing of several provisions of the state constitution roughly one hundred years ago and our results suggest that New Yorkers continue to see the region as such a special place. Four out of five respondents said that acid rain was a problem for the national government, or state and national government together. Fewer than one person in fifty said that acid rain is not a government problem, despite the fact that everyone was explicitly given the option to indicate if they agreed with the statement that "Acid rain is not the government's problem, and the government should stay out."

As might be expected, the respondents were nearly unanimous that "if cost were not a factor" we should have additional pollution control devices to reduce the amount of acid rain. But the introduction of a significant cost factor did not overwhelm the preference for "cleaning up." Specifically, we asked:

Experts estimate that the required pollution controls [needed to reduce acid rain] could be quite costly for companies to install. These costs, passed along to consumers, could mean that the electric companies might have to raise their average bill 25 dollars per month. In your opinion, is it worth the cost of clean up, or is it just too costly?

Almost half (49.5 percent) indicated that it is worth the cost of clean up while less than one-third said that it was not. More than 15 percent said that "it depends" or that they "didn't know." Residents of the

Adirondacks were statistically indistinguishable from the residents from the rest of the State in their response to this question.

The 25 dollar per month increase is far greater than what the actual increases in electricity costs are estimated to be and is far from negligible. For example, the New York State Power Pool, a consortium of New York's electric companies, estimated that reductions in emissions on the order of 30 percent would cost roughly $1.31 to $17.90 per month, depending upon the technology adopted.[15] The 25 dollar figure is certainly large enough to speak forcefully for the claim that New York residents see acid rain as a very pressing problem which needs to be alleviated by their government even if the solution costs real money.

THE EFFECTS OF ACID RAIN: THE INDUSTRY VIEW

The public's understanding is but one element in the policy debate surrounding acidic deposition. Industry leaders are another. If they were convinced that no problem exists, then the policy discussion would be severely affected. This reason alone would justify an attempt to learn the views of industry. Our decision to actually interview industry leaders, though, was even more heavily influenced by our review of the scientific literature. The uncertainty in that literature and the absence of true field investigations caused us to question whether we could get a complete picture of the extent to which acid deposition was producing effects which simply had not shown up in the literature. Affected industries should be able to fill such a gap.

Industries and industry leaders were selected for inclusion on the basis of whether they had the potential for giving us an experientially based insight about the effects of acid deposition in New York. Forest products, agriculture, building materials, human health, real estate, and recreation industries formed the core for our inquiries. We used lists of industry organizations generated in a variety of ways from state government agencies (e.g., registered lobbyists and constituent organizations) and from telephone directories in metropolitan areas to identify specific groups and individuals. In addition an effort was made in each interview to secure the names of complementary organizations that might prove knowledgeable about the effects of acid rain on New York industry. Over fifty interviews were conducted with leaders in potentially affected industries.

Each respondent was asked a series of loosely structured questions about their organization, their industry, and their knowledge of the effects of acid precipitation in their industry. The interviews were lengthy, usually exceeding 90 minutes. The respondents were candid and they displayed a high level of sophistication about acid deposition. Many respondents knew the names of one or more researchers in the area of acid deposition. Many had read scientific articles on the subject and virtually all knew the name of someone they could contact for more information on scientifically complex matters as they related to their industry. It was not unusual for the respondents to think in terms of a specific university as a source of information upon which they could easily call.

Nevertheless, it was apparent from the very beginning that our respondents were reluctant to translate their awareness of acid deposition into detailed estimates of the effects of acid deposition on their firm or industry. Across the board, the respondents were of the opinion that assessment was premature, that university and other scientists must be the source of basic knowledge, and that relevant scientific knowledge would be available to their industry through existing, reasonably well established channels. Generally, industry did not see acid precipitation as an issue which required them to take ameliorative action immediately.

Responses to our inquiries about acid deposition varied by industry. In those industries which have large companies and/or capital requirements, the respondents were more attentive to the scientific community and more knowledgeable about acid deposition. Similarly, those industries which historically have strong ties to the agricultural and technical colleges have a great deal of knowledge. Indeed, the extent to which the research and personnel of these colleges permeates industries which center on agriculture and forestry is quite remarkable. When the scientists at those well connected schools indicate that acid deposition is or is not a problem in New York, the affected industry will know immediately and most of the industry will accept the university judgment.

Consider the forest products industry. The forest products industry in New York consists of two major economic segments, wood for fiber and wood for furniture, construction, and so forth. The value of the hardwoods is substantially higher than that of the softer woods and hardwood accounts for about three-fourths of the wood value harvested in the State. While acid deposition is an issue on the minds of nearly everyone connected with the forest products industry, the concern is markedly reduced among those whose primary economic interest is hardwoods outside of the Adirondack region. In effect, this means that acid deposition is not thought to be a major problem for the sawmills in the southwestern portion of the State nor is it thought to be a major concern for economically small segments of the industry such as maple (syrup) producers and Christmas tree growers.

The best understanding of and most concern about acid deposition within the forest products industry comes from the pulp and paper producers. These companies usually have extensive holdings, particularly in the Adirondacks. The fact that pulp and paper mills are extremely expensive and have a long payback period means that decisions about fiber availability vis-à-vis a specific mill site are of paramount concern in this segment of the industry. Many of the companies have large scale forest management programs which include company holdings, leased holdings, direct purchase of fiber, and complex programs of forest management. Scientific forest management designed to produce maximum long-term yield seems to be the basic policy throughout this portion of the industry. This perspective means that a great deal of attention can sensibly be devoted to issues which will not be fully addressed in the immediate future. Moreover, the slow growth of the forest means that environmental effects are known only by means of careful, well designed research.

The pulp and paper company representatives we interviewed were extremely aware of the scientific examination of acid deposition. They cited numerous laboratory studies, published and unpublished field research, conferences attended, conversations with academic and industry researchers, and personal experience on the subject. While these industry representatives talked of the problem of acid deposition in species, soil, and location-specific terms, their considered professional judgment was that there is reason for concern and that scientific knowledge permits no conclusion at this time.

Our findings concerning agriculture are less extensive. Agriculture is a major industry in New York. Dairy farms, fruit orchards and vineyards, and various grain and vegetable farms are abundant. A network of information is created by county extension workers who attempt to bridge the gap between scientific norms and the production decisions of the farmer. Extension agents are intimately acquainted with the details of plant diseases, nutrient needs, and soil chemistry. It might have been expected that knowledge about the effects of acid deposition on agriculture would have been widespread. It was not. Farmers and farm organizations had only anecdotal evidence about harm or benefits attributable to acid deposition.

Acid is known to affect building materials, but we were able to discover very little about the effects of acid deposition from the building industry. Acid deposition does not appear to be of major concern and no documentation of possible effects or systematic research was known to them. For example, the home builders of New York have no policy on construction which takes into account possible effects of acid deposition nor were they aware of research which would cause them to adopt such a policy.

Concerning human health effects, acid deposition has the potential for affecting the availability of minerals and metals in the water as well as being an issue of water quality in its own right. There is almost no concern about the effects of acid deposition on the water supply of New York within the water supply industry.

Fishing groups see the issue of acid deposition as having esthetic and economic importance. Unless there are fish, fishermen's dollars will go elsewhere. The documentation of the dollars involved does not come from the fishermen themselves. Here, too, we have better information from the research community than from those who are engaged in the industry of sport and recreational fishing.

We conducted two interviews with representatives of the real estate industry. Our inquiries focused on the effects of acid deposition on the real estate sold in the Adirondack Region. Both of the industry represntatives interviewed expressed personal concern about the possible effects of acid deposition on real estate sales. Neither believed that it had any noticeable impact upon real estate or prices. The explanations offered for this non-effect differed. The limits on land use established by the Adirondack Park Agency were offered as reasons why the going price was already low, making additional adverse effects difficult to measure. The effects of an economic boom surrounding the recent Lake Placid Olympic Games was cited as a reason why any downward price pressure would not be apparent.

What our interviews with representatives from New York industry reveal is substantial concern about acid deposition in a wide range of potentially affected industries. The people we interviewed were knowledgeable, but the knowledge in the field is knowledge gained from researchers. There is little doubt that industry does not generally see evidence which warrants direct action at this time, yet no one is willing to deny the existence of a potentially serious problem whose dimensions are not yet known. At the same time, there is widespread support in industry for more research.

ECONOMIC AND SOCIAL COSTS: A ROUGH ASSESSMENT

The policy maker needs to move beyond the brief catalogue of scientific, popular, and industry viewpoints we have presented thus far.

The first step beyond the catalogue is to assess the economic impact of acidic deposition. It must be acknowledged, however, that the lack of firm physical scientific evidence prevents solidly grounded analysis. Nevertheless, several attempts have been made to report results for specific aspects of the larger problem.

Kamya, Mann, Denimarck, and Renshaw undertook to discover if those sub regions of the Adirondacks which had a high incidence of acidified lakes were suffering economic losses. The areas with acidified lakes have suffered economic decline in excess of that which can be explained by other variables, but no attempt was made to assign a specific dollar loss attributable to that general economic decline.[16]

In another inquiry, Kamya, Mann, and Renshaw undertook a dose-response study of New York's forest product industry. Using estimates of possible damage rates gleaned from previous research as a guide, they posit a 1 to 10 percent reduction in the growth of marketable wood products. At 1 percent, this would be a loss of 23.1 million dollars annually, 66 percent of which would be in paper and allied products, 19 percent in furniture, and the remainder in other wood products. The loss in forest growth would translate into lowered employment and earnings, with large dollar losses in the metropolitan counties of New York where paper products are used in printing and other manufacturing.[17]

Vrooman and Brown conducted a statistical study which related shore-line property values to lakes which were acidified in the Adirondacks. They hoped, of course, to be able to estimate the loss in lakefront values caused by acidification. The basic finding was that property values were unaffected.[18]

Page conducted a study of the economic impact of nitrogen and sulfur oxides and ozone on selected agricultural production in the Northeast. He assumed a reduction in production of between 6 and 12 percent for four crops—hay, corn, soybeans, and wheat. Supply elasticities were estimated, but the results were found to be insensitive to the supply elasticities. Losses in the five states, including New York, were estimated to be about 65 million dollars yearly.[19]

Menz and Mullen estimated fishing losses due to acid rain for the Adirondacks. Using New York angler interviews, and the loss in consumer surplus, the yearly losses were estimated to be between 2.5 and 8.2 million dollars.[20]

These six New York studies need to be placed in context. Crocker estimated that 5 billion dollars in damages was due to sulfur oxides for the eastern portion of the nation. The National Research Council estimated the national damages from nitrogen oxide emissions at 1.7

billion dollars. The Organization for Economic Cooperation and Development (OECD) estimated that a 37 percent reduction in sulfur oxide emissions below 1974 levels of the United States and other OECD countries would produce costs approaching 3 billion dollars and benefits of 2 to 19 billion dollars.[21]

The imprecision, incompleteness, variation, and lack of comparability in these estimates raise doubts as to their usefulness. Without solid, comprehensive evidence about damages, these estimates are more interesting than convincing. The problem is far larger than the specific difficulties in the existing literature. If it were not, a simple call for more, better economic research would be in order. The difficulty is that the basic form of economic analysis—a comparison of benefits and costs—is deficient in the context of an assessment of acid rain.

The usual strategy would be to examine the costs and benefits which accrue to proposed solutions to the acid deposition "problem." These proposed solutions typically take the form of prevention, diversion, or amelioration. Prevention would focus on limiting the generation of the primary pollutants thought to produce acidic deposition, e.g., sulfur oxides. Diversion would center on having the acid deposition take place where it would do little harm. We might make the acid fall over the North Atlantic Ocean, for example. An ameliorative solution would treat the effects of acidic deposition. If acidic deposition alters the acidity of a lake and if increased acidity causes fish to die, an ameliorative solution would be to chemically lower the acidity and, thereby, reduce the negative effects of acidic deposition.

As a general matter, the costs of the various solutions are somewhat easier to assess than are the benefits which result. We may not know whether the fish in some remote Adirondack lake are saved by reducing the production of sulfur oxides in a specific coal-fired electric generating plant in Ohio because of the scientific complexities involved in tracking the emissions, but we probably can determine how much it costs to wash the coal and put scrubbers on the smokestack to accomplish a specified level of reduced output. This results in a bias against action. And the bias against action is exacerbated as well. For instance, the inherently problematic nature of attempts to assess the value of unique goods such as a landmark building, intangibles such as "the view," and non-market commodities such as a shortened or degraded human life, is intimately interwoven with attempts to calculate the benefits of action in this area.

More importantly, the effects of acidic deposition may not be directly proportional to increases in acidification. Initial, small increases in acidity may do more damage than subsequent large increases i.e., there may be diminishing marginal effects. Such effects can serve to produce erroneous prices for the calculation of benefits in traditional benefit/ cost analyses. If the present environment is less than pristine, this produces special problems in the analysis. A large reduction in acidic deposition will have very little effect in an already dirty environment. Only after major efforts are made, and major costs are incurred, will large benefits begin to appear. When simple benefit/cost techniques are employed in such situations, inappropriate triage decisions are encouraged. Some areas are permitted to remain "dirty" because acid deposition has been too great for too long.

Of greater consequence is the possibility that some damage which occurs might be irreversible. In such a situation the conventional analyses also will mistakenly point away from action. The usual techniques assume that benefits given up today can be recaptured at some identifiable cost at sometime in the future. If acid deposition damages an agricultural crop and if we fail to address the problem immediately, we still can make up the shortfall next year by planting more seed, using more fertilizer, and cutting back on sulfur emissions. But the world of acid deposition may not work that way. Treating a lake with lime, for example, will lower the acidity levels, thus reversing the effects of acidity, but we are less than certain that such a treatment will reduce the volume of toxic metals. If the effects of acidic deposition are not reversible, then we properly adjust our analysis to lower our tolerance to the risks attributable to making an analytical mistake by placing a higher cost on these uncertain effects (i.e., to become risk averse). If present action or inaction forecloses future attempts to improve the environment, we might want to proceed differently than if the environment only is harmed temporarily.

The problems of diminishing marginal effects and irreversibility are also part of a larger set of problems associated with benefit/cost analyses of environmental quality. In benefit/cost analysis the emphasis is typically on the rate of environmental degradation rather than on the absolute level of environmental quality. Strong theoretical results in microeconomics indicate that erroneous pricing always will be the case in such situations and that the resultant suggestion will be to produce more degradation than is optimal (economically justifiable).[22]

POLICY MAKING: ACID RAIN

Neo-classical economics argues that a natural resource, such as soil productivity or oil, can never be depleted in an open market. Increasing resource scarcity will increase price, thereby decreasing the quantity used and causing technologically produced substitutes (e.g., hydroponics or coal) increasingly to be used, instead. Government intervention in the market is said to interfere with this efficient allocation of resources by upsetting the pricing of those resources and encouraging both overuse (range land) and underuse (forest) of natural resources. The privatization of resources will make better—more market oriented—decisions. Much of the argument is based on the concept of the "misuse of the commons." Each individual farmer gains by letting his cows graze on the commons. Yet, if all farmers follow this strategy, the commons will be overgrazed. Social policy must, therefore, cause the costs of overgrazing to be internalized, or privatized, so that the individual, self-interested, decisions of the farmers serve the collective good.

The "tragedy of the commons" idea is used by both those seeking greater controls and by those seeking greater privatization. The former wish to punish the free riders, the polluters, while the latter want to punish those who trespass on private property, the regulators. Both rely on the coercive state. They differ only as to who owns the property that is being protected.[23]

Acid deposition is different from the commons not only because the effects of acid deposition are not as easily known as the effects of overgrazing, but because the source of the damage is unknown and possibly unknowable. Furthermore, tragic as the loss of the commons is, the grass can be replaced. Acid deposition may not work that way. Finally, we are without easy technologically developable substitutes for clean air, land, and water.

Clearly, each of these observations forces us well beyond the limits of our evidence and knowledge. But such is often the world of the policymaker. The fact that substantial disagreement exists over such basic items as the definition of acid deposition invites controversy in the policy arena. Without agreement on the basic science, assessments of economic and social impact are made more problematic than usual. And herein lies the basic point concerning acid deposition. We have no scientific certainty.

This transforms the problem from a question of science to a question of preference. If nothing is done, the current sensibilities of New Yorkers will be violated. They stand ready to pay substantial costs to solve what they see as a serious problem while at the same time believing that many of the usual tradeoffs between the economy and the environment are illusory, forced choices.

Even if their view that "something should be done" is given a high governmental priority, it is not completely clear how to proceed. If areas such as the Adirondacks display more apparent effect due to acidic deposition, it is not even clear at this point if it is because there is more damage in this region than in others or because the region is so much more pristine that a small amount of damage which would go unnoticed elsewhere is highly visible. If it is the former, policies which are ameliorative or diversionary are in order. If it is the latter, prevention should be of higher priority.

Moreover, a decision about whether the Adirondack region is the uniquely vulnerable or simply the uniquely visible victim will affect who is to bear the burden and obtain the benefits associated with all proposed solutions. Those who suffer from the region's vulnerability are often entitled to societal compensation while those affected by merely visible damage often must give way to harder political and economic realities.

In the national debate on acid deposition, the proposed solutions are of the sort which concentrate on the reduction of emission (prevention) and which presume that acidic deposition is the result of the long-range transportation of chemically transformed pollutants. In these constructions the Midwest and Appalachian regions will be asked to incur costs to satisfy the preferences of those in the Northeast. The Midwest will see jobs given over to those who mine Western coal, which is generally lower in sulfur than Midwestern coal. (Of course, if the assumption about long-range transportation is incorrect, the Northeast does not gain despite the losses incurred by others.)

The terms of that debate reflect the recent history of air quality legislation. In the past 20 years several pieces of federal air quality legislation have been enacted. The first federal legislation concerned exclusively with air pollution was passed in 1955. The 1963 Clean Air Act built upon the 1955 legislation by adding local air pollution control program grants to the research, data collection, and technical assistance provided by the 1955 legislation. In 1965 motor vehicle emission control legislation was passed into law. The 1970 Clean Air Act required the Environmental Protection Agency (EPA) to establish national air quality standards and states to develop implementation plans. The 1977 Clean Air Act is the most recent legislation. It provides for reviews of ambient air quality standards. None of these federal laws explicitly address acid rain because they focus on pollution from local sources. Acid deposition is long distance pollution—local emissions whose total effects are not felt locally.

Similarly, most major cities have laws which address local air quality. Chicago and Cincinnati have local air quality laws dating back to 1881. Almost all of the largest thirty cities in the United States had enacted legislation concerning air quality by 1912. But the local focus of such laws virtually excludes, by definition, a consideration of acid rain.

In contrast New York state has explicitly attempted to regulate acid deposition. New York's law, signed by Governor Cuomo in August, 1984, requires a 245,000 ton cut in sulfur dioxide and nitrogen dioxide emissions in the State from 1980 levels. This is a reduction of about one-third and is in addition to the 50 percent reduction in emissions from 1968 to 1980 that is attributable to various causes, including a decline in manufacturing in the State. The State's legislation is modeled on a federal legislative proposal which has been stalled in the Congress (S. 768). Earlier, Minnesota and Wisconsin passed legislation capping sulfur emissions, and California and Washington are considering acid rain limiting legislation at this time.

RECOMMENDATIONS AND CONCLUSIONS

Economists and other analysts may find it confusing that acid rain deposition legislation was enacted by a state rather than the federal government. Clearly long-range air pollution is a national problem and not easily controlled by state or local governments. We can offer four reasons for state initiatives.

The dollar cost of reducing acid deposition in a specific "receiving" state is small compared to Ohio or Kentucky or the nation. A state can enact a policy sooner than the national government if its costs for doing so are relatively low. The recent legislation in New York is expected to cost the average 500 KWH family user about $.40 per month in additional electricity costs, and large industrial users about 45 to 80 dollars per month—a small cost compared to Ohio's possible loss in jobs.

Secondly, partisanship and politics, governors attempting to claim the attention of the nation play a role. A Republican in the White House brings forth innovative policies by Democratic governors, just as a Democrat in the White House might encourage Republican governors to innovate.

Third, the pristine character of the Adirondacks and timely analyses by Gene Likens and Carl Schofield and the New York State Department of Environmental Conservation brought attention to the problem of acid deposition in New York before other states. From the standpoint of the need for progressive legislation, the benefit of having a pristine environment cannot be over emphasized.

Finally, technology is a significant factor. New York is in the position to substitute increasing amounts of Canadian hydro-power electricity for New York's high sulfur coal and oil produced electricity. Canada, of course, is not only a source of cheap electricity but also both a source and a recipient of sulfur and nitrogen oxide emissions. Possibly 30 percent of the acid deposition in New York is from Canada. And from 3 to 7 percent of Canada's problem originates in New York.[24] In light of this fact, it would seem that New York could, by its negotiations on Canadian electricity purchases, urge Canada to reduce its smelter and other sources of sulfur or nitrogen oxide emissions. Obviously, Canada cannot be blackmailed into such a policy, any more than could Cuba or France be blackmailed through foreign trade to implement domestic policies. But what cannot be done in the glare of the TV camera might be done by quiet negotiations. We suggest that both national governments and state and provincial governments quietly negotiate a reduction in Canadian acid emissions in line with the reductions in the various states, beginning with New York.

The scientist, both physical and social, is trained to seek additional information. Conclusions prior to the time when that last bit of information is obtained are suspect. In the case of acid rain it is obvious that to wait for more data on the processes and effect of acid deposition is to violate the very real human concerns expressed by the public. Immediate action is preferred. The public's willingness to pay considerably more than what actually is required to reduce acid deposition considerably is strong evidence that it is risk averse, not that it is irrational. Delay motivated by the desire to collect additional information ignores the costs of delay itself. We would urge policy makers to reflect on the possible irreparable harm inflicted in the interim. In this way we can all move toward an improvement in air quality.

VII

Foreign Models for State Initiatives

SIXTEEN

Industrial Democracy and Reindustrialization:

Cross-Cultural Perspectives

Alvin Magid

The philosophical roots of industrial democracy can be traced back
to the Industrial Revolution. For some, the coming age aroused
fears that the nation-state and the nascent factory system would succeed
to the detriment of myriad smaller communities which had long been
organized on ties of personal loyalty, on small trade, and on the routine
of manual labor. The principle of industrial democracy was born partly
of a notion that participatory democracy on a broad front must assert
itself against the organizational power of the modern state and of
industry and commerce.[1]

In contemporary America, participatory democracy is fed by various
elements of discontent. An important one concerns the growing dissatisfaction of industrial labor with how industrial workplaces are
organized. For example, many workers greatly distrust the industrial
organization philosophy known as Taylorism. Named for Frederick
Winslow Taylor, a turn-of-the-century social theorist, Taylorism asserts
that the job performance of industrial labor will be adequate where
reasonable wages are paid as compensation for the numbing hierarchism
of the factory, with its emphasis upon the scientific organization of
work based on repetitive tasks and detailed instructions.[2] Wages and
working conditions have since improved significantly, fueled mainly by
the interaction of trade unions, management, and government. U.S.
industries nevertheless continue to experience growing alienation of

workers and decline of the work ethic among them; their absenteeism is increasing and their productivity is falling.

Proponents of industrial democracy contend that traditional incentives, such as wages, fringe benefits, promotions, dismissals, and superiors' instructions, are not adequate. They have more confidence in worker participation in industrial decision making as a strategy for improving the quality of worklife and stimulating worker/decision makers to act more responsibly in the interest of greater productivity.[3] Some advocates of industrial democracy believe that labor will be more efficient in a participatory environment where resourcefulness and inventiveness are rewarded, not detailing the tasks performed by fellow workers. Labor productivity is expected to grow with the loosening of organizational fetters.[4] Even in management circles there is some qualified support for the notion of worker-participation-as-incentive.[5]

FACTORS INFLUENCING INDUSTRIAL DEMOCRACY IN REINDUSTRIALIZATION

Dissatisfaction with the quality of worklife is, by numerous accounts, endemic in American society.[6] Partly for that reason, and partly because many Americans feel themselves powerless to check the tedium at work, ideas for workplace reform advanced on behalf of any segment of the labor force are not likely to attract wide support. For example, the issue of dysfunction in the organization of the industrial workplace has yet to win over a large constituency to industrial democracy. The forces of bureaucratization, professionalization, specialization, and centralized control in U.S. industry are all geared to promote rationalization based on a particular model of efficient human behavior. They prevail over a countervailing derationalization whose stress is upon debureaucratization, deprofessionalization, and democratization.[7]

But there is more reason to anticipate a growing interest in this country in the principle of industrial democracy spurred by the play of economic forces at the local, regional, national, and international levels than by ennui in the workplace. Already those forces are seen to threaten an increasing number of American industrial workers as well as the survival of many communities tied to a traditional factory system economy.

Among the more significant economic forces that cast a long shadow over the landscape of American industry are the soaring deficits in international trade and the federal budget; high U.S. interest rates; American and Japanese industrial joint ventures; plant closings, particularly in the sunset states of the Northeast and Midwest; and the mobility of capital to the sunbelt states of the South and Southwest, to the Far East, and to the Third World. A brief comment on these matters is in order.

The United States in International Trade

The position of the United States in international trade and finance deteriorated significantly in the period 1981–1984. Although at the beginning of the quadrennium the external trade in goods and services was substantially in balance, by the end of 1984 the U.S. trade deficit amounted to more than 123 billion dollars and the federal budget deficit topped 200 billion dollars. If left unchanged, the Reagan Administration's policy of tying control of deficits principally to the engine of economic growth could result in a trade deficit of 250 billion dollars annually by the end of the president's second term, along with a federal budget deficit far exceeding that level. This augurs deep concern, not least of all for the industrial labor sector.

The Loss of Jobs

At least two million jobs were lost in 1981–1984 in the export sector of U.S. industry, and a substantial part of the production of American-based multinational firms was transferred abroad. In the third quarter of 1984 growth in domestic demand outpaced growth in the gross national product by a ratio of 3:1, a robust 5.7 percent and a sluggish 1.9 percent, respectively. The imported goods needed to meet much of that demand provided a further stimulus to imports.

The Trade Deficit

The United States emerged at the end of the quadrennium as a leading debtor in the international community after borrowing at least 100 billion dollars annually to finance its huge trade deficit. Because domestic savings will probably be inadequate to finance private investment and to rectify imbalances in international trade and the federal budget, foreign sources will increasingly finance total demand. Dependence on those sources to supply and fund a substantial part of total demand will doubtless exacerbate the deficits and imperil U.S. economic stability.

Borrowing and Interest Rates

Dependence on borrowing at home and abroad will keep U.S. interest rates high. Consequently, a large pool of mobile international funds will be drawn into dollar assets, causing the dollar to be greatly overvalued in the international economy. American exports, moreover, will continue to be priced out of world markets. In effect, the United States will persist in heavily taxing its own exports while subsidizing imports through fluctuations in the exchange rate. Among the principal losers will be American industrial labor, particularly in the export sector.

Relations Between the United States and Japan

The United States and Japan are closely linked as military allies and trading partners, but their relationship has become increasingly strained. Militarily, the United States continues to press its Asian ally for a significant increase in outlays, despite Japanese constitutional restrictions and their unwritten rule that limits the annual military appropriation to a maximum 1 percent of the gross national product. The United States contends that the economic prosperity of Japan is facilitated by the costly security shield it provides its ally. For trade, the relationship continues to favor Japan. The U.S. trade deficit will exceed 30 billion dollars in 1984, and it is expected to reach 40 billion dollars by the end of the following year.

Faced with growing U.S. protectionist sentiment, Japan has cautiously agreed to work at closing the trade gap. Besides adopting voluntary quotas for key exports, the Japanese have begun to transfer some of their industrial production to the United States (utilizing American labor and management personnel) and to lower their own protectionist barriers against the import of American goods and services. If broadened, these concessions may grant significant relief to American industry— and its workforce—in both the domestic economy and the export sector. One other apparent concession, however, may have an offsetting effect. New and anticipated joint ventures for the manufacture of such items as automobiles, computers, photographic equipment, airplanes, machine tools, and robots are being organized according to a division of labor that favors Japanese workers over their American counterparts.[8] Accordingly, responsibility for product design, assembly, and marketing is assigned principally to the American partner; the Japanese dominate the production process and so command the bulk of the joint-venture workforce. Automation of the assembly function over time can be expected to reduce still further the input of American labor. In sum, the establishment of joint ventures as part of a larger strategy to correct the imbalance in United States-Japanese trade, an innovation in corporate bilateralism, may impose a considerable hardship upon American industrial labor.

American Labor and Reindustrialization

For most industrial workers in the United States, the arcana of deficits, high interest rates, overheated currencies, and transnational corporate alliances are best understood in terms of their overall impact on the lives of individuals and of communities. Few workers are unaware that over the last decade millions of jobs have been drained from the older U.S. industrial cities and towns, from the Northeast and Midwest and also increasingly from smokestack communities elsewhere in America.[9] The process has been discernible in workforce reductions and in permanent plant contractions and closings. As the line of dispirited jobless—and often unemployable—industrial workers has lengthened, their communities across America have come to suffer a corresponding diminution of economic security.

Some critics hold that this development has its roots in a larger strategy for deindustrializing the United States through domestic corporate mergers, plant closings, community abandonment, and by scrapping basic industry.[10] From their ranks comes the call for an ambitious countervailing radicalism to reindustrialize America, which includes an industrial democracy strategy to promote worker and community ownership of industry with worker and community owners exercising direct, permanent control over management.[11] In this view, workers and their communities can ill afford to assume that only unprofitable industries will contract and expire, that there will always be private investors to rescue profitable or potentially profitable industries faced with either contingency, and that a class of peripatetic high-level managers can operate industries more efficiently and more profitably than local workers and managers.[12]

The search for a radical solution based on a kind of 'reindustrial' democratic philosophy evokes the old clarion call for a participatory democracy that weighs against institutional gigantism in modern life. Such a proposed solution warrants particular consideration in those older industrial areas of the country where the question of reindustrialization is high on the public agenda. One such area is New York State. Accordingly, what follows is a brief survey of various instances of applied industrial democracy in the United States and abroad, identifying some implications for reindustrialization in this state.

WORKER OWNERSHIP AND LABOR-MANAGEMENT COOPERATION: INDUSTRIAL DEMOCRACY IN THE UNITED STATES

Various strategies have been adopted in the United States to foster industrial democracy. In this section, we shall highlight two basic approaches: worker ownership and labor-management cooperation.

Worker Ownership

There is a well documented, if not well known, tradition in American society of worker and, to a lesser extent, of municipal ownership of industry.[13] Before the Civil War, it was not uncommon for a few workers to join together as the owners of some light industry. In the last quarter of the nineteenth century, organized labor in the United States began to show interest in worker ownership. In the 1880s the Knights of Labor, for example, founded more than a hundred cooperatives in mining, shoe manufacturing, and other industries. At their initiative, a central organ, the General Cooperative Board, was created to educate members in the arcana of management and finance and to promote the cooperative idea among artisans, farmers, and shopkeepers.[14] But the notion that ordinary workers should have control over their workplace *and* their companies was destined to be undercut by the philosophy of Taylorism in American industry.

In recent years, there has been a revival of interest in worker ownership. Some have been drawn to it principally as a means of preventing plant closings, with their harsh effects upon individuals and communities. Others look to worker ownership to realize a more just capitalism. For example, in the 1960s, to promote economic equity and industrial peace as barriers to socialism, San Francisco attorney Louis O. Kelso formulated a rudimentary scheme based on the idea of an employee stock option plan (ESOP).[15] Kelso calculated that employee-shareholders who received dividend checks and a retirement income from company stock would have a deeper attachment to their companies and would, moreover, exert a greater effort to enhance productivity. By 1973, the ESOP idea's strong advocate in government, Senator Russell Long (Dem.-Louisiana), was working hard as Chairman of the Senate Finance Committee to promote ESOPs through revision of the federal tax code. By 1980 there were as many as 3,000 such plans in the United States, and the number continues to grow.[16]

At this juncture it is important to distinguish between *worker participation in corporate ownership* (via ESOP shareholding) and *worker participation in corporate management.* Closely examined, ESOPs are less instruments of worker control than plans for deferred compensation. They operate as follows. A company creates an employee stock option trust, and banks lend it money to buy company stock and other assets. The company makes payments to the trust to retire debt. As loans are repaid, the trust allocates to employees company stock that is vested in the names of the employee-shareholders for a prescribed period of time—usually a decade—based on a formula which takes into account wages and length of service. Upon retirement, workers receive their share of stock. From a tax perspective, the arrangement benefits all the principals. Companies can take deductions for cash dividends paid to the ESOP, and banks are rewarded by not having to pay income taxes on half the interest they collect on loans to ESOPs.

The federal tax code has been revised over the years to enhance the attractiveness of ESOPs. For example, the "leveraged ESOP" allows interest *and* principal to be deducted where the trust borrows from banks, collateralizing loans with company assets, stock, and credit. In a new twist unanticipated by the Congress, management in large industrial companies can reorganize as a "leveraged ESOP" in order to head off unwelcome corporate takeovers.[17] In that event, the position of management is likely to be strengthened at the expense of employees in the newly-created ESOP. Employee-shareholders who fear that the takeover will result in a decreased workforce are often more concerned with their own job security than with profiting from a stock sale. They do not sell their shares and are then expected to affirm their gratitude for the failed takeover by deepening their attachment to the company and its triumphant management.

But, following Louis O. Kelso, if ESOPs grant industrial workers a piece of the corporation, they do not guarantee employee-shareholders a key role in the management function.[18] There are now only a few ESOP companies in which the workers own a majority of the voting stock. Among the more than 7,000 partially or wholly employee-owned companies in the United States (some 3,000 of which, as we have seen, are ESOPs) probably no more than 500 grant to low-level workers a key role in the management process.[19] Worker participation in management is usually limited to activities on the shop-floor, with control of the decision-making process for product design, manufacture, and marketing generally held tightly by higher-level, professional managers. The power and privileges of management in ESOP companies are further enhanced by the propensity of trustees to exercise workers' voting rights without prior consultation. Because many years are likely to pass before workers acquire majority ownership of an ESOP company, they are expected to wield little power and influence in management affairs.[20] In some cases management has refrained from embracing the ESOP option, despite its lucrative tax aspect, where there is fear of the workers' growing strength.

There are other serious drawbacks in the ESOP approach to industrial democracy and worker participation. First, financing is not easily available to buy out companies for the purpose of transforming them into ESOPs. The problem is especially acute where government and the private sector are reluctant to make grants or loans to failing companies.[21] Second, still feeling alienated from management despite their shareholder status, workers in ESOP companies may want to reap a quick profit by selling out to private investors. The impulse to sell is apt to be strong among those workers who are nearing retirement age, who are confident that the new owners will not effect a sharp reduction in the workforce, or who are reluctant to forego wage and fringe benefits in order to reinvest profits in needed plant modernization. Selling off ESOP companies is a further check on the development of a worker-manager ethos in the industrial sector. And it is a risky course of action. The sale to private investors of companies whose profitability has been restored under worker ownership may promote the very condition—plant closings—which originally impelled workers to become corporate owners. Third, feeling themselves threatened by a new form of industrial organization favoring labor-management cooperation over the old system of adversarial relationships, trade unions tend to regard ESOPs with skepticism or outright hostility. These traditional representatives of labor are also likely to fear that the new arrangement will cause workers to lose the hard-won benefits of collective bargaining.[22] Relations may consequently deteriorate within ESOP companies in the triangular network formed of workers, management, and trade unions. Finally, there is the considerable risk to workers—especially older ones—where pension funds are used as the principal source of capital to finance an ESOP buy out. The bankruptcy of an ESOP company is liable to cause great hardship for retired workers unprotected by a pension plan.

Labor-Management Cooperation

It can fairly be said of industrial democracy in contemporary America that opportunity and adversity, not principle, are the mothers of invention because of many recent decisions that led to the establishment of ESOPs. The primary goal has usually been to improve the financial condition of a company, to increase the productivity of its workers, to avert plant closings, or to repulse a hostile buy out. In devising strategies for worker ownership based on ESOPs the principals have rarely been motivated to secure for industrial workers a key role in corporate decision making.

As with ESOPs, the approach to industrial democracy based on institutions of labor-management cooperation has not often achieved for workers a place next to upper management in the corridors of corporate power. Here, too, the emphasis has been essentially pragmatic, seeking primarily to improve the quality of labor-management relations as part of the search for industrial peace and/or to arrest industrial decline with its baleful effect on local communities. If dealing with adversity in industrial and community life through labor-management cooperation has not given ordinary workers a leading role in organizational decision making, it has in some cases at least enabled them to widen their scope of participation. One such case centers on factory workers in Jamestown, a small manufacturing city near the western border of New York State.[23]

The Jamestown Area Labor-Management Committee (JALMC) was created in the early 1970s to help vitalize that community by arresting the erosion of its industrial base, particularly in furniture manufacturing and metal works. The Committee was organized through the cooperation of labor, management, and a progressive city administration headed by Mayor Stanley Lundine. Their goals were to save jobs threatened by plant closings; to establish problem-solving projects at the plant level based on the cooperation of labor and management with the assistance of professional staff members of JALMC; to train union and management personnel to eventually take over the facilitating role of JALMC in their own company or in other local companies; to organize training programs throughout the Jamestown area and enlarge the base of skills for local industry; and to develop joint projects with other community organizations, including the public school system, the public junior college, and the county development agency. It was agreed from the outset that JALMC would preempt neither the collective bargaining role of the unions nor the mediation role of federal and state agencies. Moreover, it was stressed that the Committee would be essentially facilitative, with JALMC doing its work through personal contacts, persuasion, and mobilization of requisite financing.[24] The Committee received strong encouragement along these lines from its various consultants, who included Eric Trist, a leading behavioral scientist and founder of the Tavistock Work Research Institute in London, and William F. Whyte, a distinguished sociologist, as well as some of his colleagues at the New York State School for Industrial and Labor

Relations at Cornell University. By the end of the 1970s, JALMC had managed by trial and error to become institutionalized in the Jamestown area on the base of permanent labor-management committees in various plants. It had established an impressive record of helping to build trust in a community known for its poor labor-management relations and had enlarged the job base in companies the Committee had assisted. Over time, management in those companies came increasingly to include its workers in decision making on such matters as shop-floor procedures and plant design.[25] The Jamestown approach to institutionalizing labor-management cooperation has been adopted by several communities throughout the United States.[26]

CROSS-CULTURAL PERSPECTIVES ON INDUSTRIAL DEMOCRACY

Proponents of industrial democracy in the United States have long been attentive to kindred developments abroad. In the four decades after the Second World War, European initiatives have strengthened that conception, particularly in the industrial sector of the economy.[27] Among the most important—and influential—are those in Sweden, Spain, and Yugoslavia. They merit examination here.

Sweden

Implementation of diverse programs for industrial democracy in Sweden over the last few decades reflects the play of forces in the workplace and throughout society. Together these forces marked an historic irony. Just when liberal social values were coming to dominate important spheres of life, e.g., education, the family, and a state increasingly tied to a welfare ethos, industrial management was promoting even more aggressively the values of efficiency and hard work to outproduce international competitors. As pressure mounted to increase productivity, so, too, did the level of personal stress.[28] Gaining their voice through the trade unions and a socialist government in power, workers responded by protesting against an industrial order which appeared to them to be incompatible with the new liberalization in Swedish society. As absenteeism and job-turnover both escalated (the latter exacerbated by a law which protected workers from losing their rights with transfer between companies, and by another law which sharply reduced the pool of foreign labor) Swedish industry felt compelled to seek relief with a strategy of industrial democracy. Throughout the country, hundreds of programs were established, some based on new labor-management committees, others on reorganization of the workplace to enhance job satisfaction without sacrificing the value of worker efficiency in the prevailing system of capitalist production.[29]

The automobile industry helped spearhead this development. Volvo, for example, reorganized several of its plants to promote the semi-autonomy of work groups based on the tradition of skilled craftsmanship. These groups were empowered to set their own work pace and to determine the schedule for coffee breaks. Organized on fewer than a dozen workers, each group was made responsible for its own quality control, for maintaining an inventory of tools, and for processing the raw materials.

Newer Volvo plants, like the one at Kalmar, were designed to promote job satisfaction as a concomitant of worker efficiency. Constructed without a traditional assembly line and illuminated partly by the sun's rays, Volvo/Kalmar underlined the need for an environment in which autonomous and semi-autonomous groups would be able to function in unaccustomed comfort. Light and color held sway in the plant, with the noise level reduced significantly. In place of an assembly line, there was an electrically-driven carrier system. Each car in production was given its separate carrier, controlled either by a central computer or by the workers themselves. Each work group moved the carrier through its area on the shop-floor either by setting the timing of the carrier to resemble the movement of a traditional assembly line (allowing each worker to attend to his own repetitive task) or by adjusting the carrier to stop in the work area or to move through it at a slow pace (allowing the whole group to work together on a car). So long as they met their hourly quota for production, the Kalmar work groups could decide on task assignment and on coffee break scheduling. Saab, another leading manufacturer of automobiles in Sweden, has experimented with similar programs based on the principle of industrial democracy.

In sum, the Swedish automobile industry evinces a mixed character, with its traditional assembly line and its innovative work regimens. In other Swedish industries many companies with plants organized on assembly line production have introduced labor-management committees to deal essentially with shop-floor activities. Companies such as Volvo and Saab provide in individual plants the alternatives of assembly-line-like production and democratization of the workplace. They emphasize giving workers the opportunity to organize their production on either the traditional or the non-traditional mode, or on a combination of the two. While there is some evidence of increased job satisfaction among Swedish workers using this more flexible approach, discontent continues to be voiced over the monotony that is intrinsic in the industrial workplace. Finally, it should be noted that democratization has not been extended to the upper reaches of corporate management. Shop-floor innovations in Swedish industry have come by a 'top-down' process, allowing management to retain control over key decisions relating to design, manufacture, and marketing of product.

Spain

The exemplar of industrial democracy based on voluntary cooperatives using the technical methods of modern industry can be found in Spain, in the small Basque city of Mondragón.[30] As with any commercial partnership, the members of the cooperative movement in Mondragón use their own resources to provide part of the business capital in which they retain full ownership rights. Within quite strict limits, additional funds can be obtained for investment purposes from the movement's own savings bank, the *Caja Laboral Popular*. (The *Caja*, which exists principally to help finance cooperatives, receives its funds from the savings deposits of the population in the Basque region.)

Most of the workers employed by a cooperative in Mondragón are members of that cooperative. They have equal rights in the organization, including the right to participate in meetings of the workers' assembly and to elect the supervisory board of the enterprise. The board, in turn, appoints the management. Wage differentials for the members of a cooperative are set according to occupational skills and job responsibilities. Wage rates for manual laborers are related to the rates of local trade unions in private industry. Wages are paid in advance. At the conclusion of each accounting period the members divide up any surplus revenue which may have accumulated over costs. Costs are calculated on wage advances, depreciation, and taxes. A part of the surplus is expended as interest on the members' capital. Most of the interest, which is paid at a minimum annual rate of 6 percent, can be drawn out by the members in cash. What remains of the surplus is then allocated as follows: 10 percent is paid to the members in proportion to their earnings; about 30 percent is held back as reserve and social funds; and the balance is added to the members' capital accounts in proportion to their earnings. Capital accounts are periodically revalued consistent with inflation. Only upon their retirement can the members withdraw funds from these accounts. In sharp contrast with the system of ESOP companies in the United States, the Mondragón system virtually ensures that its cooperative enterprises will not be sold off to private investors. As we shall see, the successful growth of

Mondragón enterprises builds pressure not to sell those units, but to have them spin off other cooperatives to function efficiently on a smaller scale.

The Mondragón system was conceived by a Roman Catholic priest, José María Arizmendi, who settled in the city in 1941. Even before his death in 1976, Father Arizmendi was able to institutionalize the cooperative movement he had founded on the key Basque values of democratic association, hard work and thrift, and craftsmanship. What sets Mondragón apart from other capitalist enterprises are its roots in an inspiring ideology and in Basque nationalism. The ideology of cooperation works together with local nationalism to provide an abundant supply of workers and management personnel. Able managers are willing to work for less in Mondragón than their counterparts earn in the private sector.

As part of its extensive institutional framework, the cooperative movement in Mondragón has spawned an array of support services. The movement has its own technical school and a polytechnic institute with university-level courses. There is an institute for research and development to advise the individual cooperatives on innovations in products and in manufacturing processes. The Management Services Division in the *Caja Laboral Popular* advises all new cooperatives on development planning; existing cooperatives often solicit advice from the division on how to improve their performance. Near the end of the 1970s, the Management Services Division in the *Caja* had more than 100 economists, engineers, attorneys, and other technical experts on its full-time staff. All together, these support services play a key role in launching new cooperatives, supplying them with a large pool of skilled workers, managers, and technicians, arranging for finance, and advising on product design, manufacture, and marketing.

Mondragón launched its first industrial cooperative in 1956, with five employees. Nearly three decades later, at least 87 cooperatives have 18,000 employees and gross annual sales amounting to 1.7 billion dollars. The largest cooperative, Ulgor, manufacturing household durables, employed nearly 4,000 people in 1979. Ulgor currently leads Spain in the production of refrigerators and stoves. Other cooperatives manufacture such items as construction materials, electronic equipment, and foundry products. Mondragón is an extraordinarily dynamic system, having succeeded through the 1960s and 1970s in creating annually about three new cooperatives. (By the end of the latter decade, it had suffered only one failure, a fishermen's cooperative.) Eight hundred new jobs were created annually in the period 1961–1976. The cooperative movement has had a robust return on capital, with a five-year average of 18 percent. The Basque region's great confidence in the movement is evidenced by the fact that by 1978 the *Caja Laboral Popular* had more than 300,000 depositor accounts and assets of 2.1 billion dollars. For almost two decades following the movement's establishment in Mondragón, the *Caja* was content merely to respond to proposals to create new enterprises either by arranging for them to be spun off existing enterprises or by helping to finance new ones. But with the rapid growth of its assets, the cooperative bank felt compelled to adopt a more aggressive program for developing new enterprises, some more capital-intensive than their predecessors and requiring higher levels of skill and training. The drive to increase the number of enterprises has met several critical needs. By identifying and promoting new areas for productive investment, the *Caja* has carved out for itself a key role in the social and economic development of the entire Basque region.[31] By helping to finance more capital-intensive enterprises, the *Caja* has strongly encouraged skilled workers and technicians to remain in the region. Finally, the Mondragón system has demonstrated an admirable flexibility in responding to worker pressure to correct some of the Taylorist attributes particularly of the larger industrial cooperatives. The correctives include creating many new cooperatives in other than the assembly line mode, with employment rolls close to a few hundred workers for each new unit; restructuring work patterns in existing enterprises to enhance job satisfaction; and revising the wage rate system. While the largest cooperative, Ulgor, has spun off a half-dozen co-operatives of modest size, this giant organization has yet to restructure itself as other than an unpopular traditional assembly line industry.

Yugoslavia

Yugoslavia represents a singular case of industrial democracy. Where institutions embodying that principle do exist, they are apt to be found at random in capitalist economies, as islands in a sea of enterprises organized on the authoritarian lines of Taylorist scientific management. In Yugoslavia, by contrast, the notion of industrial democracy is included in the concept of democratic self-management, usually vaguely-defined.[32] Industrial democracy is, in effect, democratic self-management in the industrial sector.

Because democratic self-management is at the core of the official Marxist ideology, whose repository is the ruling Communist League in the one-party Yugoslav state, that concept is the basis on which economic and political life formally turns. Almost all the industrial and service sectors along with nearly 20 percent of agriculture are nominally controlled by institutions of democratic self-management. Together with an array of sociopolitical organizations and communities of interest, the institutions of democratic self-management in the economic sphere are, in turn, linked through a delegate system to the organs of government at the *opština* (commune), municipal, republic, and federal levels.[33]

Economic enterprises in Yugoslavia are called "organizations of associated labor," not "cooperatives," because ordinarily the members of a cooperative retain individual rights over their investment of capital in the organization.[34] (The Mondragón system is an example.) In contrast, all enterprises in Yugoslavia which employ more than a few workers are, by law, socially owned. As such, they operate as institutions of democratic self-management.

The notion of democratic self-management is derived from Marxist texts which antedate Yugoslav socialism and from the society's own historical experience. The Partisan resistance movement led by Marshal Josip Broz Tito during the Second World War had perforce to lay the groundwork for its national and social revolution along Marxist lines against the backdrop of the struggle against the German and Italian invaders. Of necessity, the resistance movement had to pursue its multifarious goals with a highly decentralized, mobile organization which stressed initiative-taking and self-reliance. After surviving the war years those values were then subordinated for a brief time to the Stalinist values of centralized party and state control, nationalization of the industrial and service sectors, and collectivization of agriculture. Over several decades following the break with Stalin's Cominform in 1948, Yugoslavia evolved by stages to its present status as a democratic self-management society. The process was fueled partly by the need to explain the expulsion from the Soviet bloc and to frame a distinctive Marxist socialism for an economically underdeveloped country cleaved deeply along the cross-cutting lines of nationality, region, and religion.[35] In short, democratic self-management was imposed on Yugoslavia by a political leadership that wanted simultaneously to promote economic modernization within a heterogeneous society marked by zones of uneven development and to legitimize both the ruling Marxist ideology and the various key groups in the party, the state organization, and the economic and cultural spheres which had come to dominate public life. The commitment to democratic self-management was also reinforced by political strains in the Yugoslav Federation, among factions tied to competing national and regional interests. In time, the ruling Titoist coterie sought to regulate the factional conflict by devolving party and state power to the republic, municipal, and commune levels. Central authority was further weakened by instituting at the center of both party and state the principle that collective leadership is based on rotation.[36] It was hoped that divisive tendencies in Yugoslav society could be checked by a combination of devolution, collective leadership, and democratic self-management—all the while achieving economic progress on a wide front, and especially in the industrial sector.

By law, Yugoslav industrial workers have full management rights, including the right to allocate the net income of their enterprises either to themselves or to collective consumption or savings.[37] Workers are no longer obliged to pay interest on capital invested in their enterprises. In effect, they are able to use without charge the inherited capital of the enterprises, which is augmented by reinvested income and by loans made initially by the government and now increasingly by the socially-owned banks. In theory, management in Yugoslavia resembles that found in the Mondragón cooperatives, with great decision-making authority lodged in workers' councils in the areas of production and marketing and in the selection of senior management personnel. In fact, decision making in those key areas is dominated by management boards and enterprise directors, whose real power derives from the alliances they strike with the management of banks and with party and government officials at the commune, municipal, and republic levels.[38] As a consequence, decisions relating to the industrial economy, including income-distribution, are affected by the political need for the wealthy republics to transfer part of their resources to less-developed areas in the south and by the autarkic tendencies which mark economic decision making at the republic and even the commune levels.[39] The principle of a unified market economy in Yugoslavia is more often honored in the breach.[40]

The Yugoslav case differs from that of Mondragón, moreover, in that workers in the former make no initial contribution to the equity of their enterprises, nor are they required to pay an official fee for job entry. (Corruption in the form of illegal fees plays an important role in Yugoslavia, where the official unemployment rate exceeds 15 percent. Similar fees often are also paid to secure an apartment through the enterprises in which workers are employed.[41]) Because society is deemed to own most of the economic resources in the country, workers enjoy some part of their enterprises' savings just so long as they are employed by them. They cease to derive benefits from enterprise savings upon their retirement, death, or transfer to another enterprise.

Despite the great human and financial resources which are invested in operating (and trying to export) the Yugoslav system of democratic self-management, it continues to suffer widespread declining vitality.[42] The post-war drive to create a modern industrial society has left—

mostly private—agriculture to stagnate.[43] Food imports increase, exacerbating the strain on limited hard-currency reserves.[44] As alienation spreads, worker productivity decreases and absenteeism increases. Economic crimes abound in industrial plants, where many workers steal expensive tools and materials for use in their "second jobs" as private mechanics and artisans. Also, erosion of labor discipline is evidenced in numerous illegal strikes and in the many free-riders in the workplace.[45] A large body of empirical research by Yugoslav and other scholars documents the growing cynicism among workers about democratic self-management institutions. Workers' councils are widely perceived as unable to deal with the vagaries of economic decision making when management hoards vital information. Worker delegates at the commune, municipal, and republic levels of government tend to be perceived by their blue collar colleagues as self-interested political opportunists.

The deepening malaise in the industrial workforce and among the general population in Yugoslavia is fueled also by key economic factors. Although a decade ago the thriving economy was bolstered by foreign credits, it reels now from an official inflation rate of at least 60 percent and a hard-currency debt of nearly 20 billion dollars. Over the last few years, the export trade has continued to falter even while the dinar has plummeted against the dollar. The economic recession in Western Europe has caused thousands of Yugoslav "guest workers" to return home to an uncertain future. The growing number of returnees threatens Yugoslavia with a sharp decline in hard-currency remittances. Many Yugoslavs project their own flagging spirit onto a society faced with mounting problems, at once economic and political, domestic and international. Their hopes are not bouyed by a political leadership which persists in using ideology as a means of marshalling power and fails to heed its own call for austerity.

INDUSTRIAL DEMOCRACY IN A STRATEGY FOR REINDUSTRIALIZATION

In assessing the role that industrial democracy might play in some larger strategy for reindustrialization—in New York State and elsewhere in the United States—it is well to recall the evolution over two centuries of our dominant modes of production. Before the Civil War, American industry was organized on a relatively small scale, with its base in skill-intensive craft activities. In the next half-century, the primacy of that mode of production was effectively challenged by the rise of large-scale mass-production factories. But in establishing their own economic

393

ascendancy, assembly line industries never did manage to sweep away entirely the ideology of craft-production based on skilled craftsmanship. Nor were they able to wholly displace the organizational foundation for that ideology. Indeed, the older tradition survived alongside its aggressive rival down to the contemporary period. By the 1970s the metalworking industry in this country was still operating mostly in that tradition. And notwithstanding its vaunted gigantism organized on assembly line production, 20 percent of the steel industry's output was based on mini-mills. The vitality of the older tradition is also evident in the spread of high-technology industries throughout the United States. High-technology industries rely on a craft-based, skill-intensive workforce. Encouraged by innovations in computer technology and by the general inability of mass-production companies to adapt swiftly to changing currents in manufacture and trade, the newcomers organized on a smaller scale have found their niche in an American economy more and more demanding of specialized product and service.[46]

The historical record yields these important lessons—modes of production will vary according to social needs tied to technological innovation and, in the process of change, old and new modes will likely fuse with each other, interpenetrate, or coexist, thereby avoiding a head-on clash that would otherwise culminate in displacement. Greater flexibility must underpin a strategy for reindustrialization that is intended to avoid displacement. Taking the long view, it is clear that the system of mass-production assembly line industry rooted in Taylorist scientific management need not define modern industrial organization. It is rather one way to conceive such organization. Evidence of the greater value of a mixed approach can be found in the experience of Volvo and Saab in Sweden, of the Mondragón cooperatives in Spain, and of democratic self-management in Yugoslavia. Whatever success the two Swedish industrial giants and the Basque cooperatives have had with their own variants of industrial democracy may be ascribed substantially to obviating the numbing effects of a Taylorist monolithism, i.e., they anchored their industrial organization in a process of choosing from among alternative modes of production. Democratic self-management and economic development in Yugoslavia, by contrast, have both foundered principally on a rigid institutionalism tightly held by the imperatives of ideology and political power. The constricting character of the Yugoslav system can perhaps best be conveyed by noting this difference with Mondragón. Whereas the Basque cooperative movement has grown by creating more specialized cooperatives of small scale, Yugoslav industry has courted stultification by emphasizing gigantism around the enlargement of existing enterprises. Mondragón's efforts have been crowned by an impressive rate of job-development and by increasing efficiency, productivity, and job satisfaction in the workplace.

Reindustrialization based partly at least on a growing base of small-scale capital- and skill-intensive industries appears, on the record of Mondragón and high-technology enterprises in the United States, to hold out the promise that major objectives of industrial democracy will be achieved—greater autonomy in the workplace along with enhanced job satisfaction. It is reasonable to expect that in those industries requiring ever higher levels of skill and training and a more self-regulating work regimen, a kind of self-correcting mechanism will improve the overall quality of worklife. For the large body of shop-level workers who will likely remain in, or enter, mass-production industries, the experiences of Volvo and Saab in Sweden and of the Jamestown Area Labor-Management Committee in western New York State indicate that careful redesign of repetitive work regimens and of physical plants can elevate job satisfaction and the quality of work. It should also be noted that a growing number of workers in Yugoslavia's mostly non-high-technology industrial sector advocates reforming the system of democratic self-management to provide for their own greater control over workplace activities.

But here a caveat is in order. Any decision about modes of production in a particular industrial plant, old, new, or redesigned, should take into account the preferences and capabilities of workers. Replacing relatively simple repetitive work with the complexity and individual responsibility that inevitably attends industrial workplace democratization will doubtless be more attractive to some workers than to others. Mismatching worker preferences and capabilities with modes of industrial production is liable to reduce job satisfaction and worker efficiency.

Two items in the industrial democracy agenda merit particular comment: worker participation in corporate ownership and worker participation in corporate management. As previously noted, they have grown disproportionately in the United States. Worker ownership increases with the spread of employee stock option plans, but upper management retains its virtual monopoly over decision making for product design, manufacture, and marketing. Given industrial management's ease of mobility, the risks associated with ESOPs appear to be far greater for labor than for its superiors. And compounding their burden, workers concerned with job security have often had to accept a shrunken paycheck as ESOP employee-shareholders. Small wonder that many such workers and their advocates bristle over the arrangement, suspecting that ESOPs are designed more to discipline labor than to promote either worker ownership or power-sharing with management.[47]

Neither the cases of Volvo and Saab in Sweden nor the Yugoslav system of democratic self-management signal a way for American industrial workers—who may wish to do so—to enter the halls of corporate decision making. In the experience of Mondragón, however, we encounter a basis for cautious optimism. Basque cooperative workers own their enterprises, and they wield influence upon management decisions. Management at Mondragón finds itself increasingly pressured by workers to increase the material rewards of ownership if not to establish a duopoly of power. While rooted in the culture of Basque society, the cooperative system there might usefully be adapted in several of its key aspects to conditions elsewhere.

Worker cooperatives organized as part of a reindustrialization strategy particularly for U.S. enterprises of small scale would vitalize the principle of industrial democracy as they joined together with other small companies to spearhead the process of job development. Realistically, however, it is well to recall that Mondragón has succeeded partly because it has managed over several decades to strengthen the identification of cooperative members with their enterprises and because it has pioneered an array of supportive institutions—a bank, a research and development facility, and educational and training centers from which the Basque cooperative movement continues to draw creative energy and material assistance.[48] In recent years in the United States, there has been some discussion in private and in political circles of the possible benefits of launching a cooperative movement within the industrial sector—with its own energizing institutions, including a chartered bank. With or without that innovation, it is a healthy sign indeed that those who would frame a strategy for reindustrialization in New York State and elsewhere recognize that its success is conditional, among other things, on a pluralism of organizational forms and functions shaped always by trial and error.

Notes

CHAPTER ONE: SOLVING THE DILEMMA OF STATESMANSHIP: REINDUSTRIALIZATION THROUGH AN EVOLVING DEMOCRATIC PLAN

1. For example, see Hugh L. Carey's *The New York State Economy in the 1980's: A Program for Economic Growth* (1981); *Building From Strength: A Program for Economic Growth and Opportunity* (1982); and *A Strategy for Developing Technology-Based Industry in New York* (1982); Mario M. Cuomo, *Message to the Legislature* (1983, 1984, and 1985). Copies of these documents can be obtained from the Office of the Governor of New York State or the New York State Archives, Cultural Education Center, Empire State Plaza, Albany, New York, 12230.

2. The analysis of New York's economy in this section is based upon the following documentation:

   (a) Aaron S. Gurwitz, Kathleen Auda, and William Greer, "Federal R & D and Defense Outlays in New York State," Federal Reserve Bank of New York *Regional Economic Studies* (February, 1984).

   (b) *1983 Annual Report,* Economic Development Administration, U.S. Department of Commerce, Washington, D.C. (1983).

   (c) Robert Meyer, *Corporate Headquarters in New York State 1983,* Research Report Number 83-11, Division of Economic Research and Statistics, New York State Department of Commerce (August, 1984).

   (d) *Business Statistics New York State: Annual Summary 1972-1980,* New York State Department of Commerce, Bureau of Business Research.

   (e) New York State Business Fact Book, 1983 Supplement, New York State Department of Commerce.

   (f) *1980-82 Big Gains for Small Business in New York State,* Subcommittee on Small Business, New York State Assembly (December, 1982).

   (g) *The Economic Eclipse of New York State: The Shadow is Passing,* New York State Senate Research Service, Task Force on Critical Problems (March, 1981).

   (h) *An Economic Review of New York State 1970-1982,* New York State Department of Commerce, Bureau of Business Research (March, 1983).

   (i) *1983 Annual Report,* New York State Assembly Committee on Commerce, Industry and Economic Development (November, 1983).

   (j) William Schweke and Robert Friedman, "The Debate Over 'Who Generates Jobs?' " *Entrepreneurial Economy* (February, 1983).

   (k) David L. Birch, "Who Creates Jobs?" *Public Interest* (Fall, 1981); and "Generating New Jobs: Are Government Incentives Effective?" *Commentary* (July, 1979).

   (l) Richard Alba, *The Impact of Migration on New York State,* a report published by the Public Policy Institute of the Business Council of New York State (Albany, 1984).

3. See footnote 2, entries (b), (c), (d), (e), (g), (h).

4. *Ibid.*

5. *Ibid.*

6. *Ibid.*

7. *Ibid.*

8. See footnote 2, entries (d), (g), and (h).

9. See footnote 2, entry (g), particularly pp. 29–53.

10. *Ibid.,* particularly pp. 23–26.

11. *Ibid.,* particularly pp. 33–50.

12. *Ibid.*

13. *Ibid.,* particularly pp. 29–31.

14. See the studies by the Conference of State Manufacturers' Associations and by Felecian F. Foltman cited in footnote 2, entry (g), pp. 29–31.

15. See footnote 2, entry (g), pp. 100–103.

16. Interview with Mr. Frank Mauro, Secretary, New York Assembly Ways and Means Committee, December 15, 1984. See also the remarks by New York State Senator Joseph Pisani, "Opening Statements of the Joint Senate-Assembly Commerce Committee Hearing on the Governor's [1981] Economic Message" (Albany: March 18, 1981), p. 2.

17. Hugh L. Carey, *The New York State Economy in the 1980's: A Program for Economic Growth* (1981) and *Building From Strength: A Program for Economic Growth and Productivity* (1982). (Copies of these documents can be obtained from the New York State Archives, Cultural Education Center, Empire State Plaza, Albany, New York, 12230.); "Opening Statements of the Joint Senate-Assembly Commerce Committee Hearing on the Governor's [1981] Economic Message" (Albany: March 18, 1981) and "A Public Hearing on the Governor's 1982 Economic Message: A Review of Assumptions and Economic Projections" (Albany: March 23, 1982).

18. *Building From Strength, op. cit.,* p. 5.

19. See footnote 2, entries (j) and (k), and the study by Peter M. Allaman and David Birch cited in footnote 2, entry (g), p. 9.

20. See *Building From Strength, op. cit.,* pp. 38–46; "Summary of the Economic Impact of the Small Business Investment Corporation Program," a report published by Deloitte Haskins and Sells and Arthur D. Little, Inc., National Association of Small Business Investment Companies (October, 1981); Governor's Public Investment Task Force, "Final Report" (October, 1981); and footnote 2, entry (f).

21. See *Building From Strength, op. cit.,* pp. 34–47; and footnote 2, entry (f), particularly pp. 7–46.

22. *Ibid.*

23. Memorandum, Executive Chamber, New York State, "High Technology Industries—Summary," June 30, 1978.

24. *Ibid.,* p. 2.

25. For example, see *ibid;* "Briefing Paper for the Meeting of the Governor's Advisory Council on High Technology," March 2, 1979; and "Summary of the Meeting of the Governor's Advisory Council on High Technology," updated (published sometime in March, 1979). Available from the New York State Science and Technology Foundation, Albany, New York.

26. Memorandum, June 30, 1978, *op. cit.,* p. 2.

27. Regarding the controversy, see George Gilder, "The U.S. Semiconductor Industry Rivals the Growth of the Japanese Economy as the Greatest Success Story of Our Times," *Policy Review* (Winter, 1984), 27; Regis McKenna, "Sustaining the Innovation Process in America," *The Industrial Policy Debate,* Chalmers Johnson, ed. (San Francisco: ICS. 1984); Richard R. Nelson, *High-Technology Policies: A Five-Nation Comparison* (Washington, D.C.: AEI, 1984).

28. See the "Briefing Paper" of March 2, 1979, *op. cit.*

29. See "Revitalizing the Science and Technology Foundation," November 15, 1978, one of the several working papers generated by the High Technology Opportunities Task Force. Available from the New York State Science and Technology Foundation, Albany, New York.

30. See "Suggested Work Program for the High Technology Opportunities Task Force," Fall, 1978. Available from the New York State Science and Technology Foundation, Albany, New York.

31. See "New York State Centers for Advanced Technology." Available from the New York State Science and Technology Foundation, Albany, New York.

32. Chapter 561 of the Laws of 1982.

33. The Job Training Partnership Act (JTPA, P. L. 97–300) was enacted by the U.S. Congress in October, 1982.

34. JTPA (P. L. 97–300), Title I.

35. Compare, for example, the Carey and Cuomo documents cited in footnote 1.

36. See, for example, "Cuomo at midterm: style or substance?" *Times Union* (Albany: December 30, 1984), p. 8.

37. Mario M. Cuomo, *Message to the Legislature* (1984), p. 13.

38. *Ibid.,* p. 12.

39. As far as I am able to determine, the "partnership" concept first appears during the Carey administration in early 1979 as a centerpiece of economic revitalization policy (see "Briefing Paper for the Meeting of the Governor's Advisory Council on High Technology," *op. cit.*). From that time on it appears regularly in economic policy statements and programs issued by the executive branch until Mario Cuomo raised it to the level of a formal organizing principal of strategic economic planning in 1983 (see his *Message to the Legislature,* p. 6).

40. The decisive redefinition of economic policy discourse in this area occurs in Hugh Carey, *A Strategy for Developing Technology-Based Industry in New York,* October 12, 1982. In particular, see Carey's definition of a "technology-based industry," p. 2.

41. See "The Innovation Finance Corporation: A New Source of Capital for New Technology in New York State," Office of the Governor of New York State, April, 1984.

42. For instance, see Governor Cuomo's *Message to the Legislature* (1984), pp. 13–14.

43. See "Report on the Implementation of the JTPA," Executive Chamber, September 21, 1984, and "Job Training," New York State Assembly Ways and Means Committee, November 19, 1984.

44. See Governor Cuomo's *Message to the Legislature* (1983).

45. See *The Role of the New York State Urban Development Corporation in the State's High Technology Strategy: A Report to the Governor,* prepared by the New York State Urban

Development Corporation in Association with the UDC High Technology Advisory Council, December, 1983.

46. *Ibid.,* pp. 11–39.

47. For example, see Carey's *Building from Strength: A Program for Economic Growth and Opportunity* (1982).

48. *Report of the Working Group on Adaptation of Older Industries,* Economic Development Subcabinet, October 5, 1984.

49. *Ibid.,* p. 2.

50. *Ibid.,* pp. 5–6, 15–16.

51. *Ibid.,* pp. 7–9.

52. *Ibid.,* p. 10.

53. Mario M. Cuomo, *Message to the Legislature* (1985), p. 6.

54. On the strategic importance of new institutional forms to technological development, see "Location of High Technology Firms and Regional Economic Development," Joint Economic Committee, Congress of the United States (Washington, D.C.: U.S. Government Printing Office, June 1, 1982), pp. 39–40.

55. Mario M. Cuomo, *Message to the Legislature* (1983), p. 6.

56. Robert B. Reich, *The Next American Frontier* (New York: Penguin, 1984), pp. 3–21.

57. *Ibid.,* particularly pp. 246–251.

58. Mario M. Cuomo, *Message to the Legislature* (1985), p. 14.

59. The allusion here is to theorists as different as Comte, Tocqueville, Marx, Weber, Lukacs, Ellul, Marcuse, and Habermas.

60. See, for example, Reich, *op. cit.,* especially chapter XI, or Michael J. Piore and Charles F. Sabel, *The Second Industrial Divide* (New York: Basic Books, 1984), also chapter 11.

61. Felix G. Rohatyn, *The Twenty-Year Century* (New York: Random House, 1983), pp. 83–84.

62. Mario M. Cuomo, *Message to the Legislature* (1984), p. 15.

63. *Ibid.*

64. Dr. Hugh O'Neill, Deputy Secretary for Economic Development, at a conference on "The Impact of State Policy on Growth Industries and Mature Industries in New York," March 8, 1985.

CHAPTER TWO: IMPORTS AND APPAREL: FROM RICHES TO RAGS

1. "How to Rescue a Drowning Economy," *New York Review of Books* (April 1, 1982), pp. 3–4.

2. "Playing Tag with Japan," *New York Review of Books* (June 24, 1982), p. 40.

3. All figures on import penetration and joblessness, ILGWU Research Department.

4. All figures on New York State are taken from the New York State Department of Labor, *Report on the Garment Industry in New York State,* Publication No. B-231, February 1, 1982.

5. *Ibid.,* p. 17.

6. Sol C. Chaikin, Testimony before the Subcommittee on Economic Stabilization of the Committee on Banking, Finance and Urban Affairs, U.S. House of Representatives, January 31, 1984.

7. Springfield, Massachusetts, *Daily News* (March 3, 1983), p. 10.

8. Files, ILGWU Political/Education Department.

9. Kitty G. Dickerson, "Imported Versus U.S.-Produced Apparel: Consumer Views and Buying Patterns," *Home Economic Research Journal* (March, 1982).

10. United States International Trade Commission, *Emerging Textile-Exporting Countries,* USITC Publication 1273 (August, 1982), p. A-20.

11. ILGWU Research Department.

12. David Ricardo, *The Principles of Political Economy and Taxation* (New York: Dent Dutton, 1973), p. 82 (italics added).

13. World Bank, *The Changing Composition of Developing Country Exports,* Working Paper No. 314 (January, 1979), p. 17.

14. *Ibid.,* p. 18.

15. "Putting on the Style" (September 4, 1981), p. 56.

16. Bob Gatty, "Textile Trade: The Battle to Bring Imports into Balance," *Du Pont Context* (1983), p. 14.

17. November 12, 1980, p. D18.

18. *Manchester Guardian Weekly* (May 18, 1980), p. 12.

19. *Ibid.*

20. USITC, *Emerging Textile-Exporting Countries, op. cit.,* p. A-303.

21. December 12, 1978, p. 1.

22. Calculations based on U.S. Bureau of the Census data supplied by the ILGWU Research Department.

23. *Emerging Textile-Exporting Countries, op. cit.,* p. A-315.

24. "Employing China's Millions," *The Economist* (February 16, 1980), p. 108.

25. *Women's Wear Daily* (November 7. 1979), p. 48.

26. *Women's Wear Daily* (December 19, 1978), p. 1.

27. *Emerging Textile-Exporting Countries, op. cit.,* p. A-63.

28. *Ibid.,* p. A-73.

29. Reprinted in *Manchester Guardian Weekly* (January 8, 1978), p. 17.

30. *Manchester Guardian Weekly* (February 22, 1976), p. 17.

31. *Ibid.* (May 1, 1977), p. 8.

32. August 25, 1980, p. A21.

33. *The Economist* (December 29, 1979), p. Singapore Survey 9.

34. September 4, 1981, p. 50.

35. July 22, 1981, p. 50.

36. Sol C. Chaikin, Testimony, Subcommittee on Economic Stabilization.

37. Sol C. Chaikin, Testimony before the Trade Subcommittee of the Committee on Ways and Means, U.S. House of Representatives, March 16, 1983.

38. *Congressional Record* (September 27, 1977), p. H-31087.

39. Reich, *New York Review,* p. 40.

40. Sol C. Chaikin, "The Impact of Exports on the American Economy," *USA Today* (January, 1979), p. 18.

41. *The Economist* (February 19, 1983), pp. 74–75.

42. *Ibid.* (March 17, 1984), pp. 70–71.

43. Edward A. Feigenbaum and Pamela McCorduck, *The Fifth Generation* (Reading, Massachusetts: Addison-Wesley, 1983), p. 126.

44. *Ibid.,* p. 221.

45. Subcommittee on Trade of the Committee on Ways and Means, U.S. House of Representatives, *Task Force Report on United States—Japan Trade* (Washington: Government Printing Office, 1979), p. 51.

46. Joint Economic Committee, Congress of the United States, *Anticipating Disruptive Imports* (Washington: Government Printing Office, 1978), p. 15.

47. March 19, 1983, p. 1.

48. *Ibid.*

49. *Ibid.*

50. I wish to note that while my views have been influenced by my work with the International Ladies' Garment Workers' Union, they should not be identified necessarily with the official positions of the Union.

CHAPTER THREE: INDUSTRIAL DEVOLUTION IN NEW YORK STATE

1. D. Massey and R. Meegan, "Industrial Restructuring versus the Cities," *Urban Studies* (1978), 15, pp. 273–88; Stephen Fothergill and Graham Gudgin, *Unequal Growth: Urban and Regional Employment Change in the U.K.* (London: Heinemann Educational Books, Ltd., 1982); Alan R. Townsend, *The Impacts of Recession* (London: Croom Helm, 1982).

2. David L. Barkley and Arnold Pausen, "Patterns in the Openings and Closings of Manufacturing Plants in Rural Areas of Iowa," North Central Regional Center for Rural Development at Iowa State University (May 1979); Barry Bluestone and Bennett Harrison, *Capital Mobility and Economic Dislocation* (Washington, D.C.: Progressive Alliance, 1982).

3. Daniel Bell, *The Coming of Post-Industrial Society* (New York: Basic Books, 1983); R. D. Norton and J. Rees, "The Product Cycle and the Spatial Decentralization of American Manufacturing," *Regional Studies,* (1979), 13, pp. 141–151.

4. R. Struyk and F. James, *Intrametropolitan Industrial Location* (New York: D. C. Heath, 1975).

5. R. Barnet and W. Mueller, *Global Reach* (New York: Basic Books, 1974); Barry Bluestone and Bennett Harrison, *op. cit.;* Alan R. Townsend, *op. cit.;* Illinois Advisory Committee, "Employment Opportunity and Industrial Decline in Illinois" (Report to the Illinois State Legislature, 1980); A. Hochner and J. Zibman, "Plant Closings and Job Loss in Philadelphia," American Sociological Association Meetings (Toronto, 1981); William H. Lazonick, "Competition, Specialization, and Industrial Decline," *Journal of Economic History* (March, 1981), p. 41; R. Hayes and W. Abernathy, "Managing Our Way to Economic Decline," *Harvard Business Review* (July–August 1980), p. 58.

CHAPTER FOUR: TRENDS IN MANUFACTURING EMPLOYMENT AND REFLECTIONS ON INFRASTRUCTURE INVESTMENT, TAX AND EXPENDITURE POLICY IN NEW YORK STATE.

1. Benjamin H. Stevens, "Regional Cost Equalization and the Potential for Manufacturing Recovery in the Industrial North." A paper presented at a conference on "Economic Prospects of the Northeast" held at SUNY-Albany, April 16 and 17, 1982.

2. Phil Keisling, "Industrial America's Suicide Pact," *The Washington Monthly* (December 1982), p. 29.

3. John P. Shelton, "Allocative Efficiency vs. 'X-Efficiency': Comment," *American Economic Review* (December 1967), pp. 1252–58.

4. Bennett Harrison, "Increasing Instability and Inequality in the 'revival' of the New England Economy." A paper presented at a conference on "Economic Prospects of the Northeast," SUNY-Albany, April 16 and 17, 1982.

5. See Gerard Bray, "Fulton Co. is Skin Deep in Foreign Competition," *Times Union* (January 16, 1983), p. F-7.

6. Carter Goodrich, *Government Promotion of American Canals and Railroads, 1800–1890* (New York: Columbia University Press, 1960), p. 287.

7. *Ibid.*, p. 55.

8. *New York State Energy Master Plan II,* Vol. 2, Draft Report, August 1981, pp. 479–80.

9. The Batten Kill Railroad Co. might be considered an interesting prototype of the new short line railroads to be spawned in the future. See "New Railroad is a Man's Dream," *Times Union* (October 23, 1982), p. A-11; and Robert Hershey, "Little Railroads that Think They Can," *New York Times* (September 19, 1983), p. F1.

10. James Cook, "Change Causing Industrial Slowdown—Microelectronics Takes Bigger Role in All Industries," *Times Union* (February 6, 1983), pp. E-9 and E-10.

11. Pierre du Pont IV, "Going to Work on Unemployment: Training a Priority to Meet Challenge," *Times Union* (February 6, 1983), pp. B1 and B6.

12. "Are Whizzes Washed Up at 35? To Compete, Says an M.I.T. Study, They Need to Keep Retraining," *Time Magazine* (October 18, 1982). Reprinted in *MIT News* (January 1983), p. 6.

13. Gerald S. Schatz, "Scientific Equipment in the Universities: Obsolete and Deteriorating," *SUNY Research* (February 1983), pp. 3–6.

14. "Math, Science Ability Down; Blacks Reading Level Up," *Times Union* (February 8, 1983), p. D12.

15. Margaret A. Farrell, "Education Falls Short in High-Technology Preparation," *Times Union* (February 6, 1983), pp. B7 and B6.

16. Edward F. Renshaw, "Conserving Water Through Pricing," *Journal of the American Water Works Association* (January 1982), pp. 2–5.

17. C. S. Russell, *Drought and Water Supply* (Baltimore: Johns Hopkins Press, 1970).

18. U.S. Army Corps of Engineers, "Urban Water Study, Buffalo, New York," Final Report August 1981, Volume I, pp. 7–13 and Volume II, pp. A-7-1–16.

19. Report to the Governor by the Council on State Priorities, Albany, New York, 1982, p. 220.

20. Edward Renshaw, "The Economics of Congestion," *The Southern Economic Journal* (April, 1962), pp. 372–77.

21. Leonard Sahling, "Are State and City Corporate Income Taxes Stifling Investment in New York?" *Quarterly Review*, Federal Reserve Bank of New York, Winter 1978–79, pp. 41–48.

22. *New York State Energy Master Plan II*, Volume 2, p. 624.

23. Edward Renshaw, "Public Utilities and the Promotion of District Heating," *Public Utilities Fortnightly*, July 17, 1980, pp. 26–32 and "Retrofitting Existing New York City Power Plants for District Heating: Technical and Economic Analysis," New York State Energy Research and Development Authority, April, 1981.

24. "Mini-mills Pose Added Threat to Ailing Big Steel," *Times Union* (January 27, 1983), p. B11.

25. Edward Renshaw, "Power Exchanges and Public Authorities to Distribute the Benefits of Low Cost Hydro Power More Widely," *Electric Rate Making* (June, 1982), pp. 36–39.

26. Herbert F. Baum, "Free Public Transport," *Journal of Transport Economics and Policy* (January, 1973), pp. 3–19; Frank J. Prail, "Study Dispels a Theory about Transit," *The New York Times* (October 19, 1971), pp. 1 and 65; Eric Schenker and John Wilson, "The Use of Public Mass Transportation in the Major Metropolitan Areas of the United States," *Land Economics* (1976), pp. 361–67; and M. Wahl, "Users of Urban Transportation Services and Their Income Circumstances," *Traffic Quarterly* (1970), p. 43.

27. For a more general discussion of employment multiplier models, see Edward Renshaw and Michael Dimmit, "A Note on the Government Employment Multiplier," *Nebraska Journal of Economics and Business* (Summer 1977), pp. 47–56.

CHAPTER FIVE: STRATEGIC PLANNING IN A WHITE COLLAR CITY: THE CASE OF ALBANY

1. For an introduction to the application of strategic planning in the private sector, see George Steiner, *Strategic Planning: What Every Manager Must Know* (New York: Free Press, 1979); and H. Igor Ansoff, *Strategic Management* (London: MacMillan, 1979). Strategic planning has been attacked in recent years, however, as corporations have become disillusioned with remote staffs of overly quantitative professional planners. See Walter Kiechel III, "Corporate Strategists Come Under Fire," *Fortune* (December 27, 1982); and "The New Breed of Strategic Planner," *Business Week* (September 17, 1984), pp. 62–68.

2. For an introduction to the application of strategic planning techniques in the public sector, see John B. Olson and Douglas C. Eadie, *The Game Plan: Governance with Foresight* (Washington, D.C.: Council of State Planning Agencies, 1982); and *Strategies for Cities and Counties: A Strategic Planning Guide* (Washington, D.C.: Public Technology, Inc., 1984). See also the annotated bibliography, *Strategies for Cities and Counties: A Literature Review* (Washington, D.C.: Public Technology, Inc., February, 1984).

3. *San Francisco's Strategic Plan: Making a Great City Greater* (San Francisco: Arthur Andersen and Co., February, 1983). For a summary of the San Francisco plan, see the special issue of *San Francisco Business* (February 1983), 18, 2.

4. For a useful summary of these basic forecasting techniques, see Olson and Eadie, *op. cit.,* pp. 21–28. For the application of forecasting techniques to problems of government, see the Committee on Energy and Commerce of the U.S. House of Representatives, *Foresight in the Private Sector: How Can Government Use It?* (Washington, D.C.: U.S. Government Printing Office, January, 1983).

5. Joint Economic Committee, Congress of the United States, *Trends in the Fiscal Condition of Cities: 1981–1983* (Washington, D.C.: U.S. Government Printing Office, November 1983), p. 19.

6. *Strategies for Cities and Counties: A Strategic Planning Guide, op. cit.,* p. 1.

7. The tendency to view local governments like a private corporation is reflected in political science by the change from pluralist to market approaches to urban politics. See Paul Peterson, *City Limits* (Chicago: University of Chicago Press, 1981).

8. Todd Swanstrom and Willard Bruce, *The Present Condition of Downtown Albany* (Albany: Albany Strategic Planning Project, April 1984), p. 25.

9. U.S. Bureau of Census, 1980 Census of Population and Housing, Albany-Schenectady-Troy, N.Y. Standard Metropolitan Statistical Area and U.S. Summary (Washington, D.C.: U.S. Government Printing Office, 1983).

10. U.S. Bureau of the Census, *Census of Retail Trade: Major Retail Centers, 1958 and 1977* (Washington, D.C.: U.S. Government Printing Office).

11. U.S. Bureau of the Census, *1954 (and 1977) Census of Manufacturing* (Washington, D.C.: U.S. Government Printing Office).

12. U.S. Bureau of the Census, *1950 Census of Population, Albany, New York Census Tracts* (Albany: Council of Community Services, n.d.) and U.S. Bureau of the Census, *1980 Census of Population and Housing, Albany-Schenectady-Troy, N.Y. Standard Metropolitan Statistical Area* (Washington, D.C.: U.S. Government Printing Office, July 1983).

13. U.S. Bureau of the Census, *1958 (and 1977) Census of Selected Services for New York State* (Washington, D.C.: U.S. Government Printing Office).

14. U.S. Bureau of the Census, *1970 (and 1980) Census of Population and Housing, Census Tracts, Albany-Schenectady-Troy, N.Y. Standard Metropolitan Statistical Area* (Washington, D.C.: U.S. Government Printing Office).

15. *Strategic Planning: Some Basic Trends Facing the City of Albany* (Albany: Albany Strategic Planning Project, March 13, 1984), p. 8.

16. For an introduction to the theory of dual labor markets, primary and secondary, see Michael J. Piore, "The Dual Labor Market: Theory and Implications," and Michael Reich, David M. Gordon, and Richard C. Edwards, "A Theory of Labor Market Segmentation," both in *Problems in Political Economy: An Urban Perspective,* David M. Gordon, ed. (Lexington, Mass.: D. C. Heath, 1977), pp. 93–97 and 108–113, respectively.

17. Department of Assessment and Taxation, City of Albany, *Annual Report, 1975–1983* (Albany: Department of Assessment and Taxation).

18. Benjamin Bridges, Jr., "State and Local Inducements for Industry: Part II," *Locational Analysis for Manufacturing,* Gerald Karaska and David Bramhall, eds. (Cambridge, Mass.: M.I.T. Press, 1969), p. 177.

19. For summaries of the evidence, see Bennett Harrison and Sandra Kanter, "The Great State Robbery," *Working Papers* (Spring 1976), p. 63; and John F. Due, "Studies of State-Local Tax Influences on Location of Industry," *National Tax Journal* (1961), 14, pp. 165–168.

20. Quoted in Robert Goodman, *The Last Entrepreneurs* (New York: Simon and Schuster, 1979), pp. 43–44.

21. *Local Economic Development Tools and Techniques* (Washington, D.C.: U.S. Department of Housing and Urban Development and U.S. Department of Commerce, 1979), p. 51.

22. Intradepartmental Memorandum from Jerry Finch to Carol Bellamy, September 21, 1981, p. 3. Cited in Frank Domurad and Ruth Messinger, *Citizen Program to Eliminate the Gap* (New York: The City Project, 1983), p. 26.

23. New York Office of the Comptroller, Bureau of Performance Analysis, *Performance Audit of the Industrial and Commercial Incentive Board* (March 12, 1979). Quote is from the official news release on the report (March 22, 1979).

24. David Gordon, *The Working Poor: Towards a State Agenda* (Washington, D.C.: Council of State Planning Agencies, 1979).

25. For a history of economic base theory see Richard B. Andrews, "Mechanics of the Urban Economic Base: Historical Development of the Base Concept," in *The Techniques of Urban Economic Analysis,* Ralph W. Pfouts, ed. (West Trenton, N.J.: Chanler-Davis, 1960), pp. 5–17.

26. For an insightful discussion of the new service economy see Thomas M. Stanback, Jr., *Services: The New Economy* (Totowa, N.J.: Allanheld, Osmun, 1983).

27. See Jean Gottman, "Urban Centrality and the Interweaving of Quaternary Activities," *Ekistics* (April, 1970), 29, 173, pp. 322–331; and Jean Gottman, *The Coming of the Transactional City* (College Park, Maryland: Institute for Urban Studies, 1983).

28. John Boffa, "Rich, Fat and Old," *Empire State Report* (March, 1983), p. 35.

29. *Survey of Office Space in Albany County* (Albany: Downtown Albany Development Corporation, 1982).

30. Jane Jacobs, *The Death and Life of Great American Cities* (New York: Random House, 1961), p. 14.

31. James W. Rouse, "The Case for Vision," in *Rebuilding America's Cities: Roads to Recovery,* Paul R. Porter and David C. Sweet, eds. (New Brunswick, N.J.: Center for Urban Policy Research, 1984), p. 22.

32. Displacement has become a national issue. HUD estimates that 500,000 households are affected annually. A report highly critical of the HUD study estimated that almost twice as many households are involved. See U.S. Department of Housing and Urban Development, Office of Policy Development and Research, *Displacement Report* (Washington, D.C.: HUD, 1979); and Richard T. LeGates and Chester Hartman, "Displacement," *Clearinghouse Review* (July, 1981), 15, 3.

CHAPTER SIX: ECONOMIC DEVELOPMENT PROSPECTS FOR NEW YORK'S ST. LAWRENCE RIVER BASIN

1. *New York State Business Fact Book,* 1981 Supplement (Albany, Department of Commerce), p. 19.

2. *Courier-Freeman* (Potsdam, N.Y.: January 22, 1983).

3. Comptroller General of the United States, *Insights Into Major Urban Development Action Grant Issues* (Gaithersburg, M.D.: General Accounting Office, 1984).

4. The Foreign Trade Zone Act of 1934, as amended, "authorizes the establishment of designated geographic areas of the United States, called foreign trade zones, into which foreign goods may be brought without payment of duties and with a minimum of the paperwork required by U.S. Customs. Such goods, which may be further processed in the zones, may be exported without incurring customs duties or may be entered into the customs territory of the United States upon payment of applicable duties." U.S. General Accounting Office, *Foreign Trade Zone Growth Primarily Benefits Users Who Import for Domestic Commerce*, a Report to the Chairman of the House Ways and Means Committee, March 2, 1984, p. 1.

CHAPTER SEVEN: LOCAL ECONOMIC DEVELOPMENT AND THE STATE

1. In one example with which the author is familiar, SEQR was used to delay the rezoning of a parcel of land in an area of expensive homes for use as sites for even more expensive homes. Ultimately, the objections raised under SEQR were found to have been adequately addressed under normal zoning procedures.

2. Of course, most such moves also involve an expansion. The incentive is not usually enough to overcome, by itself, the costs associated with a move. In one case, however, a firm actually moved from one building in a locality to another building in the same locality. The result, of course, is also due in part to the tax laws which induce increased property transfers.

3. In one case in the City of Buffalo, two developers were given cash, bonding, and tax incentives to build two new hotels. These new hotels undoubtedly contributed to the removal of the Statler Hotel.

4. Examples of such aid include training and product fairs.

5. See Charles N. Tiebout, "A Pure Theory of Local Expenditures," *Journal of Political Economy* (October, 1956), 64, pp. 416–24.

6. An analysis of the various choices made by communities in Western New York is given in Southwick, "Inter-Jurisdictional Competition and Cooperation Among Local Government," *Journal of New York State Economics Association* (1981), XI, pp. 72–80. A variety of service levels for several government services as well as different tax levels were found. These clearly appealed to different market segments.

7. See Robert J. Vaughn, "State Tax Incentives: How Effective Are They?" *Commentary* (July, 1979).

8. See David Birch, "Generating New Jobs: Are Government Incentives Effective?" *Commentary* (July, 1979).

9. See Bruce G. Posner, "A Report on the States," *INC.* (October, 1982), pp. 95–99.

CHAPTER EIGHT: THE CHANGING IMPACT OF INTERNATIONAL TRADE ON THE ECONOMY OF NEW YORK STATE

1.   The employment and earnings statistics cited in the next few pages are taken from the statistical series published by the U.S. Bureau of the Census, from the U.S. and the New York State Departments of Labor and of Commerce, and the 1983–84 *New York State Statistical Yearbook* (Albany: Rockefeller Institute, 1983). Also used are the New York State *Business Fact Book* and *Business Statistics* issued by the Office of the Governor, 1984.

2.   A study was made of the *Fortune 500* list of the largest U.S. Corporations by Regina Armstrong, "The Role of National Corporations in New York City's Economy," in *New York City's Changing Economic Base,* Benjamin J. Klabaner, ed. (New York: Pica, 1981). She reported that 136 of the 500 largest companies maintained headquarters in New York in the late 1960s, but that a decade later only half of them were still in place. Corporate flight caused more concern for prestige than jobs since corporate staff accounted for only 11 percent of New York City's employment while small businesses provided 65 percent. Going beyond the top 500, 369 corporate HQs stayed in the City. Each managed 1 billion dollars a year or more in business and together they accounted for 10 percent of the Nation's GNP. They included a considerable number of MNCs—especially in oil, computers, banking, and high value-added manufacturing. See in the same volume, Matthew Drennan, "The Apple's Core: New York City's Export Industries;" and Maurice Ballabon, "The Role of New York City's Foreign Exports in Local Manufacturing."

3.   Each year a survey is published by Business International, the most recent being *The Effects of U.S. Corporate Foreign Investment* (New York, 1984). From a sample of 56 MNCs, the surveyed companies in 1980–82 recorded 305 billion dollars in business (34 percent of it to non-U.S. customers) and they held 22 percent of the book value of all American DFI overseas. While employment in U.S. manufacturing fell by 13 percent between 1980–82, for the 56 companies in the sample it fell by only 9.6 percent. The inference, which will later be questioned, is that MNCs on aggregate do not export jobs and that, in fact, they add to the stock of jobs at home more rapidly than non-MNC firms.

4.   Sources for population and employment are the same as in note 1, above; also Richard Alba, *The Impact of Migration on New York State,* a report issued by the Public Policy Institute of the Business Council of New York State (Albany: 1984).

5.   There was a sharp contraction in State spending after Governor Rockefeller left office. In his 15 years he had pushed spending from its historic position of 130 percent greater per capita than the rest of the U.S. to a high of 165 percent. His successors brought it down to 140 percent and pledged to cap tax levels at 8 percent of statewide income, but the tax burden was still greater than in 48 other states. See the "Charts on New York State and Local Government Spending," *Quarterly Review* of the Federal Reserve Bank of New York (Spring, 1983), 8, 1. With a median personal income tax of $107 per $1,000 for all 50 states, New Yorkers paid $156 p.a. (or 146 percent more) in 1984.

6.   The U.S. Bureau of Census published projections in 1983 to the year 2000, based to a large extent on the shift of work and people away from the Snowbelt and into the Sunbelt. It estimated that the total U.S. population will increase by 18 percent to 267.5 million, but that New York will lose 17 percent of its 17.6 million and end the decade

with 15 million people. States in the South will grow by 37 percent, the West and Arizona will add even more, and New York will finish as the fourth largest state after California, Texas, and Florida. See the *Provisional Projections of the Population of the States* as summarized in the *New York Times* (Sept. 8, 1983). It added that the Northeast would have the oldest population, with 15 percent over the age of 64, and the West will have the youngest. The relative decline of New York is presented graphically in Gregory Jackson and George Masnick, "Take another look at regional U.S. growth," *Harvard Business Review* (March–April, 1983), 61, 2.

7. Several states in the Northeast and the Midwest are trying to halt the abandonment of aging plant. They want to force companies to disclose plans to close plant several years ahead of time, and to pay at least 90 days of health insurance coverage, and possibly pension payments, too, for redundant workers (*Business Week*, August 20, 1984). A similar plan was adopted by the 10 countries in the EEC. It was bitterly contested by business, and especially by MNC's, as an expensive infringement on business rights. They warned that if it were ever adopted, the plan would deter investment of new corporate funds. See Richard P. Walter, "The Vredeling Proposal," *International Tax and Business Lawyer* (Summer, 1983), 1, 1.

8. Bennett Harrison and Barry Bluestone have condemned the consequences of dismantling high paying manufacturing plant and replacing them with poorly paid jobs in the service sectors. Nationwide, between 1979 and 1984, 2.4 million blue-collar workers lost employment while 4 million were added to service industries that pay considerably lower wages. Since the 1960s, 67 percent of all new jobs have been created in sectors that pay less than $13,000 a year (in 1980 dollars), or one-half of the median family wage in the U.S. The estimate of the Bureau of Labor Statistics is that this trend will accelerate and that the largest number of new jobs will be filled by janitors, fast-food workers, nurses' aides and clerical workers, and certainly not by high-technology industries. The two authors cited above argue that entry into middle-class income brackets will become increasingly difficult, that structural change might reduce the number of unemployed but it will leave more people impoverished, and that poverty will be increasingly feminized. See *The Deindustrialization of America* (New York: Basic Books, 1982).

9. Two surveys were published in the *New York Times* (July 10, 1983 and May 20, 1984) of the loss of high-paying jobs in manufacturing industries—such as steel, automobiles, and petrochemicals—in New York. In 1983, Genesee, Erie, and Niagara Counties reported unemployment far exceeding the national average (at about 13.7 percent) as plants were closed by Bethlehem Steel, General Motors, and Ashland Petroleum. Governor Cuomo asked for Federal aid to help fund unemployment insurance and job retraining and for more of the military budget to be allocated to New York. His appeals were not heeded. Only 1 percent of the State's workforce is employed in defense industries, and New York pays considerably more in Federal tax revenues than it proportionately receives in Federal procurement or defence expenditures. See the monograph, *Federal R & D and Defense Outlays in NYS*, issued by the Federal Reserve Bank of New York (February, 1984).

10. An estimate of the changing structure of the workforce appears in Marvin J. Cetron, "Getting Ready for the Jobs of the Future," *Forbes* (June, 1983), 17, 3. He calculated that by the year 2000 manufacturing will decline from 20 percent to 11 percent of employment, that the service sector will increase from 68 to 86 percent, that "full

employment" rates will reach 8.5 percent without work, and that U.S. households with two incomes will increase from 45 to 75 percent. "Structural employment" will have a severe impact on printing and a wide range of machine operators as computers and robots take over their jobs. A considerable increase in technicians' work will occur in computer, paralegal, and business services, as well as in fast food chains and health care, all of which are poorly paid. A major effort clearly must be started for job retraining programs to upgrade labor skills and productivity. So far only a weak start has been made.

11. *Wall Street Journal* (May 1, 1984). The inference drawn from the article is the conventional complaint that New York has not created a "favorable climate" for business investment. A more optimistic view was taken in the outstanding essays published a decade ago by Eli Ginzberg, *et al.* in *New York is Very Much Alive* (New York: McGraw-Hill, 1973).

12. A summary of the report by the New York State Department of Labor was given in the Albany press (*Knickerbocker News,* May 25, 1983).

13. The doubling in the ratio of foreign trade to GNP between 1970 and 1980 is noted in the *Annual Survey of Manufacturers* (Washington, D.C.: U.S. Department of Commerce, 1982). Also noted were the 4.8 million jobs, 2.8 million of which were in manufacturing, that were directly related to U.S. export activity, and the estimate that 28,000 jobs were financed by each additional 1 billion dollars of export trade. See also Robert A. Feldman, "Dollar Appreciation, Foreign Trade, and the U.S. Economy," *Quarterly Review* of the Federal Reserve Bank of New York (Summer 1982), 7, 2.

14. The literature on MNC operations and the redeployment of their DFI to match changing conditions in world trade and money markets is extensive. For an updating on MNCs in theory and practice see the distinguished essays in *The Multinational Corporation in the 1980s,* Charles P. Kindleberger and David P. Audretch, eds. (Cambridge, MA.: M.I.T. Press, 1983).

15. For the year 1980 the IMF estimated that global merchandise exports amounted to 1,870 billion. Of that worldwide total, one-third came from service and income payments earned by MNCs. The 200 billion of DFI owned by American MNCs accounted for 27 percent of all U.S. assets overseas, the 100 billion of foreign MNCs investment in the U.S. accounted for all 15 percent of all foreign assets held in the U.S., the remainder in each category appearing in portfolio holdings, Treasury bills and short-term capital. See the *World Perspectives* series issued by the Conference Board (New York: October 1983), 75.

16. See the *Annual Survey of Manufactures* (New York State Department of Commerce, 1982). In 1980 13.5 percent of New York manufactures were related to export trade or support activities, along with 12.2 percent of all employment in manufacturing industries. For later data see "New York Exports a Variety of Manufactures," *Business America* (July 9, 1984), 7, 14.

17. For a preliminary review of New York's potential to match the rapid growth of U.S. export trade, see Walter Goldstein, "Rx for New York's Economy: More World Trade, Less Welfare," *Empire State Report* (October, 1983), 9, 10.

18. It is difficult to draw up a balance sheet of the benefits generated by the MNCs as against the power that they can exercise by threatening to become "runaway industries." On the positive side they can bring valuable investment, employment, export earnings, and R & D. On the negative side, they can abruptly shift capital and jobs, leaving the "host

country" with idle workers and closed plant. See my assessment, "The MNC and World Trade," *The MNC and Social Change,* David E. Apter and Louis W. Goodman, eds. (New York: Praeger, 1976).

19. A list of the states receiving incoming foreign DFI may be found in the *World Perspectives* series of the Conference Board (February, 1983 and 1984), 71 and 78.

20. *Ibid.* The book value of DFI held in the U.S. must be distinguished from three other forms of investment accounting: (1) the market value, assessed at current prices, of plant and equipment owned by foreign firms; (2) the annual value of shipments or sales generated by affiliate plant; and (3) the capital worth of portfolio or minority investments in affiliate firms, when foreign interests hold less than 10 percent of equity. Eighty-five percent of foreign capital in the U.S. appear in the third category, and here it could be liquidated if the dollar and placements in the U.S. were to lose their high value.

21. The figures for foreign companies operating in the U.S. are taken from the *Survey of Current Business* (U.S. Dept. of Commerce, May 1984), 45, 5; from the unpublished economic development studies compiled by the Port Authority of New York and New Jersey (March and November, 1983); and from *New York—The International State* (New York State Department of Commerce, February, 1985).

22. *Ibid.* A detailed breakdown of DFI by country of origin, by SIC industrial classification, and geographical distribution in the U.S. is given in the updated development study of the U.S. Department of Commerce, *State Export Series: New York* (August, 1984).

23. A breakdown of foreign DFI across the U.S. between 1960 and 1982, and of the yearly additions of investment in 1981 and 1982, appears in the *U.S. Abstract of Statistics* (Washington, D.C.: 1984), and in the sources cited in footnote 21.

24. The income from DFI overseas brought 23 billion dollars (or a 10 percent return on investment) in 1982 to the U.S., while foreign investment in the U.S. earned 5 billion dollars in income (or a 5 percent return). See the sources listed in footnote 19.

25. The liquidation, whether threatened or actual, of foreign holdings in the U.S. is a matter of acute concern to many State governments. Hard data is difficult to find but many cases have been reported of foreign subsidiaries being sold or closed down in various states despite the efforts of "host" governments to maintain their operations. To cite just one example, British Petroleum, an MNC half-owned at the time by the British government, sold off many of its interests in Sinclair Oil and Standard Oil of Ohio in order to concentrate its capital in the Alaska pipeline and the rich oil fields of Prudhoe Bay on the North Slope.

26. The record of MNCs pulling out or selling off their overseas operations gives reason to fear their footloose mobility. When a severe economic downturn occurred in Italy in the 1960s, the runaway companies included such giant firms as GE, BP, Siemens, and Total. In most cases they fled to cheap wage economies in Spain, South East Asia, and Eastern Europe. For a fuller listing see footnote 18.

27. Data cited was drawn from *World Perspectives* (February and August, 1982), 65 and 68. Included in the survey were 3,540 U.S. parent MNCs with a total in 1977 of 24,666 affiliates overseas. Their affiliates accounted for nearly 34 percent of all U.S. export incomes, thus confirming that success in export trade is largely correlated with the size of the firm (87 percent of U.S. manufactured exports came from firms with 1,000 employees or more, most of which were MNCs). Two other points were noted for the years under review, 1977–80. In U.S. export-related industries employment grew by 42.7 percent and

manufacturing shipments by 83.2 percent, while in non-export sectors the respective figures were only 5.5 and 36.1 percent.

28. Every year *Fortune* magazine lists not only the largest and the most profitable companies in the U.S. economy, and abroad, too, but also the "50 Leading Exporters" (August 6, 1984). The 50 listed, with only a few exceptions, are giant MNCs (GM, Boeing, Ford, GE and IBM top the list and 9 of the 50 have HQs in New York). The rank order of export sales varies with world market conditions. Exxon, Caterpillar Tractor, Phillips and Occidental Petroleum descended in the rank order from the year before (August 8, 1983), but the larger MNCs increased their proportion of foreign over domestic sales, despite the 25 percent rise over the year in dollar exchange rates.

29. See the sources in footnotes 19 and 21. It also should be added that labor rates climbed more rapidly in the leading OECD countries than in the U.S. during the 1970s as the dollar lost value, thus boosting the U.S. export sector into the fastest growing segment of the U.S. economy. See *World Perspectives* (April, 1982 and August, 1983), 66 and 74.

30. Data drawn from the Port Authority of New York and New Jersey, *The Regional Economy: 1983 Review and 1984 Outlook;* and from footnote 21.

31. *Ibid.* It was also noted that the high value of the dollar cost the U.S. a loss of 2.3 percent in real GNP and well over 1 million jobs between 1980 and 1983. The full impact of deregulating international banking has yet to be determined.

32. Data on the potential default by foreign borrowers and the possible impact of their refusal to reschedule sovereign debt appear in Walter Goldstein, "The World Debt Crisis," *International Tax and Business Lawyer* (University of California, Winter, 1985), 3, 1.

33. The exposed position of the New York banks in their poorly secured loans to the Third World debtors is examined in William R. Cline, *International Debt and the Stability of the World Economy* (Washington, D.C.: Institute for International Economics, 1983).

34. See the report issued by the New York State Department of Commerce, *The Evolving Telecommunications Industry* (1982), for an impressive array of investment and employment inputs in the New York economy. For data on universities and research activities see footnote 1.

35. See the excellent articles by Robert A. Feldman and Allen J. Proctor, "U.S. International Trade in Services," *Quarterly Review of the Federal Reserve Bank of New York* (Spring, 1983), 8, 1; Joan E. Spero, "Information: The Policy Void," *Foreign Policy* (Fall, 1982), 48; and *World Perspectives* (October, 1983), 75.

36. Operational statistics appear in *VIA* (June, 1984), 36, 6, published by the Port Authority of New York and New Jersey, and in the sources of footnote 21.

37. *Ibid;* and U.S. Department of Commerce, Bureau of the Census, *U.S. Export and Import Trade, 1983.*

38. *Ibid.*

39. *Ibid.*

40. See the special study of the Port Authority *The Arts as an Industry* (1983); and *Business Week* (October 8, 1984). It is estimated that 2.5 million of the 17 million tourists visiting New York in 1983 came from overseas. Many came because of the 1,900 arts

institutions in the region. The arts accounted for an economic input of 5.6 billion a year, together with 117,000 jobs and 2 billion dollars in personal income.

41. Many appeals were made to the U.S. International Trade Commission to halt or to penalize the "dumping" of foreign goods in the U.S. at prices lower than factor cost. The subsidizing of foreign exports also moved U.S. industries to seek counterprotection through quotas, nontariff barriers, and other forms of trade shelters. See two useful articles in *Foreign Affairs*, Robert R. Reich, "Beyond Free Trade" and John Zysman and Stephen S. Cohen, "Open Trade and Competitive Industry" (Spring and Summer, 1983), 63, 3 and 4.

42. The composition of U.S. exports and imports changed radically in the 1980s. In 1970 the U.S. enjoyed a trade balance in manufactures of 12 billion dollars, but in the 1980s the negative balance mounted and by 1984 the deficit exceeded 120 billion a year. The dollar rose in the 1980s by 45 percent and it was estimated that 3 million jobs in the U.S. were lost to the fierce competition offered by foreign imports. In 1984 imports took over 25 percent of U.S. domestic steel sales, 23 percent of automobiles, and 41.5 percent of machine tools. See the *New York Times* (September 23, 1984).

43. A diversified and extended analysis of the U.S. record in competing with foreign trade appears in Robert R. Reich, *The Next American Frontier* (New York: Times Books, 1983).

44. *Ibid.*, and John Hein, *The Dollar and U.S. Exports* (New York: The Conference Board, 1984).

45. The debate over industrial policy has been conducted to a great extent by policy analysts, macroeconomic theorists, and political scientists innocent of business experience. The argument that the free market must make policy is advanced by Kevin Phillips, *Staying on Top: The Business Case for a National Industrial Strategy* (New York: Random House, 1984). The argument for some form of state intervention and coordinated planning is pursued by Robert B. Reich, *op. cit.;* Ira C. Magaziner and Robert B. Reich, *Minding America's Business: The Decline and Rise of the American Economy* (New York: Harcourt Brace Jovanovich, 1982); Lester Thurow, *The Zero Sum Society* (New York: Basic Books, 1980).

46. The ability of the MNC to transfer assembly line production processes, R&D technology, and manufacturing employment to cheap wage countries is evaluated by Robert Reich, *op. cit.* His data on the export of manufacturing jobs conflicts with the estimates of the MNCs job expansion at home published by Business International, footnote 3.

47. For the export successes of American MNCs, see footnotes 27 and 28.

48. A range of mercantile measures has been adopted by "host" countries to try and limit the freedom of foreign MNCs and their footloose affiliates to maneuver. Many of them were unsuccessful. The ten nations in the EEC argued over a set of rules to forestall or delay plant closings, despite angry protests from American MNCs, and several States in the U.S. now seek to copy the EEC model. See Richard P. Walker, "The Vredeling Proposal," *International Tax and Business Lawyer* (Summer 1983), 1, 1.

49. Several dramatic clashes occurred in recent years. It was alleged that First National Bank of New York (Citibank) and Exxon had understated their tax obligations at home and overseas, and the joint venture plant built in California by GM and Toyota refused to accept union bargaining rights. But in no case has a MNC ever been forced to build a

new plant, or to keep open an old one, when it was determined to move out of a "host" country.

50. See the sources in footnotes 21 and 22.

51. A sustained argument is made against state intervention in the market—either to subsidize winners and sunrise industries or to bury losers and sunset companies—by Robert Z. Lawrence, *Can America Compete?* (Washington, D.C.: Brookings Institution, 1984). He challenges the gloomy analyses of the structural changes and the manufacturing setbacks afflicting U.S. industry, and he questions the wisdom of Felix Rohatyn's proposal to create a new Reconstruction Finance Corporation to serve as a public investment bank. Lawrence and many other free market theorists of industrial policy see no need for government to reduce the costs or to increase the availability of capital for pioneering companies, and they reject any suggestion of collective economic planning. So, too, does Charles L. Schultze in "Industrial Policy: A Dissent," *The Brookings Review* (Fall, 1983), 2, 1.

52. Lawrence, *op. cit.,* insists that the U.S. has increased its production of manufacturing goods with a variety of non-tariff barriers and other import restrictions. In 1980 only 20 percent of goods were protected, but by 1983 the proportion had risen to 35 percent. Reeling from the effects of high interest and exchange rates, he argues, U.S. protectionism has in fact provided an aggressive form of industrial policy, and he urges that it should be dismantled to "liberalize" the U.S. economy.

53. Several models have been devised in recent years to test propositions regarding the potential for growth and capital input into specific industrial sectors. See the Regional Planning Association, *Economic Development and Public Infrastructure Investment for the New York Urban Region* (New York: 1982); and Aaron S. Gurwitz, "New York State's Economic Turnaround: Services or Manufacturing," *Quarterly Review of the Federal Reserve Bank of New York* (Autumn, 1983), 8, 3.

54. In 1981 New York spent 190 percent more than the rest of the U.S. on welfare transfers, 150 percent more on health and hospitals, 125 percent more on education, and 255 percent more on debt interest (see the source in footnote 5). These payments had been considerably scaled back after 1974 when Governor Carey introduced his first austerity budget. His aim had been to cap the continuous rise in State spending, to rescue New York City from possible bankruptcy, and to improve the "business climate." Unfortunately, the cutback in Federal spending on welfare and social services has added to the hardship inflicted by capping State expenditures, many of which were funded by Federal grants-in-aid. For an assessment of these program reductions, see *The Reagan Experiment: An Examination of Economic and Social Policies,* John L. Palmer and Isabel V. Sawhill, eds. (Washington, D.C.: Urban Institute, 1982); and Robert J. Lampman, "Economic and Social Policies Under the Reagan Administration, *Journal of Social Policy* (1983), 12, 3.

55. A useful note about state efforts to promote economic development—in Rhode Island, California, and Massachusetts—appears in the constructive suggestions offered by Glenn Yago and Richard McGahey, "Can the Empire State Strike Back?," *New York Affairs* (1980), 8, 3.

56. A series of articles on Economic Development in New York, including an appraisal of increased spending on education, infrastructure, and enterprise zones, is to be found in the special issue of *New York Affairs* (1983), 7, 4.

CHAPTER NINE: FOREIGN DIRECT INVESTMENT AND REGIONAL DEVELOPMENT: THE CASE OF CANADIAN INVESTMENT IN NEW YORK STATE

1. Economists attribute the decline in the competitive position of the United States during the last three decades, especially in the manufacturing sector, to the decline in the United States' share of the World's capital stock and to the decline in its expenditure on R & D. It has been estimated that the rates of growth of capital, skilled labor, and R & D scientists between 1963 and 1980 in the United States stood at 1.4, 1.0, and −1.1 percent, respectively. The comparable figures for Japan are 8.3, 2.7, and 5.1 percent, and for West Germany are 3.1, 2.5, and 5.6 percent. See, for example, John Muth and Peter Morici, *Changing Patterns of United States Industrial Activity and Comparative Advantage* (Washington, D.C.: National Planning Association, 1983).

2. The type of foreign investment emphasized in this paper is on foreign direct investment in manufacturing. As opposed to either portfolio investment or investment in real property, foreign direct investment in manufacturing is responsible for a larger multiplier or turnover effect and this contributes to increasing income, employment, and economic growth.

3. Data compiled by *Statistics Canada* indicate that in 1976 Ontario and Quebec possessed 63 percent of the Canadian population, and that in 1978 72 percent of Canada's total labor force in the secondary sector was located in these two provinces, Toronto and Montreal controlled 74 percent of manufacturing revenues, and 72 percent of Canadian domestic and foreign assets were controlled by the financial institutions located in these two cities.

4. Figures provided by the New York State Department of Commerce indicate that there were 251 cases of foreign investment in manufacturing with the reported value of 1.13 billion dollars (reported by 98 firms) and employing 14,877 New Yorkers (reported by 114 firms) between 1976 and 1982. Canada ranked first in the number of firms investing in New York and the number of jobs created in New York by foreign firms, and ranked third in terms of the value of investment after Great Britain and West Germany.

5. The importance of New York's international dimension was given a further boost recently when Governor Cuomo, in his ("State of the State") *Message to the Legislature* on January 4, 1984, announced the establishment of a State World Trade Council under the chairmanship of former Governor Hugh L. Carey. The Council's task will be to increase exports from the State and attract foreign investment into New York.

6. The New York State Department of Commerce identified 127 Canadian companies operating in the State as of January 1, 1983. This figure was a result of a special survey Commerce conducted in 1982, and only those firms were included that responded to the survey. According to this survey, Canada ranked third in the number of New York State operations, second in the number of workers employed, and fifth in the value of the investment that stood at 182.6 million dollars. New York State Department of Commerce, *Foreign Direct Investment in New York State By County, as of January 1, 1983* (Division of Economic Research and Statistics, August 19, 1983).

7. Both of the questionnaires were developed after extensive consultations with individuals having expertise in marketing survey research and project evaluations. While

415

methodological problems were not all resolved in conducting the study, individuals knowledgeable of mail surveys suggest that a response rate over 30 percent is quite respectable. In fact, in a 1983 survey of foreign-owned firms operating in New York City conducted for the New York City Chamber of Commerce, Main Hurdman, one of the world's largest accounting firms, mailed 1,160 questionnaires and received 381 responses yielding a rate of 33 percent. In light of that fact, and considering the limitations of a small research team with limited resources, our response rate of 46 percent appears very satisfactory.

8.   It may be of interest to note that the New York Department of Commerce survey revealed that between 1980–82, a total of 56 Canadian manufacturing affiliates either established operations (32), expanded (17), or were involved in acquisitions (7) in New York. This activity equalled 44.4 percent of all foreign investment announcements. The total Canadian investment reported was 128.9 million dollars, and these projects were expected to create almost 2,900 jobs. See *Foreign Direct Investment in New York State by County, As of January 1, 1983, op. cit.*

9.   Isaiah A. Litvak and Christopher J. Maule, "The Emerging Challenge of Canadian Direct Investment Abroad," in K. C. Dhawan, Hamid Etemad, and Richard W. Wright, eds. *International Businesses: A Canadian Perspective* (Don Mills, Ontario: Addison Wesley, 1981), pp. 337–357.

10.   Isaiah A. Litvak and Christopher J. Maule, "Canadian Small Business Investment in the United States—Corporate Forms and Characteristics," in *ibid.,* pp. 358–375.

11.   Our findings confirm a 1983 report by the Conference Board stating that "New York has capitalized on its skilled workforce and proximity to Canada to attract a large number of foreign companies." Though we do not know the relative importance of either as reported by the survey, our own findings put the proximity to Canada as the decisive locational consideration after Canadians made the decision to invest in the United States. Similarly, in our survey, access to highways turns out to be far more important than a skilled labor force, a finding not only contrary to that of the Conference Board but also to our own earlier findings. We suspect, however, that the large percentage of processing, warehousing, wholesale, and retail businesses may have something to do with this result. See Rom Chugh and Prem Gandhi, *Canadian Investment in Northern New York: Some Empirical Findings* (Albany: The Nelson A. Rockefeller Institute of Government Working Papers, September, 1982), 2.

12.   Conversation with Mr. Harold Thompson, New York State Representative in Montreal. At the same time, during the course of our survey, we noticed a direct telephone link between some Canadian companies in Western New York and their Canadian headquarters in Ontario. See also Litvak and Maule, *op. cit.*

13.   Though we have often heard that New York's high taxes serve as a disincentive to private investment and that the State's business lobbying groups certainly have made lower taxes one of the themes in their lobbying efforts, we are not sure of the relative importance of taxes in locational analysis. In a recent survey of 408 senior engineering students by the Public Policy Institute of the Business Council of New York State, it was found that 85 percent believed the State's tax levels to be an obstacle to taking a job in New York despite the high salaries offered and the superior quality of life (*Times Union,* May 25, 1984). Yet in the published literature on business locational preferences, tax considerations are only marginal. In our estimation, factors such as market potential and

higher sales are more important as an incentive than higher taxes are as a disincentive for business to locate or to expand. See Litvak and Maule, *op. cit.,* and also Chugh and Gandhi, *op. cit.*

14. Besides surveying the Canadian companies and the communities in New York State during the course of this study, we conferred with many members of the State's government, business and political community. Our analysis and the policy recommendations we offer have benefited from such conversations and may reflect our understanding of their concerns.

CHAPTER TEN: BUILDING THE TWENTIETH-CENTURY PUBLIC WORKS MACHINE: ROBERT MOSES AND THE PUBLIC AUTHORITY.

1. David C. Perry and Alfred J. Watkins, "Regional Change and the Impacts of Uneven Urban Development," *Rise of the Sunbelt Cities,* David C. Perry and Alfred J. Watkins, eds. (Beverly Hills: Sage Publications, 1977); James O'Connor, *The Fiscal Crisis of the State* (New York: St. Martin's Press, 1973); *The Fiscal Crisis of American Cities: Essays on the Political Economy of Urban America with Special Reference to New York,* Roger Alcaly and Donald Mermelstein, eds. (New York: Vintage, 1976).

2. Pat Choate and Susan Walters, *America in Ruins: Beyond the Public Works Barrel* (Washington, D.C.: Council of State Planning Agencies, 1981); *America's Urban Capital Stock,* George Peterson, series editor (Washington, D.C.: Urban Institute, 1979), six volumes; Nan Humphrey and Peter Wilson, *Capital Stock Condition in Twenty-Eight Cities* (Washington, D.C.: Urban Institute, February 15, 1980).

3. Annmarie Walsh, "The Authorities: $24 Billion Debt and Still Growing," *Empire State Report* (July, 1983).

4. "Statewide Public Authorities: A Fourth Branch of Government?" A Report by the Office of the New York State Comptroller, 1974.

5. *Restoring Credit and Confidence: A Reform Program for New York State and Its Public Authorities.* Report to the Governor by the New York State Moreland Act Commission on the Urban Development Corporation and other State Financing Agencies, March 31, 1976: 9.

6. This quote is taken from a confidential report written in 1982 for the Legislative Commission on Economy and Efficiency in Government. The author of the report lists the "profound and threatening ways" in which the public authority in New York State has changed as: (1) the increased "scale of authority operations" (2) the widened scope of authority operations; and (3) the growth of financial problems of public authorities in New York State, particularly the Urban Development Corporation which defaulted on note payments in 1975.

7. For a general discussion of the institution of the public authority see Annmarie Walsh, *The Public's Business: The Politics and Practices of Public Corporations* (Cambridge: MIT Press, 1978); Robert G. Smith, *Ad-Hoc Governments: Special Purpose Transportation Authorities in the U.S. and Britain* (Beverly Hills: Sage Publications, 1974); Robert G. Smith, *Public Authorities, Special Districts and Local Government* (Washington, D.C.: National

Association of Counties Research Foundation, 1964); and Jerome J. Shestack, "The Public Authority," *University of Pennsylvania Law Review* (1957), 105. For a discussion of the public authority in New York State, see William Quirk and Leon E. Wein, "A Short Constitutional History of Entities Commonly Known as Authorities," *Cornell Law Review* (1971), 56; and State of New York, Temporary State Commission on Coordination of State Activities, *Staff Report on Public Authorities Under New York State* (Albany: Williams Press, 1956). With respect to authorities in New York City, emphasizing the Triborough Bridge and Tunnel Authority and the Port of New York Authority, see Michael N. Danielson and Jameson W. Doig, *New York: The Politics of Urban Regional Development* (Berkeley: University of California Press, 1982), particularly chapters four through seven; Jameson W. Doig, *Metropolitan Transportation Politics and the New York Region* (New York: Columbia University Press, 1966); Herbert Kaufman, "Gotham in the Air Age," *Public Administration and Policy Development: A Case Book,* Harold Stein, ed. (New York: Harcourt, Brace, 1952); Wallace Sayre and Herbert Kaufman, *Governing New York City: Politics in the Metropolis* (New York: W. W. Norton and Company, 1965), pp. 320–348.

8.   In September of 1982, the School of Architecture and Environmental Design at SUNY of Buffalo was granted exclusive permission to review, organize, and research the files of Robert Moses and the Triborough Bridge and Tunnel Authority. These files document close to half a century of public infrastructure development in New York City and State. Indices to the TBTA Archives and the Upstate Robert Moses Papers will be published in the Summer of 1984 by the authors of this paper through the School of Architecture and Environmental Design.

9.   Annmarie Walsh, *The Public's Business: The Politics and Practices of Government Corporations* (Cambridge, MA.: MIT Press, 1980).

10.   Robert A. Caro, *The Power Broker: Robert Moses and the Fall of New York* (New York: Alfred A. Knopf, 1974).

11.   Austin J. Tobin, "Authorities as a Governmental Technique," paper presented at Rutgers University, March 26, 1953.

12.   Lincoln Gordon, *The Public Corporation in Great Britain* (New York: Oxford University Press, 1938); cited in Austin, *op. cit.,* p. 3.

13.   David C. Perry, "Efficiency: Political Economy of Public Authorities," paper delivered at the 54th Annual Southwest Social Science Association Meeting, Forth Worth, Texas, March 24, 1984.

14.   *Report of the Constitutional Convention Committee* (1938), XI, p. 240; cited in the *Staff Report on Public Authorities Under New York State* issued by the Temporary State Commission on Coordination of State Activities, March 21, 1956, p. 15.

15.   State of New York, Temporary State Commission on the Coordination of State Activities, *Staff Report on Public Authorities under New York State* (Albany: Williams Press, 1956), p. 18.

16.   Shestack, *op. cit.* p. 556; and Jerome J. Shestack, "An Analysis of Authorities: Traditional and Multicountry," *Michigan Law Review* (1976), 71, pp. 1387–1388.

17.   *Ibid.,* p. 1388.

18.   Robert G. Smith, *Ad-Hoc Governments: Special Purpose Transportation Authorities in the United States and Britain* (Beverley Hills, Sage Publications, 1974), p. 108.

19.   *Ibid.,* p. 228.

20. Shestack, "The Public Authority," *op. cit.,* p. 556.

21. For example, the Governors of New York and New Jersey can veto Port of New York Authority Board Minutes. Also, the New York City Board of Estimate and Apportionment must approve land acquisition in New York City for TBTA projects.

22. Brochure issued to commemorate the fifth anniversary of the Triborough Bridge, July 11, 1941.

23. Horace A. Davis, "Borrowing Machines," *National Municipal Review* (June, 1935), pp. 328–344.

24. Caro, *op. cit.*

25. *Civil Engineering* (August 1936), p. 515.

26. Brochure issued for 5th Anniversary of the Triborough Bridge, July 11, 1941, New York, p. 9.

27. Caro, *op. cit.*

28. James Hoey to Mayor John P. O'Brien, March 23, 1933.

29. *Ibid.*

30. Moses to Hoey, March 24, 1933.

31. Laws of New York, 1933, Chapter 145.

32. Circular, undated; Moses to Lewis L. Delafield, March 30, 1933; George Combs to Gordon G. Battle, September 11, 1933.

33. Draft attached to memo of May 11, 1933, Moses to Battle.

34. Jesse Jones, *50 Billion Dollars,* p. 3.

35. Battle to Moses, May 26, 1933.

36. H. R. 5755, Public No. 67, 73d Congress, Title II.

37. Circular, undated, also cited in footnote 32.

38. TBA Policy Memo, "Memorandum as to Triborough Bridge Financing," May 29, 1933.

39. "Application by Triborough Bridge Authority to Federal Emergency Administration of Public Works for Loan and Grant," June 21, 1933.

40. Moses to George McAneny, April 19, 1933.

41. Battle to Moses, August 25, 1933.

42. Battle to Mayor O'Brien, November 27, 1933.

43. There was a correspondence in January of 1934 between Mayor LaGuardia and the current Board members of the TBA leading to the filing of formal charges of misconduct against Fred C. Lemmerman and John Stratton O'Leary. The letters suggest that although there were definite grounds for charges, these may have been trumped up in a deliberate attempt to clear the TBA board to make room for Moses' appointees.

44. In an interesting footnote to Moses' appointment of the TBA Board, Moses requested in a memo dated January 15, 1934, a legal opinion from Raymond McNulty, legal counsel to the Long Island Park Commission, as to whether the chairmanship of the TBA could be transferred. McNulty advised him that this course of action was doubtful. To avoid any legal problems, Moses simply had the by-laws of the TBA rewritten shortly after his appointment, making the Secretary the Chief Executive Officer and divesting those executive powers from the office of the Chairman of the Authority.

45. Robert Moses, *Public Works: A Dangerous Trade* (New York: McGraw Hill Inc., 1970), p. 163.

46. Triborough Bridge Authority, *The Triborough Bridge: A Modern Metropolitan Traffic Artery* (July 1, 1936), p. 13.

47. Harold L. Ickes, *The Secret Diary of Harold L. Ickes: The First Thousand Days—1932—1936* (New York: Simon and Schuster, 1953); cited in Moses, *Public Works, op. cit.,* pp. 165–182.

48. Loan Agreement between the Triborough Bridge Authority and the United States of America, September 1, 1933.

49. Caro, *op. cit.,* p. 341.

50. Edward G. Griffin to Moses, February 26, 1935.

51. O. H. Ammann to Paul Loeser, February 25, 1935.

52. Griffin to Delafield, March 4, 1936.

53. Delafield to Griffin, March 51, 1936.

54. Moses to George McLaughlin, June 12, 1936.

55. *Ibid.*

56. Griffin to Moses, February 26, 1935.

57. Loeser to RFC, March 9, 1936; RFC to Loeser, March 17, 1936; Loeser to Wharton Green, PWA Resident Project Engineer, March 9, 1936; Green to Loeser, March 19, 1936.

58. William Draper of Dillon, Read & Company to Moses, June 2, 1936.

59. Moses to McLaughlin, June 12, 1936.

60. Laws of New York 1936, Chapter 555.

61. Caro, writing from the benefit of hindsight, claims that the revenue generated by the Triborough Bridge would have meant a short life for the TBA. A letter from Loeser to Morton Macartney, December 16, 1936, giving traffic and revenue estimates for the bridge's first six months of operation, indicates revenues were indeed beyond expectations.

62. Moses to Michael J. Madigan, December 7, 1936.

63. This quote appears in a letter Moses drafted in December 1936 to Jesse Jones. The final version was mailed on January 28, 1937, the day on which the amendment actually passed in the State Legislature. While the written record of the correspondence between the TBA and the RFC is sparse, there is mention of phone conversations and it is reasonable to assume that the two men were in contact with each other.

64. By April 24, 1937, the RFC had acquired all 35 million dollars in Triborough Bridge Bonds originally held by the PWA.

65. Moses to Jones, December 1936, *op. cit.*

66. Laws of New York 1937, Chapter 3.

67. *Ibid* (italics added).

68. *Ibid.*

69. *Ibid* (italics added).

70. Caro, *op. cit.,* pp. 623–631.

71. Moses to Jones, January 28, 1937.

72. Moses to Draper of Dillon, Read & Co., February 3, 1937.

73. Moses to Jones, April 9, 1937. By "past relations with this organization [PWA]," Moses was referring to the political antagonism created over the Order 129 incident.

74. *Ibid.*

75. Moses to Jones, April 16, 1937.

76. Dillon, Read & Co. to Moses, May 4, 1937; Loeser to Jones, May 5, 1937.

77. The historical progression by which the TBA became the TBTA was as follows: In 1938, the Henry Hudson Parkway Authority and the Marine Parkway Authority merged to become the New York City Parkway Authority. The Parkway Authority was then merged with the TBA in 1940. In 1946, the TBA and the New York City Tunnel Authority, which was created from the Queens-Midtown Tunnel Authority, merged creating the TBTA.

78. City of New York, *Arterial Progress* (November 8, 1965), p. 24.

79. Sayre and Kaufman, *op. cit.,* Robert C. Wood, *1400 Governments* (Cambridge, M.A.: Harvard University Press, 1961); Doig and Danielson, *op. cit.*

80. "State Mandates," in New York State, *Report of the Temporary State Commission on State and Local Finances* (March 31, 1975), 3, p. 61.

81. Walsh, *The Public's Business, op. cit.,* p. 6.

CHAPTER ELEVEN: THE CENTER FOR INDUSTRIAL INNOVATION AT RPI: CRITICAL REFLECTIONS ON NEW YORK'S ECONOMIC RECOVERY

1. Langdon Winner, *Autonomous Technology: Technics Out-of-Control as a Theme in Political Thought* (Cambridge, M.A.: MIT Press, 1977); Francois Hetman, *Society and the Assessment of Technology* (Paris: Organization for Economic Cooperation and Development, 1973).

2. Murray Edelman, *Politics as Symbolic Action: Mass Arousal and Quiescence* (New York: Academic Press, 1971); *The Symbolic Uses of Politics* (Chicago: University of Illinois Press, 1964).

3. Ira C. Magaziner and Robert B. Reich, *Minding America's Business: The Decline and Rise of the American Economy* (New York: Vintage Books, 1982), pp. 11–29.

4. *Ibid.,* pp. 11–29.

5. Battelle-Columbus Laboratories, *Development of High Technology Industries in New York State,* prepared for the New York State Science and Technology Foundation (Columbus, Ohio: 1982). The five volumes of the Battelle Study are:

   1. *Special Report I: High Technology: The Private Industry Perspective, A Feasibility Analysis for New York State;*

   2. *Special Report III: The Development of Research and Science Parks: Problems and Potentials;*

   3. *Special Report IV: Identification of High Technology Industries;*

   4. *Special Report V: The Higher Education System in New York and its Potential Role in Economic Development;*

   5. *Final Summary Report: a Strategy for the Development of High Technology Activities in New York State.*

6. Hugh L. Carey, *A Strategy for Developing Technology-Based Industry in New York,* Albany, New York, Office of the Governor, October 12, 1982.

7. Quoted from the CII bill, *McKinney's Session Laws of New York,* 1982, p. 1492.

8. Carey, *op. cit.,* p. 1; and Battelle Columbus Labs, *op. cit., passim.*

9. Governor's Advisory Council, "Briefing Paper for the Meeting of the Governor's Advisory Council on High Technology," Albany, New York, March 2, 1979.

10. The memo subsequently became Carey, *op. cit.*

11. Mr. Low's thoughts on these issues are presented in George Low, "The Organization of Industrial Relationships in Universities," presented at the National Conference on University-Corporate Relations in Science and Technology, University of Pennsylvania, December 15, 1982; available from the Office of University Relations, Rensselaer Polytechnic Institute, Troy, New York, 12181.

12. Marvin Harris, *America Now: The Anthropology of a Changing Culture* (New York: Simon & Schuster, 1981), p. 44.

13. Barry Bluestone and Bennett Harrison, *The Deindustrialization of America* (New York: Basic Books, 1982), p. 95.

14. Harry Braverman, *Labor and Monopoly Capital: The Degradation of Work in the Twentieth Century* (New York: Monthly Review Press, 1974); Bluestone, *op. cit.;* Michael Cooley, *Architect or Bee: The Human Technology Relationship* (Boston: South End Press, 1982); Judith Merkle, *Management and Ideology: The Legacy of the International Scientific Management Movement* (Berkeley: University of California Press, 1980).

15. Bluestone and Harrison, *op. cit.,* p. 95.

16. *Ibid.*

17. *Ibid,* p. 165.

18. Richard J. Barnet, *The Lean Years: Politics in an Age of Scarcity* (New York: Simon & Schuster, 1980).

19. Willis W. Harman, *An Incomplete Guide to the Future* (Stanford, C.A.: The Portable Stanford, 1976), pp. 54–55.

20. Cited in *ibid.,* p. 26.

21. Harris, *op. cit.*

22. Cooley, *op. cit.,* p. 94.

23. Battelle Columbus Labs, *op. cit.,* 5, p. III-8.

24. *Ibid.,* 4.

25. Carey, *op. cit.,* pp. 9–10.

26. Colin Norman, *Microelectronics at Work: Productivity and Jobs in the World Economy* (Washington, D.C.: Worldwatch Institute, 1980), pp. 29–51.

27. *Ibid.,* p. 33.

28. General Accounting Office, *Advances in Automation Prompt Concern Over Increased U.S. Unemployment* (Washington, D.C.: 1982).

29. Norman, *op. cit.,* p. 40.

30. Mark Kramer, "The Ruination of the Tomato," *The Atlantic Monthly* (January, 1980), pp. 72–77.

31. Bernard Taper, "The Bittersweet Harvest," *Science 80* (November, 1980), pp. 79–84.

32. *Ibid.,* p. 81.

33. Alan Wolfe, *America's Impasse* (New York: Pantheon Books, 1981).

34. Thomas Dye, *Understanding Public Policy* (Englewood Cliffs, N.J.: Prentice-Hall, 1973), p. 315.

35. *Wall Street Journal* (October 27, 1982).

36. Herman Kahn, *Toward the Year 2000,* pp. 12–16.

27. Ronald Brickman, "Public Controversies Over Toxic Chemicals in Four National Settings: Science as Cause or Cure," presented at the Annual Meeting of the Society for the Social Studies of Science (4S) (Philadelphia, PA.: October 28–31, 1982).

38. Edelman, *The Symbolic Use of Politics, op. cit.,* p. 4.

39. *Ibid.,* pp. 164–165.

40. *Ibid.,* p. 23.

APPENDIX: BATTELLE STUDY VARIABLES

Projected Growth
Adjusted Average Annual Growth 1980–85
Input/Output, Shipments

Employment Trends
Regional Growth Percent Change, 1972–77
New York Growth Percent Change, 1970–78, 1979–80
United States Growth Percent Change, 1970–78, 1979–80
New York Standard Industrial Classification as Percent of United States SIC 1980, Difference from 1979

Earnings Comparison
New York Average Weekly Pay Percent Change, 1979–80
New York SIC to United States SIC Index 1980
New York SIC to Total New York Manufacturing Index, 1980

Establishment Trends
Percent Change in Number
United States, 1970–78
New York, 1970–78
New York Establishments as Percent of United States SIC, 1970, 1978
Percent Change in Number
United States, 1977–80
New York, 1979–80

Shipment Trends
United States Annual Average Change, 1977–80
United States SIC as Percent of Total United States Manufacturing 1980, Percent Change 1977–80

Research and Development Expenditures as Percent of Sales

Market Size: Percent of Shipments Transported
300–999 Miles

1000 or More Miles

Typical Energy Requirements

SOURCE: Battelle Columbus Laboratories, *Development of High Technology Industries in New York State: Special Report IV* (Prepared for the New York State Science and Technology Foundation, 1982), pp. 2–65.

CHAPTER TWELVE: REINDUSTRIALIZATION IN NEW YORK: THE ROLE OF THE STATE UNIVERSITY

1. As examples:
   a. Max L. Carey, "Occupational Employment Growth Through 1990," *Monthly Labor Review* (U.S. Department of Labor, Bureau of Labor Statistics, August, 1981).
   b. William R. Upthegrove, "Engineering Manpower Issues: Must it Always be Feast or Famine?," paper prepared for Business Higher Education Forum, Cleveland, Ohio, October, 1980.
   c. Shirley M. Hufstedleer and Donald N. Langeberg, *Science and Engineering Education for the 1980s and Beyond,* a report prepared for President Carter by the National Science Foundation and the Department of Education, October, 1980.
   d. Russell C. McGregor, *The Doctoral Shortage in Engineering: A Growing Crisis,* a report prepared for the National Association of State Universities and Land Grant Colleges, Washington, D.C., 1981.
   e. *A Call for Action to Reduce the Engineering Shortage,* American Electronics Association, August, 1981.

2. *Investment Needs: Engineering and the Engineering Technologies,* a report prepared for the Trustees of State University of New York, SUNY staff, Albany, New York, January 26, 1982.

3. Russell C. McGregor, *The Doctoral Shortage in Engineering: A Growing Crisis,* a report prepared for the National Association of State Universities and Land Grant Colleges, Washington, D.C., 1981, p. 5.

4. *Report on the Quality of Engineering Education,* Commission on Education for the Engineering Professions, National Association of State Universities and Land Grant Colleges, Washington, D.C., November 7, 1982.

5. *Ibid.,* p. 24.

6. Lois Peters and Herbert Fusfeld, "Current U.S. University–Industry Research Connections," *University–Industry Research Relationships,* National Science Board, National Science Foundation, Washington D.C., 1982, from table 6, p. 21.

7. Cited in *High Technology, The Private Industry Perspective, A Feasibility Analysis for New York State,* Battelle Columbus Laboratories, Columbus, Ohio, April, 1982.

8. This information is extracted from computerized grant and contract information files of the SUNY Research Foundation, compiled by the author.

9. *International Competition in Advanced Technology: Decisions for America*, a report of the Committee on Advanced Technology Competition and the Industrialized Allies, National Academy of Sciences, Washington, D.C., March, 1983, p. 11.

CHAPTER THIRTEEN: DEFENSE PROCUREMENT AND THE REINDUSTRIALIZATION OF NEW YORK STATE

1. Data used to derive these estimates are published in New York State Department of Commerce, Bureau of Business Research, *Business Statistics: Annual Summary 1973–1981, 1974–1982 and 1975–1983*, Albany, New York, pp. 6–7.

2. *Ibid.*, p. 8.

3. Aaron S. Gurwitz, "New York State's Economic Turnaround: Services or Manufacturing," Federal Reserve Bank of New York, *Quarterly Review* (Autumn, 1983), p. 34.

4. Directorate for Information Operations and Reports (DIOR). *Department of Defense Prime Contract Awards Over $10,000 By State, County, Contractor, and Place (New York)*, Fiscal Years 1981, 1982, 1983, The Pentagon, Washington, D.C.

5. Gurwitz, *op. cit.*, pp. 30–31.

6. New York State Department of Commerce, *op. cit.*, p. 6.

7. Bureau of the Census, *Statistical Abstract of the United States, 1982–1983* (103rd ed.) Washington, D.C., p. 13.

8. *Ibid.*, p. 427.

9. For a summary of these conditions see Roy Bahl, *Financing State and Local Government in the 1980s* (New York: Oxford University Press, 1984), chapters 5 and 6.

10. Yanklevich, Skelly and White, Inc., *Research to Support New York State's Economic Development Activities*, Vol. I, "Management Summary," February, 1978, p. 2; cited in Joseph M. Heikoff, "Management Perceptions of the Business Climate in New York State," Graduate School of Public Affairs, State University of New York at Albany, Albany, New York, 1979, pp. 3–6 (unpublished).

11. These figures were provided by the National Tax Foundation, personal conversations, April, 1984.

12. Estimated from the Bureau of the Census, *Federal Expenditures By State*, Fiscal Years 1981, 1982, and 1983, Washington D.C., p. 1. Figures adjusted for exclusion of postal expenditures and federal retirement outlays.

13. Frans Seastrand, *The Flow of Federal Funds to New York State, 1976–1980, With an Evaluation of Senator Moynihan's Study New York State and the Federal Fisc: VI*, Research Report no. 82–7, New York State Department of Commerce, Division of Economic Research and Statistics, Albany, New York, p. 3.

14. James E. Ryan, *Federal Fiscal Policy and Employment in New York State: 1981–1983*, The Nelson A. Rockefeller Institute of Government, State University of New York, Albany, New York, November 1984, pp. 29–33.

15. Thomas J. Anton, "The Regional Distribution of Federal Expenditures 1971–1980," *National Tax Journal* (December, 1983), 4, pp. 429–442.

16. *Federal Expenditures by State, op. cit.*, pp. 14, 15, 16.

17. *Ibid.*, pp. 18, 19, 20. Net value differs in percentages, see note 4.

18. Estimated from the sum of procurement expenditures, salaries and grants to state and local governments in *Federal Expenditures by State* for Fiscal Year 1981, 1982, and 1983. Transfer payments take up almost half of the federal budget but cannot be properly compared with GNP. Individuals who receive these payments may purchase goods and services of their choice. However, to count transfer as part of GNP would be to double count, since these transfers are counted at the time they are used to purchase goods and services.

19. Federal Procurement Data Center, *Standard Report: Fiscal Year 1983 Fourth Quarter Report,* Washington, D.C., April 1, 1984, p. 2.

20. *Ibid.,* p. 6.

21. *Federal Expenditures by State: Fiscal Year 1983,* p. 1.

22. Roger E. Bolton, "Defense Spending: Burden or Prop," *Defense and Disarmament: The Economics of Transition,* Roger E. Bolton, ed. (Englewood Cliffs, N.J.: Prentice-Hall, 1966), pp. 1–10.

23. *Ibid.,* pp. 1–4.

24. From a speech by President Eisenhower, quoted in Charles Hitch and Roland McKean, *The Economics of Defense in the Nuclear Age* (Cambridge, M.A.: Harvard University Press, 1961), p. 4.

25. Barry Bluestone and Bennet Harrison, *The Deindustrialization of America* (New York: Basic Books, 1982), pp. 3–48.

26. Bluestone and Harrison, pp. 49–63.

27. Paul Seabury, "Industrial Policy and National Defense," *The Industrial Policy Debate,* Chalmers Johnson, ed. (San Francisco: Institute for Contemporary Studies, 1984), pp. 195–216.

28. Roger E. Bolton, *Defense Purchases and Regional Growth* (Washington, D.C.: Brookings, 1966), pp. 92–93.

29. *Ibid.,* p. 142.

30. *Ibid.,* p. 143.

31. Quoted in Charles J. Hitch, "The Defense Sector: Its Impact," *The Defense Sector and the American Economy* (New York: New York University Press, 1968), p. 53.

32. Bolton, *Defense Purchases, op. cit.,* p. 142.

33. *Ibid.,* pp. 144–145.

34. Northeast-Midwest Congressional Coalition, Northeast-Midwest Senate Coalition, Northeast-Midwest Institute, Budget Analysis Series, *Selected Budget Briefs: A Regional Analysis of President Reagan's Fiscal 1984 Budget* (Washington, D.C., February, 1984), p. 1.5.

35. Murray L. Weidenbaum, "Industrial Adjustments to Military Expenditure Shifts and Cutbacks," *The Economic Consequences of Reduced Military Spending,* Bernard Udis, ed. (Lexington, M.A.: Lexington Books, 1973), p. 271.

36. Federal Procurement Data Center, *op. cit., p.* 17.

37. *See footnote 28.*

38. *See Federal Procurement Data Center, op. cit.,* information on DLA procurement, p. 5.

39. *Ibid.,* p. 7.

40. *Ibid.,* p. 17.

41. *Ibid.,* p. 29.

42. *Ibid.*, pp. 25, 29, 95.

43. Edward B. Roberts, *The Dynamics of Research and Development* (New York: Harper and Row, 1964), pp. 81–85.

44. Regis McKenna, "Sustaining the Innovation Process in America," in Johnson, *op. cit.*, pp. 136–137.

45. Calspan received $14 million in Fiscal Year 1981 and $18 million in Fiscal Year 1983. Sierra Research Corporation received $40 million in Fiscal Year 1981 and $60 million in Fiscal Year 1983. See *DIOR, op. cit.*, 1981 and 1983.

46. Gurwitz, *op. cit.*, p. 33–34.

47. Federal Procurement Data Center, *op. cit.*, p. 9.

48. New York State Department of Commerce, Bureau of Business Statistics, *Business Statistics: Annual Summary 1975–1983*, pp. 6–7.

49. Ryan, *op. cit.*, pp. 36–43.

50. *DIOR, op. cit.*, 1981 and 1983.

51. Aaron S. Gurwitz, Kathleen Auda, and William Greer, *Federal R & D and Defense Outlays in New York State*, Regional Economic Studies of the Federal Reserve Bank of New York, February, 1984, p. 13.

52. *Federal Expenditures by State, Fiscal Year 1983*, p. 20.

53. Ryan, *op. cit.*, p. 32.

APPENDIX:

The estimates for the increases necessary to halt the decline of the manufacturing sector are based on the ratio of the dollar value of total sales in the State to the number of total employment positions in the State. The dollar value of retail sales is published by the New York State Department of Commerce. Wholesale trade data was not available for the years 1981 through 1983 at the time of this writing. However, historically wholesale trade has had a dollar value of approximately twice retail sales dollar value and this fact was used in the following estimates. Hence, for example, total sales for the year 1981 were estimated at $209.9 billion (Retail sales dollar value = $69.97 billion and wholesale trade value = 2 × $69.97 billion). The total published number of workers for the year 1981 is 7.281 million. The ratio of total sales to workers is calculated as being $37,400/worker. Data for the years 1981 and 1983 are as follows:

	1982	1983
Estimated Total Sales	$221.2 billion	$244.7 billion
Total Employment	7.263 million	7.206 million
Sales/Worker ratio	$30,455/worker	$29,500/worker

Defense procurement contracts are treated as sales made by state firms to the Department of Defense. However, given the capital intensiveness of most manufacturing performed on behalf of the DOD, I used a figure ($60,000) which is approximately twice the three year average of sales needed to support a worker in order to adjust for this factor. Personal conversations with executives from defense firms indicate that this figure is realistic. Firm

427

specific ratios of sales to workers produce dollar values ranging from $50,000 per worker to $78,000 per worker for Fiscal Year 1983.

CHAPTER FOURTEEN; OLD FEDERALISM AND NEW FEDERALISM IN NEW YORK STATE

1. Wallace Oates, *Fiscal Federalism* (New York: Harcourt Brace and Jovanovich, Inc., 1972), pp. 21–30.

2. It should also be noted that, as a result of both greater progressivity and a more inclusive and meaningful tax base, vertical and horizontal equity considerations are better satisfied at the federal level than at state and local levels. See Wallace Oates, "An Economist's Perspective on Fiscal Federalism," *The Political Economy of Fiscal Federalism*, Wallace Oates, ed. (Lexington, M.A.: Lexington Books, 1977).

3. Mancur Olsen and Richard Zeckhauser, "An Economic Theory of Alliances," *Review of Economics and Statistics* (August, 1966), 48, pp. 266–79.

4. This is a restatement of the Decentralization Theorem found in Oates, *Fiscal Federalism, op. cit.,* p. 35.

5. Of course, some or all of the variation in taxes and expenditure levels across communities may be capitalized into land values mitigating some of the economic incentive to exercise residential choice.

6. Albert O. Hirschman, *Exit, Voice, and Loyalty: Responses to Decline in Firms, Organizations, and States* (Cambridge: Harvard University Press, 1970).

7. An interesting alternative rationale for intergovernmental grants-in-aid can be found in an article by Winer. He argues that the post-war rapid growth in Canadian federal expenditures stemmed from the federal government's efforts to associate itself with the provision of social services in an area in which the provinces had primary constitutional and historical responsibilities. Provincial governments were "forced" to accept grants-in-aid to effectively block tax-shifting across jurisdictions, thus allowing the federal government entry into this single most important area of public sector growth. Stanley L. Winer, "Some Evidence on the Effect of the Separation of Spending and Taxing Decisions," *Carleton Economic Papers* (Ottawa: Carleton University, 1979), pp. 80–81.

8. This is a theoretical proposition which has been put to empirical test many times. Generally, the ability of higher levels of government to affect service levels and expenditures in lower levels of government through intergovernmental aid has been documented. However, this ability to induce recipient governments to alter service and expenditure levels is not as powerful as one might expect, due primarily to local governments' abilities to "funge" aid dollars. Edward M. Gramlich, "Intergovernmental Grants: A Review of the Empirical Literature," in Oates, *The Political Economy of Fiscal Federalism, op. cit.*

9. Dennis R. Young, "Productivity Effects of State Formula Grants," a paper presented to the Public Choice Society, New Orleans, March, 1978.

10. David R. Beam, "Economic Theory as Policy Prescription: Pessimistic Findings on Optimizing Grants," Advisory Commission on Intergovernmental Relations, Washington, D.C., 1978 and Gramlich, *op. cit.*

11. William Niskanen, *Bureaucracy and Representative Government* (New York: Aldine Publishing Co., 1971); and Richard Wagner, "Revenue Sharing, Fiscal Illusion, and Budgetary Choice," *Public Choice* (1977), 25, pp. 45–61.

12. Richard H. Silkman and Dennis R. Young, "X-Efficiency and State Formula Grants," *The National Tax Journal* (September, 1982), 35, 3, pp. 383–97; and Richard H. Silkman and Dennis R. Young, "X-Efficiency, State Formula Grants and Public Library Systems," *Perspectives in Local Finance and Public Policy,* John M. Quigley, ed. (Connecticut: JAI Press, 1983).

13. Advisory Commission on Intergovernmental Relations, "An Agenda for American Federalism: Restoring the Confidence and Competence," Washington, D.C., 1981.

14. Government Accounting Office, "Lessons Learned from Past Block Grants: Implications for Congressional Oversight," Washington, D.C., 1982.

15. *The Reagan Experiment,* John L. Palmer and Isabel V. Sawhill, eds. (Washington, D.C.: The Urban Institute, 1982).

16. For example, Governor Milliken of Michigan has estimated that ERTA will cost his state approximately 5 million dollars due to exemptions for interest on all-savers certificates, 10 million dollars due to liberalized pensions and retirement provisions, and 20 million dollars due to the new ACRS and other business provisions per year in lost sales tax revenues. Advisory Commission on Intergovernmental Relations, *Intergovernmental Perspective* (Summer, 1982), 8, 3.

17. See Palmer and Sawhill, *op. cit.*

18. National Governor's Association, "The Proposed FY 1983 Federal Budget: Impact on the States," National Conference of State Legislatures, Washington, D.C., February, 1982.

19. George Peterson, "The State and Local Sector," in Palmer and Sawhill, *op. cit.*

20. Joint Committee on Taxation, "Summary of H.R. 4242: The Economic Recovery Tax Act of 1981," U.S. Congress, Washington, D.C., August 1981.

21. Advisory Commission on Intergovernmental Relations, 1982.

22. Albert J. Davis, "New Federalism—A Shifting of Responsibilities and Taxes," *Proceedings of the National Tax Association,* forthcoming.

23. Government Accounting Office, *op. cit.,* p. 62.

24. Government Accounting Office, *op. cit.,* cover.

25. It should be noted that each of the nine block grants does require annual or biennial reports and/or fiscal audits. However, it is interesting and indicative of the overall thrust of the legislation that in Community Service and Low-Income Energy Assistance the annual reports are public but not directed to any federal agency.

26. *Statistical Abstract of the United States,* U.S. Department of Commerce, Washington, D.C., 1979.

27. Of course, some of this impact has been mitigated by the Tax Equity and Fiscal Responsibility Act of 1982 and is likely to be further reduced by tax increases proposed in this year's congress.

28. Peterson, *op. cit.*

29. The potential for such switching is quite large. For example, in 1979 245 million dollars of day care services under Title XX nationwide went to AFDC recipients. In New York State, of the 87,701 estimated recipients of day care services funded in whole or in

part through Title XX in 1981–82, 29,968 or 34.2 percent were AFDC eligible. *Consolidated Services Plan—1982,* New York State Department of Social Services, Albany, 1983.

30. *Ibid.*

31. This would result from the fact that the federal tax structure is somewhat more progressive than state tax structures and substantially more progressive than local tax systems which rely to a great extent on property taxes.

32. *Consolidated Services Plan—1982, ibid.*

CHAPTER FIFTEEN: ACID RAIN: PUBLIC POLICY IN THE FACE OF UNCERTAINTY

1. P. A. Sabatier and D. A. Mazmanian, *Can Regulation Work? The Implementation of the 1972 California Coastal Zone Initiative* (New York: Plenum Press, 1983).

2. *Acid Precipitation Research Needs Conference Proceedings,* V. A. Mohnen and J. W. Geis, eds. College of Environmental Science and Forestry, State University of New York, Syracuse, New York, 1981. Acidity is measured on a logarithmic pH scale. A pH of 7 is neutral. A pH of 1.0 is very acidic (battery acid), while a pH of 14.0 is very alkaline (lye). A pH of 5.7 is considered "normal" for rain and a pH of 4.7 is ten times more acidic than normal rain.

3. Phase II Interim Working Paper, Impact Assessment Working Group I, U.S.—Canada Memorandum of Intent on Transboundary Air Pollution, October, 1981. National Research Council, *Atmosphere-Biosphere Interactions: Toward a Better Understanding of the Ecological Consequences of Fossil Fuel Combustion* (Washington: National Academy Press, 1981).

4. N. R. Glass, D. E. Arnold, J. N. Galloway, G. R. Hendrey, J. J. Lee, W. W. McFee, S. A. Norton, C. F. Powers, D. L. Rambo, C. L. Schofield, "Effects of Acid Precipitation," *Environmental Science and Technology* (1982), 16, pp. 163–169.

5. M. H. Pfeiffer and P. J. Festa, *Acidity Status of Lakes in the Adirondack Region of New York in Relation to Fish Resources, Progress Report* (Albany, New York: New York State Department of Environmental Conservation, 1980). C. L. Schofield, "Lake Acidification in the Adirondack Mountains of New York: Causes and Consequences," *Proceedings of the First International Symposium on Acid Precipitation and the Forest Ecosystem, General Technical Report NE-23,* L. S. Dochinger and T. S. Seliga, eds. (Columbus, Ohio: USDA Forest Service, 1976).

6. New York State Department of Environmental Conservation, *Acidity Status Update of Lakes and Streams in New York State* (Albany, New York: New York State Department of Environmental Conservation, 1984).

7. H. W. Vogelman, "Catastrophe on Camel's Hump," *Natural History* (1982), 91, pp. 8–14; L. R. Ember, "Acid Rain Implicated in Forest Die-back," *Chemical Engineering News* (November 22, 1982), pp. 25–26.

8. D. J. Raynal, J. R. Roman, and W. M. Eichenlaub, "Response of Tree Seedlings to Acid Precipitation—I & II. Effect of Simulated Acidified Canopy Throughfall on Sugar Maple Seedling Growth," *Environmental and Experimental Botany* (March, 1982), 22, pp. 385–392; J. R. Roman and D. J. Raynal, "Effects of Acid Precipitation on Vegetation,"

Actual and Potential Effects of Acid Precipitation on a Forest Ecosystem (Albany, New York: New York State Energy Research and Development Authority, 1980).

9. C. J. Wang, D. J. Raynal, A. L. Leaf, and P. D. Manion, "Actual and Potential Effects of Acid Precipitation on an Adirondack Forest," *NYSERDA 80–28* (Albany, New York: New York State Energy Research and Development Authority, 1980).

10. Mohnen and Geis, *op. cit.*

11. P. L. Forsline and W. J. Kender, "The Effects of Acid Rain on Fruit Crops," *Proceedings of the New York State Symposium on Acid Deposition,* Center for Environmental Research, Cornell University, Ithaca, New York, January, 1982.

12. N. S. Baer and S. M. Berman, "Marble Tombstones in National Cemeteries as Indicators of Stone Damage: General Methods," Seventy-sixth Annual Meeting of the Air Pollution Control Association, Atlanta, Georgia, 1983.

13. F. B. Taylor, "A Cooperative Study of the Effects of Acid Rain on Water Supplies," New England Water Works Association, Dedham, Massachusetts, 1983. G. W. Fuhs and R. A. Olsen, *Acid Precipitation Effects on Drinking Water in the Adirondack Mountains of New York State* (Albany, New York: New York State Department of Health, 1979).

14. This survey was conducted by Gordon S. Black Associates of Rochester, New York, based upon a sample design and survey instrument constructed by us. A more complete report of the results of the survey can be found in R. Hedges and P. Wissel, "Public Perceptions of Acid Deposition: A Survey of New York Residents," *Economic Impact Study of Acid Precipitation* (Albany: Center for Financial Management, State University of New York at Albany, 1983).

15. New York Power Pool, *The Cost Impact of Acid Rain Legislation on the Member Electric Systems of the New York Power Pool* (Albany, New York: 1983).

16. M. Kamya, M. Mann, and E. Renshaw, "Acid Lakes and Population Growth," and P. Denimarck and E. Renshaw, "Sulfur Dioxide and Population Growth for Large Cities," *Economic Impact Study of Acid Precipitation, op. cit.*

17. M. Kamya, M. Mann, and E. Renshaw, "The Possible Economic Impact in New York State of Acid Deposition on the Forest Ecosystem," *Economic Impact Study of Acid Precipitation, op. cit.*

18. D. Vrooman and W. Brown, "Acidity and the Value of Waterfront Properties in the Adirondack Park Region," (St. Lawrence University, Canton, New York: 1982), unpublished paper.

19. W. P. Page, "Electricity Generation, Acid Rain, and Regional Economic Agricultural Losses," Fourteenth Annual Conference of the Institute of Public Utilities, Williamsburg, Virginia, 1982.

20. F. C. Menz and J. K. Mullen, "Acidification Impact on Fisheries: Substitution and the Valuation of Recreation Resources," Annual Meeting of the American Chemical Society, Las Vegas, Nevada, 1982.

21. E. Renshaw, M. Mann, and M. Kamya, "Review of the Literature," *Economic Impact Study of Acid Precipitation, op. cit.*

22. D. Pearce, "The Limits of Cost-Benefit Analysis as a Guide to Environmental Policy," *Kyklos* (1976), 29, pp. 97–111; and E. G. Farnworthe, T. H. Tidrick, C. F.

Jordan, and W. M. Smathers, "The Value of Natural Ecosystems: An Economic and Ecological Framework," *Environmental Conservation* (1981), 8, pp. 275–282.

23. C. F. Runge, "The Fallacy of Privatization," *Journal of Contemporary Studies* (1984), 7, pp. 89–100.

24. New York Department of Environmental Conservation, *Acid Rain: A Policy for New York State to Reduce Sulfur Dioxide Emissions. Draft Environmental Impact Statement* (Albany, New York: New York State Department of Environmental Conservation, 1984).

CHAPTER SIXTEEN: INDUSTRIAL DEMOCRACY AND REINDUSTRIALIZATION: CROSS-CULTURAL PERSPECTIVES

1. Jean-Jacques Rousseau, *The Social Contract* (London: Penguin, 1968), Bk. I, Chs. 7 and 8, Bk. II, Ch. 3, Bk. III, Ch. 18; John Stuart Mill, *Considerations on Representative Government* (London: Routledge, 1905), p. 114; Carole Pateman, *Participation and Democratic Theory* (Cambridge: Cambridge University, 1970), pp. 1–111; Charles E. Lindblom, *Politics and Markets: The World's Political-Economic Systems* (New York: Basic, 1977), pp. 331–334.

2. Frederick Winslow Taylor, *Principles of Scientific Management* (New York: Harper and Row, 1947), pp. 41–47.

3. Graham Wootton, *Workers, Unions, and the State* (New York: Schocken, 1967), p. 106ff.; Paul Blumberg, *Industrial Democracy* (New York: Schocken, 1969), Chs. 5 and 6.

4. Lindblom, *op. cit.,* p. 332.

5. John M. Roach, *Worker Participation: New Voices in Management* (New York: Conference Board, 1973), pp. 1–43.

6. George Ritzer, *Working: Conflict and Change* (Englewood Cliffs, N.J.: Prentice-Hall, 1972), pp. 139–325; Studs Terkel, *Working: People Talk About What They Do All Day And How They Feel About What They Do* (New York: Pantheon, 1974).

7. Ritzer, *op. cit.,* p. 3–67.

8. Robert B. Reich, "Japan Inc., U.S.A.," *The New Republic* (November 26, 1984), pp. 19–23.

9. With regard to the American South, see, for example, "Town Built By Textile Mill Faces Future Without It," *New York Times* (December 22, 1984), p. 8; "To Save Jobs, Union Urges New Use of Plant," *New York Times* (December 27, 1984), p. A/11.

10. Barry Bluestone and Bennett Harrison, *The Deindustrialization of America: Plant Closings, Community Abandonment, and the Dismantling of Basic Industry* (New York: Basic, 1982).

11. *Ibid.,* pp. 193–264.

12. William Foote Whyte *et. al., Worker Participation and Ownership: Cooperative Strategies for Strengthening Local Communities* (Ithaca, N.Y.: ILR, 1983), pp. 56–58.

13. Martin Carnoy and Derek Shearer, *Economic Democracy* (White Plains, N.Y.: M. E. Sharpe, 1980); *Socialism and the Cities,* Bruce M. Stave, ed. (Port Washington, N.Y.: Kennikat, 1975).

14. Joseph Rayback, *A History of American Labor* (New York: Free Press, 1966), p. 160.

15. Louis O. Kelso and Patricia Hetter, *Two-Factor Theory: The Economics of Reality, How To Turn Eighty Million Workers Into Capitalists on Borrowed Money* (New York: Random House, 1967).

16. U.S. Congress, Joint Economic Committee, 94th Congress, 2nd Session,"Broadening the Ownership of New Capital: ESOPs and Other Alternatives" (Washington, D.C.: U.S. Government Printing Office, 1976), pp. 1–62; U.S. Senate, Select Committee on Small Business, 96th Congress, 2nd Session, "The Role of the Federal Government in Employee Ownership of Business" (Washington, D.C.: U.S. Government Printing Office, 1980), pp. iii–vii, 1–27.

17. "The New Role for ESOPs," *New York Times* (January 2, 1985), p. D/1.

18. Kelso and Hetter, *op. cit.*, pp. 82–92.

19. "Employee-Owned Companies and Their Fates," *New York Times* (December 30, 1985), p. IV/3.

20. John Simmons and William Mares, *Working Together* (New York: Knopf, 1983), pp. 116–135.

21. See footnote 16; also U.S. Congress, 95th Congress, 2nd Session, "Employee-Community Ownership to Save Jobs When Firms Shut Down," *Congressional Record* (June 19, 1978), pp. E3325–E3328.

22. Bluestone and Harrison, *op. cit.*, p. 261.

23. Whyte *et. al., op. cit.*, pp. 6–54; Simmons and Mares, *op. cit.*, pp. 80–95.

24. Whyte *et. al., op. cit.*, p. 8.

25. *Ibid.*, pp. 6–54.

26. Simmons and Mares, *op. cit.*, p. 95.

27. Attention has been focused especially on Western Europe, the birthplace of the Industrial Revolution and the spawning ground for an antidotal notion of participatory democracy. See the opening paragraph to this essay and footnote 1.

28. Lars Bjork, "An Experiment in Work Satisfaction," *Scientific American* (March, 1975), 232, p. 17.

29. Ritzer, *op. cit.*, pp. 399–407.

30. H. Thomas and C. Logan, *Mondragón: An Economic Analysis* (London: Allen and Unwin, 1982); Ana Gutierrez Johnson and William Foote Whyte, "The Mondragón System of Worker Production Cooperatives," *Industrial and Labor Relations Review* (October, 1977), 31, 1, pp. 18–30; Simmons and Mares, *op. cit.*, pp. 136–144.

31. Profitability is not the principal factor in decisions regarding the establishment of new cooperatives. Greater weight attaches to the interests and needs of the members and to the long-term implications of investment decisions for regional development. Johnson and Whyte, *op. cit.*, p. 28.

32. The problem of conceptual ambiguity in the Yugoslav system of democratic self-management is underlined in Pavao Novosel, "Komunikacija i Razvoj: Jedna jugoslavenska perspektiva" ("Communication and Development: A Yugoslav Perspective"), *Informatologia Yugoslavica* (1982), 14, 3–4, pp. 209–224. The evolution of democratic self-management in the industrial sector is examined by the International Labour Office, *Workers' Management in Yugoslavia* (Geneva: I.L.O., 1962); "Workers' Participation in Management: Country

Studies Series, Yugoslavia (No. 9)," *International Institute for Labour Studies Review* (1972), 9, pp. 129–172; Najdan Pašić, Stanislav Grozdanić, and Milorad Radevic, *Workers' Management in Yugoslavia: Recent Development and Trends* (Geneva: International Labour Office, 1982).

33. The Socialist Alliance of Working People and the Veterans' Association are the two leading sociopolitical organizations. Communities of interest are based on schools, medical facilities, and art, cultural, and research institutes. The Yugoslav Federation includes more than 500 communes, six republics (Slovenia, Croatia, Serbia, Bosnia'/Hercegovina, Montenegro, and Macedonia), and two autonomous regions within the Serbian Republic (Kosovo bordering on Albania, and Vojvodina).

34. The status of labor in the Yugoslav system is outlined in great detail in *The Associated Labour Act* (Ljubljana, Slovenian Republic: Dopisna Delavska Univerza, 1977).

35. The political development of Yugoslavia in the post-war era is surveyed in A. Ross Johnson, *The Transformation of Communist Ideology: The Yugoslav Case, 1945–1953* (Cambridge: Massachusetts Institute of Technology, 1972); Bogdan Denis Denitch, *The Legitimation of a Revolution: The Yugoslav Case* (New Haven: Yale University, 1976); Steven L. Burg, *Conflict and Cohesion in Socialist Yugoslavia: Political Decision-Making Since 1966* (Princeton: Princeton University, 1983). For a useful overview of the factors of nationality, region, and religion in Yugoslavia, see Koča Jončić, *Narodnosti u Jugoslaviji (Nationalities in Yugoslavia)* (Belgrade: Jugoslovenska Stvarnost, ca. 1982).

36. Two executive groups form the apex of the party and state hierarchies at the federal level in Yugoslavia. Each group has members drawn from the six republics and two autonomous regions in the Yugoslav Federation. There is a rotating presidency in each group.

37. Taxes are levied upon economic organizations and the workers in order to support a wide array of social services and also government administration at the various levels.

38. See footnote 33.

39. The more developed areas are Slovenia and Croatia (along with the autonomous region of Vojvodina, a prosperous agricultural area within the Serbian Republic). The less-developed areas are the autonomous region of Kosovo within the Serbian Republic, Macedonia, Montenegro, and Bosnia/Hercegovina.

40. The absence of a unified market economy is underlined in the report and recommendations of the Kraigher Commission established to propose a long-term economic stabilization program for Yugoslavia. See Dokumenti Komisije, *Book 4: Zaklünji Deo Dugorocnog Programa Ekonomske Stabilizacije* (Beograd: Centar Za Radnicko Samoupravljane, 1983), pp. 281–344.

41. The preoccupation many urban-dwellers have with the matter of securing adequate housing in a tight market is examined by the writer in a forthcoming book, *I Work, I Manage: Profiles in Yugoslav Socialism*.

42. Yugoslavia, in both the bilateral and multilateral aspects of its foreign policy of nonalignment, seeks to promote the idea of democratic self-management. Many academicians and research institutes are also involved in that activity. See, for example, *Workers' Self-Management and Participation in Decision-Making as a Factor of Social Change and Economic Progress in Developing Countries: National Reports Vol. II: Algeria, Guyana, India, and Tanzania* (Ljubljana, Slovenian Republic: International Center for Public Enterprises in Developing Countries, 1981).

43. At the end of the Second World War, only 30 percent of the population of Yugoslavia lived in cities and large towns. Four decades later, only 30 percent of the population live in the countryside. Farmsteads organized on a legal maximum of 10 hectares are often tended by elderly peasants, their sons having moved away to the cities and towns. Where relatively young family members continue to live on farms, they are apt to be part-time farmers engaged in full-time factory or commercial work. The Kraigher Commission (see footnote 40) stressed the need to vitalize private agriculture in Yugoslavia as part of a comprehensive strategy aimed at rural development.

44. Petroleum imports also soak up a major part of the hard currency reserves.

45. Most strikes are of short duration, a few hours or a few days. Strikers' demands are usually met in order to resume factory operations.

46. The changing pattern of production modes in the United States is examined in Michael J. Piore and Charles F. Sabel, *The Second Industrial Divide: Possibilities for Prosperity* (New York: Basic, 1984).

47. See, for example, the cases of the Weirton (W. Va.) Steel Corporation and the Rath Packing Company of Cedar Rapids, Iowa, in "Employees Make A Go of Weirton," *New York Times* (January 6, 1985), p. III/4; "Worker-Owned Plant Fights for Survival in Court in Iowa," *New York Times* (January 13, 1985), p. I/18; and "Worker-Owned Rath Packing May Be at End of a Long Road," *New York Times* (February 15, 1985), p. 16.

48. One indicator of this can be found in the low incidence of serious labor conflicts and strikes. With only a few exceptions, such conflicts and strikes have occurred in Ulgor, the giant industrial cooperative with a work regimen still based largely on the Taylorist philosophy. For example, upper management is appointed by the workers and it, in turn, appoints supervisory personnel. Many of these lower-level supervisors continue to exercise their responsibilities in an unpopular authoritarian manner. See Johnson and Whyte, *op. cit.,* p. 25.

Contributors

Michael Black Rensselaer Polytechnic Institute
Prem Gandhi State University of New York College at Plattsburgh
Barry Gewen International Ladies Garment Workers' Union
Walter Goldstein State University of New York at Albany
Roman Hedges State University of New York at Albany
John W. Kalas State University of New York Research Foundation
Mark J. Kasoff State University of New York College at Potsdam
Hyman Korman State University of New York at Stony Brook
Gail Lerner State University of New York at Stony Brook
Jon J. Lines State University of New York at Buffalo
Alvin Magid State University of New York at Albany
Ellen L. Parker State University of New York at Buffalo
David C. Perry State University of New York at Buffalo
Donald J. Reeb State University of New York at Albany
Edward F. Renshaw State University of New York at Albany
James E. Ryan State University of New York at Albany
Morton Schoolman State University of New York at Albany
Michael Schwartz State University of New York at Stony Brook
Charlene Seifert State University of New York at Stony Brook
Richard H. Silkman State University of New York at Binghamton
Mark D. Soskin State University of New York College at Potsdam
Lawrence Southwick, Jr. State University of New York at Buffalo
Todd Swanstrom State University of New York at Albany
Richard Worthington Rensselaer Polytechnic Institute
Sen-Yuan Wu State University of New York at Stony Brook
Glenn Yago State University of New York at Stony Brook

437

Index

439

Index

"Partnership", 24–28, 32–43, 47–49, 101, 261, 274–275, 286, 300–306, 326
(see also Industrial targeting in university, public and private sector cooperation)
Pašić, Najdan, 434
Pateman, Carole, 432
Pausen, Arnold, 402
Pearce, D., 431
Perry, David C., 417, 418
Peters, Lois, 424
Peterson, George, 417, 429
Peterson, Paul, 405
Pfeiffer, M.H., 430
Pfouts, Ralph W., 406
Phillips, Kevin, 413
Piore, Michael J., 400, 405, 435
Pisani, Joseph, 398
Plant closings, 34–36, 75–79, 176, 378, 381–384
  and apparel industry, 88
  and contractions, 80–88
  and employment, 81–87
  and expansions, 80–87
  and openings, 80–87
Porter, Paul R., 406
Posner, Bruce G., 407
Powers, C.F., 430
Prail, Frank J., 404
Proctor, Allen J., 412

Quigley, John, 429
Quirk, William, 418

Radevic, Milorad, 434
Rambo, D.L., 430
Rayback, Joseph, 433
Raynal, D.J., 430, 431
Reagan, Ronald, 75, 331, 340–344, 347, 353, 379
Rees, J., 402
Regulatory policy, 16–18, 150, 220, 225–226, 317, 370–374
  and economic development, 16–18, 148, 155
  and industrial migration, 149
  and industrial targeting, 16–18
Reich, Michael, 405
Reich, Robert B., 40, 53, 54, 68, 71, 258, 259, 400, 401, 413, 421, 432
Renshaw, Edward, 368, 403, 404, 431
Rhodes, Frank H.T., 264
Ricardo, David, 59, 73, 401
Ritzer, George, 432, 433
Roach, John M., 432
Roberts, Edward B., 427
Rockefeller, Nelson, 408
Rohatyn, Felix, 44, 400

Roman, J.R., 430
Roosevelt, Franklin D., 235–238, 244
Rouse, James, 129, 406
Rousseau, Jean-Jacques, 432
Runge, C.F., 432
Russell, C.S., 103, 403
Ryan, James E., 425, 427

Sabatier, P.A., 430
Sabel, Charles F., 400, 435
Sahling, Leonard, 404
Sawhill, Isabel V., 414, 429
Sayre, Wallace, 418, 421
Schatz, Gerald S., 403
Schenker, Eric, 404
Schofield, C.L., 430
Schultze, Charles L., 414
Schweke, William, 397
Seabury, Paul, 426
Shearer, Derek, 432
Shelton, John P., 403
Shestack, Jerome J., 418, 419
Seliga, T.S., 430
Silkman, Richard H., 429
Simmons, John, 433
Smathers, W.M., 432
Smith, Adam, 73
Smith, Robert G., 417, 418
Smulin, Louis, 101
Spero, Joan E., 412
Stanback, Thomas M., 406
Stave, Bruce M., 432
Stein, Harold, 418
Steiner, George, 404
Sterens, Benjamin H., 403
Strichman, George A., 262
Structural dislocation, 39, 55, 67–69, 76, 272–275, 289–293
  in apparel industry, 54, 55, 56, 67
  (see also High technology and industrial targeting)
Struyk, R., 402
Swanstrom, Todd, 405
Sweet, David C., 406
Symbolic politics, 275–278

Taper, Bernard, 422
Tax policy, 11–17, 23, 35, 43, 91, 92, 105–109, 111, 113, 123–127, 141, 149–156, 160–162, 206, 226, 234–237, 268, 283, 380
  and New Federalism, 332–355
Taylor, F.B., 431
Taylor, Frederick Winslow, 377, 382, 390, 344
Terkel, Studs, 432
Thompson, Harold, 416

442

22463
26779